Small Firms and the Environment in Developing Countries

Collective Impacts, Collective Action

Allen Blackman

<small>EDITOR</small>

<small>RESOURCES FOR THE FUTURE</small>

Washington, DC, USA

An RFF Press book
Published by Resources for the Future
1616 P Street NW
Washington, DC 20036–1400
USA
www.rffpress.org

Library of Congress Cataloging-in-Publication Data
Small firms and the environment in developing countries: collective impacts, collective action / Allen Blackman, editor.
    p. cm.
    ISBN 1-933115-28-9 (hardcover : alk paper) ---- ISBN 1-933115-29-7 (pbk. : alk. paper)
    1. Small business--Environmental aspects--Developing countries. 2. Industries--Environmental aspects--Developing countries--Case studies. I. Blackman, Allen.
    HD2346.5.B53 2005
    338.6'42'091724--dc22   2005020490

The paper in this book meets the guidelines for permanence and durability of the Committee on Production Guidelines for Book Longevity of the Council on Library Resources. This book was typeset by Maggie Powell. It was copyedited by Paula Berard. Cover photo, "Brick Abstract," taken in San Miguel de Allende, Mexico by Mike Goldstein, Travel Text & Photography, photographersdirect.com. Cover design by Marc Alain Meadows, Meadows Design Office Inc., www.mdomedia.com.

The findings, interpretations, and conclusions offered in this publication are those of the contributors. They do not necessarily represent the views of Resources for the Future, its directors, or its officers.

ISBN 1-933115-28-9 (cloth)   ISBN 1-933115-29-7 (paper)

About Resources for the Future *and* RFF Press

RESOURCES FOR THE FUTURE (RFF) improves environmental and natural resource policymaking worldwide through independent social science research of the highest caliber. Founded in 1952, RFF pioneered the application of economics as a tool for developing more effective policy about the use and conservation of natural resources. Its scholars continue to employ social science methods to analyze critical issues concerning pollution control, energy policy, land and water use, hazardous waste, climate change, biodiversity, and the environmental challenges of developing countries.

RFF PRESS supports the mission of RFF by publishing book-length works that present a broad range of approaches to the study of natural resources and the environment. Its authors and editors include RFF staff, researchers from the larger academic and policy communities, and journalists. Audiences for publications by RFF Press include all of the participants in the policymaking process—scholars, the media, advocacy groups, NGOs, professionals in business and government, and the public.

Dedication

For my brother, Ed.

Acknowledgments

I am grateful to the Tinker Foundation for financial support; the chapter authors for their excellent contributions and patience with reviews and revisions; Paula Bérard, Grace Hill, Meg Keller, and Don Reisman at RFF Press for their skillful editorial assistance; and two anonymous reviewers for their helpful suggestions. I'm also indebted to Geoff Bannister, Mike Batz, Dave Evans, Arne Kildegaard, Steve Newbold, and Jhih-Shyang Shih for collaborating in the research that motivated this book. My biggest debt, however, is to Clara and my family for their love and support.

Contents

About the Contributors

KULSUM AHMED is lead environmental specialist at the World Bank and team leader for the environmental institutions and governance program and environmental health program in the Environment Department. She has considerable experience as an operations task manager, and previously worked in the Latin America Regional Office. Among other tasks, she led the team that prepared the Bank's first policy reform loan to integrate environmental issues in key sectors of the Mexican economy.

GEOFFREY J. BANNISTER is senior economist in the International Monetary Fund's International Capital Markets department. His recent research has focused on international trade and finance with particular focus on capital flows into emerging markets. He has published in a number of economics journals and has been a consultant to the Harvard Institute for International Development, the World Bank, the Inter-American Development Bank, and a number of other international organizations.

BRUNO BARBIER is a researcher at the International Center for Agronomic Research and Development (CIRAD). He was a post-doctoral fellow at the International Food Policy Research Institute and a scientist at the International Center for Tropical Agriculture (CIAT). His articles have been published in *Agricultural Systems* and *Agricultural Economics*.

MICHAEL B. BATZ is a research associate at Resources for the Future. His primary research interests include creating risk and decision analysis tools for reducing foodborne disease, valuing human health impacts from environmental risks, modeling spatial land-use decisions using empirical and game theoretic approaches, and improving regulation through the quantitative treatment of uncertainty. His book credits include co-authorship of *Superfund's Future: What Will It Cost?*

ALLEN BLACKMAN is an economist and fellow at Resources for the Future. His research focuses on environmental issues in developing countries, particularly small-scale polluters, forest conservation, and innovative environmental management strategies. He has worked as an adjunct professor at Georgetown University, a research fellow at the UCSD Center for U.S. Mexican Studies, and a consultant to multilateral development banks. His articles have been published in the *American Journal of Agricultural Economics*, the *Journal of Environmental Economics and Management*, and *World Development*, among other journals.

JOSEPH COOK is a doctoral student in the Department of Environmental Sciences and Engineering at the University of North Carolina at Chapel Hill. His recent research has focused on measuring demand for next-generation vaccines in Vietnam, India, and Mozambique. He has also worked on the design of financing systems for solid waste services, and helped re-evaluate the Melamchi water supply project in Nepal for the Asian Development Bank.

MICHAEL CROW is a senior associate at The Cadmus Group, specializing in an innovative approach to small-business regulation called the Environmental Results Program. He has advised international aid agencies on improving assistance to small enterprises. He recently served on the Board of Regents for the Multi-State Working Group's Policy Academy on Environmental Management Tools. *Environmental Forum*, *Environmental Engineering and Policy*, and *The Environmental Law Reporter* have published his research.

DAVID A. EVANS is a research associate at Resources for the Future and a doctoral candidate in the Department of Economics at the University of Maryland. His primary research interest is the design and effects of pollution control policies, with particular attention to the efficacy of emissions trading programs in the United States. His recent research also includes the study and application of methods to value non-market goods.

JOSÉ MANUEL GONZALEZ is a watershed management project coordinator for Tropical Agriculture Higher Education and Research Center (CATIE) in Honduras. He has served as Director of Agroindustry with the Taiwan cooperation project in Turrialba, Costa Rica; Director of Projects for the Honduran Coffee Institute (IHCafe); and Research Assistant at CATIE in Turrialba, Costa Rica. He has published articles in *Revista Ahprocafe* and *El Boletín Informativo Del Café*.

ROBERT R. HEARNE is assistant professor in the Department of Agribusiness and Applied Economics at North Dakota State University. His research focuses on water resources management, water markets, and institutional change. He recently served as professor at the Tropical Agriculture Higher Education and Research Center (CATIE) in Turrialba, Costa Rica. His articles have been published in *Water Resources Research*, *Water Policy*, *The Journal of Environmental Management*, and *Agricultural Economics*.

LORAINE KENNEDY is a research fellow at the CNRS (Centre National de la Recherche Scientifique) in France. She has published articles in *World Development* and *Revue Tiers Monde*, and co-edited a volume for the UNESCO-MOST program comparing spatial dynamics of industrialization in Asia. Forthcoming is an edited volume on the strategies of small producers in emerging economies (Mexico, Brazil and India) as they adapt to global markets.

ALAN J. KRUPNICK is director and senior fellow in the Quality of the Environment Division at Resources for the Future. His recent research focuses on estimating the willingness to pay for health and environmental improvements, both in developed and developing countries, and on improving methods of cost-benefit analysis of environmental programs. He has published over 50 scholarly articles and regularly works for multinational development banks.

PETER LANJOUW is a lead economist in the Development Economics Research Group of the World Bank. He has taught at the *Vrije* (Free) University of Amsterdam, the University of Namur, Belgium, and the Foundation for the Advanced Study of International Development (FASID) in Japan. He is an associate editor of the *Journal of African Economies*. He has published widely on issues associated with poverty and inequality in developing countries.

RICHARD D. MORGENSTERN is an economist and senior fellow at Resources for the Future, and focuses on the costs, benefits, and design of environmental policies in the United States and abroad. His research interests include conventional types of pollution as well as global climate change. Prior to joining RFF, he served in senior policy positions in both the U.S. Environmental Protection Agency and the U.S. Department of State.

STEPHEN NEWBOLD is an ecologist at the U.S. Environmental Protection Agency's National Center for Environmental Economics. The primary focus of his current research is combining ecological modeling and economic valuation for environmental policy evaluation. He has published articles in *Ecological Applications, Ecological Modeling and Assessment*, and the *Journal of the American Water Resources Association*.

JHIH-SHYANG SHIH is a fellow at Resources for the Future. His research focuses on ozone and fine particulate control strategies, renewable energy, and community water systems. He has worked as an instructor at Johns Hopkins University and a research associate at Carnegie Mellon University. His articles have appeared in the *Review of Economics and Statistics*, the *Journal of Environmental Economics and Management* and the *Journal of Environmental Management,* among other journals.

G. SIVALINGAM is a professor and holds the Chair in Business at Monash University, Malaysia. He is also the Director of the Malaysian Business Unit, School of Business and Economics, Monash University. He is the author of *Competition Policy in the ASEAN Countries, Modern Portfolio Management, Export Processing Zones in Malaysia,* and *Malaysia's Agricultural Transformation.*

JEFFREY R. VINCENT is a professor of natural resource economics in the Graduate School of International Relations & Pacific Studies at the University of California, San Diego. He also serves as environmental research director in the University of California's Institute on Global Conflict and Cooperation. He is lead author of *Managing Natural Wealth: Environment and Development in Malaysia*, editor of the 3-volume *Handbook of Environmental Economics*, and editor of *Natural Resource Accounting and Economic Development*.

XUEHUA ZHANG is a doctoral candidate in the Interdisciplinary Graduate Program in Environmental Resources (IPER) at Stanford University. Her recent research focuses on the impact of lawsuits on local environmental enforcement in China. She has worked as an engineer at the Chengdu Environmental Protection Bureau, a consultant for the World Bank, and a research assistant for Resources for the Future.

CHAPTER I

Introduction

Small Firms and the Environment

Allen Blackman

IN MOST DEVELOPING COUNTRIES, well over 90% of private enterprises employ fewer than 50 workers. Small firms (SFs) perform a number of vital economic functions. Perhaps most important, they provide jobs. As Table 1-1 illustrates, SFs generate more than half of total employment in countries with per capita GNP under US$1,000. In addition, according to conventional wisdom, they foster entrepreneurship, enhance the economy's ability to respond quickly to changing market conditions, and help to alleviate poverty by employing the particularly poor.

In light of these perceived benefits, programs promoting SFs have become a cornerstone of modern economic development policy. Most domestic, bilateral, and multilateral economic development authorities target SFs for subsidies, tax breaks, and regulatory exemptions. For example, in 2002, the World Bank provided almost $3 billion to support SFs in developing countries, much of it in credit subsidies (Ayyagari et al. 2003). Academics share policymakers' interest in SFs and have generated an extensive literature on the topic (e.g., Snodgrass and Biggs 1996; Van Dijk and Rabellotti 1997; Liedholm and Mead 1999). Key themes include the contribution of SFs to employment and income generation, the dynamics of SF birth and growth, SF industrial organization, the performance of specific SF clusters, the effectiveness of SF promotion policies, and collective action among SFs.

Although most of the attention devoted to SFs over the past two decades has focused on economic concerns, increasingly, both policymakers and academics are exploring the link between SFs and the environment. As a result, a nascent literature on the topic is emerging that addresses three fundamental questions.

First, how important is SF pollution? Specifically, are the environmental damages these firms generate comparable in magnitude to those that large firms generate? Do they disproportionately affect particularly vulnerable populations? The answers are not obvious. The sheer number of SFs in poor countries practically guarantees that they have some environmental impacts. Also, even casual travelers

Table 1-1. *Employment in Cottage, Small, Medium, and Large Firms in 34 Countries*

GNP per capita[a] ($)	Number of countries	Percentage of total employment			
		Cottage (1–4 employees)	Small (5–19 employees)	Medium (20–99 employees)	Large (100+ employees)
100–500	6	64	7	4	25
500–1000	7	41	12	10	37
1000–2000	7	11	13	14	61
2000–5000	9	8	11	17	64
5000+	5	4	6	20	70

[a]The World Bank uses GNP per capita to categorize countries as follows: "low income," $765 or less; "lower middle income," $766–$3035; "upper middle income," $3036–$9385, and "high income," $9386 or more.

Source: Snodgrass and Biggs (1996).

to developing countries can witness severe pollution problems caused by clusters of particularly dirty SFs, such as leather tanneries and brickkilns, which are typically located in poor residential neighborhoods. But on the other hand, although SFs are exceptionally plentiful, they are, after all, small and are often engaged in relatively clean activities, such as trade and services.

Second, will forcing SFs to comply with environmental regulations exacerbate unemployment and poverty? Many believe that regulatory authorities should let such firms slip through their nets in order to promote social equity. They argue that because SFs tend to operate on extremely thin profit margins, forcing them to comply with environmental regulations would cause a significant percentage to fail and would exacerbate unemployment among the poor. Similar arguments are widely used to justify providing subsidies and regulatory exemptions to SFs.

Third, what policy options are available to control SF pollution? It is not clear that environmental regulatory authorities have the ability to compel small firms to pollute less, at least not using conventional approaches. In many developing countries, a host of financial, institutional, and political factors hamstring environmental regulation: Fiscal and technical resources for environmental protection are in short supply; environmental regulatory institutions as well as complementary judicial, legislative, and data collection institutions are weaker than those in industrialized countries; requisite physical infrastructure, such as hazardous and solid waste treatment facilities, are scarce; public sentiment favors economic development over environmental protection; and environmental advocacy—historically a critical stimulus to effective environmental regulation—is less prevalent than in industrialized countries (World Bank 2000; Blackman and Sisto 2005).

As daunting as these constraints are, regulating SFs poses a number of additional challenges. As a group, SFs are costly to regulate by conventional means simply because they are so numerous. Conventional regulatory approaches require environmental authorities to perform certain administrative tasks for each firm they target for enforcement. These tasks include permitting, periodic monitoring, and sometimes sanctioning. Obviously, the more firms authorities target, the greater their total administrative costs. Hence, for regulators, the administrative cost per unit of pollution may be significantly higher for small firms than for large ones. SFs are also particularly difficult to regulate because many are informal, that is, unregistered and virtually anonymous to the state. As a result, they are difficult to identify, much less permit, monitor, and sanction. In addition, most SFs are relatively hard pressed to comply with environmental regulations. Investments in pollution control and prevention require both financial capital and employees with some training or experience in environmental management. But most SFs have relatively little of either commodity. Finally, environmental regulators often have particular difficulty mustering political support for cracking down on SFs. As noted above, SFs are widely viewed as an economic safety net for the poor. Hence, again, given all of these obstacles to regulating SFs, conventional approaches may not be effective and efficient.

The purpose of this book is to collect some of the best examples of the emerging literature on these three "focus" questions. The questions serve as an organizing framework for the book. As we shall see, for the most part, the answers provided by the case studies suggest that in a variety of circumstances, SFs are an appropriate target for environmental management effort: They can generate environmental damages on a par with those from large firms, can cut emissions without serious economic consequences, and can be induced to do so using a variety of innovative pollution-control strategies. Virtually all of the case studies break new ground either by covering previously untouched topics—for example, the use of environmental management systems by SFs in developing countries—or by covering more established topics with unprecedented depth and rigor.

The remainder of the chapter is organized as follows. The second section discusses the definition of the term *small firm*. The third section reviews the findings of the existing literature on the link between SFs and the environment. The last section summarizes and discusses Chapters 2–12 of this volume.

Defining *Small Firm*

Small firm is one of several related terms used in the literature. Others include *small and medium enterprise* (SME), *microenterprise* (ME), *micro and small enterprise* (MSE), and *small-scale enterprise* (SSE). No standard definitions of these terms exist. In fact, the usual definitions of these terms do not all use the same criteria (e.g., number of employees, total assets, or total annual sales). As others have pointed out, while this diversity of terms and definitions makes comparisons across case studies difficult, it is in a sense appropriate since SFs in different sectors and different countries are heterogeneous in employment, physical size, capitalization, human capital, and levels of technology (Hallberg 2000; Hillary 2000). For example, a small computer software company in India is likely to be vastly different from a street merchant in El Salvador. Also, size definitions depend on the context—a firm that is relatively small in relation to the size of the economy in a middle-income developing country will not be so small in a low-income country.

Having said this, the World Bank definitions are perhaps as commonly used as any in the literature. The World Bank defines a *microenterprise* as a firm with up to 10 workers, total assets up to $100,000, and total annual sales up to $100,000; a *small enterprise* as a firm with up to 50 employees, total assets up to $3 million, and total sales up to $3 million; and a *medium enterprise* as a firm with up to 300 employees, total assets up to $15 million, and total sales up to $15 million.[1] The chapters in this book use different terms and definitions. To facilitate comparisons and to prevent confusion, we have compiled these terms and definitions in Appendix 1-1.

The Literature

Although still relatively thin, the literature on the link between SFs and the environment has grown significantly over the past decade. To provide readers with context for the case studies presented in this book, this section presents a brief summary of this literature. We omit the findings of the case studies included in this volume as they are summarized at the end of this chapter. We use the three focus questions listed above as an organizing framework.

How Important Is Small-Firm Pollution?

In an early review of the literature on SFs and the environment, Kent (1991) noted that two schools of thought had emerged on the importance of SFs as polluters, an observation that remains accurate today. One school holds that SFs are less important sources of pollution than large firms for a number of reasons. Many SFs are engaged in relatively clean activities such as trade and services, and SFs that do work in dirty economic sectors often do not produce the bulk of output or pollution in these sectors, even though they may outnumber large firms (Bartone and Benavides 1997; Scott 2000; Dasgupta et al. 2002). In addition, many SFs are dispersed throughout rural areas where local ecosystems are capable of absorbing pollution and where human exposure is limited (Kent 1991). Finally, SFs have self-interested reasons to cut pollution. Namely, they operate on thin profit margins and generally try to reduce waste as much as possible to cut input and energy costs (Villarán et al. 1991; Mubvami 1992). Also, owners and mangers of SFs tend to live near their businesses and are reluctant to "dirty their own backyards" (Kent 1991). It is widely acknowledged that whether or not most SFs create significant pollution problems, some clearly have positive environmental impacts. Most important are SFs that engage in recycling (Meyer 1987).

A less optimistic school of thought emphasizes that whether or not SFs are more important than large firms as contributors to total national pollution loads, they clearly can have severe environmental impacts—at the local level if not at the national level—that merit attention from environmental authorities. Three factors contribute to this capability. First, although many SFs operate in relatively clean sectors, many others do not. For example, in Kenya, firms with fewer than

50 employees make up 99% of all enterprises, and more than a quarter of them are engaged in manufacturing (Frijns and van Vliet 1999). In a sample of eight developing countries studied by Mead and Liedholm (1998), between 15% and 64% of SFs were engaged in manufacturing.

Second, although direct measurements are scarce, the weight of evidence suggests that compared to large firms engaged in the same dirty activities, SFs are more pollution-intensive. Moreover, SFs generally do not invest in pollution control because regulatory pressure to do so is limited, financial and human capital are scarce, and abatement equipment usually entails economies of scale—that is, it is not particularly cost-effective unless used by large firms or groups of SFs (Hamza 1991; Kent 1991; Dasgupta et al. 2002).[2]

Third, case studies almost invariably find that the SF pollution disproportionately affects the poor who are particularly vulnerable because they have a limited ability to avoid pollution or to treat pollution-related health problems (Dasgupta 1997, 2000; Bartone and Benavides 1997).[3] SFs tend to cluster together in low-income residential neighborhoods. For example, Dasgupta (1997) reports that lead smelters in Calcutta are concentrated in three lower-class residential neighborhoods. Just as important, in many cases, the principal victims of SF pollution are often SF employees (Atambo 1995; Bartone and Benavides 1997).

Most research agrees that most severe SF pollution problems are found in a relatively short list of economic sectors: auto repair, battery production and recycling, brick and tile making, charcoal making, dyestuffs manufacture, electroplating, food processing, leather tanning, metalworking, mining, painting and printing, vehicle repair, wet end textile operations (e.g., bleaching, dyeing, and finishing), and wood and metal finishing.

Will Forcing SFs To Comply with Environmental Regulations Exacerbate Unemployment and Poverty?

Few researchers have tackled the question of whether forcing SFs in developing countries to comply with environmental regulations exacerbates unemployment and poverty. The scant evidence that does exist is mixed. Dasgupta (1997, 2000) argues that in India, several dramatic and sudden efforts in the mid-1990s to force clusters of dirty SFs to comply with environmental regulations led to significant job losses among the urban poor. Similarly, Frijns and van Vliet (1999) argue that environmental standards for SFs should be less stringent than for large firms to "balance jobs and the environment." (See also, Wells 2000).

On the other hand, however, Tendler (2002) argues that numerous case studies suggest that SFs are able to meet the challenge of newly imposed regulations—including environmental regulations—without suffering significant economic harm. In fact, she argues that the process of rising to this challenge has enabled SFs to become more efficient, to improve product quality, and to identify new markets.

What Policy Options Are Available To Control SF Pollution?

We differentiate between *conventional* and *alternative* pollution-control policies. Public-sector authorities take the lead in implementing the former, whereas private-sector entities typically take the lead in implementing the latter, often in partnership with public-sector authorities.

Conventional Regulatory Policies. Conventional environmental regulatory policies are typically categorized according to three criteria: (1) whether they dictate firms' abatement decisions or simply create financial incentives for abatement, (2) whether they require the regulator to monitor emissions, and (3) whether they involve government investment in abatement. Policies that dictate abatement decisions are known as *command-and-control* instruments, whereas those that create financial incentives for abatement are referred to as *economic incentive* instruments. Policies that require the regulator to monitor emissions are called *direct* instruments, whereas those that do not are called *indirect* instruments (Eskeland and Jimenez 1992). Examples of these different types of policies are given in the top three rows of Table 1-2.

Which of these policies are likely to be effective in controlling SF pollution? As noted above, in developing countries, financial, institutional, and political factors hamper environmental regulation. Given these constraints, most scholars agree that direct economic incentive and command-and-control instruments are difficult (although not impossible) to implement, even when applied to large firms in developing countries, because regulators typically do not have the wherewithal to reliably measure emissions and to impose sanctions accordingly (Blackman and Harrington 2000; Bell and Russell 2002; West and Wolverton forthcoming). If these instruments are problematic for large firms in developing countries, then they are even more problematic for SFs since, as discussed above, SFs are particularly difficult to regulate. Thus, in most cases, the menu of feasible conventional policy options for controlling SF pollution will be limited to the items in gray in Table 1-2: indirect command-and-control and economic incentive policies and

Table 1-2. *Conventional Pollution-Control Instruments*

	Direct	Indirect
Command-and-control	• Emissions standard[a]	• Technology & process standards[b] • Relocation
Economic incentive	• Emissions fee[c] • Marketable permits[e]	• Green taxes[d] • Green subsidies[f]
Government investment		• Communal treatment facilities • Information campaigns[g]

[a]Cap on level of emissions.
[b]Requirement for a specific abatement technology or element of the production process.
[c]Fee charged per unit of emissions.
[d]Tax on dirty inputs or outputs.
[e]Allowances to emit a specified amount of pollution, which may be traded with other firms.
[f]Subsidy to clean inputs or outputs.
[g]Disseminate information about compliance.
Note: Gray indicates feasible instruments for controlling small firm pollution.

government investment. The next three subsections briefly discuss the literature on each of these approaches.

Indirect Command-and-Control Policies. To be effective, command-and-control policies require a central authority to identify and keep track of targeted polluters. Therefore, a common recommendation in applying such policies to SFs is to develop a complete registry of these firms. However, this seemingly simple step can prove problematic, as many SFs are informal and have incentives to retain their anonymity to avoid costly taxes and regulation of all types (Hilson 2002).

Technology and Process Standards. Technology standards require firms to invest in certain types of pollution-control devices. Compared to direct command-and-control policies, such standards demand relatively little of regulators. Regulators need not measure and record polluting emissions. Rather they must only check to see that the requisite equipment has been installed and is operated regularly. Even so, as Dasgupta (1997, 2000) argues forcefully, technology standards can be problematic for a number of reasons. First, compelling SFs to adopt specified abatement devices is often difficult because these devices are generally designed for large firms and entail scales of operations and levels of technical expertise that are beyond the reach of many SFs. Also, the devices may simply be too expensive for SFs, which typically have limited retained earnings and poor access to credit.[4] In any case, SFs usually have scant access to information about various technological options for pollution control. Perhaps most damning, Dasgupta writes that even when SFs do install abatement technologies, they often have a minimal impact because the firms operate them incorrectly or infrequently to save on operating costs. Finally, Dasgupta notes that technology standards create no incentives for firms to adopt pollution-prevention measures.

Whereas technology standards entail investing in new abatement equipment, process standards typically mandate specific elements of the production process. For example, a process standard may require firms to substitute clean inputs for dirty ones. Monitoring compliance is generally more costly for process standards than for technology standards.

Relocation. Relocating SFs to industrial parks or remote areas may serve three purposes: improving the access of SFs to communal waste-treatment facilities (discussed below), reducing the number of people exposed to SF emissions, and providing SFs with secure land tenure, which, according to some researchers, improves incentives for pollution control (Sethuraman and Ahmed 1992; Perera and Amin 1996). Unfortunately, relocation is generally costly, in part because it increases SFs' transportation costs by moving them away from the neighborhoods where their customers and employees live (Omuta 1986). In addition, although relocation may reduce human exposure to SF emissions, it does not, in itself, cut emissions (Dasgupta 2000).

Indirect Economic Incentive Policies. Empirical research on the use of economic incentive policies to control SF pollution is limited. The work of Biller and co-authors (1994 and 1995) aside, the following discussion is drawn mainly from the literature on the use of economic incentives in developing countries.

Input Taxes. Taxing dirty inputs to discourage their use is a popular policy recommendation in countries where direct command-and-control and economic incentive policies are impractical. In general, input taxes are relatively easy to administer because in most cases, reasonably effective tax collection agencies already exist (Eskeland and Devarajan 1996). Input taxes have the additional benefit of generating revenue that can be used to defray administrative or abatement costs.

Unfortunately, however, these taxes have a number of well-known disadvantages, whether applied to large or small firms (Blackman and Harrington 2000). Most important, because input taxes do not target polluting emissions directly, they do not create incentives for pollution control per se. For example, a tax on a highly polluting variety of coal creates incentives for firms to switch to cleaner varieties but does not create incentives to install pollution-abatement devices. Second, for input taxes to be effective, firms must have access to less-polluting substitutes at reasonable prices. Otherwise, the tax will simply raise producers' costs without changing their behavior or, worse, will cause them to switch to even dirtier inputs (Biller and Quintero 1995). Third, ubiquitous black markets make it difficult to target taxes to specific economic activities. As a result, to tax the use of a dirty input (e.g., chrome) by a specific type of firm (e.g., tanneries), regulators would have to impose an economy-wide tax on the input, raising costs to firms that use the input in an environmentally benign manner as well as to those who do not.

Input Subsidies. Rather than taxing dirty inputs and investments, policymakers have the option of subsidizing clean ones. Such subsidies can take many forms, including tax relief, loan guarantees, and low-interest loans. The obvious advantage of subsidies is that they are likely to be supported, not opposed, by the private sector, whereas the obvious drawback is that they drain scarce fiscal resources.

Government Investment. Communal Waste Treatment Facilities. The one SF pollution-control strategy that has probably received most attention in the literature is the construction of communal treatment facilities for solid and liquid wastes (Okasaki 1987; Chiu and Tsang 1990; O'Connor 1996).[5]

Communal treatment has a number of characteristics that make it particularly appropriate for SFs (Bartone and Benavides 1997). First, such facilities capture economies of scale in treating wastes. Also, communal treatment can overcome important barriers to individual waste treatment, including a lack of financial capital, technological know-how, and physical space. Finally, communal treatment significantly cuts regulators' administrative and monitoring costs by enabling them to interact with conglomerations of SFs rather than individual firms.

However, communal treatment has a number of important disadvantages as well (O'Connor 1996; Dasgupta 2000). First, it is costly. Not only is constructing and operating communal facilities expensive, but so is getting SF wastes to the facilities, either by relocating SFs to industrial parks, connecting them to the treatment facility by pipe, or trucking wastes to the facility. Second, when user fees are instituted to finance the operating costs of the treatment facility, polluters may revert to illegal dumping. Even if polluters are not charged fees, they may still dump their wastes because using treatment facilities generally raises operating costs. Third, communal treatment creates no incentives for pollution prevention.

Finally, SFs may be averse to cooperating with their business rivals to manage communal treatment facilities.

Information Dissemination. Case studies often find that SFs lack the basic information about environmental regulations and the technological options for complying with them. The usual lesson drawn from such case studies is that environmental management authorities need to remedy this knowledge gap, preferably by working with private-sector organizations that represent SFs (Hamza 1991; Dasgupta 1997, 2000).

Alternative Pollution-Control Policies. *Clean Technologies and Waste Minimization.* Clean technologies and waste minimization are both types of pollution prevention—they reduce the amount of hazardous substances released into waste streams by increasing the efficiency with which firms use raw materials, energy, and other resources. Clean technologies generally entail a more radical change than waste minimization. Both clean technologies and waste minimization ideally lower a firm's operating costs. However, both also entail fixed set-up costs, including nonpecuniary learning and transaction costs. Although polluters typically pay the bulk of these fixed costs, public-sector authorities often contribute by providing cheap credit and technical extension. Also, public-sector authorities sometimes invest in research and development in clean technologies.

Clean technologies have received considerable attention in the literature as a means of furthering pollution control in developing countries where regulatory capacity is weak. Because these technologies can reduce operating costs and boost profits, the hope is that firms will adopt them voluntarily or at least with minimal prodding. For example, Hilson (2002) describes efforts to convince small-scale miners in Africa to use simple retorts to recover mercury used to leach gold, an expensive input that is largely wasted by small-scale miners. Notwithstanding its promise, clean technological change faces a number of barriers. Most of the literature argues that clean technologies will not diffuse widely unless they significantly boost profits (see Chapter 9 for a dissenting view). Given that many SFs have minimal retained earnings and limited access to credit, this implies that adopting clean technologies must involve low fixed costs and must significantly reduce operating costs (Kent 1991; Bartone and Benavides 1997). A second obstacle is that SFs typically lack information about clean technologies (Frijns and van Vliet 1999).

Several researchers have noted that even if no privately profitable clean technologies are readily available, simple low-cost waste minimization measures, such as recycling waste streams, often are available (Chiu 1987; Bartone and Benavides 1997; Van Berkel 2004). In large firms, environmental management systems (EMSs) have historically proven an important means of promoting environmental good housekeeping. EMSs are established sets of management procedures aimed at ensuring that environmental issues are systematically identified, controlled, and monitored. Unfortunately, little research has addressed the question of whether EMSs are appropriate for SFs in developing countries.

Informal Regulation. Informal regulation refers to pressure for improved environmental performance placed on polluters by private-sector agents, such as neighborhood organizations, nongovernmental organizations, trade unions, customers, supply chains, and competitors (Pargal and Wheeler 1996; World Bank 2000). An important means of ratcheting up informal regulatory pressure is to disseminate information on the environmental performance of polluting firms and on the human health benefits of pollution control (Tietenberg 1998). Given the challenges that public-sector regulators face in controlling emissions from SFs, informal regulation is attracting increasing attention as a promising alternative approach. Frijns and van Vliet (1999) write that trade associations, downstream buyers, and neighboring firms are most likely to be effective in applying informal regulatory pressure to SFs. Biller (1994) advocates using supply chains to apply informal regulatory pressure when SFs sell intermediate inputs, such as tanned hides or bricks. Specifically, he suggests that regulators mandate boycotts of particularly dirty SFs by larger downstream buyers. He argues that such initiatives can be effective because they focus regulatory effort away from SFs onto larger firms, which are easier to identify, monitor, and sanction. Scott (2000) writes that informal regulation depends critically on raising general awareness of environmental issues in affected communities. According to Biller (1994), families of SF workers and owners ought to be targeted for the dissemination of information about the health impacts of pollution because they work and live close to their firms' pollution.

Overview of the Chapters

Of the remaining chapters of the book, Chapters 2 and 3 focus mainly on the first two questions posed above: How important is small-firm pollution? and Will forcing SFs to comply with environmental regulations exacerbate unemployment and poverty? The remaining nine case studies focus principally—although not exclusively—on the third question: What policy options are available to control SF pollution?

The case studies are diverse. They are drawn from six countries—China, Ecuador, Honduras, India, Malaysia, and Mexico—and from a variety of economic sectors, including agriculture, ceramics, leather tanning, and textiles. Each case study addressing the third (policy options) question focuses on a different approach or concern, for example: economic incentives, collective action, and environmental management systems. The titles of the chapters identify the country, sector, and topic addressed.

Chapter 2

Both Chapter 2 by Allen Blackman and coauthors and Chapter 3 by Peter Lanjouw investigate the question of whether the damages from SF pollution are comparable in magnitude to those from large firms and whether these damages are visited on particularly vulnerable populations. Both chapters bring unprecedented rigor to this contentious issue. In Chapter 2, Blackman et al. use a series of specially parameterized air dispersion, health effects, and valuation models to develop detailed estimates of the benefits and costs of controlling air pollution from a collection of several hundred small-scale informal brickkilns in Ciudad Juárez, Mexico. The kilns are a notorious source of air pollution due to their reliance on cheap, dirty fuels such as scrap wood and used tires. For comparison's sake, the authors also estimate the benefits and costs of controlling air pollution from two of the city's leading formal industrial polluters. They find that the annual net benefits (benefits minus costs) of controlling brickkiln emissions are quite substantial—in the tens of millions of dollars—and exceed those for the two formal industrial facilities by a significant margin. Moreover, the authors find that a disproportionate number of the illnesses and premature mortalities caused by air pollution from brickkilns are likely occur in the poor residential neighborhoods surrounding the kilns. These results suggest that in some cases, at least, there is a strong argument for policymakers to allocate scarce pollution-control resources to SFs as well as to large firms.

Chapter 3

While the second chapter offers an in-depth analysis of the relative importance of pollution from a particular cluster of SFs in a particular city, Chapter 3, by Peter Lanjouw, presents a less detailed but broader analysis of the importance of pollution from all SFs in a particular country—Ecuador. The general conclusions of the two chapters are complementary. Lanjouw finds that in certain economic sectors, such as ceramics, leather tanning, printing, and textiles, SFs have serious environmental impacts, especially on the health of their employees and neighbors. Moreover, in several of these sectors, SFs, *not* large firms, produce the lion's share of output and therefore generate the lion's share of total pollution loads, a finding that contrasts sharply with assumptions in some of the previous literature.

In addition to analyzing the magnitude and incidence of SF environmental impacts in Ecuador, Lanjouw's chapter also addresses the second focus question: Will forcing SFs to comply with environmental regulations exacerbate unemployment and poverty? Of all three focus questions, this one has received the least attention. Lanjouw presents detailed data and econometric simulations to demonstrate that in Ecuador, only a small percentage of the poor work in dirty SFs; and they tend to be literate, to live in cities, and to have other characteristics that would make it relatively easy for them to find new work if stricter regulation put their current employers out of business. Hence, strictly regulating SFs would likely only exacerbate poverty to a modest degree.

Chapter 4

In this chapter, Allen Blackman examines how various policy options have fared in independent efforts to control emissions from informal, small-scale brickkilns in four cities in northern Mexico. Each of these efforts relied on a different combination of policy instruments—including command-and-control process standards, clean technological change, and relocation—and each met with varying degrees of success. The main findings from these case studies are as follows. First, when SFs create severe pollution problems, the firms are typically quite numerous, and therefore, politically powerful. As a result, they are usually able to block implementation of pollution-control strategies such as physical relocation, which require them to pay significant costs. Second, conventional command-and-control process and technology standards are usually quite difficult—although not impossible—to enforce. A necessary condition for success is to rely on peer monitoring, that is, recruiting private-sector stakeholders, such as trade and neighborhood organizations, to assume some of the burden of monitoring SFs. In other words, to be feasible, formal regulation must be buttressed by informal regulation. Third, efforts to create financial disincentives for pollution by boycotting goods sold by particularly polluting firms are simply unenforceable—monitoring is too difficult, and cheating is too easy. Finally, nongovernmental organizations may be best suited to lead efforts to control SF pollution by virtue of their ability to engage informal firms, draw on public sympathy, and sidestep politics and bureaucracy.

Chapter 5

As noted above, empirical research on the use of economic incentive policies to control SF pollution is quite limited. This chapter, by Jeffrey Vincent and G. Sivalingam, fills this gap. It evaluates three economic incentive instruments used by Malaysian regulatory authorities to control pollution from textile and metal-finishing SFs: national tax breaks for environmental expenditures, user fees for a national center for toxic and hazardous waste management, and user fees for a communal wastewater treatment plant in an industrial park for electroplaters. The authors find that enforcement of environmental regulations is the key to explaining the performance of the three policies. Weak enforcement has undermined the two national economic incentive policies, whereas unusually strict enforcement has made the user fees in the electroplater industrial park quite effective. According to Vincent and Sivalingam, the important message is not that economic incentive instruments have no role to play in managing pollution from SFs, but rather that the design of these instruments must take into account the limitations of a country's regulatory system, a message that echoes the aforementioned literature on the use of direct economic incentives in developing countries.

Chapter 6

In this chapter, Loraine Kennedy delves into a topic that is virtually untouched in the SF literature—cooperation among SFs in environmental management. Kennedy reports on an environmental regulatory crackdown aimed at controlling water pollution from approximately 600 mostly small-scale leather tanneries clustered in and around five towns in the Palar Valley of Tamil Nadu, a center of Indian leather tanning. The crackdown was spurred by a 1996 Indian Supreme Court order requiring the Palar Valley leather tanneries to use wastewater treatment equipment. In response, over the relatively short period of about a year, more than three-quarters of the tanneries formed groups to build common effluent treatment plants (CETPs). In Kennedy's view, more than any other factor, joint action enabled the tanners to respond successfully to the 1996 court order, and her chapter concentrates on understanding the factors that facilitated it. She finds that social ties among tanners contributed mightily—virtually all tannery owners belonged to the region's Muslim minority, a tightly knit social group. Also, many of the tanners had a history of cooperating to form integrated supply chains. Finally, the industrial organization of the Palar Valley tanning clusters facilitated joint action. For example, in 1996, most tanneries were eager to join CETPs because they were quite small and lacked the financial and technical wherewithal to build their own individual effluent treatment plants (IETPs).

Chapter 7

Here Kulsum Ahmed sheds light on two important but little-researched policy options for controlling SF pollution: environmental management systems (EMSs) and the use of supply chains to mentor SFs.[6] Ahmed evaluates an innovative World Bank sponsored pilot project designed to help SFs in Guadalajara, Jalisco (Mexico) adopt ISO 14001 certified EMSs. The project recruited 11 large-scale firms to mentor 22 SFs that supplied them with intermediate products. The large firms were thought to have unique leverage over their SF suppliers. The project had mixed success. On the positive side, six of the SFs completed formal preaudits for ISO 14001 certification and many of the participants reported significant improvements in environmental and economic performance. On the negative side, however, several of the participants dropped out of the program, and the involvement of those that remained tailed off somewhat over time. Ahmed draws a number of lessons from the pilot project. For example, she writes that EMSs—and in particular ISO 14001 systems—clearly have the potential to improve the environmental performance of SFs. However, to be effective, they must tie into the overall business strategy of the SF, e.g., expansion of market opportunities. In addition, she concludes that the leverage of large firms—particularly in recruiting SFs to participate in EMS training—can be quite important.

Chapter 8

In this chapter, Michael Crow and Michael Batz present a case study that sheds light on the economic consequences of forcing SFs to comply with environmental regulations. Their historical and retrospective analysis is a useful complement to Lanjouw's hypothetical and prospective analysis in Chapter 3. Crow and Batz report on the fallout from a 1996 court decision effectively ordering a cluster of more than 800 mostly small-scale bleachers and dyers in Tirupur, Tamil Nadu (India's knitwear capital) to begin treating their wastewater.

Crow and Batz find that even though the court order spurred significant investments in pollution control, it did not impair the economic performance of the knitwear cluster. They argue that the main reason is that bleachers and dyers in Tirupur relied heavily on collective institutions—namely trade associations and CETPs—to provide the political and legal representation, technical assistance, and financing needed to comply with the court order. Both this chapter and Chapter 6 on tanneries in the Palar Valley examine a court-ordered regulatory crackdown in India, and both find that collective action enabled SFs to survive. However, Kennedy focuses on identifying the socioeconomic factors that facilitated SF cooperation, whereas Crow and Batz explore the effects of tighter regulation on SFs' economic performance.

Chapter 9

In this chapter, Allen Blackman and Geoffrey Bannister examine the potential for two alternative pollution-control instruments—clean technological change and informal regulation—to improve SF environmental management. Blackman and Bannister provide a more in-depth look at one of the four case studies discussed in Chapter 4: a mid-1990s effort to promote the adoption of clean-burning propane by 330 small-scale brickmakers in Ciudad Juárez, Chihuahua (Mexico). Unique among studies of clean technology adoption by SFs, this chapter presents an econometric analysis of original survey data. The purpose is to identify the key factors that motivated more than half of the brickmakers in Ciudad Juárez to voluntarily adopt propane, despite the fact that adoption significantly raised production costs.

Blackman and Bannister find that the three most important drivers of propane adoption were the brickmakers' exposure to informal regulatory pressure applied by competing firms and private-sector local organizations; their education; and their awareness of the health benefits of propane. Surprisingly, these results imply that it is possible to successfully promote the adoption of a clean technology by intensely competitive SFs even when the new technology significantly raises variable costs. Perhaps more important, the econometric results demonstrate that informal regulation can generate strong incentives for SFs to adopt clean technologies. Finally, the results imply that training and education, in particular the dissemination of information about the health risks associated with dirty technologies, can be an effective means of promoting adoption.

Chapter 10

Here Allen Blackman presents a second case study of how clean technological change can help stem pollution from a large urban cluster of dirty SFs. This case study concerns small and medium-scale leather tanneries in León, Guanajuato—Mexico's leather capital. Totaling well over a thousand, the tanneries are a major contributor to pollution of surface and groundwater in the Lerma-Chapala River basin. Efforts to mitigate the problem using conventional regulation have failed repeatedly, and the only significant progress to date has resulted from the voluntary adoption of clean technologies. Blackman presents original survey data on the adoption of five such clean technologies by 137 tanneries. These data suggest that instead of pressure applied by regulators of private-sector organizations—a driver of clean technological change among brickmakers in the Ciudad Juárez—the key factor driving clean technological change in León has been the bottom-up dissemination of information about the cost and quality benefits of the technologies. The chapter concludes with a number of hypotheses about the reasons the brick-kiln and tannery case studies generated different results.

Chapter 11

In this chapter, Robert Hearne, José Manuel Gonzalez, and Bruno Barbier consider how international trade can serve both as a barrier to—and potentially an impetus for—improving the environmental performance of SFs. This topic is new to the literature. The authors examine the problem of water pollution generated by coffee processing in Honduras. Currently, more than 40,000 small-scale coffee growers located in remote mountainous areas process their harvest by hand and, in doing so, dump untreated organic wastes and wastewater directly into streams and rivers. Given the number and location of the small mills, environmental regulations governing coffee processing are virtually impossible to enforce. Its adverse environmental consequences aside, this decentralized processing system also impairs coffee quality because small mills skimp on quality control. As a result, Honduran coffee fetches a price on the world market that is 8–16% below average international prices.

A widely recognized solution to both the adverse environmental and economic consequences of on-farm coffee processing is to switch to a system of centralized processing facilities. Hearne et al. assess the feasibility of building such a system in a specific watershed in Honduras. Using a linear programming model in combination with financial analysis, they conclude that because centralized processing would improve coffee quality and eliminate the price penalty currently imposed on Honduran growers, both growers' and middlemen's profits under the new system would at least match their current profits, and the new centralized processing plants would be able to break even. The authors also consider potential solutions to some of the practical problems that would be involved in a switch to a centralized processing system, such as financing the set-up costs and enforcing environmental regulations.

Chapter 12

In this chapter, Richard Morgenstern, Alan Krupnick, and Xuehua Zhang present a case study that examines the potential for funding SF pollution-control projects by linking them with efforts to stem global warming, another topic that is new to the literature. The rationale for such a strategy is compelling. Developing countries are a major source of the greenhouse gases that cause global warming. As a result, they are increasingly being integrated into international efforts to slow climate change. For example, the clean development mechanism (CDM) of the Kyoto Protocol allows industrialized countries to meet their commitments to slow emissions of greenhouse gases by, in effect, paying for projects that cut emissions of these gases in developing countries. Yet such projects are uncommon in developing countries—policymakers there are understandably much more concerned with cutting emissions of conventional air pollutants, such as sulfur dioxide, which have immediate and dramatic impacts on human health. Fortunately, however, investments that cut conventional pollutants typically also cut greenhouse gases—that is, they have *ancillary carbon benefits*. Hence, it might be possible for policymakers in developing countries to obtain much-needed financing for conventional pollution-control projects from the CDM and other international climate-change programs.

Morgenstern et al. present a case study that sheds light on the practicality of this funding strategy. They examine a program aimed at cutting sulfur dioxide emissions from more than 250 small-scale coal-fired boilers in a central district of Taiyuan, Shanxi, China, a city plagued by severe air pollution. Using original survey data, Morgenstern et al. find that the program reduced carbon dioxide emissions from the targeted small boilers by a substantial amount: 50–95%. Moreover, they conclude that if extended to cover a larger area, the program could eliminate as much as 15% of the total carbon emissions from the Taiyuan area and, as a result, could well be appropriate for inclusion in the CDM or similar programs.

Notes

1. For additional definitions see Hillary (2000).

2. For a dissenting view, see Scott (2000).

3. Not all the literature agrees on this point, however. For example, using county-level data, Dasgupta et al. (2002) examine the contribution of small and large plants to particulate air pollution and to premature human mortality in Brazil. They find that although small plants are more likely than large plants to be pollution-intensive and to be located in low-income areas, large plants, not small ones, are responsible for most of the particulate-related mortality in both low- and high-income areas because they generate most of the particulate emissions in both types of areas.

4. For example, a package of pollution-control technologies offered for sale to small-scale lead smelters in Calcutta cost sums equal to twice the annual turnover of some of the targeted firms (Dasgupta 1997).

5. When built to serve a large group of polluters—for example, all those in a metropolitan area—communal waste treatment facilities are generally planned, financed, and operated by public-sector authorities. However, when built for smaller groups of firms, the firms themselves usually play a more prominent role. Hence, communal waste treatment could be classified as either a "conventional" or an "alternative" policy. We treat it as the former, because public-sector funds and planning usually play major roles in all manner of communal facilities—even those spearheaded by relatively small groups of polluters.

6. The use of supply chains to mentor SFs is an increasingly popular topic, but to my knowledge, has not previously been examined in the developing country context. For a discussion of the role that supply chains can play in improving SF environmental management in industrialized countries, see Tunnessen (2000).

References

Atambo, H. 1995. Work and Hazards in Jua Kali Industries in Kenya. *African Newsletter on Occupational Health and Safety* 5(2), International Labor Organization.

Ayyagari, M., T. Beck, and A. Demirgüç-Kunt. 2003. Small and Medium Enterprises across the Globe: A New Data Base. World Bank Policy Research Paper 3127 (August).

Bartone, C.R., and L. Benavides. 1997. Local Management of Hazardous Wastes from Small-Scale and Cottage Industries. *Waste Management & Research* 15(1): 3-21.

Bell, R.G., and C. Russell. 2002. Environmental Policy for Developing Countries. *Issues in Science and Technology* Spring: 63–70.

Biller, D. 1994. Informal Gold Mining and Mercury Pollution in Brazil. Policy Research Paper 1304. World Bank: Washington, DC.

Biller, D., and J.D. Quintero. 1995. Policy Options To Address Informal Sector Contamination in Latin America: The Case of Leather Tanneries in Bogotá, Colombia. LATEN Dissemination Note 14, Washington, DC: World Bank.

Blackman A., and W. Harrington. 2000. The Use of Economic Incentives in Developing Countries: International Experience with Industrial Air Pollution. *Journal of Environment and Development* 9(1): 5–44.

Blackman, A., and N. Sisto. 2005. Muddling Through While Environmental Regulatory Capacity Evolves: What Role for Voluntary Agreements? Resources for the Future Discussion Paper 05–16.

Chiu, H. 1987. Pollution Control: A Blessing in Disguise? *Industry and Environment* 10: 3–5.

Chiu, H., and K. Tsang. 1990. Reduction of Treatment Costs by Using Communal Treatment Facilities. *Waste Management and Research* 8: 165–67.

Dasgupta, N. 1997. Greening Small Recycling Firms: The Case of Lead Smelting Units in Calcutta. *Environment and Urbanization* 9(2): 289–305.

———. 2000. Environmental Enforcement and Small Industries in India: Reworking the Problem in the Poverty Context. *World Development* 28(5): 945–67.

Dasgupta, S., R.E.B. Lucas, and D. Wheeler. 2002. Small Plants, Pollution and Poverty: New Evidence from Brazil and Mexico. *Environment and Development Economics* 7(2): 365–81.

Eskeland, G., and E. Jimenez. 1992. Policy Instruments for Pollution Control in Developing Countries. *World Bank Research Observer* 7(2): 145–69.

Eskeland, G., and S. Devarajan. 1996. *Taxing Bads by Taxing Goods: Pollution Control with Presumptive Charges.* Washington, DC: World Bank.

Frijns, J., and B. van Vliet. 1999. Small-Scale Industries and Cleaner Production Strategies. *World Development* 27(6): 967–83.

Hallberg, K. 2000. A Market-Oriented Strategy for Small and Medium-Scale Enterprises. International Finance Corporation discussion paper number 40.

Hamza, A. 1991. *Impacts of Industrial and Small-Scale Manufacturing Wastes on Urban Environment in Developing Countries.* Review prepared for the UMP/UNCHS, Nairobi (September).

Hillary, R. 2000. Introduction. In *Small and Medium-Sized Enterprises and the Environment: Business Imperatives,* edited by R. Hillary. Sheffield, U.K.: Greenleaf Publishing.

Hilson, G. 2002. Small-Scale Mining in Africa: Tackling Pressing Environmental Problems with Improved Strategy. *Journal of Environment and Development* 11(2): 149–74.

Kent, L. 1991. *The Relationship between Small Enterprises and Environmental Degradation in the Developing World (with Emphasis on Asia).* Washington, DC: U.S. Agency for International Development.

Liedholm, C., and D. Mead. 1999. *Small Enterprises and Economic Development: The Dynamics of Micro and Small Enterprises.* New York: Routledge.

Mead, D., and C. Liedholm. 1998. The Dynamics of Micro and Small Enterprises in Developing Countries. *World Development* 26(1): 61–74.

Meyer, G. 1987. Waste Recycling as a Livelihood in the Informal Sector: The Example of Refuse Collectors in Cairo. *Applied Geography* 30: 82–92.

Mubvami, T. 1992. Hazardous Waste Monument for Small-Scale Manufacturing and Cottage Industries in Urban Areas of Zimbabwe. Case study prepared for the Urban Management Programme/United Nations Centre for Human Settlements, Nairobi, Kenya, October.

O'Connor, D. 1996. *Managing the Environment with Rapid Industrialization: Lessons from the East Asian Experience.* Paris: Organisation for Economic Co-operation and Development.

Okasaki, M. 1987. Pollution Abatement and Control Technologies for Small and Medium Scale Metal Finishing Industry. *Industry and Environment* 10: 23–28.

Omuta, G. 1986. The Urban Informal Sector and Environmental Sanitation in Nigeria: The Needless Conflict. *Habitat International* 10(3): 179–87.

Pargal, S., and D. Wheeler. 1996. Informal Regulation of Industrial Pollution in Developing Countries: Evidence from Indonesia. *Journal of Political Economy* 104(6): 1314–27.

Perera, L., and A. Amin. 1996. Accommodating the Informal Sector: A Strategy for Urban Environmental Management. *Journal of Environmental Management* 46: 3–14.

Scott, A. 2000. Small-Scale Enterprises and the Environment in Developing Countries. In *Small and Medium-Sized Enterprises and the Environment: Business Imperatives,* edited by R. Hillary. Sheffield, U.K.: Greenleaf Publishing.

Sethuraman, S.V., and A. Ahmed. 1992. Urbanization, Employment and the Environment. In *Environment, Employment and Development*, edited by A.S. Bhalla. pp. 121–41, Geneva: International Labour Organization.

Snodgrass, D., and T. Biggs. 1996. *Industrialization and the Small Firm: Patterns and Policies*. San Francisco: International Center for Economic Growth.

Tendler, J. 2002. Small Firms, the Informal Sector, and the Devil's Deal. *IDS Bulletin* 33(3).

Tietenberg, T. 1998. Public Disclosure for Pollution Control. *Environmental and Resource Economics* 11(3/4): 587–602.

Tunnessen, W.W. III. 2000. The Mentoring of Small and Medium-Sized Enterprises. In *Small and Medium-Sized Enterprises and the Environment: Business Imperatives*, edited by R. Hillary. Sheffield, U.K.: Greenleaf Publishing.

Van Berkel, R. 2004. Assessment of the Impact of the DESIRE Project on the Uptake of Waste Minimization in Small Scale Industries in India (1993–1997). *Journal of Cleaner Production* 12(3): 269–81.

Van Dijk, M., and R. Rabellotti (eds.). 1997. *Enterprise Clusters and Networks in Developing Countries*. EADI Book Series 20. Frank Cass: London.

Villarán, F., J.C. Cabrera, and E. Saldivar. 1991. Hazardous Wastes and Emissions from Small-Scale Industry in Lima, Peru. Case study prepared for the Urban Management Programme/United Nations Centre for Human Settlements, Nairobi, August.

Wells, J. 2000. Environmental Concerns and Responses in Small-Scale Stone Quarries in Nairobi. *Small Enterprise Development* 11(2): 28–38.

West, S., and A. Wolverton. Forthcoming. Market-Based Incentives for Pollution Control in Latin America. In *Environmental Issues in Latin America and the Caribbean*, edited by A. Romero and S. West. Dordercht: Springer Press.

World Bank. 2000. *Greening Industry: New Roles for Communities, Markets, and Governments*. New York: Oxford University Press.

Appendix 1-1. *Terms Describing Firm Size Used by Chapter Authors*

Chapter	Terms used	Defined as
2	"informal" firm	No explicit definition is provided. However, original survey data (described in Chapter 9) indicates that the average informal brickkiln in Ciudad Juárez employs six workers.
3	"small scale enterprise (SSE)"	Firm with 10 or fewer employees.
4	"informal" firm	No explicit definition is provided. However, original survey data (described in Chapter 9) indicates that the average informal brickkiln in Ciudad Juárez employs six workers.
5	"small and medium enterprise" (SME) and "small-scale industry" (SSI)	The Malaysian government defines an SME as a firm having up to 150 full-time employees and annual sales of up to US$ 6.6 million. It defines an SSI as a firm having 50 or fewer full-time employees.
6	"small scale enterprise (SSE)"	No explicit definition is provided. However, Table 6-1 classifies 460 tanneries in five towns in the Palar Valley as "very small," "small," "medium," and "large" based on the tonnage of raw hide processed per day. 84% of the tanneries are classified as "very small" or "small."
7	"small and medium enterprise" (SME)	The Mexican government defines an SME as a firm with 250 or fewer employees. The chapter describes a pilot project involving a group of 22 firms ranging in size from 3 to 230 employees.
8	"small and medium enterprise" (SME) and "small scale industry" (SSI)	No explicit definition of SME is provided. Prior to 1999, the Indian government defined an SSI as a firm with 10–49 employees. Since 1999, it has defined an SSI as a firm with capital less than Rs 50 million (US$ 1.2 million). The chapter authors report that of the bleachers and dyers in Tirupur, 72% have 25 or fewer workers, and 96% have 100 or fewer.
9	"informal" firm	No explicit definition is provided. However, original survey data indicates that the average informal brickkiln in Ciudad Juárez employs six workers.
10	small-scale enterprise (SSE)	No explicit definition is provided. However, on average the León tanneries surveyed for this article have 16 employees.
11	acreage and output used to describe farm size	92% of coffee farmers in Honduras plant less than 7 hectares and produce less than 4500 kg of coffee.
12	"small" boilers	The pollution-control program analyzed in this chapter defined "small" boilers as those with output less than 2 tones per hour.

CHAPTER 2

The Benefits and Costs of Controlling Small-Firm Pollution

Informal Brickmaking in Ciudad Juárez, Mexico

Allen Blackman, Stephen Newbold, Jhih-Shyang Shih, David A. Evans, Joseph Cook, and Michael Batz

IN DEVELOPING COUNTRIES, population growth, rural-to-urban migration, and regulation have spurred the rapid expansion of an urban informal sector made up of low-technology microenterprises largely operating outside the purview of the state. Today, the informal sector accounts for more than half of nonagricultural employment and contributes between one-quarter and three-quarters of gross domestic product in both Latin America and Africa (Ranis and Stewart 1994; Schneider and Enste 2000). Once popularly viewed as an economic backwater—a collection of street merchants transitioning to salaried jobs—the informal sector is now recognized as a hotbed of entrepreneurship and innovation (De Soto 1989).

Unfortunately, for all its economic benefits, there are good reasons to suspect that the expansion of the informal sector is having significant environmental impacts. As discussed in Chapter 1, small firms—especially informal ones—are exceptionally numerous, sometimes quite dirty, and typically situated in poor residential areas.

Nevertheless, policymakers have thus far paid little attention to informal polluters. Industrial environmental management efforts in developing countries have generally focused exclusively on large formal facilities. In part, this bias stems from the perceived difficulty of regulating numerous small firms. But a second reason may simply be that the problem is not well understood, that is, policymakers lack information on the magnitude and incidence of the environmental damages caused by informal firms, and on the costs of mitigating these damages. Little research has been conducted to fill this gap. Collecting the requisite data is difficult because informal firms are, by their nature, wary of recordkeeping and monitoring.

Portions of this article are to be published in *Environment and Development Economics* as "Benefits and Costs of Informal Sector Pollution Control: Mexican Brick Kilns."

This chapter presents a cost–benefit analysis of four strategies for reducing air pollution from a collection of approximately 330 informal brickkilns in Ciudad Juárez, Mexico. Our analysis takes advantage of data on U.S.–Mexico border environmental problems collected in the wake of the 1992 North American Free Trade Agreement. We also compare the net benefits (benefits minus costs) of controlling brickkiln emissions to estimates of the net benefits of controlling emissions from two of the city's leading formal industrial polluters.

We find that brickkiln emissions are responsible for serious health damages, including more than a dozen premature mortalities per year. As a result, the net benefits of three of the four emission-control strategies for brickkilns are positive and quite large—in the tens of millions of dollars. We also find that the net benefits of controlling emissions from brickkilns exceed net benefits of controlling emissions from formal factories by a considerable margin, although the size of this margin depends critically on the actual level of pollution abatement in formal factories. These findings suggest that, in some cases, the conventional allocation of regulatory resources across formal and informal polluters may be suboptimal.

A number of caveats are in order. First, to make the analysis tractable, we neglect a number of factors. Although the emission sources we analyze generate a variety of pollutants, we focus solely on particulate matter smaller than 10 micrometers (PM_{10}) because it is thought to be responsible for a large proportion of the total noncarcinogenic adverse health effects of air pollution (Pope et al. 1995) and because its effects on human health are relatively well understood. In addition, we neglect both secondary PM_{10} (formed when pollutants such as nitrogen oxides and sulfur dioxide undergo chemical reactions in the atmosphere) and long-range transport of particulate matter because, as discussed in the section called Air Dispersion Model, neither is likely to be important in our case study. Also, we limit our attention to the effects of PM_{10} on human morbidity and mortality. We do not consider the effects on visibility, material damages, or nonuse values. Finally, we restrict attention to human morbidity and mortality in Ciudad Juárez and omit estimates of the (far less severe) damages in El Paso, Texas—Juárez's nearby sister city.[1] Given that we restrict attention to one type of pollutant, one category of adverse impacts, and a subset of the affected population, our estimates of the net benefits of controlling air pollution are a lower bound on the total value of the net benefits.

Second, data limitations constrain our analysis somewhat. Most importantly, data on Mexican formal industrial facilities is extremely tightly held. Therefore, as discussed below, PM_{10} emissions and abatement costs for the two formal factories in our sample are estimated rather than measured. These estimated data are adequate for our purpose—to convey a general sense of how net benefits of controlling emissions from formal factories compare with the (more precisely measured) net benefits of controlling emissions from informal firms.

Third, our analysis of abatement costs ignores implementation costs—the costs that regulators pay to compel firms to abate pollution—because these costs are highly uncertain and difficult to measure. In the informal sector, implementation costs are likely to be significant. We return to this issue in the conclusion.

The main objective of this chapter is to demonstrate that a class of fixed pollution sources that has thus far received little attention can be responsible for significant environmental damages and may in some circumstances be a more appropriate target for pollution-control efforts than the usual suspects—large industrial plants. To our knowledge, this is the first rigorous analysis of the benefits and costs of informal-sector pollution control. The literature on informal-sector pollution problems is quite thin. Most of it relies on case studies and focuses either on distinguishing between successful and unsuccessful environmental management strategies (Biller and Quintero 1995; Perera and Amin 1996; Chapter 4 in this book) or on identifying the drivers of informal firms' environmental performance (Chapter 9 in this book). The literature on the link between small firms and the environment is somewhat more robust. (See Chapter 1 for a review.)

To understand the organization of this chapter, it is helpful to provide a brief overview of the four-step method used to estimate the net benefits of investing in a specific control strategy to cut PM_{10} pollution from an emission source. First, we use a specially parameterized air dispersion model to gauge the extent to which the control strategy improves air quality in Ciudad Juárez. Second, we use a health effects model to estimate how many cases of human mortality and morbidity are avoided each year as a result of this improved air quality. Third, we use a valuation model to calculate the dollar value of the avoided mortality and morbidity. Finally, to arrive at net benefits, we calculate the annualized costs of the control strategy and subtract them from our estimate of the dollar value of benefits.

The remainder of the chapter is organized as follows. The next section briefly discusses air pollution in Ciudad Juárez and presents aggregated emissions inventory data to demonstrate that the city's informal brickkilns are a leading source of air pollution. The section after that (titled Informal Brickkilns) provides background on informal brickkilns and presents data needed to estimate the net benefit of controlling PM_{10} emissions from these sources, including emissions characteristics for the four control strategies and the annualized costs of each strategy. The next section (titled Formal Industrial Sources) provides similar information for two formal-sector facilities. The following section (titled Benefits Estimates) discusses the air dispersion, health effects, and valuation models used to estimate the benefits of pollution abatement. The next section presents our results, and the last section considers the policy implications of our findings.

Air Pollution in Ciudad Juárez

A sprawling industrial city with a population of more than 1.2 million, Ciudad Juárez has the worst air pollution on the U.S.–Mexico border. The city violates Mexican federal ambient air quality standards for PM_{10}, ozone, and carbon monoxide. Geography exacerbates the problem: Ciudad Juárez is located in a high mountain valley, which traps air pollution and gives rise to temperature inversions. Surveys show that the city's residents are more concerned about air pollution than any other environmental problem (JAC 1999).

According to official 1996 emission inventory data—the Sistema Nacional de Información de Fuentes Fijas (SNIFF) for the state of Chihuahua (Gobierno del Estado de Chihuahua 1998)—automobiles and trucks are the leading source of anthropogenic air pollution in Ciudad Juárez (Table 2-1).[2] Unfortunately, for a

Table 2-1. *Sectoral Contributions to Total Anthropogenic Air Pollution in Ciudad Juárez*

Sector	Pollutant					
	PM	SO$_2$	CO	NO$_x$	HC	All*
Informal brickmaking (%)	16	43	0	0	2	1
Other industry (%)	14	17	0	5	3	1
Services (%)	3	2	0	3	23	4
Transportation (%)	68	38	99	92	72	95
All (%)	100	100	100	100	100	100
Total (tons)	1,510	4,144	452,762	26,115	76,134	560,667

*Total tons of PM, SO$_2$, CO, NO$_x$, and HC.

Note: PM = particulate matter; SO$_2$ = sulfur dioxide; CO = carbon monoxide; NO$_x$ = nitrogen oxides; and HC = hydrocarbons.

Source: Gobierno del Estado de Chihuahua 1998.

variety of technological and political reasons, such sources are notoriously difficult to control (Harrington and McConnell 2003). Industry is also a leading source of air pollution. Although Ciudad Juárez is home to more than 250 *maquiladoras*—foreign-owned plants that have located in the city to reduce labor costs—surprisingly, a collection of 330 informal brickkilns are the city's leading source of industrial air pollution. They contribute 16% of all particulate matter pollution and 43% of all sulfur dioxide. These statistics alone suggest that in Ciudad Juárez, the informal sector deserves serious consideration as a potential target for pollution control efforts.

Informal Brickkilns

Description

Ciudad Juárez's informal brickkilns mainly supply construction companies specializing in low-cost housing. The typical informal brickkiln is a 10-meter-square primitive adobe structure that holds 10,000 bricks, employs six people, generates profits on the order of US$100 per month, and is fired two times a month with scrap wood, sawdust, and other rubbish. Brickkilns use no pollution-control devices whatsoever (Blackman and Bannister 1997). The location of the kilns within the city exacerbates their adverse effect on human health: They are clustered in seven poor neighborhoods, most of which are residential (Figure 2-1).[3] As discussed in Chapter 4, past efforts to control emissions from Ciudad Juárez's brickkilns have met with decidely mixed success.

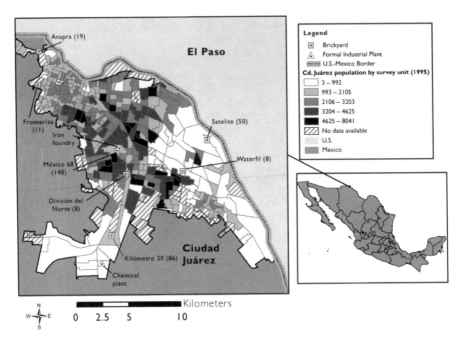

Figure 2-1. *Brickyards, Formal Industrial Facilities, and Population in Ciudad Juárez*

Data

Two types of data are required to estimate the net benefits of reducing PM_{10} emissions from informal brickkilns: data on the emissions characteristics of brickkilns (e.g., dimensions, locations, emission rates, emission velocities, and plume temperatures) and data on the efficacy and costs of appropriate emission-control strategies. In general, we have used relatively conservative data, that is, data that yield the lowest average annual ambient concentrations of PM_{10} and the highest annualized costs. Data on brickkiln emission characteristics were obtained from studies conducted by local universities and interviews with local stakeholders (Table 2-2). Note that we report probability distributions for several parameters. As discussed in the section on uncertainty below, these probability distributions are used to perform Monte Carlo simulations that account for some of the uncertainty associated with source emission characteristics.

As for data on emissions abatement, we model the four control strategies that have received considerable attention from local stakeholders: NMSU kilns, natural gas, relocation, and no-burn days (see, e.g., JAC 1999).

NMSU Kilns. Researchers at New Mexico State University (NMSU) have designed a low-cost, low-technology pollution-control technology that involves replacing traditional open-topped kilns with pairs of domed kilns connected by an underground tunnel fitted with clay-filled screens. NMSU kilns have been found to reduce emissions of PM_{10} by 99.5% (Avila et al. 1999). This design is particularly

Table 2-2. *Brickkiln Emission Characteristics*

Characteristic	Unit	Parameter or distribution	Source
Kiln radius (traditional kiln)	m	1.75	Bruce (1999)
Kiln radius (NMSU kiln)	m	0.37	Bruce (1999)
Kiln height	m	3.0	Avila et al. (1999)
Emission velocity (traditional kiln)	m/s	0.5	Bruce (1999)
Emission velocity (NMSU kiln)	m/s	1.0	Bruce (1999)
Plume temperature (traditional kiln)	degrees K	573	Bruce (1999)
Plume temperature (NMSU kiln)	degrees K	333	Bruce (1999)
Peak emission rate of total dry aerosols 0.5–20 μm in diameter[a]	g/s	$N(7.83, 2.89)$[b]	Bruce (1999)
Average emission rate/peak rate[a]	—	$T(0.2, 0.3, 0.4)$[c]	Bruce (1999)
Grams of PM10/grams total dry aerosols[a]	—	$N(0.7, 0.1)$[b]	U.S. EPA (1995)
Firings/month April–September[a]	—	2	Alfaro (2000a)
Firings/month October–May[a]	—	1	Alfaro (2000a)
Hours/firing (traditional kiln)[a]	hours	17	Alfaro (2000a)
Hours/firing (NMSU kiln)[a]	hours	8.5	Avila et al. (1999)
Number of kilns	—	See Fig. 2-1	Tarin (2000)
Location of kilns	—	See Fig. 2-1	Valenzuela (2000)

Note: NMSU = New Mexico State University.

[a]Used to calculate total emissions.

[b]$N(\mu,\sigma)$ = normal distribution with μ = mean and σ = standard deviation.

[c]$T(m_1,m_2,m_3)$= triangular distribution with m_1 = minimum, m_2 = mode, and m_3 = maximum.

promising because it uses low-cost, readily available materials and because it cuts fuel costs by approximately 50%.

Natural Gas. Natural gas burns as cleanly as propane but is considerably less expensive. Like propane, it can be used effectively in existing traditional kilns and requires a minimal investment on the part of individual brickmakers. However, whereas propane can be distributed in portable tanks, natural gas requires dedicated pipelines and decompressors—infrastructure that would have to be built to service the brickyards. We assume that switching to natural gas would eliminate 99.9% of PM_{10} emissions.

Relocation. Moving kilns away from densely populated residential neighborhoods is frequently advocated as a means of reducing exposure to kiln emissions. In 1999, 16 brickkilns in a centrally located brickyard called Francisco Villa were relocated to Kilometro 20, the brickyard furthest from Ciudad Juárez's population centers and the one brickyard in which land is plentiful. (Figure 2-1). We model this scenario as a wholesale relocation of all the kilns in Ciudad Juárez to Kilometro 20.

No-Burn Days. Because the transport of kiln emissions depends on weather conditions, requiring brickmakers to forego firing on days with certain weather conditions can significantly reduce exposure to these emissions. El Paso currently has a "no-burn days" program that prohibits open-air fires during certain weather conditions, and there has been some discussion of enforcing such restrictions in Ciudad Juárez. We model this scenario as a prohibition of firing on days with low wind speed and high air stability—conditions correlated with high particulate exposure (see Appendix 2-1 for a more detailed description of our methodology). Because enforcement of no-burn days is bound to be imperfect, we assume that only half of the kilns scheduled to fire on no-burn days actually forego firing.

We consider a uniform application of these strategies across brickyards and within brickyards. For example, for the natural gas strategy, we assume that all kilns in all seven brickyards switch. Thus, for policy purposes, we effectively treat all brickmakers in Ciudad Juárez as a single emission source. The principal reason is that brickmaking—like most informal activities with low barriers to entry profit margins—is intensely competitive. Therefore, as previous emission-control projects have demonstrated, policy scenarios in which only a portion of the city's brickmakers adopt a cost-increasing or cost-decreasing pollution-control strategy are not sustainable, as the adopters are at a cost advantage or disadvantage (see Chapter 9 in this book).

Table 2-3 gives the annualized costs of each of the control strategies. For the NMSU kilns strategy, the sole cost is that of building modified kilns. For the natural gas strategy, capital costs per kiln are based on RFF survey data on the conversion of kilns to propane in the early 1990s. Like conversion to propane,

Table 2-3. *Annualized Costs of Pollution-Control Strategies for Brickkilns (1999 US$ unless otherwise noted)*

Cost category	NMSU kilns	Natural gas	Relocation	No-burn days
Capital				
Present value per kiln	3,000[a,b]	349[c]	6,000[a,b]	0
Present value infrastructure	0	1,002,005[a]	0	0
Lifetime of capital (years)	10[c]	20	10[c]	—
Annual costs ($r = 12\%$)	175,214	149,553	350,429	0
Operations and maintenance				
Per kiln	0	0	0	0
Infrastructure	0	100,000[d]	0	24,692[e]
Total costs	175,214	249,553	350,429	24,692

[a]Alfaro (1995) and (2000b).
[b]Marquez (2000).
[c]RFF (1995).
[d]Johnson(2000).
[e]Reynoso (2000).

conversion to natural gas requires investments in a burner and modifications that enable the kiln to withstand higher temperatures. For the relocation strategy, we assume that capital costs are made up of two elements: the financing needed to relocate brickmakers' homes ($4,500) and that needed to build a new kiln ($1,500). Our costs for the no-burn days strategy are based on the administrative costs of a similar program in El Paso. This program entails labor costs only: one person-hour per day is devoted to monitoring weather data, and five person-days are devoted to enforcement for each no-burn day declared. We assume Mexican regulatory labor costs at $40,000 per person-year.[4]

Formal Industrial Sources

Ideally, to assess the relative importance of controlling emissions from informal sources, we would simply compare estimates of the net benefits of cutting brick-kiln PM_{10} with estimates of the net benefits of controlling emissions from an array of formal-sector sources in the city. Unfortunately, however, emissions and abatement cost data for formal sources in Ciudad Juárez either do not exist or are extremely tightly held. Therefore, we have developed net benefit estimates for a small sample of (two) formal sources using U.S. Environmental Protection Agency models. In doing so, we have taken care to minimize the likelihood that our methods bias these estimates downward and thereby inappropriately lead to a finding that net benefits of controlling brickkiln PM_{10} are relatively high by comparison. Specifically, we have purposely chosen to estimate emissions from formal-sector sources that have much higher PM_{10} emissions than most formal facilities in the airshed.[5] In addition, given uncertainty about abatement investments at the two plants, we present a variety of net benefit estimates based on different assumptions about such investments.

Although questions have been raised about the reliability of the facility-level data in the SNIFF emissions inventory—the reason we use U.S. Environmental Protection Agency models instead of these data to estimate PM_{10} emissions—an alternative ranking of local emission sources is lacking and, therefore, we rely on the SNIFF to identify the city's top seven industrial sources of PM_{10}. In the summer of 2001, we interviewed managers and engineers of these plants (both in person and by telephone) in an attempt to obtain production data needed to estimate PM_{10} emissions and abatement costs. Two of these seven facilities provided us with the requisite data: a U.S.-owned gray iron foundry and a Belgian-owned chemical plant. The iron foundry produces table bases. It employs about 140 workers and is located in an industrial park in a densely populated central section of Ciudad Juárez (Figure 2-1). The chemical plant mainly produces hydrofluoric acid. It employs about 150 workers and is located in the sparsely populated southern section of the city.

We used U.S. Environmental Protection Agency emissions factors to estimate emissions from each particulate-intensive production process in the iron foundry and chemical plant (U.S. EPA 1995).[6] Based on engineering estimates and historical emissions data, these emissions factors are widely used by regulatory agencies around the world to estimate plant-level emissions. The data required to use the emissions factors include the type of output, the scale of production, and the type of production technology. We obtained these data from plant managers.

An important element of uncertainty in estimating emissions at the two formal plants concerns their actual levels of pollution abatement. In Mexico, as in many developing countries, pollution-control regulations are fairly stringent. Noncompliance is widespread, however (Dasgupta et al. 2000). Both the iron foundry and chemical plant claim to comply fully with pollution-control regulations and—given that *maquiladoras* on the U.S.–Mexico border are subject to considerable scrutiny—these claims may well be valid. Unfortunately, we are not able to verify these claims; reliable plant-level data on pollution abatement are tightly held, as are monitoring data collected by Mexican regulatory authorities. Given this uncertainty—and given that our goal is to estimate net benefits for *typical* formal industrial facilities, which may not comply with pollution-control regulations—we estimate emissions for the iron foundry and chemical plant assuming alternatively that they have installed (1) all of the pollution-control equipment standard in similar U.S. plants and (2) no pollution-control equipment whatsoever. Table 2-4 presents estimated emissions rates for the two plants and for the brickkilns. Note that particulate emissions from the chemical plant are significantly higher than emissions from the iron foundry.

In addition to PM_{10} emissions, our air dispersion model requires detailed source-specific data on stack heights, emission velocities, and plume temperatures.

Table 2-4. *Estimated Annual PM_{10} Emissions from Formal and Informal Sources (tons)*

Facility/process	Emissions	
	No controls	U.S. controls
Iron foundry		
Induction furnace	4.43	0.89
Pouring/cooling	11.28	0.56
Shakeout	12.26	0.61
Sand handling	13.78	0.69
Cleaning/finishing	0.37	0.02
Total	42.12	2.77
Chemical plant		
Fluorspar drying	748.70	7.49
Fluorspar handling	598.00	5.985
Fluorspar transfer	60.00	11.97
Total	1,406.70	25.45
Brickkilns	596.19	n/a

Sources: U.S. EPA 1995 for industrial facilities; parameters in Table 2-2 for brickkilns.

Managers of the two formal plants did not provide these parameters. Therefore, we estimated them using publicly available data on U.S. gray iron foundries and hydrofluoric acid plants (U.S. EPA 2001).

We used U.S. Environmental Protection Agency (EPA) spreadsheet models (U.S. EPA 1998a; 1999b) along with documentation on various techniques for controlling particulate emissions (U.S. EPA 1998b) to estimate the costs of the particulate-control equipment likely to be found at the iron foundry and chemical plant (Table 2-5). Based on vendor quotes, these spreadsheet models estimate the annual costs of installing and operating various types of abatement equipment to control emissions from specified production processes at specified types of plants. The data inputs required for these models (including engineering design values, operating statistics, electricity prices, and waste disposal costs) were obtained from a variety of sources, including interviews with plant managers; operating permits for U.S. plants with identical outputs and similar scales; INEGI, the International Energy Agency; and interviews with waste disposal officials in Ciudad Juárez.

Benefits Estimates

The benefits of pollution control for an emissions source, or collection of sources, are the difference between the damages associated with uncontrolled PM_{10} emissions and the damages associated with controlled PM_{10} emissions. To estimate damages for each scenario, we use three models. First, we use a specially parameterized air dispersion model to estimate our sample sources' contributions to annual average ambient levels of PM_{10} at thousands of locations in Ciudad Juárez. Next,

Table 2-5. *Annualized Costs of Installing PM_{10} Abatement Equipment Standard at U.S. Plants in Mexican Formal Industrial Facilities (1999 US$)*

Facility/process	Abatement device	Annual cost
Iron foundry		
Induction furnace	Pulse jet bag house	13,395
Pouring/cooling	Pulse jet bag house	34,109
Shakeout	Shaker bag house	1,152
Sand handling	Pulse jet bag house	1,164
Cleaning/finishing	Shaker bag house	54
Total		49,874
Chemical plant		
Fluorspar drying	Pulse jet bag house	10,955
Fluorspar handling	Pulse jet bag house	8,750
Fluorspar transfer	Pulse jet bag house	8,281
Total		27,986

Sources: U.S. EPA 1998a; 1998b; and 1999b.

we use a health effects model to estimate the number of cases of human mortality and morbidity that result from this pollution each year. Finally, we use a valuation model to calculate the dollar values of these health effects. Having estimated the annual benefits of each of our control strategies, we compare them to annualized costs. This section discusses each of these models.[7]

Air Dispersion Model

The U.S. EPA's Industrial Source Complex Short Term 3 (ISCST3) Gaussian plume air dispersion model uses data on emissions source characteristics, local meteorology, and local topography to estimate average hourly, daily, and annual concentrations of primary PM_{10} due to a specific source in a defined study area. It has been one of the U.S. EPA's chief tools for investigating violations of ambient air quality standards (Riswadkar and Kumar, 1994).[8] Note that the ISCST3 model does not have the capability to handle secondary PM_{10} (formed when pollutants such as nitrogen oxides and sulfur dioxide undergo chemical reactions in the atmosphere) or long-range transport of PM_{10}. However, neither phenomenon is likely to be important in our case study.[9]

We use the ISCST3 model to estimate annual average concentrations of primary PM_{10} due to each of our study sources—brickkilns, the iron foundry, and the chemical plant—at 4,026 arbitrarily chosen receptor locations in the study area.[10] Table 2-6 details the meteorological and topographical data used to parameterize the ISCST3 model. Regarding the former, the ISCST3 model uses one specific year's worth of hourly data on temperature, wind speed, wind direction, and mixing height.

Health Effects Model

To estimate exposure to the PM_{10} emitted by the various sources, we use INEGI population data at the level of survey units called areas geoestadísticas básicas (AGEBs). Like census tracts in the United States, AGEBs vary in both size and population (Figure 2-1).[11] We assign the inhabitants of each AGEB a distance-weighted average of PM_{10} concentrations predicted by the ISCST3 model at all receptor locations within 800 m of the center of the AGEB.[12] Next we estimate the health effects of this exposure using concentration–response (CR) coefficients reported in the epidemiological literature. CR coefficients indicate the expected change in the number of cases of some health endpoint due to a marginal change in the ambient concentration of a particular air pollutant. We model nine different health endpoints:

- mortalities (MORTs);
- respiratory hospital admissions (RHAs);
- emergency room visits (ERVs);
- adult respiratory symptom days (ARSDs);
- adult restricted-activity days (ARADs);
- asthma attacks (AAs);
- child chronic bronchitis (CCBs);

Table 2-6. *Meteorological and Topographical Data*

Data	Unit	Source
Temperature (hourly)	degrees K	NCDC 2000
Wind speed	m/s	NCDC 2000
Random flow vector	degrees	NCDC 2000
Stability category	—	NCDC 2000
Mixing height	m	U.S. EPA 2000
Topography	m	INEGI 1992

- child chronic cough cases (CCCs); and
- adult chronic bronchitis cases (ACBs).

We make the conventional assumption that these health effects are linear functions of PM_{10} exposure levels (see, e.g., U.S. EPA 1999a).[13] Hence, health effects are calculated as

$$H_i = CR_i \times \sum_{j=1}^{J} (\overline{C}_j \times Pop_j)$$

where

H_i = the number of cases of health endpoint i;
CR_i = the concentration response coefficient for health endpoint i;
$\overline{C}_j$ = the estimated average annual concentration of PM_{10} from emissions source for survey unit j; and
Pop_j = the population in survey unit j.

Table 2-7 presents the parameters used in the health effects model. As discussed in the section titled Valuation Model, mortality effects—not morbidity effects—dominate the total benefits estimates because of the relatively high monetary value assigned to the avoidance of premature mortality, therefore by far the most important CR coefficient in Table 2-7 is that for mortality. We make the relatively conservative assumption—based on a number of U.S. studies (Ostro 1994)—that a 10-μg/m^3 change in daily PM_{10} results in a 1% annual increase in the mortality rate.[14] A discussion of the remaining CR coefficients in Table 2-7 can be found in Chapter 8 of Bloyd et al. (1996).

A challenge in estimating morbidity damages is identifying a set of endpoints that reflects the full range of identified adverse health effects but that avoids double counting. For example, there is a potential for double counting if adult restricted-activity days that result from relatively acute symptoms are also counted as adult respiratory symptom days that result from all types of symptoms. We have dealt with this issue in the conventional manner—by restricting some endpoints to subpopulations, subtracting potentially overlapping categories of endpoints, and

Table 2-7. Health Effects Model Inputs

	Parameter	Units	Value or distribution	Source
	CR coefficients			
CR_{MORT}	Mortality	% change mortality rate/($\mu g/m^3$)	N(1m, 300u)	Krupnick, 1996
CR_{RHA}	Respiratory hospital admissions	admissions/yr/($\mu g/m^3$)/person	N(102u, 62.5u)	Plagiannakos and Parker, 1988[a]
CR_{ERV}	Emergency room visits	visits/yr/($\mu g/m^3$)/person	N(235.4u, 128.3u)	Samet et al., 1981
CR_{ARSD}	Adult respiratory symptom days[b]	days/yr/($\mu g/m^3$)/adult[c]	N(0.247, 0.059)	Krupnick et al., 1990
CR_{ARAD}	Adult restricted activity days[d]	days/yr/($\mu g/m^3$)/nonasthmatic adult	N(0.0575, 0.0275)	Ostro, 1987
CR_{AA}	Asthma attacks[e]	attacks/day/($\mu g/m^3$)/asthmatic person	N(912u,450u)	Ostro et al., 1991
CR_{CCB}	Child chronic bronchitis	cases/yr/($\mu g/m^3$)/child[c]	N(1.59m, 805u)	Dockery et al., 1989
CR_{CCC}	Child chronic cough	cases/yr/($\mu g/m^3$)/child[c]	N(1.84m, 924u)	Dockery et al., 1989
CR_{ACB}	Adult chronic bronchitis	cases/yr/($\mu g/m^3$)/adult[c]	N(61.5u, 30.7u)	Abbey et al., 1993
	Population data			
	Ciudad Juárez, 1995	persons/survey unit	—	INEGI, 1995
	Other parameters			
	Baseline mortality rate in Chihuahua, 1997	deaths/1000 persons/year	5.506	INEGI, 2000
	Fraction of population asthmatic		0.05 (U.S. rate)	Bloyd et al., 1996
	Work loss days per ERV	days	1.28	Chestnut and Rowe, 1988
	Work loss days per RHA	days	9.30	Heart, Lung and Blood Institute, 1992

[a] We convert the relationship between annual RHAs and annual SO_4 concentrations in Plagiannakos and Parker (1988) to a relationship between RHAs and annual PM_{10} concentrations using the standard ratio of SO_4 to PM_{10} reported in Lee et al. (1994, Part III).

[b] To avoid double counting ARSDs, ARADs, and AAs, we define ARSDs as the total number of ARSDs predicted by CR_{ARSD} minus the sum of ARADs and AAs.

[c] Adults are defined as persons older than 17.

[d] To avoid double counting ARADs and AAs, we restrict ARADs to nonasthmatic persons. The data used to estimate CR_{ARSD} omited cases that results in hospital admissions and emergency room visits, and therefore, double counting ARADs, RHAs, and ERVs is not a concern.

[e] Double counting AAs, RHAs, and ERVs is not likely to be significant because only 0.5% of AAs result in RHAs and ERVs (Bloyd et al. 1996).

Notes: N(μ,σ) = normal distribution where μ = mean and σ = standard deviation. m = 10^{-3}; u = 10^{-6}

carefully selecting how each endpoint is valued. Appendix 2-1 details our methodology.

Valuation Model

To estimate the monetary values of health damages avoided by reducing PM_{10} emissions from our sample sources, we use a combination of the following:

1. willingness to pay (WTP) figures obtained from the economics literature, i.e., a "benefits transfer" approach,
2. estimates of the value of work loss days based on average daily wages in Ciudad Juárez, and
3. estimates of health care costs based on the value of work loss days (Table 2-8).

Because more than three-quarters of the total estimated benefits arise from premature mortalities avoided, by far the most important parameter in the valuation model is the value of a statistical life. We use a discrete distribution—$1.9 million (33%), $3.8 million (34%), and $7.5 million (33%)—from Hagler Bailly, Inc. (1991). This distribution is relatively conservative. For example, the U.S. EPA used a mean value of $4.8 million per mortality avoided to assess the benefits of the Clean Air Act (see U.S. EPA 1999a, Appendix H-8). The parameters used to value respiratory hospital admissions and emergency room visits are estimates of medical costs associated with each endpoint. These estimates are based on workday-equivalent conversion factors taken from a study for Santiago, Chile (World Bank 1994). We also use conversion factors to estimate the value of child chronic cough. A discussion of the remaining valuation parameters can be found in Chapter 9 of Bloyd et al. (1996).

Unfortunately, to our knowledge, direct estimates of Mexican WTP for reductions in the health endpoints considered in this chapter are not yet available. Therefore, we use WTP parameters (for adult respiratory symptom days, adult reduced-activity days, asthma attacks, and chronic bronchitis) based on U.S. studies. But given that average income adjusted for purchasing power parity is approximately four times as high in the United States as in Mexico, Mexican WTP may be lower than U.S. WTP.[15] Cultural factors may also cause WTP in the two countries to differ. To account for international differences in WTP, we use three different values for Mexican WTP based on three different assumptions about the elasticity (E) of WTP with respect to income.[16] We assume alternatively that E = 1, E = 0.33, and E = 0. For example, E = 0.33 implies that if average per capita income adjusted for purchasing power parity is 10% lower in Mexico than in the United States, then WTP is 3.3% lower. An E between 0.2 and 0.5 is supported by some studies that look at differences in WTP across income groups (Loehman et al. 1979; Alberini et al. 1997). Thus, the middle value of the discrete probability distribution we use to value premature mortality in Mexico is $3.80 million, assuming that E = 0; $2.42 million, assuming that E = 0.33; and $0.97 million, assuming that E = 1.

Table 2-8. *Benefits Valuation Model Inputs (1999 US$)*

	Parameter (value of)	Units	Value or distribution	Source
VSL	statistical life	millions $/ statistical life	Prtb(1.9,3.8,7.5) (0.33,0.34,0.33)	Hagler Bailly, Inc. 1991
Val$_{RHA}$	respiratory hospital admissions	$/case	43.6 days × Val$_{WLD}$	World Bank 1994
Val$_{ERV}$	emergency room visits	$/case	2.2 days × Val$_{WLD}$	World Bank 1994
Val$_{ARSD}$	adult respiratory symptom days	$/case/individual	b(6)	Krupnick and Kopp 1988
Val$_{ARAD}$	adult restricted activity days	$/case/individual	62.09	Krupnick and Kopp 1988
Val$_{AA}$	asthma attacks	$/case	U(13,62)	Rowe and Chestnut 1985
Val$_{CCB}$	child chronic bronchitiss	$/case	166	Krupnick and Cropper 1989
Val$_{CCC}$	child chronic cough	$/case	0.12 × Val$_{WLD}$	Ostro 1994
Val$_{ACB}$	adult chronic bronchitis	$/case	N(9887,3666)	Krupnick and Cropper 1989
Val$_{WLD}$	work loss days	$/day	17	INEGI 1995

Notes: Prtb(a)(p) = discrete probability distribution where a = vector of outcomes and p = vector of probabilities for outcomes. N(μ,σ) = normal distribution where μ = mean and σ = standard deviation. U(a, b) = uniform distribution where a = lower bound and b = upper bound. b(a) = beta distribution with central value of a.

Uncertainty

We use Monte Carlo simulation to account for uncertainty associated with the parameterization of the air dispersion, health effects, and benefits valuation models. That is, where data on probability distributions is available, we treat model parameters as distributions and we use these distributions to generate 95% confidence intervals for model outputs. In our air dispersion model for brickkilns, we have data on probability distributions of the peak emission rate of total dry aerosols, the ratio between peak and average emission rates, and the fraction of total aerosols that is PM$_{10}$. In our air dispersion model for the two formal industrial facilities, we have data on probability distribution of emission rates. In our health effects model, for each of our nine concentration–response coefficients, we use mean values and standard deviations reported in the literature, and—unless the literature dictates otherwise—assume normal distributions. Finally, for our benefits valuation model, we have information on the probability distributions of the value of a statistical life, the value of an adult respiratory symptom day, the value of an asthma attack, and the value of adult chronic bronchitis.

Results

Brickkilns

The air dispersion model results suggest that brickkilns' impacts are highly localized geographically. Figure 2-2, a concentration profile for PM_{10} emissions from the brickyard Mexico 68 on a due north transect, shows that brickkilns primarily affect PM_{10} concentrations within 500 m. This result stems from the fact that brickkilns have low stack heights and emission velocities.

The health effects model suggests that brickkilns have significant effects on mortality and morbidity (Table 2-9). Most important, the model's mean prediction is that brickkiln emissions are responsible for 14 premature mortalities per year. Note that the predicted health effects pass an internal consistency check in the sense that they are related to each other in a reasonable way. For instance, the model predicts more than twice as many emergency room visits as respiratory hospital admissions, and more than twice as many adult respiratory symptom days as adult restricted-activity days.

The first row of Table 2-10 presents our estimates of the value of annual morbidity and mortality due to uncontrolled brickkiln emissions. (We discuss the remainder of Table 2-10 in the next section, called Informal vs. Formal Sources). We report three sets of mean estimates based on different assumptions about the elasticity of WTP with respect to income. To illustrate the variation in our estimates, we also present the 95% confidence interval for the middle elasticity case. Even when this elasticity is assumed to be quite high ($E = 1.0$), the mean estimate is more than $19 million. Assuming a middle elasticity value ($E = 0.33$), the mean estimate is $47 million. Assuming that Mexicans and U.S. citizens have the same WTP ($E = 0$), the mean estimate is more than $74 million. Note that reduced

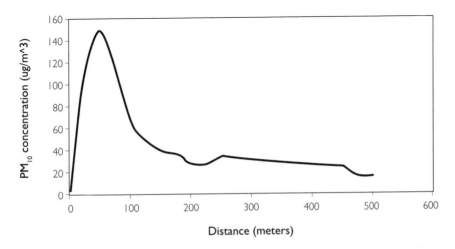

Figure 2-2. *Profile of Brickkiln PM_{10} Concentration Downwind of Mexico 68*

Table 2-9. *Annual Health Effects of Uncontrolled PM$_{10}$ Emissions from Brickkilns (mean values and 95% confidence intervals)*

Health endpoint	Number of cases		
	Low	Mean	High
Mortality	2.5	14.1	31
Respiratory hospital admissions	0	262	770
Emergency room visits	0	607	1,719
Work loss days	0	3,216	8,500
Adult respiratory symptom days	91,610	376,600	794,000
Adult restricted activity days	2,704	138,000	349,100
Asthma attacks	180	42,680	108,600
Child chronic bronchitis	0	1,637	4,416
Child chronic cough	0	1,878	5,017
Adult chronic bronchitis	0	93	242

Source: The model in this chapter.

mortality is by far the largest component of benefits, accounting for more than 80% of the total.

Table 2-11 presents estimates of the annual net benefits of each of the four brickkiln pollution control strategies, allowing for three different values of E. For each value of E, the ranking of the control strategies is the same: the net benefits of natural gas and NMSU kilns are virtually the same, the net benefits of relocation are about half that of natural gas, and the net benefits of no-burn days are about one fiftieth that of natural gas. Natural gas and NMSU kilns have the highest net benefits because they are most effective at reducing PM$_{10}$ emissions. Relocation is ranked third because the total benefits of this strategy are about half those for natural gas, while the costs are the highest of any of the four strategies. The no-burn days strategy is ranked last because it generates the lowest total benefits—less than one-hundredth of those associated with natural gas.

The mean annual net benefits of all four strategies are quite large for each of the three assumptions about the value of E. Assuming that $E = 0.33$, the mean annual net benefits range from $47 million for natural gas to $1 million for no-burn days. Even the lowest estimates—those at the low end of the 95% confidence interval given $E = 1$—are positive for all of the control strategies.

Informal vs. Formal Sources

Table 2-10 presents estimates of the annual value of health damages due to PM$_{10}$ emissions from the formal plants given two alternative emission-control scenarios: absolutely no emission controls and U.S.-level controls. In addition, the table presents the average for these two scenarios.

We begin with two points that are fairly obvious, but important nonetheless. First, the health damages associated with the chemical plant are much higher

Table 2-10. *Value of Annual Morbidity and Mortality Due to (i) Uncontrolled PM$_{10}$ Emissions from Brickkilns and (ii) Controlled and Uncontrolled PM$_{10}$ Emissions from Formal Industrial Facilities (1999 US$; mean values and 95% confidence intervals)*

Source	(E = 1.0) Mean	Low	Value (E = 0.33) Mean	High	(E = 0) Mean
Brickkilns	19,110,000	4,460,000	47,360,000	141,200,000	74,210,000
Iron foundry					
U.S.-level controls	116,200	52,450	287,900	712,200	451,100
No controls	1,958,000	884,000	4,851,000	12,000,000	7,602,000
Average[a]	1,037,100	468,225	2,569,450	6,356,100	4,026,550
Chemical plant					
U.S.-level controls	236,600	106,900	586,300	1,450,000	918,700
No controls	11,920,000	5,382,000	29,530,000	73,040,000	46,270,000
Average[a]	6,078,300	2,744,450	15,058,150	37,245,000	23,594,350

[a]Average of "no controls" and "U.S.-level controls" scenarios.

Note: E = the elasticity of WTP (willingness to pay) with respect to income adjusted for purchasing power parity.

Source: RFF model.

than those associated with the iron foundry. The main reason is simply that the chemical plant emits far more PM$_{10}$ (Table 2-4). Second, the health damages from uncontrolled emissions are much higher than for controlled emissions—17 times higher for the iron foundry and 50 times higher for the chemical plant. Thus, the magnitude of the health damages the formal plants generate depends critically on their investments in pollution control.

A comparison of the damages from the formal plants and from the brickkilns reveals that the former are significantly smaller than the latter, regardless of the assumption made about the level of pollution abatement at the two formal plants (Table 2-10). If we assume that the formal plants have installed abatement devices standard in the U.S., and if $E = 0.33$, then the mean value of total damages generated by the iron foundry ($0.6 million) and the chemical plant ($0.3 million) are each approximately 1% of damages due to brickkilns ($47 million). If we assume, alternatively, that emissions from the formal plants are completely uncontrolled, then these percentages are 10% and 62%.

Given this disparity in damages—and the fact that the costs of PM$_{10}$ emission controls are relatively small in comparison to the benefits—it is not surprising that the net benefits of most of the emission-control strategies for brickkilns are significantly higher than the net benefits of installing U.S. levels of emission controls at the formal plants. Table 2-11 presents estimates of the net benefits of installing emission controls standard in the U.S. at the two formal plants given two alternative assumptions about the baseline level of pollution control (i.e., the existing

Table 2-11. *Annual Net Benefits of Pollution-Control Strategies for Brickkilns and Formal Industrial Facilities (benefits less costs in 1999 US$ mean values and 95% confidence intervals)*

E	Scenario	Brickkilns				Iron foundry		Chemical plant	
		Natural gas	NMSU kilns	Relocation	No-burn days	Baseline = no controls[a]	Baseline = 50% U.S. controls[b]	Baseline = no controls[a]	Baseline = 50% U.S. controls[b]
0	High	220,729,247	219,532,786	126,279,571	4,275,308	17,644,126	8,822,063	112,199,014	56,099,507
	Mean	73,886,237	73,447,986	42,139,571	1,435,308	7,101,026	3,550,513	45,323,314	22,661,657
	Low	6,765,425	6,745,386	3,668,571	114,308	1,257,636	628,818	8,267,914	4,133,957
0.33	High	140,809,247	140,072,486	80,499,571	2,775,308	11,237,926	5,618,963	71,562,014	35,781,007
	Mean	47,063,087	46,810,286	26,759,571	905,308	4,513,226	2,256,613	28,915,714	14,457,857
	Low	4,205,987	4,220,326	2,202,571	63,308	781,676	390,838	5,247,114	2,623,557
1	High	56,643,497	56,390,686	32,249,571	1,095,308	4,502,926	2,251,463	28,837,114	14,418,557
	Mean	18,841,337	18,783,686	10,588,571	345,308	1,791,926	895,963	11,655,414	5,827,707
	Low	1,512,683	1,563,176	659,071	9,308	280,766	140,383	2,069,524	1,034,762

[a]Net benefit of installing and operating PM$_{10}$ control equipment standard in a similar U.S. plant assuming baseline is no controls.

[b]Net benefit of installing and operating PM$_{10}$ control equipment standard in a similar U.S. plant assuming baseline is equipment sufficient to achieve 50% of abatement that would result from U.S.-level controls.

Note: E = the elasticity of willingness to pay with respect to income adjusted for purchasing power parity.

Source: RFF model.

level of abatement before installing any new equipment): absolutely no controls and average controls, that is, the investment needed to eliminate 50% of the emissions eliminated by U.S.-level controls. We assume that the annualized costs in the second scenario are half of those in the first. To simplify the comparison, we restrict attention to the mean values of total benefits and assume $E = 0.33$.

Of the various pollution-control scenarios for formal plants included in Table 2-11, the greatest net benefits—$29 million—result from installing U.S.-level controls at the chemical plant, assuming a baseline of absolutely no emission controls. These net benefits are just 62% of the net benefits of converting traditional brickkilns to natural gas or replacing them with NMSU kilns. Assuming a more realistic average baseline level of control, the net benefits of installing U.S.-level controls in the chemical plant are just 31% of the net benefits of converting traditional brickkilns to natural gas or replacing them with NMSU kilns.

The net benefits of installing U.S.-level controls at the iron foundry are an order of magnitude lower than the net benefits of installing the same controls at the chemical plant. Assuming a baseline of absolutely no emission control, the net benefits of installing U.S.-level controls at the iron foundry are $5 million, just 10% of the net benefits of converting traditional brickkilns to natural gas or replacing them with NMSU kilns. Assuming a more realistic average baseline, the net benefits of installing U.S.-level controls at the iron foundry are $2 million, just 5% of the net benefits of converting traditional brickkilns to natural gas or replacing them with NMSU kilns.

Conclusion

We have used a specially parameterized air dispersion model in combination with concentration–response coefficients and benefits transfer methods to estimate the net benefits of controlling PM_{10} from a collection of informal brickkilns and two formal industrial facilities in Ciudad Juárez. Our two principal findings are as follows. First, given a wide range of modeling assumptions, the benefits of three of four control strategies for brickkilns—NMSU kilns, natural gas, and relocation— are considerably higher than the costs. Second, the net benefits of these three strategies exceed the net benefits of controlling emissions from the two formal facilities by a considerable margin. However, the size of this margin depends critically on the baseline level of pollution abatement in formal factories. In addition, we found that health damages from brickkiln emissions are spatially concentrated in the poor residential neighborhoods surrounding the largest brickyards. What are the policy implications of these findings?

The fact that our estimates of the net benefits of controlling brickkiln emissions are positive and quite large strongly suggests that, in general, policymakers should at least include clusters of informal polluters among those industrial emission sources they consider to be potential targets for pollution-control initiatives. However, the fact that the net benefits of controlling brickkiln emissions exceed those for two leading formal industrial sources of air pollution does not necessarily suggest that, in general, policymakers will want to shift scarce pollution-control resources away from industrial facilities and toward clusters of informal polluters.

In deciding how to allocate pollution-control resources, policymakers must consider not only health benefits and abatement costs—the two components of our net benefits estimates—but also implementation costs—the costs environmental management authorities incur in monitoring environmental performance, prosecuting noncompliance, and, in certain cases, subsidizing abatement costs by, for example, educating managers of informal firms about the requirements and options for abatement and providing equipment and financial assistance. As noted in the opening paragraphs of this chapter, developing prospective estimates of implementation costs is difficult and is outside the scope of this study. However, there is good reason to expect these costs to be higher for clusters of informal polluters than for formal industrial facilities. Often, informal firms are difficult to identify. Even if they can be identified, monitoring numerous tiny firms may simply be impractical for chronically understaffed and underfunded municipal regulatory agencies. In addition, requiring cash-strapped informal firms to bear the costs of pollution control may be unrealistic. Finally, and perhaps most important, it may be difficult to generate the political will to impose costs on firms which, as a principal employer of the urban poor, are seen to perform a vital distributional function.

That said, there is little reason to believe that implementation costs for informal sources are, in general, prohibitive. Recent case studies—including companion research on brickkilns in northern Mexico—have demonstrated that a number of strategies can be used to lower implementation costs in the informal sector (World Bank 2000a; Chapters 4, 6, and 7 in this book). A common element of many of these strategies is recruiting local stakeholders—including communities affected by informal-sector pollution, organizations representing the informal firms, competitors, and upstream and downstream business contacts—to pressure polluters to cut emissions, to monitor their environmental performance, and, in some cases, to subsidize their investments in pollution abatement—in effect to undertake many of the functions traditionally performed by public-sector regulators. For example, in past efforts to convert brickkilns in Ciudad Juárez to clean-burning propane, neighborhood organizations and trade unions pressured brickmakers to switch and monitored their progress. Also, local propane companies subsidized investments in propane burners. The key to motivating stakeholders to undertake these tasks is often improving public awareness of, and appreciation for, informal-sector pollution problems. Studies like this one may be able to contribute to this effort by demonstrating that informal polluters can generate severe health damages and that these damages may be disproportionately visited on those living nearby.

Appendix 2-1

Selection of No-Burn Days

To select no-burn days, we first identified weather conditions that were correlated with high exposure to kiln emissions in 1990, our sample weather year. We did this by regressing total daily exposure from brickkilns predicted by our air dispersion model onto actual daily averages of five weather variables. We found that wind speed was significantly negatively correlated with exposure, and stability was significantly positively correlated with exposure. Next we identified all those days in our sample on which wind speed was at least one standard deviation below the annual average and stability was at least one standard deviation above the annual average. Using these criteria, we selected 23 days.

Methods Used To Avoid Double Counting Health Damages

To avoid double counting adult restricted-activity days and asthma attacks, we restrict the former to nonasthmatic adults. To avoid double counting adult respiratory symptom days, adult restricted-activity days, and asthma attacks, we define adult respiratory symptom days as the difference between total adult respiratory symptom days estimated by the coefficient reported in Table 2-8, and the sum of adult restricted-activity days and asthma attacks days experienced by adults. To avoid double counting respiratory hospital admissions and emergency room visits, we use estimated medical costs to value these endpoints (a necessity in any case because WTP estimates for these endpoints do not exist). Note that most emergency room visits do not actually result in respiratory hospital admissions, and hospitals typically charge for each separately. We avoid double counting adult restricted-activity days and hospital visits because the data used to estimate the CR coefficient for adult restricted-activity days omits hospital and emergency room days. Finally, the potential for double counting asthma attacks and hospital visits is small because an estimated 0.5% of asthma attacks actually result in hospitalization (Bloyd et al. 1996, 9–18).

Notes

1. Levels of morbidity and mortality due to brickkiln PM_{10} in El Paso are about a seventh of levels in Ciudad Juárez. For a longer version of this chapter that includes El Paso in estimates of health damages and discusses the cross-border implications of the cost–benefit analysis, see Blackman et al. (2003).

2. Naturally occurring particulates from wind erosion and unpaved roads are an important source of particulate matter. However, such particulate matter is principally made up of large particles, which are relatively benign epidemiologically. Smaller particulates related to combustion are much more dangerous because they are inhaled deeply into the lungs (Cifuentes et al. 2000; Laden et al. 2000).

3. When brickmakers squatted in these neighborhoods 25 or 30 years ago, all were situated on the outskirts of the city. Today, however, most have been enveloped by urban sprawl.

4. We ignore the effects of NMSU kilns and natural gas on variable production costs. The former strategy would reduce variable costs because it cuts fuel costs by approximately 50%, whereas the latter strategy would raise variable costs because natural gas is more expensive than traditional fuel. We assume that given uniform application of these control strategies across all brickyards, prices in the highly competitive market for bricks adjust to offset the changes in variable costs. A more rigorous evaluation of these market effects is beyond the scope of this study.

5. Although we know little about how abatement costs at our two sample plants compare to costs at other plants, we do know that abatement costs are relatively unimportant in estimating net benefits because benefits of controlling PM_{10} pollution are two to three orders of magnitude higher than the costs (Table 2-4 and 2-5).

6. In the gray iron foundry, the principal sources of PM_{10} emissions are, in order of magnitude, pouring and cooling of molten iron, handling of sand used to make molds, shaking sand from the molds, cleaning and finishing of cast iron, and operating induction furnaces. The bulk of the chemical plant's PM_{10} emissions come from the use of fluorspar, the principal material used in the manufacture of hydrofluoric acid. In particular, PM_{10} is emitted in drying, handling, and transferring fluorspar.

7. Our health effects and valuation models draw on the Tracking and Analysis Framework (TAF), an integrated tool for cost–benefit analysis developed in part by Resources for the Future (Bloyd et al. 1996).

8. Model selection was based on the Guidelines on Air Quality Models (CFR 1997). More sophisticated 3-D models (such as CIT and UAM) require meteorological and emissions inventory data that are not available at this time. In validating a number of different air dispersion models, Patel and Kumar (1998) conclude that the ISCST model had the best overall performance.

9. Brickkilns in Ciudad Juárez are unlikely to produce significant secondary PM_{10} because they rely mainly on biomass fuel, which contains minimal sulfur that could be converted to sulfur oxide during combustion and because they are fired at temperatures far too low to generate nitrogen oxides. The kilns are also unlikely to contribute to long-range transport of PM_{10} because they do not have smokestacks. As Figure 2-2 demonstrates, kiln PM_{10} concentrations drop off dramatically within 300 meters of the source. Our two formal-sector sources are also unlikely to generate significant secondary PM_{10} or long-range transport. As Table 2-6 demonstrates, more than 99% of PM_{10} emitted by both facilities results from handling of various materials at ground level, not combustion. The only combustion-related source at either facility is an induction furnace at the iron foundry. Although this source may produce some secondary particulate matter, it has a smokestack that is just 35 feet high (compared to power plants—a notorious source of long-range transport of particulate matter—which typically have stacks 10 times this height) and is unlikely to result in long-range transport.

10. The receptor locations were chosen by mapping a 365-meter rectangular grid onto the study area, that is, grid points are 365 meters apart. As discussed in the next subsection, this spatial detail is needed to estimate human exposure to this air pollution.

11. AGEB size averages 564,572 m^2 with a standard deviation of 783,681 m^2. The smallest AGEB is 5,980 m^2, and the largest is 8,082,810 m^2. AGEB population averages 2,216 with a standard deviation of 1,387. The smallest AGEB has only 3 inhabitants, and the largest, 8,041.

12. We do not assign the inhabitants of each AGEB the average of PM_{10} concentrations predicted by the ISCST3 model at all receptor locations within the AGEB because this method would generate unrealistic spikes in exposure in several small AGEBs where there are a limited number of (arbitrarily located) receptor points, one of which happens to be close to an emission source. The alternative method we use avoids such spikes and results in more conservative exposure estimates.

13. This has the somewhat counterintuitive implication that every microgram per cubic meter increase in concentration of PM_{10} has the same marginal health effect regardless of the baseline concentration of PM_{10}. Whereas some researchers have postulated that the baseline concentration of PM_{10} matters because the relationship between ambient levels of air pollution and human health entails thresholds, the evidence for such nonlinearities is not strong (Krupnick 1996).

14. The CR mortality coefficient we use is virtually identical to a weighted average drawn from 40 studies from all over the world that was used by World Bank (Cesar 2002) to estimate mortality due to PM_{10} in Mexico City. Our CR mortality coefficient is relatively conservative. For example, in estimating the costs and benefits of the Clean Air Act, the U.S. EPA relied on a large-scale study that followed a sample population over time and found that a 10-$\mu g/m^3$ change in PM_{10} results in a 3.6% annual increase in the mortality rate (Pope et al. 1995; U.S. EPA 1999a).

Other U.S. cohort studies find even larger effects (e.g., Dockery et al. 1993). A weighted average of Mexican studies used by Evans et al. (2000) to estimate mortality due to PM_{10} in Mexico City (1.4%) is also larger than the mortality CR coefficient we use.

15. In 1998, per capita gross national product adjusted for purchasing power parity was $29,240 in the United States and $7,450 in Mexico (World Bank 2000b).

16. The empirical foundations of this second-best approach to estimating international differences in WTP can be legitimately questioned. Evidence on the topic is sparse. Chestnut et al. (1999) find that median WTP to avoid respiratory symptoms is higher in Thailand than one would expect from U.S. studies. See also Alberini et al. (1997).

References

Abbey, D., F. Petersen, P. Mills, and W. Beeson. 1993. Long-Term Ambient Concentrations of Total Suspended Particulates, Ozone and Sulfur Dioxide and Respiratory Symptoms in a Non-Smoking Population. *Archives of Environmental Health* 48(1): 33–46.

Alberini, A., M. Cropper, T. Fu, A. Krupnick, J. Liu, D. Shaw, and W. Harrington. 1997. Valuing Health Effects of Air Pollution in Developing Countries: The Case of Taiwan. *Journal of Environmental Economics and Management* 34(2): 107–26.

Alfaro, F. 1995. Personal communication with Allen Blackman. Federación Mexicana de Asociaciones Privadas de Salud y Desarrollo Comunitario. Ciudad Juárez, Chihuaua, 19 July.

———. 2000a. Personal communication with Joe Cook. Federación Mexicana de Asociaciones Privadas de Salud y Desarrollo Comunitario. Ciudad Juárez, Chihuaua, 23 March.

———. 2000b. Personal communication with Joe Cook. Federación Mexicana de Asociaciones Privadas de Salud y Desarrollo Comunitario. Ciudad Juárez, Chihuaua, 24 April.

Avila, L., C. Bruce, E. Chavez, A. Lara, and R. Marquez. 1999. A Sustainable Solution to the Air Pollution Problem Caused by Low-Technology Brick Kilns. Unpublished report. Las Cruces, NM: New Mexico State University.

Biller, D., and J.D. Quintero. 1995. Policy Options To Address Informal Sector Contamination in Latin America: The Case of Leather Tanneries in Bogota, Colombia. LATEN Dissemination Note #14. Washington, DC: World Bank.

Blackman, A., and G. Bannister. 1997. Pollution Control in the Informal Sector: The Ciudad Juárez Brickmakers' Project. *Natural Resources Journal* 27(4): 829–56.

Blackman, A., S. Newbold, J.-S. Shih, J. Cook, and D. Evans. 2003. The Benefits and Costs of Informal Sector Pollution Control: Traditional Mexican Brick Kilns in Paso del Norte. Washington, DC: Resources for the Future.

Bloyd, C., et al. 1996. Tracking and Analysis Framework (TAF) Documentation and User's Guide. ANL/DIS/TM–36. Argonne, IL: Argonne National Laboratory. http://www.lumina.com/taf/index.html (accessed September 19, 2005).

Bruce, C. 1999. Aerosol Characterization of Wood-Fed Brick Kiln Effluents in Ciudad Juárez, Chihuaua, Mexico: A SCERP Project Progress Report. In *A Sustainable Solution to the Air Pollution Problem Caused by Low-Technology Brick Kilns* by L. Avila, C. Bruce, E. Chavez, A. Lara, and R. Marquez. Unpublished report. Las Cruces, NM: New Mexico State University.

CFR (40 Code of Federal Regulations). 1997. Guideline on Air Quality Models, Part. 51, Appendix W. http://www.gpoaccess.gov/cfr/index.html (accessed September 19, 2005).

Cesar, H., et al. 2002. Improving Air Quality in Metropolitan Mexico City: An Economic Evaluation. Washington, DC: World Bank.

Chestnut, L., B. Ostro, and N. Vischit-Vadakan. 1999. Transferability of Air Pollution Control Health Benefits Estimates from the United States to Developing Countries: Evidence from the Bangkok Study. *American Journal of Agricultural Economics* 79(5): 1630–35.

Chestnut, L., and R. Rowe. 1988. Ambient Particulate Matter and Ozone Benefit Analysis for Denver. Draft Report. Prepared for U.S. EPA Region 8, Denver, CO by RCG/Hagler Bailly, Inc., Boulder, CO.

Cifuentes, L.A., J.Vega, K. Kopfer, and L.B. Lave. 2000. Effect of the Fine Fraction of Particulate Matter Versus the Coarse Mass and Other Pollutants on Daily Mortality in Santiago, Chile. *Journal of the Air and Waste Management Society* 50(8): 1287–98.

Dasgupta, S., H. Hettige, and D. Wheeler. 2000. What Improves Environmental Compliance? Evidence from Mexican Industry. *Journal of Environmental Economics and Management* 39(1): 39–66.

De Soto, H. 1989. *The Other Path: The Invisible Revolution in the Third World.* New York: Harper and Row.

Dockery, D., C. Pope, X. Xu, J. Spengler, J. Ware, M. Fay, B. Ferris, Jr., and F. Speizer. 1993. An Association Between Air Pollution and Mortality in Six US Cities. *New England Journal of Medicine* 329(24): 1753–59.

Dockery, D., F. Speizer, and D. Stram. 1989. Effects of Inhalable Particles on Respiratory Health of Children. *American Review of Respiratory Diseases* 139: 587–94.

Evans, J.S., et al. 2000. Contaminación Atmosférica y Salud Humana en la Ciudad de México. MIT-IPURGAP Report No. 10. September.

Gobierno del Estado de Chihuahua. 1998. (Also, Gobierno Municipal de Juárez; Secretaría de Medio Ambiente, Recursos Naturales y Pesca; y Secretaría de Salud.) *Programa de Gestión de la Calidad del Aire de Ciudad Juárez 1998–2002.*

Harrington, W., and G. McConnell. 2003. *Motor Vehicles and the Environment.* RFF report. April. Washington, DC: Resources for the Future.

Hagler Bailly, Inc. 1991. *Valuation of Other Externalities: Air Toxics, Water Consumption, Wastewater and Land Use.* Unpublished report prepared for New England Power Service Company Boulder, CO. October.

Heart, Lung and Blood Institute. 1992. *Tenth Report of the Director, National Heart, Lung and Blood Institute: Ten-Year Review and Five-Year Plan, Volume 3: Lung Diseases.* National Institutes of Health Publication No. 84–2358. Washington, DC: Public Health Service, U.S. Department of Health and Human Services.

INEGI (Instituto Nacional de Estadistica, Geographica e Informatica). 1992. *Ciudad Juárez.* Carte Topographica H13A25. Aguascalientes, Chihuahua, Mexico: INEGI.

———. 1995. *Conteo de Poblacion y Vivienda 1995. Resultados Definitivos.* Chihuahua. (CD-ROM).

———. 2000. Registered Deaths by State. http://www.inegi.gob.mx (accessed September 19, 2005).

JAC (Joint Advisory Committee for the Improvement of Air Quality in the Ciudad Juárez, Chihuahua / El Paso, Texas / Dona Aña County, New Mexico Air Basin). 1999. *Strategic Plan.* May. El Paso, TX: JAC.

Johnson, A. 2000. Personal communication with Allen Blackman. El Paso Natural Gas, El Paso, TX, 19 July.

Krupnick, A. 1996. The Health Benefits of Air Pollution Reduction in Monterrey, Mexico. Unpublished report. Washington, DC: Resources for the Future.

Krupnick, A., and M. Cropper. 1989. Social Costs of Chronic Heart and Lung Disease. *Resources* 1997, Fall.

Krupnick, A., W. Harrington, and B. Ostro. 1990. Ambient Ozone and Acute Health Effects: Evidence from Daily Data. *Journal of Environmental Economics and Management* 18(1): 1–18.

Krupnick, A., and R. Kopp. 1988. The Acute Health Benefits of Ambient Ozone Control. Appendix to *Catching Our Breath: Next Steps for Reducing Urban Ozone.* July. Washington, DC: Office of Technology Assessment, U.S. Congress.

Laden, F., L.M. Neas, D.W. Dockery, and J. Schwartz. 2000. Association of Fine Particulate Matter from Different Sources with Daily Mortality in Six U.S. Cities. *Environmental Health Perspectives* 108(10): 941–47.

Lee, R., A. Krupnick, D. Burtraw, et al. 1994. *Estimating Externalities of Electric Fuel Cycles: Analytical Methods and Issues.* Washington, DC: McGraw-Hill/Utility Data Institute.

Loehman, E., S. Berg, A. Arroyo, R. Hedinger, J. Schwartz, M. Shaw, W. Fahien, V. De, R. Fishe, D. Rio, W. Rossley, and A. Green. 1979. Distributional Analysis of Regional Benefits and Cost of Air Quality. *Journal of Environmental Economics and Management* 6(3): 222–43.

Marquez, R. 2000. Personal communication with Joe Cook. New Mexico State University, Las Cruces, NM, 9 February and 26 June.

NCDC (National Climate Data Center). 2000. http://www.ncdc.noaa.gov (accessed September 19, 2005).

Ostro, B. 1987. Air Pollution and Morbidity Revisited: A Specification Test. *Journal of Environmental Economics and Management* 14: 87–98.

———. 1994. Estimating the Health Effects of Air Pollutants: A Method with an Application to Jakarta. Policy Research Working Paper 1301. Washington, DC: World Bank.

Ostro, B., M. Lipsett, M. Wiener, and J. Selner. 1991. Asthmatic Response to Airborne Acid Aerosols. *American Journal of Public Health* 81: 694–702.

Patel, V., and A. Kumar. 1998. Evaluation of Three Air Dispersion Models: ISCST2, ISCLT2, and Screen 2 for Mercury Emissions in an Urban Area. *Environmental Monitoring and Assessment* 53(2): 259–77.

Perera, L.A.S.R., and A.T.M.N. Amin. 1996. Accommodating the Informal Sector: A Strategy for Urban Environmental Management. *Journal of Environmental Management* 46: 3–14.

Plagiannakos, T., and J. Parker. 1988. An Assessment of Air Pollution Effects on Human Health in Ontario. *Ontario Hydro*, March.

Pope, D., M. Thun, M. Namboodiri, D. Dockery, J. Evans, F. Speizer, and C. Heath. 1995. Particulate Air Pollution as a Predictor of Mortality in a Prospective Study of U.S. Adults. *American Journal of Respiratory Critical Care Medicine* 151(3): 669–74.

Ranis, G., and F. Stewart. 1994. V-Goods and the Role of the Urban Informal Sector in Development. Economic Growth Center Discussion Paper No. 724. New Haven, CT: Yale University.

Reynoso, J. 2000. Personal communication with Joe Cook. Texas Natural Resources Conservation Commission, El Paso, TX, 8 May.

RFF (Resources for the Future). 1995. Ciudad Juárez Brick Kiln Survey. Washington, DC: Resources for the Future.

Riswadkar, R., and A. Kumar. 1994. Evaluation of the Industrial Source Complex Short-term Model in a Large-Scale Multiple Source Region for Different Stability Classes. *Environmental Monitoring and Assessment* 33(1): 19–32.

Rowe, R., and L. Chestnut. 1985. Oxidants and Asthmatics in Los Angeles: A Benefits Analysis. EPA–230–07–85–010, and Addendum of March 1986, prepared by Energy and Resource Consultants, Inc., for U.S. Environmental Protection Agency, Office of Policy Analysis, Washington, DC.

Samet, J., Y. Bishop, F. Speizer, J. Spengler, and B. Ferris, Jr. 1981. The Relationship Between Air Pollution and Emergency Room Visits in an Industrial Community. *Journal of Air Pollution Control Association* 31: 236–40.

Schneider, F., and D.H. Enste. 2000. Shadow Economies Around the World: Size, Cause and Consequences. *Journal of Economic Literature* 38(1): 77–114.

Tarin, G. 2000. Personal communication with Joe Cook. Dirección Municipal de Ecología. Ciudad Juárez, Chihuahua, 1 March.

U.S. EPA (U.S. Environmental Protection Agency). 1995. *Compilation of Air Pollutant Emission Factors (AP–42), Fifth Edition, Volume I: Stationary Point and Area Sources.* Washington, DC: U.S. EPA. http://www.epa.gov/ttn/chief/ap42/ (accessed September 19, 2005).

———. 1998a. *OAQPS Control Cost Manual, Fifth Edition.* EPA 453/b–96–001. Research Triangle Park, NC: U.S. EPA Office of Air Quality and Planning. http://www.epa.gov/ttn/catc/products.html#cccinfo (accessed September 19, 2005).

———. 1998b. *Stationary Source Control Techniques Document for Fine Particulate Matter.* EPA 452/R–97–001. Research Triangle Park, NC: U.S. EPA. http://www.epa.gov/ttn/catc/dir1/finepmtech.pdf (accessed September 19, 2005).

———. 1999a. *The Benefits and Costs of the Clean Air Act 1990 to 2010.* EPA–410–R–99–001. Washington, DC: U.S. EPA. http://www.epa.gov/oar/sect812/ (accessed September 19, 2005).

———. 1999b. *'CO$T-AIR' Air Pollution Control Cost Spreadsheets (Second Edition).* Research Triangle Park, NC: U.S. EPA Office of Air Quality and Planning. http://www.epa.gov/ttn/catc/products.html#cccinfo (accessed September 19, 2005).

———. 2000. Technology Transfer Network Bulletin Board System Support Center for Regulatory Air Models (SCRAM). Washington, DC: U.S. EPA.

———. 2001. Aerometric Information Retrieval System/AIRS Facility Subsystem (AIRS/AFS). Washington, DC: U.S. EPA. http://www.epa.gov/enviro/html/airs/airs_query_java.html (accessed September 19, 2005).

Valenzuela, V. 2000. Personal communication with Allen Blackman. TCEQ (Texas Commission on Environmental Quality). El Paso, TX, 15 August.

World Bank. 1994. Chile, Managing Environmental Problems: Economic Analysis of Selected Issues. World Bank, Environmental and Urban Development Division, Country Department I, Latin America and the Caribbean Region. Washington, DC: World Bank.

———. 2000a. *Greening Industry: New Roles for Communities, Markets, and Governments*. New York: Oxford University Press.

———. 2000b. World Development Indicators. http://www.worldbank.org (accessed September 19, 2005).

CHAPTER 3

Small-Scale Industry, Poverty, and the Environment

A Case Study of Ecuador

Peter Lanjouw

SOME SMALL-SCALE INDUSTRIES in developing countries are highly pollution-intensive, when pollution is measured per unit of output. Yet, small-scale firms are rarely subject to stringent environmental regulation for a combination of reasons. First, they are thought to contribute only a small fraction to total pollution loads because their share of total output is believed to be relatively small. Second, small-scale industries are thought to fulfill an important distributional function, by providing employment to the poor. Policies that curtail their activities, it is feared, would translate directly into an increase in poverty. Third, as many small-scale enterprises operate in the informal sector, it is particularly costly to establish the monitoring and supervision capacity necessary to regulate them. These arguments have been used to make a case for excluding small-scale enterprises from environmental regulation (see, for example, Brandon 1993). By excluding such firms, it is argued, total pollution will probably not increase by much, the sector's poverty alleviation function can be preserved, and the costs associated with incorporating these firms into the regulatory purview can be avoided.

This chapter examines the above argument in the context of Ecuador, a small, middle-income developing country. It scrutinizes the different components of the overall argument, as well as the implicit assumptions on which they are based. The chapter suggests that the three pillars underlying the argument are quite fragile in the context of Ecuador. In fact, rather than the "best compromise" scenario envisaged in the above argument (where poverty alleviation objectives can be pursued at negligible environmental expense), an entirely different scenario could in fact apply: environmental regulation could result in a significant reduction of total pollution without compromising the objective of reducing poverty. The circumstances in Ecuador that lead to this conclusion can be briefly summarized.[1]

First, in Ecuador small-scale firms contribute a significant share to total pollution loads. The vast majority of the economically active population in Ecuador works in an enterprise with 10 or fewer workers. This observation clearly holds whether one considers the economically active population as a whole (i.e., including the agricultural and service sectors) or just the industrial sector. As pollution per worker coefficients are typically higher in small-scale firms than in large firms, the share of total pollution arising from small-scale firms dominates. Effective regulation of pollution-intensive small-scale firms is thus likely to make a considerable difference to total industrial pollution loads.

Second, the small-scale sector, by virtue of its overall employment levels, is important in providing employment to the poor. However, most of Ecuador's poor are found in the small-scale agricultural sector.[2] Even within the nonagricultural sector, the data indicate that a significant proportion of the poor are employed in relatively clean activities. Moreover, within the pollution-intensive subsector, an important distinction can be drawn between those activities where employees are among those at greatest risk from pollution and those where the impact of the pollution is primarily on outsiders. Poverty rates are considerably higher among the former group. This observation implies that effective regulation of pollution-intensive small-scale firms, which results in lower workplace health hazards, could have a beneficial effect on living standards of the poor.

However, active regulation of small-scale firms could clearly also reduce employment. Given the personal endowments of those who are employed in pollution-intensive small-scale firms, what kind of increase in poverty might one expect to see if pollution from this sector were closely controlled, and if this resulted in a serious contraction of employment? Because of the myriad possible indirect effects of such a policy, it is difficult to provide a full answer to this question. However, rough estimates suggest that the rise in the incidence of poverty could be fairly modest—because those who are currently employed in this sector have the endowments to also find employment outside this sector and therefore to maintain consumption levels.

Much of this chapter presents the empirical evidence that underlies the preceding arguments. We begin in the next section, however, with a brief comment on our approach to linking poverty issues with environmental and employment considerations. The following section examines the small-scale sector in the Ecuadorean economy and assesses the importance of the sector in terms of employment. In section 4, entitled Small-Scale Industry and Environmental Degradation, we consider the environmental impact of the sector. In section 5 we link small-scale enterprises to poverty. We ask in a first sub-section how significant a role this sector plays in providing employment to the poor. We then turn to the question of what might be the effect on poverty of a severe contraction in employment in pollution-intensive small-scale enterprises. The final section summarizes the discussion to point to policy implications.

Concepts of Poverty and Environmental Degradation

This chapter was written to assess the contribution of small-scale enterprises to poverty-reduction and to inquire whether, and to what extent, the simultaneous goal of environmental improvement complements or conflicts with this objective. This type of investigation can become quite awkward, and potentially misleading, unless a clear notion of poverty is spelled out from the start. In this chapter, we apply an absolute poverty criterion, in which people are judged to be poor when their consumption level falls below a poverty line that has been specified for the country as a whole and that remains unchanged (in real terms) across sectors of the economy and over time.[3] This approach can be contrasted with one where, say, attention is confined to the bottom 30% of the urban population (who may, in fact, be fairly highly ranked in the population as a whole). For example, taking such a relative poverty notion, one might decide that measures should be introduced to protect the employment of slum dwellers. This may entail withholding resources that could be directed toward the absolutely poor and may therefore constrain absolute poverty reduction, or may even result in a worsening of absolute poverty. We cannot easily justify intervening on behalf of the slum dwellers for poverty reasons, unless they are in fact *absolutely* poor, not just relatively poor in urban areas. The critical point is to retain a clear overview of poverty and consumption levels across the population as a whole and to ensure that comparisons of poverty across such groups are consistent (see Ravallion 1994 for further discussion).

In a similar vein, it is also worth considering the manner in which the environmental consequences of small-scale industrial activities should be addressed. It is clear that environmental effects can be distinguished in terms of how they are released: into the air or water or as solid wastes.[4] While we attempt to address as broad a spectrum of environmental consequences as possible, we focus on wastewater pollution in particular when we present a tentative quantitative estimate of the pollution intensity of small-scale enterprises.[5] Environmental consequences can also be distinguished in terms of their reversibility. We concentrate on environmental consequences that are relatively more difficult or costly to alleviate. (Thus, relatively little attention is paid to noise pollution, for example.) Finally, we note that environmental consequences can differ in terms of their effect on workers, nearby residents, and the population at large. We argue that when poverty links are also considered, worker health issues can be particularly relevant.

Small-Scale Industry in the Ecuadorean Economy

It is difficult to point to a single criterion that best defines a small-scale enterprise. Such firms could be distinguished from medium or large firms on the basis of employment or of turnover levels, for example. In this study, we define small-scale enterprises as those engaged in manufacturing activities employing no more than 10 workers (making no distinction between owners, family members, and other employees). This definition accounts for a large share of total employment in Ecuador, even in industrial and manufacturing sectors. Yet it defines a group that rarely comes under the purview of conventional firm-level surveys. Our definition can be applied to the household survey data, from which we draw much of our evidence. However, given that we want to cross-check with alternative data sources and that different data sources adopt different conventions, we also use alternative definitions of small-scale enterprise. We note specifically those cases where a different definition applies.

How important are small-scale enterprises in the Ecuadorean economy? There exists no nationally representative survey of small-scale enterprises, defined in the manner we have chosen, which would allow us to establish their contribution to total manufacturing. However, from the 1995 *Encuesta sobre las Condiciones de Vida* (ECV 1995), a nationally representative household survey, we can measure their share of total employment in Ecuador. Because such household surveys are not generally used to document the size distribution and structure of the manufacturing sector, it will also be necessary to devote some effort in this section to establishing the suitability of the ECV 1995 data for this purpose.

Table 3-1 indicates that, confining our attention solely to industrial and manufacturing activities, more than 300,000 Ecuadoreans were employed in firms ranging in size from 2 to 10 workers in 1995. These firms accounted for more than half (53%) of total employment in industrial and manufacturing activities in that year. Table 3-1 also allows us to compare employment data from the 1995 household survey with that from the 1993 firm-level Survey of Mining and Manufacturing carried out by the Ecuadorean National Institute of the Census and Statistics (INEC) and reported in INSOTEC (1993). This survey defines small-scale enterprises as those with 11 to 50 workers, medium-sized firms as those with 50 to 100 workers, and large firms as those with more than 100 workers. In Table 3-1

Table 3-1. *Employment in the Ecuador Industrial Sector Compared across Data Sources*

Size of establishment	Employees in industrial iector in 1993[a]	Employees in industrial sector in 1995[b]
Single worker	NA	125,047 (21%)
2–10 workers	NA	318,375 (53%)
11–50 workers	26,219	66,428 (11%)
51–100 workers	19,437	23,502 (4%)
100+ workers	76,662	71,236 (12%)
Total	122,318	604,588 (100%)
		161,166[c]

[a]The figures from the INSOTEC 1993 Survey of Mining and Manufacturing were calculated by the Instituto de Investigaciones Socio-Economicas y Tecnologicas in Quito, Ecuador.

[b]The figures for the Encuesta de Condiciones de Vida (1995) were calculated from the survey data. Employment figures from ECV 1995 are based on reported principal economic activity during the preceding week.

[c]Total including only establishments with more than 10 workers.

Note: NA means not applicable.

we see that although the ECV 1995 indicates a much higher employment level in small-scale firms, employment levels for medium and large-scale firms are quite close across the two data sources. Given that a firm-level survey might be expected to miss relatively small firms (especially those that exist in the informal sector and that may not be registered), the employment figures from the ECV 1995 appear to accord broadly with those from the firm-level survey.

In Table 3-2 we pursue the comparison between the two data sources further. In this table, we confine our attention to the small- and medium-scale enterprises, as defined by INEC. That is, we focus on the sectoral breakdown of employment in industry and manufacturing of those firms that employ from 10 to 100 workers. In Table 3-2 (as in Table 3-1), we see that total employment in such firms is higher in the ECV 1995 than in the Survey of Mining and Manufacturing of 1993. It

Table 3-2. *Employment in Medium-Sized Industry (10–100 workers) by Sector*

Sector of industrial activity	Employees in medium-sized industry in 1993[a]	Employees in medium-sized industry in 1995[b]		
		Total	Urban	Rural
Food, beverages, and tobacco	11,933 (26%)	25,144 (28%)	22,297	2,847
Textiles, clothing, and leather goods	8,976 (20%)	19,586 (22%)	15,053	4,533
Wood products and furniture	3,026 (7%)	13,200 (15%)	10,470	2,730
Paper and printing	2,806 (6%)	5,007 (6%)	4,931	76
Plastics, rubber, and chemical products	7,679 (17%)	10,057 (11%)	9,193	864
Nonmetal mineral products	2,266 (5%)	6,731 (7%)	6,635	96
Basic metal products	491 (1%)	1,435 (2%)	950	485
Metal goods and machinery	7,520 (16%)	7,845 (9%)	7,574	279
Other	959 (2%)	925 (1%)	925	0
Total	45,656 (100%)	89,930 (100%)	78,020	11,910

[a]The figures from the INSOTEC 1993 Survey of Mining and Manufacturing were calculated by the Instituto de Investigaciones Socio-Economicas y Tecnologicas in Quito, Ecuador (Survey of Mining and Manufacturing).

[b]The figures for the Encuesta de Condiciones de Vida (1995) were calculated from the survey data. Employment figures from ECV 1995 are based on reported principal economic activity during the preceding week.

is unlikely that the differing dates of the survey can explain the discrepancy. The Ecuadorean economy did not undergo any major structural changes during this time that could have led to such a dramatic increase in employment in small-scale enterprises within the industrial sector. It also appears that the discrepancy cannot be explained by a better coverage of rural areas in the ECV 1995. Even if one omits rural firms, employment levels in the ECV 1995 are much higher than those in the firm-level survey (the last two columns of Table 3-2).

One is left with the explanation that coverage of the firm-level survey was simply less comprehensive. This notion is given some support by the observation that the share of employment across different sectors is quite consistent between the two data sources. For example, both surveys indicate that just over a quarter of employment in firms of this size occurs within the food processing industry, and another fifth occurs in textiles and clothing. If one assumes that the firm-level survey failed to cover the smallest firms in particular, then this might also account for the relatively larger share of employment in wood products and furniture in the ECV 1995 and the commensurately lower share in that survey in plastics, rubber, and chemical products and in metal goods and machinery products (which are probably closer to the upper limit of our size category).

From Tables 3-1 and 3-2, we draw the conclusion that employment figures from the ECV 1995 are not out of line with firm-level surveys. As a result, we can feel some justification in scrutinizing the ECV 1995 data set more closely for levels of employment in small-scale enterprises and their principal sectors of activity (where we take our definition of small-scale firms as employing no more than 10 workers).

Table 3-3 provides a breakdown of employment by sector and size of workplace as revealed by the ECV 1995. (The survey figures have been scaled up to the national level by using the household weights that accompanied the data set.) The sector breakdown provided in Table 3-3 accords loosely with an industrial breakdown based on (two-digit) International Standard Industrial Classification (ISIC) codes.[6] Employment figures per sector apply to the principal occupation of all surveyed individuals aged 10 and above who reported working during the past week. From the last row of Table 3-3 we can see that just under half of Ecuador's total population can be defined as economically active in this way.

Also in the last row of Table 3-3, we can see that almost three-fifths of all employment in Ecuador occurs in establishments with 2–10 workers. Adding to this figure those individuals who work on their own, we find that more than three-quarters of the economically active population (77%) works in a workplace with 10 or fewer workers.[7]

Much of the total employment in Ecuador occurs in agriculture, forestry, and fishing. This sector falls out of the purview of this chapter.[8] Nonagricultural sectors that provide significant employment in Ecuador include food processing, clothing, construction, retail and wholesale commerce, hotel and restaurant operation, and certain services (such as public administration, teaching, and domestic service). The relative importance of small-scale enterprises within these sectors varies, but it is striking from Table 3-3 just how important small-scale enterprises are in the majority of sectors in the economy. Only in sectors such as oil mining, tobacco product manufacture, wood pulp and paper production, petroleum-based product

Table 3-3. *Employment Levels by Sector of Employment and Size of Establishment (principal economic activity during preceding week)*

Sector of economic activity	Total numbers of workers in the workplace (row percent)					
	One	2–10	11–50	51–100	101+	Total
Agriculture, forestry, and fishing	105,686 6.8%	1,249,735 81.4%	130,252 8.5%	19,720 1.3%	30,587 2.0%	1,535,980 100%
Extraction, mining, and quarrying	388 1.3%	14,454 48.4%	5,435 18.2%	2,307 7.7%	7,294 24.4%	29,878 100%
Industry and manufacturing	126,550 20.8%	319,541 52.4%	67,643 11.1%	23,502 3.9%	72,277 11.9%	609,513 100%
Utilities	477 3.1%	3,249 21.0%	2,396 15.5%	1,958 12.7%	7,364 47.7%	15,444 100%
Construction	18,890 7.5%	161,563 64.0%	48,424 19.2%	9,145 3.6%	14,430 5.72%	252,452 100%
Commerce and repair	269,323 24.2%	701,985 63.1%	83,634 7.5%	12,653 1.1%	45,441 4.1%	1,113,036 100%
Hotels and restaurants	8,544 7.5%	76,668 68.8%	19,464 17.0%	3,986 3.5%	3,761 3.3%	114,423 100%
Transport and communications	60,314 30.9%	85,516 43.9%	19,713 10.1%	5,236 2.7%	24,166 12.4%	194,545 100%
Financial services	750 1.6%	5,721 12.4%	5,807 12.6%	4,476 9.7%	29,513 63.8%	46,267 100%
Real estate and leasing	11,033 14.4%	35,880 46.7%	13,450 17.5%	2,233 2.9%	14,202 18.5%	76,798 100%
Administration, teaching, and other services	260,024 27.4%	282,195 29.8%	97,730 10.3%	27,257 2.9%	280,211 29.6%	947,417 100%
Other and/or not available	2,317 40.3%	1,404 24.4%	409 7.1%	0 0%	1,618 28.2%	5,748 100%
Total	864,296 17.5%	293,9911 59.5%	494,357 10.0%	112,473 2.3%	530,864 10.7%	4,941,901 100%

Source: Calculated from Encuesta de Condiciones de Vida (1995).

manufacture, gas and electricity provision, and various service sector jobs (e.g., utilities, finance, and public administration) do large-scale establishments clearly provide the bulk of total employment (Lanjouw 1997).

Small-Scale Industry and Environmental Degradation

We now inquire into the environmental threat posed by small-scale enterprises. It is not easy to arrive at a simple diagnosis of the environmental impact of various economic activities. As was discussed in the previous section, titled Concepts of Poverty and Environmental Degradation, environmental degradation can occur in many dimensions. Pollution and environmental hazards can be highly localized so that the impact is felt mainly by those working in the polluting firm. Alternatively, the firm's pollution may impinge mainly on those residing in the immediate vicinity of the polluting plant rather than on those working in it (due to effluent discharge into public water or air pollution). Finally, the pollution may be regional, national, or global rather than local and can contribute to a general deterioration of the environment that is felt by all. All three types of pollution may occur simultaneously, but to differing degrees.

In a related vein, pollution can take the form of solids, liquid, or gas. The costs associated with mitigating or eliminating the adverse effects of pollution will differ across these different types of pollution.

Typically, it is thought that small-scale enterprises (particularly those that are in the informal sector) are more likely to be using older equipment than are large firms. Given credit, managerial, and other constraints that small firms operating in the informal sector face, it is thought that such firms use older equipment, which becomes increasingly pollution-intensive with age through heavy use. The more modern equipment, which large firms operate, is also more likely to incorporate new technologies that address the environmental concerns of developed countries, where many of the new technologies are developed. There is therefore a presumption that small firms are more intensive producers of pollution than large firms.[9] In assessing the contribution of small-scale enterprises to total pollution loads, it is thus important to identify not only the kinds of environmental damage arising from activities they pursue, but also to contrast the pollution intensity of small-scale enterprises with that of large firms engaged in similar activities.

No single study for Ecuador carefully describes and analyzes the environmental implications of the different economic activities undertaken in the economy. Certainly no such study takes explicit account of the scale of operation, i.e., distinguishing the pollution "coefficients" associated with small-scale enterprises from those associated with medium and large firms. However, by bringing together results from some of the investigations on pollution and industry that have been undertaken in Ecuador, and by making some rough calculations applying pollution intensity coefficients from countries other than Ecuador, it is possible to arrive at a tentative assessment of how significant a contribution to total pollution is provided by small-scale enterprises.

In 1993, the Corporacion Nacional de Apoyo a las Unidades Populares Economicas (CONAUPE 1993), in conjunction with the Inter-American Development Bank (IDB), produced a study of the environmental impact of small-scale enterprises in Ecuador (defined as firms with no more than eight workers). They identified 24 sectors in which small-scale enterprises in Ecuador are active and are likely to have some adverse environmental impact. Within each sector, the separate tasks making up the overall production process were examined, and each task was given a qualitative grade for its overall environmental impact (from 1 to 5, with 5 indicating the most severe impact). Moreover, for each task, within each sector, an environmental grade was registered separately for a whole range of environmental dimensions.[10] Table 3-4 summarizes the findings from this qualitative study. In this table, a sector is associated with a high environmental impact for a given environmental dimension if any one task within the overall production process of that sector was given a qualitative grading of 4 or 5. For example, small-scale enterprises engaged in the manufacture of bricks are attributed a high impact on the physical landscape, on the health of workers, and on the health of local residents because at least one of the tasks that make up the process of manufacturing bricks was found to place a heavy strain on the respective environmental dimension (warranting a grade of at least 4). A medium impact in Table 3-4 is attributed to those sectors which, for a given environmental dimension, include at least one task which has received a qualitative grading of 3 (and no task received a grading of 4 or 5). Sectors have a low impact in a given environmental dimension if the highest grading received by at least one underlying task is a 1 or 2. Those sectors that have no adverse impact on a particular environmental dimension are represented with an NA.

The small-scale enterprise activities listed in Table 3-4 have been separated into two groups: those that have a significant impact on the environment and those that have a more moderate impact. This informal separation is based on the scrutiny of the different grades per environmental dimension as well as consideration of the nature of the given environmental impact. For example, a sector that exercises a high impact on workers in terms of noise pollution (such as textile and clothing production) has been designated of a moderate overall impact, whereas printing, which has a high impact on workers' health due to their exposure to chemicals such as chlorine during the bleaching process, has been designated of significant environmental impact.

It is striking from Table 3-4 how often the effect on workers' health is found to be of serious concern. In all but one of the economic activities that were designated as having a significant environmental impact, the effect on workers' health is registered as high. Many of these activities also have a high impact on other dimensions of the environment. It is also important to note that of the 24 economic sectors, three have been found to exert a medium or higher level impact on the health of *local* residents, (through contamination of local water sources and emissions of air pollution).

Among the manufacturing activities undertaken by small-scale enterprises that exert a significant impact on the more commonly discussed environmental categories (namely, air pollution, solid and liquid waste generation, and physical landscape degradation), the important ones in Ecuador include brick and tile manufacture; leather tanning; chemical and medicine production; battery repair and reconditioning; manufacture of "Panama" hats; cloth dyeing; furniture making; the manufacture of electronic, sporting, and musical equipment; and food processing.[11] It is not straightforward to relate each of these sectors of activity to the sectoral breakdown available from the ECV 1995. Lanjouw (1997) shows, on the basis of detailed tabulations from the ECV 1995, that in the case of leather tanning, the manufacture of Panama hats, furniture making, and food processing, the definitions seem broadly comparable, and it appears that the bulk of total employment in those sectors occurs among small-scale enterprises. Given the importance of small-scale enterprises in most sectors of the Ecuadorean economy, it is likely that most employment in the other activities listed above is also generated by small firms.

Given the importance of small-scale firms in terms of employment in many sectors of the Ecuadorean economy, we would expect their contribution to total

Table 3-4. Small-Scale Enterprise Activities and Environmental Degradation in Ecuador

Economic sector	Air pollution	Solid and liquid waste generation	Physical landscape	Worker health	Neighbor health	Client health	Remarks
Significant environmental impact							
Brick and roof-tile manufacture	Medium	Low	High	High	High	Low	Erosion; river contamination; sulfur and carbon smoke
Leather tanning	Low	High	NA	High	Low	Low	Animal residues and toxic chemical wastes
Chemical and medicine production	Low	Medium	NA	High	Medium	High	Toxic chemical spills and leaks; explosions
Battery repair and reconditioning	High	Low	NA	High	High	NA	Toxic liquid and solid wastes (acids and lead)
"Panama" hats	Medium	Low	NA	High	Low	Low	Sulphuric gas emissions from steaming process
Ceramics	Low	Low	NA	High	Low	Medium	Lead-based paints; toxic chemicals in glazes
Printing	Low	Low	NA	High	Low	Low	Production using toxic chemicals (e.g., chlorine)
Jewelry and glass objects	Low	Low	NA	High	Low	NA	Production of toxic chemicals (e.g., silica, heavy metals)
Agriculture	Medium	Low	High	High	Low	Medium	Deforestation; erosion; herbicides; pesticides
Dairy	Low	High	NA	Low	Low	Low	Contamination in pasteurization and removal of whey
Moderate environmental impact							
Textiles, clothing, and leather goods	Low	Low	NA	High	NA	Low	Noise from spinning and sewing machines
Cloth dyeing	Low	Medium	NA	Low	NA	NA	Chemical residues and dyes in wastewater
Furniture making	Medium	Low	High	Medium	Low	Low	Deforestation; wood dust; waste from varnishes; wax
Equipment: electronic, sporting, musical	Medium	Low	NA	Medium	Low	NA	Noise; soldering contamination; paint; insulation
Food processing	Low	Low	NA	Low	Low	Low	Heavy water use; pesticide and fertilizer residue
Restaurants	Low	Medium	NA	Low	Low	High	Residues of pesticides; waste from processing
Fisheries	NA	Low	High	Low	NA	NA	Fuel spills; fish populations; coral and reef integrity
Animal care and livestock	Low	Medium	High	Low	Low	Low	Deforestation; erosion; herbicides; spoilage of meat

Nightclubs	NA	Low	NA	Medium	Low	Medium	Alcohol poisoning; noise pollution
Distribution and sale of gasoline	Low	Low	NA	Low	Low	High	Gas leaks; exploding canisters
Cement and plaster products	Low	Low	NA	Low	Low	NA	Cement dust; liquid and solid waste
Rubber products	Low	NA	NA	Low	Low	Low	Sulfur and carbon emissions
Metal products	Low	NA	NA	Low	Low	NA	Inferior smelting and casting technology emissions
Vehicle repair	Low	Low	NA	Low	Low	NA	Oils, solvents, and paint residues in air and water

Notes: Within each sector, the activities that contribute to overall production have been scrutinized and ranked from 1 to 5 in terms of their environmental impact (along 6 possible dimensions—see below). Sectors in which at least one of these activities is associated with an impact of 4 or 5 are designated high-impact sectors. A maximum grade of 3 for any of the activities comprising a sector's range of activities results in the sector being designated a medium impact sector. Low-impact sectors are those where no activity is associated with a grade of more than 2. The six environmental dimensions are air pollution; solid and liquid waste generation; physical landscape (including flora and fauna) degradation; risk to health of workers; risk to health of neighbors; and risk to health of clients.

Source: Adapted from CONAUPE 1993, Document M.A. 4.2 *Manual de Seguimiento, Monitoreo y Evaluacion.*

pollution loads to be large (barring exceptionally low labor productivity in small-scale firms). It is difficult to demonstrate this rigorously, however. Such an exercise would entail examining all pollution-intensive sectors, identifying the degree of differences in pollution intensity (pollution per worker) between large and small firms within each sector, alongside measures of total employment in small and large firms within each sector. Such data are unavailable for Ecuador (or most other countries). Even if they were available, they would probably be controversial, given that there are so many forms of environmental degradation that cannot always be easily quantified or aggregated together.

However, as a highly tentative and exploratory exercise, we consider what rough orders of magnitude might emerge from such a calculation (Table 3-5). We make use, for this exercise, of pollution coefficients in terms of average industrial wastewater generated per worker (WAPW) in six sectors. These pollution coefficients are based on a study carried out in 1992 of 397 enterprises in Thailand, distinguishing between small-scale enterprises (up to 15 workers) and medium and large-scale firms (between 15 and 120 workers).[12] We distinguish between small and medium and large-scale firms in this exercise, rather than between small-scale and large-scale firms, because we saw in Tables 3-1 and 3-3 that only around 10% of total employment in Ecuador takes place in workplaces with more than 100 workers.

Table 3-5 confirms, at least for these six sectors, that just as small-scale firms account for the bulk of total employment in these sectors, they also account for the bulk of the industrial wastewater pollution deriving from these activities. From columns 1 and 2 of Table 3-5, we can see that pollution per worker in the larger firms is lower than in small-scale firms.[13] This is probably because larger firms are better placed to afford and operate modern technologies, which are less pollu-

Table 3-5. *Contribution to Total Industrial Wastewater Pollution by Sector, Contrasting Small-Scale Enterprises against Large Enterprises*

Description of activity	SSE WAPW (m3/day)	MLSE WAPW (m3/day)	Employment at SSEs	Employment at LSEs	Contribution by SSE to Total (%)
Vehicle repair	0.07692	0.05077	68,689	8,090	93
Food processing	0.61538	0.13109	63,279	55,451	84
Furniture making	0.03508	0.00000	70,554	7,695	100
Iron goods	0.05405	0.05243	28,212	6,052	83
Paper and pulp	0.10000	0.06070	464	3,698	17
Textiles	1.18812	0.38901	45,403	1,836	90

Notes: SSE is small-scale enterprise (up to 15 workers); WAPW is average wastewater generated per worker, MLSE is medium and large-scale enterprises (15–20 workers). Pollution coefficients correspond to the WAPW observed in Thailand in 1992. The above sectors were the only ones for which comparability between Thailand and Ecuador seemed possible.

Sources: Employment figures were obtained from ECV 1995. Pollution coefficients were obtained from a study of 397 firms in Rangsit and Suksawat, undertaken by DHV consultants, of the Netherlands, for the Thailand Institute of Scientific and Technological Research (1994).

tion-intensive. Coupling the higher pollution intensity of small-scale firms with the generally greater total employment in small-scale firms (the only exception in Table 3-5 is paper and pulp production), it comes as no surprise that the contribution of small-scale firms to total wastewater pollution dominates in these six sectors. Only in the case of paper and pulp production do large-scale firms contribute a larger share to total pollution loads from that sector than do small-scale firms, even though the larger firms are less pollution-intensive. Table 3-5 indicates that 92% of all wastewater pollution produced by these six sectors comes from small-scale enterprises.

We are far from having proved the general proposition that small-scale firms contribute more to total pollution in Ecuador than do large-scale firms. To claim this, one would need information on pollution intensity for a complete range of sectors. We would also need to replicate the analysis presented in Table 3-5 for media other than water. A large amount of information, which is currently not available, is needed before concrete statements can be made. Nevertheless, the evidence on employment in small-scale industries in Ecuador suggests that the approximate orders of magnitude presented in Table 3-5 may not be wildly out of line. This finding is in fairly stark contrast to the conventional view that large-scale enterprises account for the bulk of total pollution loads. Such a view may well be applicable for industrialized countries, where the bulk of manufacturing activity (and employment) takes place in large firms. But it requires empirical validation in developing countries such as Ecuador.

Small-Scale Enterprises and Poverty

Are Workers in Small-Scale Enterprises Poor?

In this section, we consider the question of how important small-scale enterprises are for the poor. We are particularly interested to assess the significance of those small-scale sector activities that have been found to present important environmental risks. Table 3-6 presents calculations of the incidence of poverty among the economically active population, broken down by size and sector of the workplace. Poverty rates are calculated for a high and a low poverty line, representing, respectively, a threshold below which a person can subsist, but only frugally, and a second threshold below which a person can clearly be counted among the extreme poor (able, at best, to meet his or her food requirements but with no essential non-food items). In addition to the incidence of poverty associated with different sectors of economic activity, Table 3-6 also presents figures on the fraction of the poor who are employed in those sectors.

The final row of Table 3-6 indicates that 53% of the economically active population in Ecuador had a consumption level below the high poverty line in 1995 (corresponding to a daily per capita consumption level of approximately $3 at 1995 exchange rates). With the low poverty line of roughly $1 per day, the incidence of poverty among the economically active population as a whole was about 13%.[14]

Table 3-6. *Poverty by Pollution-Intensive Employment Activity*

Sector	High poverty line Incidence	Contribution (%)	Low poverty line Incidence	Contribution (%)
Pollution-intensive SSI with significant worker health impact				
Nonmetal mineral goods, quarrying, and construction	68.0	5.59	17.4	5.97
Leather goods and tanning	58.8	0.52	18.8	0.69
Chemical products (chemical goods and medicines)	31.0	0.00	0.0	0.00
Vehicle repair (and battery reconditioning)	52.3	1.44	6.3	0.72
Woodwork and straw ("Panama" hats)	68.2	1.29	14.9	1.18
Printing	11.5	0.05	0.0	0.00
Textiles and cloth dyeing	55.0	2.99	14.3	3.21
Subtotal	60.9	11.93	14.3	11.77
Pollution-intensive SSI with moderate to low worker health impact				
Furniture making	56.6	1.52	13.1	1.45
Equipment: electronics/sporting/musical	37.9	0.08	10.6	0.09
Food processing	41.4	1.00	14.8	1.48
Hotels and restaurants	43.6	1.45	13.9	1.91
Electricity and gasoline distribution	58.3	0.04	0.0	0.00
Rubber products	75.9	0.09	46.3	0.24
Metal products	34.7	0.46	0.0	0.00
Subtotal	45.8	4.64	12.3	5.17
Other activities				
Nonpolluting small-scale industries	49.7	0.03	0.0	0.00
Domestic servants	48.6	2.60	12.5	2.78
Other small-scale services	43.2	24.74	6.4	15.29
Large-scale industry	43.3	2.72	4.3	1.13
Large-scale services	31.1	9.31	3.7	4.55
Mining	55.4	0.36	23.8	0.64
Forestry	64.5	0.13	0.8	0.01
Fishing	63.7	3.09	10.4	2.08
Agriculture	75.9	40.47	25.6	56.59
Subtotal	52.8	83.45	12.7	83.07
Total	53.2	100.00	12.8	100.0

Notes: SSI means small-scale industry. Poverty rates are calculated for the population of economically active persons. The contribution to poverty is calculated as the percentage of the total poor employed in a particular sector.

Source: Encuesta de Condiciones de Vida (1995)

Of the pollution-intensive small-scale industries with a significant worker health impact, it can be seen that the risk of poverty (applying the high poverty line criterion) is 61%, eight percentage points higher than the average for the economically active population as a whole. Among persons employed in the manufacture of nonmetal mineral goods (e.g., bricks and ceramics), in quarrying, and in construction, the risk is as high as 68%. Similarly, those active in woodworking and straw-goods manufacture are also markedly more likely to be poor than average. On the other hand, persons employed in the chemical products and printing are relatively less likely to be poor than average.

Applying the low poverty line criterion, employment in leather goods and tanning is associated with the highest risk of poverty (19%, compared to 13% on average) among the pollution-intensive small-scale industries with significant worker health impact. Whichever poverty line criterion is applied, similar sectors are associated with a high risk of poverty relative to the average, and thus it seems as though there is no sector in which the extremely poor, in particular, are concentrated.

From Table 3-6 we can see, therefore, that there is some indication that employment in pollution-intensive small-scale industries is associated with a higher than average incidence of poverty, for both the extreme poor and the moderately poor. However, because the pollution-intensive firms account for only a relatively small fraction of total employment, only around 16% of the poor in Ecuador are employed in these sectors (the column sum of the two first subtotals in the "contribution" column of Table 3-6). Roughly two-thirds of this fraction are employed in activities where the environmental risks are felt, at least in part, by the employees of the firms themselves. This is an important observation, because it is obviously somewhat inconsistent to justify nonregulation for distribution reasons when the effect is to place at risk the health of those one is aiming to assist in the first place.

Considering together pollution-intensive as well as nonpolluting activities, and combining both manufacturing and service activities, it can be seen from Table 3-6 that around 44% of the moderately poor and 35% of the extremely poor are employed in the small-scale sector as a whole. This can be compared with 12% (6%) for large-scale enterprises with the high (low) poverty line criterion and 40% (57%) for the agriculture sector. The small-scale sector as a whole is thus an important sector for the poor. However, pollution-intensive firms are only a subset of all small-scale firms and represent less than half of the sector's total contribution to poverty in Ecuador.

In sum, the data presented in Table 3-6 offer a number of important insights into the profile of poverty in Ecuador and the role of pollution-intensive small-scale industries. First, poverty in Ecuador is largely an agricultural phenomenon. The agricultural sector accounts for the largest number of the economically active poor in the country. Second, whereas those who are employed in small-scale nonagricultural enterprises also account for a significant number of the poor, the bulk of these enterprises are in the service sector and are therefore not pollution-intensive. Third, pollution-intensive small-scale enterprises employ roughly 16% of the total economically active poor in Ecuador. Fourth, pollution-intensive small-scale enterprises can be divided into two groups, depending on whether they pose significant environmental risks to their employees or not. It appears that a sizable proportion of the poor employed in pollution-intensive small-scale enterprises face serious health risks themselves. Whereas environmental regulation of small-scale enterprises can be expected to have certain employment implications, and hence an impact on the incomes of the poor, it also appears from these figures that such regulation could benefit those poor who remain employed in these firms by reducing the health risks they face. Thus, an effect for poor people on health outcomes can be expected alongside a possibly poverty-exacerbating effect via employment and incomes.

Would Workers Laid Off from Small-Scale Polluting Industries Fall into Poverty?

How large an increase in poverty might one expect to see if strict environmental regulation was extended to the small-scale sector? The answer depends on two factors. First, one needs to establish the net loss of employment associated with the introduction of environmental regulation. This itself will depend on the type of regulation imposed, the effectiveness of enforcement, and so on. Second, one must ascertain to what extent those who lose their jobs would actually fall into poverty as a result. Both are difficult to estimate as they depend on a whole range of indirect effects of regulation on the economy. For example, how is the nonpolluting sector affected by the regulation? Certain activities, e.g., recycling, may experience a surge in activity levels. Others, e.g., leather goods and tailoring, may face a sharp rise in the cost of inputs. These factors can have second-round employment effects, with concomitant poverty implications.

A rough sense of the possible orders of magnitude involved may be gained by asking the following question: Given his or her various endowments and attributes, what consumption level might a person who is employed in a pollution-intensive small-scale enterprise expect to obtain outside his or her sector of employment? To investigate this question, we use the ECV 1995 survey data to construct a model to predict what consumption level might be obtained by such an individual if he or she were to lose employment in a pollution intensive small-scale enterprise (the result, perhaps, of Draconian regulatory measures that close down the sector). In this model, we regress (log) per capita consumption on a range of individual, household, and community level characteristics for that subsample of the population aged 15 and above (both economically active and nonactive, to allow for the possibility of unemployment) that is not currently employed in a pollution-intensive small-scale activity. We then apply the parameter estimates obtained from this model to the characteristics associated with those individuals who are currently employed in the pollution-intensive small-scale industries to predict their consumption levels if they were to lose their jobs. Estimating poverty rates based on these predicted consumption levels provides an indication of the possible change in poverty that might be expected from the introduction of this proposed policy.

Before presenting the results from this exercise, there are two important sets of issues to be addressed. First, we make two rather strong assumptions. We assume the most extreme policy and ask what would be the effect on poverty given the whole-scale redundancy of all those employed in the pollution-intensive small-scale sector. A more realistic policy impact would be the loss of employment of only some individuals, as some firms closed down or contracted, rather than all. In the proposed exercise, we also assume that returns to education, unemployment rates, etc., in the sector other than the pollution-intensive small-scale sector remain entirely unchanged. This is clearly unrealistic. Although it is true that the small-scale sector is relatively small compared to the rest of the economy, a wholesale closure of this sector would lead to a surge in the number of persons looking for employment and would also change expected returns from a range of activities, and it is likely that this would have an effect on the rest of the economy. The first assumption we make exaggerates the effect of regulation, whereas the second understates its effect.

The second set of issues relates to the sample-selection adjustments that are necessary to implement our calculation.[15] Those who are employed in the pollution-intensive small-scale sector may differ from the rest of the population in terms of observed but also certain unobserved characteristics. Failure to explicitly take this possibility into account could bias our results. As a stylized illustration, suppose individuals of a certain ethnic group could only find employment in pollution-intensive activities, such as leather tanning. Suppose further that our data do not indicate the ethnic group to which individuals belong. Constructing a model estimating consumption levels in nonpolluting activities, even after controlling for observed characteristics such as education, would not provide a reliable basis on which to predict the consumption level of our specific ethnic group, were they to lose their employment in leather tanning. The unobserved factor that governs the employment rationing to which they are subjected would not be included in this regression, and our predicted estimates of consumption would therefore be overstated.

We address these sample-selection issues in the conventional manner by estimating a probit model for the probability that an individual is employed inside or outside of the polluting small-scale sector. This model is then used to construct a bias-correction term, given by the inverse Mills ratio, which is included in the regression of per capita consumption on a range of personal and household characteristics in the subsample of those not employed in the pollution-intensive small-scale sector. In predicting the consumption level of those who would lose their jobs, we apply the parameter estimates from this consumption model to the subsample of the population currently employed in the pollution-intensive sector. As the bias-correction term is significant in the consumption regression, we include it too when predicting consumption.

In Table 3-7 we present our probit estimates for sector choice. The probability of employment in pollution-intensive small-scale industry increases with age but declines beyond the age of 36 years. Females are significantly less likely to be employed in this sector. Land ownership reduces the probability of employment in this sector, although at very large landownership levels (more than 200 ha) the probability rises. Literacy raises the probability of employment in this sector, but education levels beyond secondary schooling reduce the probability of such employment. Employment in pollution-intensive small-scale activities appears to be particularly high in the urban Sierra (the regional dummy that is left out in the

64 • Peter Lanjouw

Table 3-7. *Probit Model of Employment in Pollution-Intensive Small-Scale Industry (for population aged 15 and above)*

Parameter	Coefficient	Probability value	Marginal effects
Age	0.0218	0.000	0.0037
Age squared	−0.0003	0.000	−0.00005
Female	−0.3828	0.000	−0.0651
Household size	−0.0011	0.845	−0.0002
Land owned (per capita)	−0.0186	0.003	−0.0031
Land owned squared	0.00004	0.010	0.00001
Literate	0.1249	0.134	0.0197
Highest education level achieved			
Primary schooling	0.0336	0.720	0.0057
Secondary schooling	−0.1035	0.299	−0.0170
University	−0.5352	0.000	−0.0682
Postgraduate	−0.9126	0.041	−0.0816
Other tertiary education	−0.2844	0.074	−0.0396
Other (basic) education	−0.2294	0.156	−0.0331
Vocational training	−0.1317	0.010	−0.0207
Recent migrant (past 10 years)	−0.0581	0.124	−0.0095
Quichua or Shuar speaking	−0.1056	0.144	−0.0166
Sierra			
Urban periphery	0.3182	0.002	0.0648
Rural village	−0.0078	0.910	−0.0013
Remote dwelling	−0.1213	0.012	−0.0193
Costa			
Urban	−0.0261	0.483	−0.0044
Urban periphery	−0.9674	0.001	−0.0840
Rural village	−0.1970	0.001	−0.0296
Remote dwelling	−0.6774	0.000	−0.0802
Oriente			
Urban	0.1928	0.001	0.0362
Rural village	0.0673	0.578	0.0118
Remote dwelling	−0.1876	0.059	−0.0280
Constant	−1.2747	0.000	

Notes: Marginal effects indicate discrete changes from 0 to 1 for dummy variables. Number of observations is 16,241.

Log likelihood is −5242.8812.

regressions in Table 3-7), with only those living in the urban Oriente and in rural areas around the periphery of Sierran cities having a higher likelihood of being employed in this sector. Although the rural non-farm sector has been found to be of considerable importance in Ecuador, in terms of employment and income shares (Lanjouw 1996), pollution-intensive activities in small-scale enterprises are relatively unimportant in rural areas, particularly in the more remote areas. On balance, the probit model indicates that the "profile" of those employed in the pollution-intensive small-scale sector firms does not correspond exactly to that of the poor in Ecuador more generally.[16] The fact that such workers are typically literate adult males who do not belong to the indigenous population and who reside in the urban or semi-urban Sierra region suggests that they are relatively well positioned in Ecuadorean society to escape poverty.

To aid in identification of the selection effect, we have postulated that although gender of an individual is likely to influence whether or not a person seeks work in the pollution-intensive small-scale sector, once one has controlled for education, age, and other factors, gender does not separately influence an individual's consumption level. The data support this conjecture, in that females are significantly less likely to be employed in the pollution-intensive sector, but this variable exercises no independent influence on consumption levels when included in our consumption regression.

Table 3-8 presents estimates from the consumption regression for the subsample of the population not employed in pollution-intensive small-scale industry activities. The explanatory variables influence consumption in the way one would expect. Per capita landholdings are associated with higher consumption levels (although in a nonlinear fashion, such that at landholdings of 144 ha or more, per capita consumption levels decline). Returns to education are positive and rise significantly. Controlling for other variables, the indigenous population appears to achieve significantly lower consumption levels. Rural areas, whether in the periphery of cities, in built-up rural areas, or in remote regions, are associated with significantly lower consumption levels than urban Sierra, whereas urban Costa is slightly better off than urban Sierra. The sample-selection term is significant at the 90% confidence level. This suggests that unobserved variables influence the choice of sector of employment and also affect consumption levels. Failure to adjust for this sample-selection effect would therefore bias our predicted consumption levels for those switching from the pollution-intensive sector to the nonpollution-intensive sector.

Applying these parameter estimates to data for those individuals currently employed in pollution-intensive small-scale industries yields their predicted consumption levels. We use these predictions to estimate roughly the impact on poverty of mass redundancy from the pollution-intensive small-scale sector. Table 3-9 provides poverty rate calculations on the basis of the incidence, poverty gap (FGT1), and squared poverty gap (FGT2) measures.[17] In the base case, we confine our attention to the population aged 15 and above currently employed in pollution-intensive small-scale industries. If this sector were closed down, the incidence of poverty among this subgroup would rise from 54% to 67%. This is not a negligible jump, corresponding to a net increase in the number of poor of 90,301. However, not everyone who lost his or her job in this sector would fall into poverty.[18]

Table 3-8. *OLS Regression Model of Log per Capita Consumption with Sample Selection Correction (for population aged 15 and above not employed in pollution-intensive SSI)*

Parameter	Coefficient	Huber-White Standard Errors	Probability Value
Age	0.8651	0.1375	0.000
Age squared	−0.0058	0.0016	0.000
Household size	−11.384	0.2012	0.000
Land owned (per capita)	1.5118	0.1246	0.000
Land owned squared	−0.0039	0.0005	0.000
Literate	20.036	2.7074	0.000
Highest education level achieved			
Primary schooling	4.6518	3.0141	0.123
Secondary schooling	33.490	3.2665	0.000
University	61.159	3.6761	0.000
Postgraduate	104.33	11.162	0.000
Other tertiary education	48.050	5.3253	0.000
Other (basic) education	1.7911	4.9154	0.716
Vocational training	7.1942	1.7080	0.000
Recent migrant (past 10 years)	2.0899	1.3326	0.117
Quichua or Shuar speaking	−14.534	2.6166	0.000
Sierra			
Urban periphery	−37.137	4.2766	0.000
Rural village	−13.981	2.6237	0.000
Remote dwelling	−30.654	1.9057	0.000
Costa			
Urban	5.7070	1.4044	0.000
Urban periphery	−24.084	5.3547	0.000
Rural village	−12.376	1.9554	0.000
Remote dwelling	−29.026	2.1774	0.000
Oriente			
Urban	−3.0149	2.5187	0.231
Rural village	−19.213	4.1888	0.000
Remote dwelling	−15.434	2.8671	0.000
Mills ratio	−16.122	8.3330	0.053
Constant	1153.7	3.9988	0.000

Notes: Excluded dummy is Urban Quito. Number of observations is 14,597. The adjusted R^2 is 0.4126.

Table 3-9. *Estimating the Impact of Wholesale Redundancy from the Pollution-Intensive Small-Scale Sector*

	Poverty incidence	FGT I	FGT2	No. of Poor
Population initially employed in pollution-intensive small-scale sector				
Base case	0.540	0.0271	0.0021	390,098
Estimated case	0.665	0.0266	0.0016	480,399
Change	+23%	−2%	−23%	+90,301
Population as a whole				
Base case	0.516	0.0258	0.00196	3,418,077
Estimated case	0.530	0.0257	0.00191	3,510,815
Change	+3%	−0.3%	−3%	+92,738

Note: FGT1 and FGT2 are poverty indicies defined by Foster, Greer, Therbeke (1984) that reflect how far individuals fall below the poverty line. See footnote 17.

Our rather Draconian policy measure thus seems to increase overall poverty by a rather modest amount at best. We find that the *overall* incidence of poverty rises only by three percentage points as a result of the policy (Table 3-9). Whereas 93,000 additional people would become poor, these represent only about 3% of the population aged 15 or above that was poor in the base case.

The true impact of an active policy of environmental regulation of small-scale industries seems unlikely to result in such widespread job losses within the polluting small-scale sector. Moreover, those of the poor who remain employed in this sector are likely to benefit from the reduced health hazards to which they are exposed. Thus, one can conclude from this section that the direct poverty impact of environmental regulation of this sector would appear to be fairly muted.

Indirect effects could, of course, overshadow the direct effects. There are many directions in which the indirect effects could go. For example, we saw in Table 3-7 that most of the pollution-intensive employment occurs in urban Sierra and in the rural areas immediately surrounding urban centers in this region. Although we lack the data to track down exactly where these firms are located, and whether, for example, poor communities tend to be most directly exposed to the pollution caused by small-scale firms, it seems unlikely that pollution-intensive small-scale firms are located in the most affluent parts of town. As we have already seen, a number of types of pollution-intensive firms have a damaging impact on their immediate surroundings; effective regulation of these firms is also likely to bring benefits to the poor who reside in the vicinity, in terms of cleaner water, air, and physical surroundings.

On the other hand, we have already mentioned that there may be a number of nonpolluting enterprises that depend on inputs from pollution-intensive enterprises. If the latter were to become heavily regulated, then costs in these other enterprises might rise, and total employment might fall further. Alternatively, the goods produced by pollution-intensive firms might be consumed relatively heavily by the poor. Again, if these were to rise sharply in price, then the poor would suffer disproportionately. Against this, however, one must also recognize that environmental regulation can stimulate new activities, such as recycling or the manufacture of pollution-control devices, which may in turn stimulate employment.

The full impact of regulation on poverty thus remains something of a guess. Considerably richer data and analysis are needed to arrive at credible estimates of this full impact. However, we suggest that adverse distributional consequences are not necessarily overwhelming. Arguments against regulation on equity grounds should not be accepted without question.

Summary and Policy Implications

Small-scale enterprises are not a small segment of the Ecuadorean economy. Almost 80% of total employment occurs in establishments of up to 10 workers. Hence, the notion that the bulk of pollution from a given industrial sector derives from a few large-scale firms and that small-scale firms, while intensive in pollution generation, account for only a relatively small fraction of all pollution, is not likely to apply across the board in a country like Ecuador.

The environmental threat posed by pollution-intensive enterprises in Ecuador generally takes two forms: a dangerous workplace, placing employees at risk, and local pollution affecting residents who live near the small-scale enterprise. If the employees are poor or vulnerable, then improving workplace conditions and standards in such firms could have an impact that helps poor people, at least in terms of the broader standard of living of employees, if not in terms of their income or consumption levels. If the small-scale enterprise is located in an area where those affected by the local pollution are poor, then, once again, reducing pollution will improve their living standards.

The bulk of the poor in Ecuador reside in rural areas. Few small-scale enterprises engaged in pollution-intensive manufacturing or industrial activities are located in rural regions. Within urban areas, those who are employed in the pollution-intensive firms are not generally poor in an absolute sense. In addition, in terms of their human capital endowments, age, and gender, it appears that a significant fraction of those who are employed in pollution-intensive small-scale enterprises would not inevitably fall into absolute poverty were they to lose their jobs.

The structure of the economy in Ecuador, its sources of comparative advantage, and its likely development path in the near future provide no reason to suppose that pollution-intensive activity in the future will be accounted for increasingly by large firms. Pollution-intensive activities in Ecuador are thus likely to remain heavily represented in the small-scale sector. This means that if it wishes to have a meaningful impact on total industrial pollution loads, the government must influence the polluting behavior of small-scale enterprises. We have indicated that the distributional implications of such regulation may be less adverse than might have been expected. However, direct regulation of pollution-intensive small-scale firms is, in all likelihood, costly from an administrative perspective. One important finding in this study is the sheer size of the small-scale sector. Given the importance of this sector in a country such as Ecuador (and the likelihood that much of this sector operates in the informal sector), one might ask whether it can, in fact, afford to keep all these firms outside of its regulatory purview. Expanding the tax base in the economy is an important priority in most developing countries, and to the extent that extending environmental regulation can piggyback on an expansion of financial regulation, the incremental cost of environmental regulation may therefore be less severe than expected.

Acknowledgments

I am grateful for advice and comments from Allen Blackman, David Coady, Jesko Hentschel, and Jenny Lanjouw. Javier Poggi provided valuable assistance. The views contained in this paper are my own and do not necessarily reflect the views of the World Bank or any of its affiliates. All remaining errors are my own.

Notes

1. In a companion paper, Jayaraman and Lanjouw (2004) examine similar questions in Brazil and illustrate that conclusions do appear to be country specific. This fact underlines the importance of detailed analysis of these questions on a case-by-case basis—something that this chapter hopes to encourage.

2. Environmental degradation associated with agriculture can be quite significant. However, in this chapter we are mainly concerned with small-scale industry and with the "brown-side" environmental degradation that is associated with industrial activities.

3. The poverty line that we apply corresponds to the "upper bound" methodology described in Hentschel and Lanjouw (1996) and Lanjouw and Lanjouw (2001) and applied to household survey data for Ecuador for 1995.

4. See, for example, World Bank 1992.

5. See Jayaraman and Lanjouw (2004) for a similar analysis in Brazil, in which the focus is on air pollution.

6. Lanjouw (1997) presents analogous figures at the more disaggregated 3-digit ISIC level.

7. This figure might seem high, but it is not out of line with similar estimates for other countries. For example, in its February 1997 survey of the Indian economy, the *Economist* notes that less than 10% of the economically active population in India is employed in firms with 10 or more employees (*Economist* 1997).

8. For more detailed analysis of the agricultural sector in Ecuador based on the 1994 and 1995 rounds of the Encuesta Sobre Las Condiciones de Vida, see Lanjouw (1996, 1999) on rural poverty and rural nonfarm employment, respectively.

9. In this chapter, we assume that firms with high pollution per unit of output also have high pollution-per-worker ratios. We provide some evidence to suggest that this is not unreasonable. However, it is clear that if small-scale firms are particularly labor-intensive and large firms are very capital-intensive, pollution-per-worker ratios could rank large and small firms differently than pollution-per-output ratios.

10. The 16 dimensions are air pollution; water and solid waste; land; fauna; flora; potable water; sewage; energy use; public space; waste collection; private property; workers' health; neighbors' health; clients' health; silence; and landscape. The distinctions between these dimensions are not always clear. In Table 3-4, we conflate the categories into six: air pollution; solid and liquid waste generation; physical landscape (including flora and fauna); workers health; neighbors health, and clients health.

11. These manufacturing sectors each registered at least a medium impact in terms of either air pollution, solid and liquid waste generation, or physical landscape degradation.

12. This study was prepared for the Thailand Institute of Scientific and Technological Research and was conducted by DHV Consultants, of the Netherlands, in 1994. We are unable to comment to what extent manufacturing processes in Ecuador and Thailand resemble one another. The exercise described below is clearly applicable only (and even then only tentatively) if the manufacturing processes are at least roughly similar.

13. And thus, our assumption that pollution-per-worker coefficients are qualitatively in line with pollution-per-output coefficients is not rejected in this example.

14. Poverty rates among the population of Ecuador as a whole, i.e., including also the non-economically active population, are higher by around three percentage points.

15. The issues of sample selection, which can arise in this kind of exercise, are well known and have been widely discussed. See, for example, Maddala (1983), Amemiya (1984), Greene (1993). Ravallion and Wodon (1997) provide a recent example of this approach in the context of farm versus nonfarm employment in rural Bangladesh.

16. See World Bank (1996) for a detailed profile of poverty in Ecuador based on the ECV 1994 and 1995.

17. Foster, Greer and Thorbecke (1984) define the so-called FGT class of poverty measures as

$$FGT(\alpha) = (\frac{1}{\sum w_i})\sum w_i(1-(x_i/z)^{\alpha}$$

where i is an index of individuals; z is the poverty line, x_i is per capita expenditure for those below this line; and w_i are weights that sum to the total population. The parameter α defines three different versions of the measure. It takes a value of zero for the simple poverty incidence (or "headcount index"), one for the poverty gap index (FGT1), and two for the squared poverty gap index (FGT2). The poverty incidence does not capture how far below the poverty line individuals fall. As the value of α rises, the other two FGT poverty measures attach greater weight to this distance.

18. In fact, a rather surprising observation is that both the FGT1 and FGT2 poverty measures suggest that poverty would *fall* as a result of this policy measure. It is rather difficult to explain this observation fully, although part of the explanation must certainly lie in the fact that these poverty measures are increasingly sensitive to observations in the lower end of the consumption distribution. And as the consumption regression was only able to explain around 40% of the total variation in consumption, the distribution of predicted consumption has lower variance than that of observed consumption, and consequently distribution-sensitive poverty measures are also lower than they should be.

References

Amemiya, T. 1984. Tobit Models: A Survey. *Journal of Econometrics* 24: 3–61.

Brandon, C. 1993. Towards an Environmental Strategy for Asia. World Bank Discussion Paper 227. Washington, DC: World Bank.

CONAUPE. 1993. *Microempresa y Medio Ambiente en el Ecuador: Aproximacion a las Caracteristicas Ambientales de las Microempresas Tipo III y IV en el Programa de CONAUPE.* Quito, Ecuador: CONAUPE.

Economist Magazine. 1997. February 22. London.

ECV (Encuesta Sobre las Condiciones de Vida). 1995. Instituto Nacional de Estadistica y Censo, Quito, Ecuador.

Foster, J., J. Greer, and E. Thorbecke. 1984. A Class of Decomposable Poverty measures. *Econometrica* 52 (3): 761–66.

Greene, W. 1993. *Econometric Analysis,* 2d ed. New York: Macmillan.

Hentschel, J., and P. Lanjouw. 1996. Constructing an Indicator of Consumption for the Analysis of Poverty: Principles and Illustrations with Reference to Ecuador. Living Standard Measurement Survey Working Paper No. 124. Washington, DC: World Bank.

INSOTEC. 1993. Diagnostico de la Pequeña y Mediana Industria en el Ecuador, Cuaderno de Trabajo, Instituto de Investigaciones Socio-Economicas y Tecnologicas. Quito, Ecuador: INSOTEC.

Jayaraman, R., and P. Lanjouw. 2004. Small Scale Industry, Environmental Regulation and Poverty: The Case of Brazil. *World Bank Economic Review* 18(3): 443–64.

Lanjouw, P. 1996. Pobreza Rural en Ecuador. *Questiones Economicas.* Quito, Ecuador: Banco Central.

———. 1997. Small Scale Industry, Poverty and the Environment: A Case Study of Ecuador. Working Paper No. 18, Research Project on Social and Environmental Consequences of Growth-Oriented Policies. Development Economics Research Group. Washington, DC: World Bank

———. 1999. Rural Non-Agricultural Employment and Poverty in Ecuador. *Economic Development and Cultural Change* 48(1): October.

Lanjouw, J.O., and P. Lanjouw. 2001. How To Compare Apples and Oranges: Poverty Measurement Based on Different Definitions of Consumption. *Review of Income and Wealth* 47(1): 25–42.

Maddala, G.S. 1983. *Limited-Dependent and Qualitative Variables in Econometrics.* Cambridge, U.K.: Cambridge University Press.

Ravallion, M. 1994. *Poverty Comparisons.* Chur, Switzerland: Harwood Press.

Ravallion, M., and Q. Wodon. 1997. What Are a Poor Farmer's Prospects in the Rural Non-Farm Sector? Mimeograph. Policy Research Department. Washington, DC: World Bank.

World Bank. 1992. *World Development Report 1992.* Washington DC: Oxford University Press.

World Bank 1996 'Ecuador Poverty Report' Report No 14533-EC, Washington D.C: World Bank.

CHAPTER 4

Policy Options for Controlling Small-Firm Pollution

Informal Brickmaking in Northern Mexico

Allen Blackman

AS DISCUSSED IN CHAPTER 1, for both political and economic reasons, small firms—particularly informal ones—are difficult for environmental authorities in developing countries to monitor and sanction. Therefore, conventional regulatory approaches are bound to be problematic, if not completely impractical.

In Mexico, as in developing countries around the world, small-scale traditional brickkilns are a notorious informal-sector source of urban air pollution. According to one estimate, the country is home to approximately 20,000 traditional brickkilns fired with a variety of cheap, highly polluting fuels (Johnson et al. 1994). Many large cities support several hundred. In such cities brickkilns are often a leading source of air pollution. In other cities, they mainly pose health risks to the residents of surrounding neighborhoods and to brickmakers themselves.

Efforts to control pollution from traditional kilns in Mexico have not been coordinated at the national level. Rather, individual municipalities have implemented a variety of strategies, which have met with decidedly mixed success. This mixed record provides an opportunity to study what types of policies work and what types do not. Using the menu of policy options for small-firm pollution control presented in Chapter 1 as a frame of reference, this chapter examines how various policies have fared in dealing with traditional Mexican brickmakers. We analyze pollution-control efforts in four cities in northern Mexico: Ciudad Juárez, Saltillo, Zacatecas, and Torreón. Our case studies are based on interviews with brickmakers, regulators, and other stakeholders in each city, as well as on primary and secondary documents.

Extracted from a paper previously published as Informal Sector Pollution Control: What Policy Options Do We Have? *World Development* 28(12): 2067–82, 2000.

Case Studies

The key points of the four case studies presented in this section are summarized in Table 4-1.

Ciudad Juárez[1]

Background. A sprawling border city with more than a million permanent inhabitants, Ciudad Juárez hosts approximately 330 traditional brickkilns, which are principally fired with scrap wood. Collectively, these kilns are a significant area-wide source of air pollution. They have attracted considerable attention because air quality in Ciudad Juárez and its sister city, El Paso, Texas, are among the worst in North America.[2] The kilns are also a serious local health hazard to those living in the densely populated residential neighborhoods that surround most of the city's brickyards.

In Ciudad Juárez, as in our other three study cities, a number of factors make it politically difficult to require brickmakers to bear the full costs of pollution control. Brickmaking is a significant source of employment, providing more than 2000 jobs directly and 150 jobs indirectly in transportation and wholesale. In addition, most brickmakers are impoverished. They typically live next to their kilns in rudimentary houses with no drainage or running water. Finally, brickmakers are well organized. Approximately two-thirds belong to a trade association or other local organization.

Policies. In 1989, the municipal environmental authority in Ciudad Juárez initiated a project aimed at convincing traditional brickmakers to substitute clean-burning propane for dirty fuels. This substitution amounts to clean technological change because adopting propane involves significant set-up costs and significant changes in the production process. In 1990, the Brickmakers' Project, as it came to be known, was handed off to the *Federación Mexicana de Asociaciones Privadas de Salud y Desarrollo Comunitario* (FEMAP), a private nonprofit social services organization based in Ciudad Juárez that had expertise in grassroots organizing in poor neighborhoods. FEMAP was able to attract considerable funding and participation from both sides of the border. The majority of the funding came from the Mexican government. Key Mexican participants included propane companies, and the municipal government in Ciudad Juárez, while leading U.S. participants included El Paso Natural Gas and Los Alamos National Laboratories

Participants in the Brickmakers' Project used a broad range of polices to promote propane adoption. First, they subsidized various costs associated with adoption. Propane companies made tanks and vaporizers available free of charge, and a number of organizations (including local propane companies, FEMAP, El Paso Natural Gas, and local universities) provided training. In addition, motivated by the fact that the cost of propane per unit of energy was considerably higher than the cost of traditional dirty fuels, engineers from El Paso Natural Gas, Los Alamos National Laboratories, and FEMAP devoted considerable effort to developing new energy-efficient kilns. However, most of their designs involved completely rebuilding existing kilns, a prohibitively expensive proposition for most brickmakers.

Table 4-1. Summary of Case Studies

	Ciudad Juárez	Saltillo	Zacatecas	Torreón
Background				
Approximate number of kilns	• 330	• 500	• 60	• 165
Principal traditional fuel	• scrap wood	• used tires	• used tires, scrap wood	• scrap wood, refuse
Leading source air pollution?	• reputedly	• reputedly	• no	• no
Brickmakers well-organized?	• yes	• yes	• no	• yes
Miscellaneous	• cross-border impacts	• tile exporters powerful	• kilns deemed tourist liability	• competition from neighboring cities
Policies	• Private-sector-led initiative with strong public-sector support • Clean technological change (conversion to propane) • Subsidies to fixed adoption costs • R&D in energy-efficient kilns • Process standards (ban on dirty fuels) underpinned by peer monitoring • Public education initiative • Boycott of bricks fired with dirty fuels within Juárez	• Public-sector-led initiative • Clean technological change (conversion to propane) • Subsidies to fixed adoption costs • R&D in energy-efficient kilns • Process standards (ban on exclusive use of tires) underpinned by peer monitoring and registration • Subsidies to cleaner fuels (scrap wood) • Rights for creosote distribution awarded to brickmakers' union	• Public-sector-led initiative • Clean technological change (conversion to propane) • Subsidies to fixed adoption costs • Process standard (ban on use of tires) underpinned by peer monitoring and registration • Forced relocation of certain kilns • Boycott of bricks fired with dirty fuels from neighboring towns	• Public-sector-led initiative • Clean technological change (conversion to propane) • Promised subsidies to fixed relocation and adoption costs • Privately enforced process standards (ban on use of tires, firing limits) underpinned by peer monitoring • Relocation of certain kilns
Results	• 50% adoption of propane before increases in propane prices led to 100% withdrawal from program • Drastic reduction in use of tires and plastics	• 10% adoption of propane before increases in propane prices led to 100% withdrawal from program • Moderate reduction in use of tires, drastic reduction in plastics and used motor oil	• 100% adoption of propane before increases in propane prices led to 100% withdrawal from program • Continued partial use of propane in some kilns • Reduced use of tires	• No relocation or conversion to propane • Reduction in use of tires; firing schedules enforced

Engineers also worked to develop low-cost measures for improving fuel efficiency, such as optimizing the fuel mixture, the manner in which bricks are stacked, and the way that the kiln opening is covered.

Second, project leaders worked to put in place and enforce process standards prohibiting the use of dirty fuels. In 1992, a newly elected municipal government banned the use of certain fuels. To facilitate enforcement, the new administration relied on peer monitoring. A telephone hotline was set up to register complaints about brickmakers violating the ban. Enforcement teams with the power to jail and fine violators were dispatched in response to complaints. Project organizers also encouraged local trade unions and neighborhood organizations in communities surrounding brickyards to pressure brickmakers to switch to propane. The brickmaker organizations affiliated with the dominant national political party (the Partido Revolucionario Institucional) were in general quite cooperative, enforcing strict rules on permissible fuels in some brickyards.

Third, FEMAP initiated a campaign to raise brickmakers' awareness of the health hazards associated with dirty fuels. Among the mechanisms it used were one-on-one discussions with individual brickmakers, organized training sessions, and an educational comic book.

Finally, project leaders tried to reduce competitive pressures for brickmakers to use cheap dirty fuels by intervening in the market for bricks. In March 1993, they helped to negotiate an agreement among leaders of all of the major brickmaker unions to establish a price floor high enough to allow all brickmakers to use propane. The next year, project leaders obtained a commitment from local construction companies and from INFONAVIT, the federal workers' housing agency, to boycott bricks fired with dirty fuels. Both the price floor and the boycott were quickly undone by rampant cheating.

Results. The high-water mark of the Brickmakers' Project probably occurred in the fall of 1993, when, according to most estimates, at least half of the brickmakers in Ciudad Juárez were using propane, albeit in inefficient traditional kilns that had been modified slightly to accommodate the new fuel. However, during the early 1990s, Mexico's state-run petroleum company was in the process of phasing out longstanding subsides on propane. As propane prices continued to rise in 1993 and 1994, key participants in the project began to defect: the municipal government relaxed the ban on burning debris, brickmakers began abandoning propane in droves, brickmaker organizations increasingly dropped out as they were undercut by competitors using dirty fuels, and construction companies and the federal workers' housing agency gave up the pretense of boycotting "dirty" bricks. By 1995, only a handful of brickmakers were still using propane. Despite the withdrawal from the use of propane, the Brickmakers' Project has had some lasting effects: local organizations and city officials continue to enforce a ban on the use of the dirtiest fuels, mainly tires and plastics.

Although the diffusion of propane among the brickmakers in Ciudad Juárez was limited and temporary, it nevertheless represents a significant achievement in view of the obstacles involved, especially the drastic reduction in propane subsidies. Which of the broad range of strategies used by the project were responsible? Statistical analysis of survey data described in detail in Chapter 9 suggests that three factors played a key role: peer monitoring applied by neighbors and local organizations affiliated with the city government, a growing awareness of the health risks associated with burning dirty fuels, and subsidies to the costs of propane equipment and training. Efforts to introduce new energy-efficient kilns and to intervene in the market for bricks were obviously ineffective.

Saltillo[3]

Background. An industrial city of approximately 425,000 people in the southeast corner of the state of Cohuila, Saltillo is home to approximately 500 traditional kilns, the largest collection in any of the four study cities. The majority of these kilns produce more tile than bricks.[4] Some 60–80% of the tile produced in Saltillo is exported to the United States, where it is prized as an artisanal product. The majority of Saltillo's brickmakers belong to a single union, which has considerable influence because of its large membership and ties to exporters.

Brickmakers in Saltillo rely principally on used tires for fuel. According to the Cohuila Department of Ecology, Saltillo's kilns burn 50 tons of tires per day (Cruz 1993). Supplementary fuels include scrap wood, plastics, used motor oil, and garbage. Kiln emissions are an acute problem for the poor residential neighborhoods that surround the six principal brickyards. There is some confusion regarding the contribution of traditional brickkilns to citywide pollution. Newspaper articles frequently assert that brickkilns are the leading source of Saltillo's air pollution. However, the city environmental authority claims that fixed industrial sources and a sizable vehicular fleet are the most important sources.

Policies. By 1992, worsening air pollution and growing environmental consciousness led to a general recognition that kiln emissions were a serious problem. In early 1993, the city environmental authority initiated an effort to convert traditional kilns to clean-burning propane, the same clean technology strategy adopted in Ciudad Juárez. With the financial backing of NAFIN (a federal development bank), the city government commissioned a study to develop a plan of action. The study recommended building new energy-efficient propane-burning kilns costing approximately 73,000 pesos (US$24,300) each and leasing them to brickmakers under a rent-to-own scheme.

Before this scheme could be implemented, it was cut short by the election of a new mayor in December 1993. Under the new administration, a number of elements of the program were reformed and extended, so that ultimately, as in Ciudad Juárez, a multifaceted approach was adopted. Recognizing that introducing expensive new energy-efficient kilns would be problematic given brickmakers' financial constraints, the city decided to focus instead on simply introducing propane equipment that could be used in existing kilns. Using funds provided by the state and federal governments, it set up a window at the Municipal Ecology Office to provide credit and technical extension to brickmakers adopting propane.[5] In addition, the city government promulgated process standards. In June 1994, a municipal ordinance was passed that forbade burning tires after a six-month grace period and prohibited using a number of other dirty fuels immediately (including battery cases, used motor oil, plastics, and solvents). The process standard was to be enforced by requiring all brickmakers to register with the city government. Violators were to have their kilns closed down. There was an attempt to enlist the support of brickmaker organizations in enforcing the new rules. Toward this end, the city government convened several meetings with leaders of local brickmaker organizations.

For reasons discussed below, Saltillo's propane initiative failed. Subsequently, the city focused on limiting the use of used tires for fuel. It promulgated a regulation that allowed brickmakers to use a combination of 50% tires and 50% cleaner fuels—either creosote (a low-grade petroleum distillate) or scrap wood. Peer monitoring was used to enforce this rule. Brickmakers and their neighbors in surrounding residential communities monitored emissions and reported producers who fired their kilns exclusively with tires. Violators were fined. In addition, the city set up an innovative program to subsidize the cost of relatively clean fuels: local factories provided scrap wood to brickmakers free of charge. Finally, as a gesture of goodwill, the city funded the construction of a public square with recreational facilities and market stalls for brickmakers.

Eventually, the city of Saltillo hopes to replace all dirty fuels with creosote. To promote the new fuel, the city has commissioned test firings and has made credit available. Also, it has awarded a contract for the distribution of creosote to the brickmakers' union, hoping the concession will give the union an incentive to pressure its members to adopt the fuel. Still, in July 1996, no brickmakers in Saltillo were using creosote on a regular basis.

Results. Despite the city government's efforts to induce brickmakers to switch to propane, only 14 ever received credit from the loan fund set up to finance new equipment investments, and fewer than 40 ever adopted propane. A number of factors were responsible. Most important, by the time the program had been launched in earnest, propane prices had risen dramatically relative to the price of debris due to the nationwide reductions in propane subsidies. Concerns about costs were exacerbated by a macroeconomic recession in Mexico, which made investing in a new technology especially burdensome and risky. According to the leader of the brickmakers' union, by the end of 1994, sales of bricks and tile had fallen off by as much as 70% compared to the early 1990s. In addition, there was little enforcement of the June 1994 prohibition on burning tires, despite the fact that more than 300 of approximately 500 kilns were registered (the holdouts were principally kilns in the brickyards located on the outskirts of the city). And finally, support for the project among the brickmakers was dampened by internal divisions in the brickmakers' union. In part, this was the result of rumors that bricks and tiles fired with clean fuels were of inferior quality. These rumors persisted despite the several successful test firings designed to allay these concerns. Although the propane initiative failed, other components of the city's environmental program were more successful. Most notably, there was a decline in the use of the dirtiest fuels, such as battery cases and used motor oil.

Zacatecas[6]

Background. A colonial city in north central Mexico and the capital of the state of the same name, the city of Zacatecas is a major domestic tourist attraction. With a population of a little more than 110,000, it is the smallest city in our sample. It is home to approximately 60 small-scale brickkilns, which have traditionally burned used tires, scrap wood, manure, used motor oil, and refuse. There are no unions or other local organizations to speak of among the brickmakers. Unlike kilns in Ciudad Juárez and Saltillo, those in Zacatecas are too few in number to constitute a significant source of citywide pollution. They have attracted attention because they are a health hazard to those who live nearby and because municipal authorities have deemed a cluster of kilns near the entrance of the city to be an eyesore and a threat to tourism.

Policies. In December 1992, the mayor's office initiated a series of meetings with brickmakers to address the problem of kiln emissions. The city settled on a dual policy. First, 19 kilns near the entrance of the city would be relocated. The city committed to finding a new site for these brickmakers and to providing them with credit to build new kilns. Second, all kilns remaining in the city would be converted to propane. With the assistance of two federal credit programs (NAFIN and Solidarity Enterprises), the city set up a loan fund to finance the purchase of new propane equipment. It offered three-year interest-free loans to several groups of brickmakers who were to share equipment. A firm was chosen to supply equipment and technical extension. To ensure that the propane initiative was successful, the city registered all of its brickmakers and had them sign a pledge to adopt propane as soon as financing could be arranged.

Results. Both of the program's components were ultimately carried out. The 19 kilns near the entrance to the city were relocated, although in a far more Draconian manner than originally planned. The city purchased the land where these kilns were located and summarily evicted them. The owners were given the option of purchasing land in a new (somewhat remote) site, but financing was never made available. As a result, only six brickmakers from this group eventually relocated. The others found new employment.

The propane initiative was completely, although only temporarily, successful. By early 1994, 150,000 pesos (US$50,000) in credit had been extended for the purchase of new equipment, and by the end of the year, every kiln in the city was being fired with propane. The project was so successful that plans were made to extend it to all municipalities within 100 kilometers of Zacatecas.[7]

Unfortunately, as in Ciudad Juárez, the nationwide removal of subsidies on propane that began in 1992 created strong pressures to revert to burning debris. Although Zacatecas' brickmakers did not face competition from brickmakers using cheap fuel inside the city (since all brickmakers in the city adopted propane), they did face competition from nonadopters in surrounding municipalities. To ease this pressure, the city briefly attempted to organize a boycott of bricks fired with dirty fuels. The boycott soon collapsed, however, and ultimately propane use fell off dramatically. In the summer of 1996, several brickmakers continued to use propane, but only during a brief initial phase of firing the kiln.

One positive legacy of the propane initiative is that brickmakers have reduced their use of tires. As in Saltillo and Ciudad Juárez, peer monitoring is used to enforce a ban on tires. Generally, neighbors and competitors who observe violations complain to the municipal police, who then issue a fine and temporarily close the offending kiln.

Torreón[8]

Background. A rapidly growing industrial city of 450,000 people in the southwest corner of the state of Cohuila, Torreón supports 165 traditional kilns. Most are in one centrally located neighborhood, *ejido San Antonio.* The brickmakers' principal fuels are scrap wood, pecan shells, plastics, used tires, and refuse. Virtually all brickmakers belong to one of five local organizations. The brickmakers face stiff competition from the nearby cities of Gomez Palacios and Matamoros.

Torreón has poor air quality as a result of industrial emissions and a sizable vehicular fleet. Traditional kilns are considered a significant contributor to citywide air pollution, but not a leading contributor. A more urgent concern is the threat that the kilns pose to the residents of the densely populated low-income communities that have grown up around the main brickyard in the past decade.

Policies. In 1994, the Office of Economic Development in Torreón began to develop a strategy for reducing emissions from traditional kilns. It organized a series of meetings that brought together representatives of the brickmakers' organizations, the Municipal Ecology Office, the federal environmental authority, and FEMAP, the same nongovernmental organization that organized the propane initiative in Ciudad Juárez. As in Zacatecas, a two-pronged strategy emerged: brickmakers in *ejido San Antonio* would be relocated, and clean fuels—including propane—would be introduced.

Not surprisingly, the communities surrounding *ejido San Antonio* supported relocation. In the early 1990s, they had organized demonstrations protesting kiln emissions and repeatedly petitioned the city environmental authority to address the problem. The owners of *ejido San Antonio* also supported relocation because they hoped to develop the increasingly valuable land used by the brickmakers into an industrial park.

After a study of the suitability of soils in different locations, the city chose two sites outside the city limits to use as new brickyards and pledged to subsidize relocation. It developed a package of incentives that included a half hectare of land, water rights on the land, 10,000 pesos (US$3,300) for each brickmaker (for building a new kiln), compensation for all inventory on hand on the eve of the move, and training in the use of propane. To spur a shift away from dirty fuels, the city passed regulations banning the burning of particularly dirty fuels, such as plastics.

Results. As of July 1996, four of the five brickmaker organizations active in *ejido San Antonio* had signed documents committing their members to relocation, but no brickmakers had actually relocated. The city had not yet secured the funding for the package of relocation incentives. Some brickmakers doubted that the city would keep its end of the bargain. They viewed the relocation plan as a political ploy designed to win brickmakers' votes.

Like the relocation effort, the city's clean fuels initiative has involved more talk than action. The city regulations banning dirty fuels are infrequently enforced. Not surprisingly, the city's plans to introduce propane were shelved following nation-wide reductions in propane subsidies.

The communities surrounding *ejido San Antonio* have had a more significant impact on kiln emissions than has the city government. After repeated protests, these communities have managed to get the brickmakers to agree to stop burning tires, to fire only at night (when emissions from other sources are at a minimum), and to limit the number of kilns that are fired at any given time. In addition, three of the five brickmaker organizations now enforce a prohibition on the burning of tires.

Conclusion

This section distills policy lessons from the four case studies. It makes three general observations about environmental management in the informal sector and then evaluates the performance of the various pollution-control policies described in the previous section. The main points of the discussion are summarized in Table 4-2.

The Political Economy of Policy Choice

Some pollution-control policies impose greater costs on firms than others. For example, relocation and clean technological change are relatively costly to firms compared to educational programs. Of course, subsidies can be used to reduce the costs of any policy. For example, the costs of a clean technology strategy can be reduced by subsidizing technical extension, credit and equipment.

In each of our four study cities, policymakers were only able to pursue pol-lution-control strategies that imposed significant costs on brickmakers in cities where brickmakers' political power was relatively limited. For example, in Za-catecas, brickmakers were both few in number and completely unorganized. They were unable to either prevent regulators from pursuing costly abatement strate-gies—relocation and clean technological change—or to convince them to subsi-dize their expenses. By contrast, in both Ciudad Juárez and Saltillo, brickmakers were numerous, well–organized, and politically powerful and, as a result, they were able to block costly strategies. In Ciudad Juárez, although pollution-control efforts focused on clean technological change—a relatively costly strategy—they also involved significant subsidies for equipment and technical extension. In Saltillo, regulatory authorities ultimately opted for a process standard prohibiting exclusive use of tires as fuel—a relatively low-cost strategy—and made efforts to reduce the costs of this regulation by providing brickmakers with free scrap wood and subsidizing the cost of recreational facilities and market stalls. In Torreón, which had a relatively small but geographically concentrated and politically active group

Table 4-2. *Lessons from Case Studies*

Policy	Lessons
All	• When informal polluters are numerous and/or well-organized, they can block enforcement efforts. In such cases, only combinations of policies with low private costs are likely be feasible.
	• Private-sector-led initiatives with strong public-sector support may be best suited to informal-sector pollution control.
Command-and-control	
Process standards	• Registering informal enterprises and peer monitoring are common strategies for enhancing enforceability.
	• Registration alone is not sufficient to facilitate enforcement.
	• Peer monitoring is a necessary condition for enforcement and appears to be most effective when carried out by local organizations.
Relocation	• Imposes relatively high costs on polluters and is therefore likely to meet with considerable resistance.
Economic incentives	
Green subsidies	• Without careful monitoring, subsidies may simply encourage the resale of subsidized goods.
Alternative instruments	
Clean technologies	• Technologies need not be cost-reducing to diffuse widely.
	• Subsidies to early adopters may heighten competitive pressures for further adoption.
	• Technologies must be appropriate: affordable and consistent with existing levels of technology.
	• Technologies may be derailed by input price instability.
	• Time and location matter: universal solutions are improbable.
Informal regulation	• Educational programs may bolster pollution-control efforts.
	• Boycotts are unlikely to be effective because enforcement is highly problematic.

of brickmakers, regulators promoted relocation—a costly strategy. However, they tried to do this by offering a generous incentive package rather than by threatening sanctions. Moreover, city authorities had limited success with this policy.

Thus, our case studies suggest that even though informal firms might appear to be politically ineffectual, actually they are often capable of blocking costly pollution-control policies. This is especially likely to be true in cases where informal-sector polluters have significant environmental impacts, simply because in such cases they are bound to be numerous. Hence, policymakers grappling with serious informal-sector pollution problems will generally be unable to pursue policies that impose significant costs on polluters.

The Promise of Private-Sector-Led Environmental Initiatives

If we discount the Zacatecas experience because of the relatively small number of kilns involved, then of the remaining three pollution-control initiatives, the most successful was the Ciudad Juárez Brickmakers' Project, which managed to convince more than 175 brickmakers to adopt propane, albeit for a limited time. This effort was also the only one in our sample that was led by a private-sector organization, a fact which suggests that private-sector-led initiatives hold considerable promise as a means of addressing informal-sector pollution problems.

Private-sector-led initiatives would seem to enjoy a number of advantages over state-run programs. First, the willingness of the majority of the brickmakers in Ciudad Juárez to cooperate with the project suggests that private-sector-led initiatives may be best suited to engage firms that by their nature are bound to be wary of sustained contact with regulatory authorities. Second, the enthusiasm that the Brickmakers' Project generated among funders, participants, and the public at large suggests that private-sector-led projects may be able to draw more freely on public sympathy for environmentalism than top-down bureaucratic initiatives. And finally, the project's success at consensus building among a diverse set of stakeholders suggests that private-sector-led-initiatives may be better able to sidestep the politics and bureaucracy that often plague public-sector-led initiatives. The city-led initiatives in our sample were rife with such problems. For example, in Torreón, brickmakers belonging to a union affiliated with a political party opposed to the municipal government were impelled to oppose the city's abatement initiative. Even those brickmakers who supported this initiative were reluctant to put great store in a promised package of relocation incentives for fear that it was politically motivated. In Saltillo, the propane initiative was twice disrupted by changes in the municipal government, first in December 1993 and again in December 1996. Finally, in both Zacatecas and Torreón, a difficult effort to forge a consensus among unwieldy bureaucracies in neighboring municipalities was needed to promote pollution-abatement efforts among brickmakers in each city.

The qualified success of the Ciudad Juárez Brickmakers' Project, however, does not imply that informal-sector environmental problems are best left to private-sector organizers. In all likelihood, the Ciudad Juárez Brickmakers' Project would not have had as much success without unusually strong United States and Mexican federal support and the support of the municipal and state governments. Thus, our case studies suggest that private-sector-led initiatives can work—indeed they may be more effective than public-sector initiatives—but they require strong public-sector support.

Combining Policies

As Table 4-1 illustrates, the policymakers in our four study cities used combinations of several pollution-control policies, rather than simply relying on one or two. For example, in Ciudad Juárez, the key policy was clearly clean technological change, but this policy was buttressed by a program of research and development, subsidies, an educational campaign, a boycott of brickmakers using dirty fuels, and a command-and-control prohibition of dirty fuels. The fact that pollution-control policies were not implemented one at a time makes them difficult to evaluate. Nevertheless, it is possible to draw some conclusion about each policy.

Command-and-Control Process Standards

Municipal environmental authorities in each of our four study cities promulgated command-and-control regulations prohibiting the use of certain types of fuels. In Ciudad Juárez and Zacatecas, these regulations helped to temporarily dramatically boost propane use, and in Ciudad Juárez, Zacatecas, and Torreón, they ultimately succeeded in permanently eliminating the use of particularly dirty fuels, such as plastics and used tires. Policymakers relied on two strategies to overcome the difficulty of monitoring and enforcing these regulations: registration and peer monitoring.

In Saltillo, Zacatecas, and Torreón, municipal authorities compiled registries of informal brickmakers. In Saltillo, registration was clearly futile. Brickmakers continued to violate prohibitions on burning tires with impunity. It is hard to judge the impact that registration had in Torreón because peer monitoring appears to have played a strong role in the shift away from the dirtiest fuels. By contrast, in Zacatecas, registration undoubtedly had a significant effect. For a short period, all brickmakers in the city used propane exclusively, and there is little evidence that peer monitoring or other strategies were responsible. But the success of the registration effort in Zacatecas was likely due to the fact that there were only about 60 kilns in the city. As a result, monitoring was not prohibitively costly. Also, brickmakers did not have the political power to block enforcement.

Thus, our case studies suggest that in general, simply registering informal polluters is not sufficient to facilitate enforcement of command-and-control regulations. Evidently, the fact that informal polluters are anonymous is not the principal barrier to enforcement. Rather, the key obstacles are the high cost of monitoring and the political considerations discussed above. Registering informal firms may give regulators some added leverage by laying the groundwork for inspections and fines, but it does not solve the underlying problem of too few regulatory resources chasing too many firms.

Perhaps the single most striking finding from our study is that in each study city, enforcement of command-and-control regulations depended critically on peer monitoring. In most cases, local organizations played a key role. For example, in Ciudad Juárez, trade unions and neighborhood associations imposed sanctions on brickmakers who used certain dirty fuels. In addition, to enforce a ban on burning debris, the municipal environmental authority relied on citizen complaints to identify violators. In Saltillo, the enforcement of a prohibition on the exclusive use of tires depended on peer monitoring and on the cooperation of the brickmakers' union. Similarly, in Zacatecas, brickmakers reported violations of the ban on burning tires to the city environmental authority. Finally, in Torreón, demonstrations and petitions organized by residents of the communities surrounding the main brickyard were instrumental in getting the brickmaker organizations to agree to fire only at night, to limit the number of kilns burning at any given time, and to stop burning tires.

Thus, our case studies suggest that peer monitoring is a necessary condition for effective command-and-control regulation in the informal sector. They also suggest that peer monitoring is most successful when facilitated by local organizations. It is important to note, however, that the success of this strategy in our study cities depended on the fact that neighbors could easily see or smell brickkiln emissions. Peer monitoring would probably be less effective for other types of polluters (such as leather tanneries), whose emissions are less visible.

Relocation

Relocation is probably the most costly pollution-control strategy for brickmakers. It requires them to purchase new land and build new kilns. In addition, it usually increases transportation costs because most brickmakers live next to their kilns and sell their goods locally. The only city in our sample where kilns were actually relocated was Zacatecas, which was also the only city where brickmakers had little political power. Relocation was never even seriously discussed in either Ciudad Juárez or Saltillo, cities where brickmakers have considerable political power. Thus, relocation is only feasible when regulatory authorities enjoy considerable bargaining power or have the resources to pay significant subsidies.

Input Subsidies and Taxes

There were no attempts to use input taxes or subsidies in any of our study cities. The explanation most likely has to do with a number of practical considerations. First, all the pollution-control efforts we studied were led either by municipal governments or nongovernmental organizations. Neither institution is likely to have the fiscal resources to provide substantial sustained subsidies. Second, the dirty inputs into brickmaking that are the appropriate targets for input taxes—used tires, plastic wastes, and scrap wood—are sold on informal markets, where tax collection institutions are absent and easily avoided. Third, given the level of poverty among brickmakers, attempts to subsidize clean inputs (like propane) would likely induce brickmakers to resell these inputs to make quick profits. In fact, according to regulatory authorities in Ciudad Juárez, one reason federal propane subsidies were lifted in the early 1990s was to end a rampant cross-border black market in propane. Thus, our case studies suggest that, in general, when informal polluters buy their inputs in informal markets, input taxes and subsidies are not feasible.

Boycotts

Boycotts of brickmakers using dirty fuels were attempted in two cities: Ciudad Juárez and Zacatecas. In both cases, they were utter failures. Buyers simply continued to buy bricks from whomever was selling at the best price. These experiences suggest that in most cases, contravening market forces in the informal sector simply does not work; monitoring is too difficult and cheating is too easy.

Clean Technological Change

In three of our study cities, Ciudad Juárez, Saltillo, and Zacatecas, policymakers adopted pollution-control strategies that, temporarily at least, centered around converting kilns to propane, a process that we have argued constitutes technological change. In practice, all of the propane initiatives in our study cities turned out to differ in an important way from what is conventionally thought of as clean technological change: due to reductions in propane subsidies, conversion to propane increased variable costs rather than reducing them. Nevertheless, the majority of brickmakers in two of our study cities—Ciudad Juárez and Zacatecas—adopted propane and continued to use it for over a year. This phenomenon runs counter to the conventional wisdom that to be viable, clean technologies must reduce variable costs.

Part of the explanation for this phenomenon undoubtedly has to do with the effectiveness of regulatory pressure and peer monitoring. But another part of the explanation may have to do with the interplay between competition and peer monitoring. The market for bricks is highly competitive and, as a result, brickmakers who use high-cost clean fuels are liable to be undercut by competitors using dirty fuels. Thus, initially, competition in the market for bricks seems to work against the introduction of cost-increasing clean fuels. However, our case studies suggest that, ironically, once diffusion of the clean fuel has progressed past a certain stage, competition can work *in favor* of diffusion because those who have adopted have an incentive to ensure that their competitors adopt as well. Moreover, adopters generally have some leverage over those of their competitors who are neighbors or fellow union members. This suggests that, in general, if a critical mass of informal firms can be convinced by hook or crook to adopt a cost-increasing clean technology, eventually diffusion can become self-perpetuating. One would expect this dynamic to be strongest in situations where the firms are geographically and politically unified and therefore have some influence over a relatively high percentage of their competitors, and to be weakest in situations where there are strong jurisdictional or political divisions among firms. The observed pattern of adoption in Ciudad Juárez was consistent with this story. Once an initial cadre of brickmakers had been convinced to adopt, neighbors and fellow union members quickly followed suit. The same dynamic may have been played out in Zacatecas, speeded by the fact that the entire pool of brickmakers was relatively small. The lesson for policymakers is that subsidies to early adopters may heighten pressures to adopt for other firms.

The case studies also suggest lessons concerning the types of technologies that are appropriate in the informal sector. Project leaders in Ciudad Juárez and Saltillo attempted to develop and diffuse new energy-efficient kilns. In both cities, experimental kilns were designed by highly trained engineers, involved radical departures from existing kilns, and would have required brickmakers to finance sizable investments in new equipment and in training. These efforts were unsuccessful. By contrast, with the benefit of the Ciudad Juárez experience, city authorities in Zacatecas promoted the use of low-technology, low-cost methods of firing existing traditional kilns with propane. These experiences illustrate well-established principles for introducing new technologies in low-income settings. First, to the extent possible, intended adopters should participate in designing the innovation. And second, new technologies must be "appropriate," that is, both affordable and consistent with existing levels of technology.

Finally, are there any lessons to be learned from the fact that technological change initiatives in Ciudad Juárez, Saltillo, and Zacatecas were undermined by nationwide reductions in propane subsidies? This might be seen as evidence of a failure on the part of the Mexican government to coordinate conflicting policy initiatives. Whereas the government funded efforts to convert brickmakers to propane (through Solidarity Enterprises and NAFIN), it simultaneously pursued an economic liberalization program that undermined these efforts. But this liberalization program was part of a broad economic reform, and the benefits of this reform may well have outweighed the costs, including the environmental costs. To reduce the environmental costs, the Mexican government might have subsidized propane use by those consumers who were likely to substitute into dirty fuels. However, such a policy would have been difficult to implement and almost certainly would have created a black market in subsidized propane.

Should the organizers of the propane initiatives in each city be blamed for failing to recognize that propane was an economically unsustainable option? It seems unfair to fault the organizers of the Ciudad Juárez program. Propane prices only began to rise in 1992, by which time this initiative had completely organized itself around engineering a switch to propane. But the leaders of the Saltillo and Zacatecas programs might have foreseen the difficulties of promoting propane because their projects were not launched until 1993 and 1994. Their failure to do so may have stemmed from the fact that in the early 1990s, the Ciudad Juárez experience was being widely touted as a model initiative by both its leaders and its funders. In 1994, with federal financing, the Mexican nonprofit that spearheaded the Ciudad Juárez project established ECO-TEC, a national center for brickmaking training and research that strongly advocated conversion to propane.

Hence, the demise of the propane initiatives in three of our study cities holds two lessons. First, in developing economies where input prices are often unstable, market-based technological change initiatives among enterprises that are sensitive to variations in these prices are bound to be somewhat fragile. Second, intertemporal and place-based factors matter: what works at one time and in one place will not necessarily be a universal solution.

Education Initiatives

In only one study city, Ciudad Juárez, did project leaders attempt to use an information campaign about the health hazards associated with burning dirty fuels to promote a shift to cleaner fuels. Even this campaign was limited in scope and duration.

Yet, statistical analysis of survey data from Ciudad Juárez reveals a positive correlation between awareness of the health hazards associated with burning dirty fuels and the adoption of propane (Chapter 9 in this book). This finding suggests that information campaigns regarding the health impacts of emissions can bolster pollution-control efforts.

Acknowledgments

I am grateful to the Tinker Foundation for financial support, Geoffrey Bannister for invaluable assistance with field research and primary documents and all of our interviewees in Mexico and Texas.

Notes

1. This section is based on a July 1995 survey of 95 brickmakers in Ciudad Juárez, statistical analysis of that survey data, a variety of primary and secondary documents, and interviews with Texan and Mexican stakeholders, including representatives of *Federación Mexicana de Asociaciones Privadas de Salud y Desarrollo Comunitario* (FEMAP), the Ciudad Juárez Municipal Ecology Office, and the Texas Natural Resources Conservation Commission. It is distilled from in-depth analyses of the Brickmakers' Project presented in Blackman and Bannister (1997, 1998), which contain complete bibliographic information.

2. In 1995, the city of El Paso was classified by the US Environmental Protection Agency as a moderate nonattainment area for both carbon monoxide and particulate matter, and El Paso County was classified as a serious nonattainment area for ozone.

3. This section is based on interviews with the secretary, the subdirector, and the director of the Municipal Ecology Office of Saltillo (July 16 and 17, 1996, documents provided by these three officials) and interviews with four brickmakers in the La Rosa and Guayulera districts (July 16 and 17, 1996).

4. Tiles and bricks are usually fired simultaneously. The soil in Saltillo is particularly well suited to tile making.

5. The city government established a fund of 50,000 pesos (US$17,000). The state government was recruited to provide matching funds. With the cooperation of Solidarity Enterprises, the same federal program that funded the Ciudad Juárez initiative, this funding was used to leverage a 1,000,000 peso (US$333,000) loan fund from NAFIN, the federal development bank. All of the funds were earmarked for brickmakers' investments in propane equipment.

6. This section is based on interviews with the director of the Solidarity Enterprises office in Zacatecas (July 19, 1996), primary documents and newspaper clippings provided by this office, and interviews with seven brickmakers in Zacatecas and Guadalupe (July 18 and 19, 1996).

7. The municipalities were Jerez, Ojo Caliente, Guadalupe, Tlaltenango, and Fesnillo.

8. This section is based on interviews with the director general of Economic Development and the director general of Public Services and Ecology for the Municipality of Torreón (July 23 and 24, 1996), documents provided by these officials, and interviews with five brickmakers of the *ejido San Antonio* (July 23 and 24, 1996).

References

Blackman, A., and G.J. Bannister. 1997. Pollution Control in the Informal Sector: The Ciudad Juárez Brickmakers' Project. *Natural Resources Journal* 37: 829–56.

———. 1998. Community Pressure and Clean Technology in the Informal Sector: An Econometric Analysis of the Adoption of Propane by Traditional Mexican Brickmakers. *Journal of Environmental Economics and Management* 35: 1–21.

Cruz, J.M. 1993. Proyectan Constitución de Cooperativas los Productores de Ladrilleros. El Norte de Ciudad Juárez, February 8.

Johnson, A., J. Soto, Jr., and J.B. Ward. 1994. Successful Modernization of an Ancient Industry: The Brickmakers of Ciudad Juárez, Mexico. El Paso, TX: El Paso Natural Gas. Presented at the New Mexico Conference on the Environment, April.

CHAPTER 5

Economic Incentives for Cleaner Small and Medium Enterprises

Evidence from Malaysia

Jeffrey R. Vincent and G. Sivalingam

COUNTRIES AROUND THE WORLD are increasingly experimenting with economic incentives as policy instruments for reducing industrial pollution (Panayotou 1998, Sterner 2003). Economic instruments "create financial incentives for abatement by putting an implicit or explicit price on emissions but … do not dictate abatement decisions" (Blackman and Harrington 1999, 2). Environmental economics textbooks typically focus on the twin examples of a Pigovian pollution tax as the prototypical price-based instrument and emissions trading as the prototypical quantity-based instrument. In practice, governments in both developed and developing countries have selected economic incentives from a longer menu. Examples include taxes on polluting inputs instead of pollution itself; user fees for the treatment or disposal of solid and liquid wastes of various types; deposit-refund schemes; insurance premium taxes; and fiscal incentives, or tax breaks, on pollution-control equipment (Stavins 2003).

Judging from a recent survey by Blackman (2000), relatively little has been written about applications of economic incentives to pollution from small and medium enterprises (SMEs). One apparent reason is that few countries have attempted such applications. Malaysia is an exception. As in most developing countries, command-and-control regulations remain at the core of the Malaysian government's strategy for managing industrial pollution, including pollution from SMEs. However, the government has augmented those regulations with fiscal incentives for certain types of environmental expenditures, and it has allowed private companies to charge user fees for centralized waste-treatment facilities. The fiscal incentives encompass a range of tax allowances, deductions, and exemptions. They represent subsidies for activities that reduce pollution.[1] The user fees pertain to two systems that are operating at greatly different scales: user fees for common wastewater-treatment services within an individual industrial park, and user fees for the collection, treatment, and disposal of toxic and hazardous wastes at a recently established national waste management center. In contrast to fiscal incentives, they represent applications of the "polluter pays principle."

This chapter describes and evaluates Malaysia's experience with these incentive-based approaches. It focuses on their literal incentive effect: Have they succeeded in reducing pollution from SMEs? This chapter does not consider other standard economic criteria for evaluating environmental policy instruments, such as whether they are cost-effective or whether they create dynamic incentives for technological change. We pay particular attention to the effects of these incentives on water pollution from SMEs in two industrial sectors, metal finishing and textiles. Most companies in the metal-finishing sector in Malaysia are SMEs, especially ones in the electroplating subsector. The Malaysian textiles sector is large and diverse, but most dyeing and finishing houses are SMEs. Electroplaters and dyeing and finishing houses commonly generate wastewater that is contaminated with toxic and hazardous waste, which became a major concern of the Malaysian Department of Environment (DOE) during the 1990s.

The chapter begins with a graphic analysis of the incentive effects of fiscal incentives and user fees. It then provides an overview of SMEs in the Malaysian manufacturing sector and summarizes the available quantitative information on their environmental performance. Next, the chapter presents estimates of the benefits and costs of improved environmental performance from the standpoint of SMEs. The core of the chapter then follows: a description of the main features of the fiscal incentives and user fees that have been applied in Malaysia, a review of evidence on their environmental effectiveness, and an analysis of the differences observed. The chapter concludes with a summary of the main findings and lessons for other countries.

Most of the information in the chapter was collected during 1998–99, as part of field work for a study funded by the Asian Development Bank (ADB; see International Business & Technical Consultants Inc. 1999). That study focused on water pollution from SMEs in three sectors: metal finishing, textiles, and food processing. This chapter highlights the first two sectors because they are greater sources of wastewater containing toxic and hazardous substances.

Graphic Analysis of Fiscal Incentives and User Fees

The incentive effects of stylized versions of fiscal incentives and user fees are presented in Figures 5-1 and 5-2, respectively. Figure 5-1 plots the marginal benefits and costs of water pollution reduction against the quantity of pollution reduction by an individual firm. *Pollution reduction* is understood here and in the remainder of this chapter as including both pollution prevention—modifications of manufacturing processes that reduce the amount of pollution generated—and pollution control—end-of-pipe treatment processes that remove residual pollution from a company's wastewater stream.

The vertical line s is the official discharge standard. This is the minimum amount of pollution reduction that the firm is required to make to be in compliance with pollution regulations. The downward-sloping line s^e is the effective standard, which equals the marginal value of penalties the firm expects to pay if it fails to

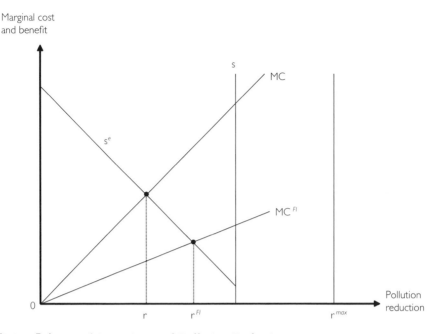

Figure 5-1. *Fiscal Incentives and Pollution Reduction*

comply.[2] It is a downward-sloping function of pollution reduction: both the risk of being caught violating the official standard and the resulting penalties are lower if the firm is closer to being in compliance. The horizontal discrepancy between s and s^e indicates that the discharge standard is not perfectly enforced. The vertical line r^{max} is the maximum amount of pollution reduction the firm can potentially achieve (i.e., the amount of pollution it discharges if it practices neither pollution prevention nor pollution control).

In the absence of fiscal incentives, the firm's before- and after-tax marginal cost curves for reducing pollution are the same and are given by MC. The firm maximizes the net benefits of pollution reduction by reducing pollution up to r, which in this example falls far short of the emission standard s. Fiscal incentives reduce the after-tax cost of marginal expenditures on pollution reduction to MC^{FI}. Now, the optimal amount of pollution reduction from the standpoint of the firm is r^{FI}. Although this remains less than s, it is greater than r. The fiscal incentives have induced the firm to come closer to being in compliance.

Figure 5-2 assumes that the firm is located in an industrial park equipped with a common wastewater-treatment plant. Wastewater from the firm is piped to the treatment plant, and the firm pays a user fee of u for every unit of pollution in its wastewater, i.e., for every unit it does not remove through pollution prevention. MC now depicts the marginal cost of just pollution prevention, since pollution control is provided by the common treatment plant. Marginal cost is drawn as being negative up to a point: In this range, pollution prevention can save the firm variable costs. Pollution prevention also involves fixed costs, however, and these cause the average total cost, ATC, to be positive at all levels of pollution prevention.

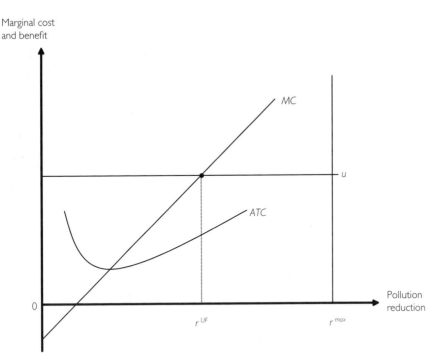

Figure 5-2. *User Fees and Pollution Prevention*

In the absence of the user fee, the firm thus has no incentive to invest in pollution prevention, despite the negative marginal costs. As long as u is greater than the minimum of ATC, however, the firm has such an incentive, because pollution prevention enables it to avoid paying user fees on pollution up to r^{UF}.[3] Hence, it pays only $u(r^{max} - r^{UF})$. If the user fee were not enforced perfectly, it would be a downward-sloping function analogous to s^e in Figure 5-1, and the amount of pollution prevention would be less than r^{UF}.

Small and Medium Enterprises in Malaysia

Basic Characteristics

The Malaysian government refers to SMEs in the manufacturing sector as "small and medium scale industries," or SMIs. It defines them as firms with up to 150 full-time employees and annual sales up to US$6.6 million.[4] It uses this definition in statistical reporting and in determining which firms qualify for certain industrial development programs. For the sake of consistency with the other chapters in this book, we will use the more familiar acronym, SMEs, to refer to companies that satisfy the Malaysian definition.

The government views SMEs as key constituents of Malaysia's manufacturing sector for both economic and social reasons. The *Second Industrial Master Plan,* which is the government's blueprint for industrial development during 1996–2005, refers to SMEs as "the critical and strategic link to develop and strengthen [manufacturing] cluster formation and increase domestic value-added" (Ministry of International Trade and Industry 1996, 403). It also notes that SMEs are an important source of employment because they are numerous and tend to be labor-intensive. SMEs accounted for 80% of registered Malaysian manufacturing establishments in 1998.

The social significance of SMEs derives from more than their employment contribution, however. Malaysia is a multiethnic society in which ethnic Chinese have historically dominated most business sectors. The government views SMEs, with their low capital and technological requirements, as providing natural entry points into the modern economy for ethnic Malays and other indigenous groups. Consequently, it offers a wide range of fiscal and financial incentives[5] to promote the creation of new SMEs and the expansion and modernization of existing ones. In 1998, it offered 14 subsidized credit schemes aimed exclusively at SMEs.

The primary source of comprehensive data on SMEs in Malaysia at the time of the ADB study was a 1993 census (PNB Corporate Development 1996). The sample frame included 11,855 manufacturing establishments. Virtually all establishments—11,292—provided full information. Although this is an impressive response rate, the companies included in the census did not represent the full range of SMEs in the manufacturing sector. The sample frame was based on the Malaysian Registry of Companies, which biased it strongly toward companies in the formal sector. Only 6% of the respondents were not listed in the registry. The census therefore omitted an unknown but probably large number of SMEs in the informal sector.

For example, according to the registry and other official information, the government estimated that there were 145 SME electroplaters operating in the country in 1998. In contrast, the Malaysian Metal Finishing Society estimated that there were in fact around 300 such companies, 200 of which were unregistered. A July 10, 1998, article in the leading Malaysian newspaper, the *New Straits Times*, reported an even higher estimate, 458 establishments. The census is therefore best interpreted as a census of formal-sector SMEs, not all SMEs.

Table 5-1 summarizes selected results from the census. The vast majority of respondents—88%—met the Ministry of International Trade and Industry's definition of a "small scale industry": a company with no more than 50 full-time employees and, at the 1993 exchange rate, annual sales of no more than $4 million.[6] As can be seen, the mean number of employees and the mean value of annual sales were both far below these cutoff values. Few of the SMEs reported having completely manual production processes, but almost half obtained their technology primarily locally. The low percentages of respondents who exported goods or had any foreign equity provide additional evidence that Malaysian SMEs had limited direct connections to the global economy. In these regards, Malaysian small-scale manufacturing enterprises are probably not dissimilar from small-scale manufacturing enterprises in other countries.

Table 5-1. *Characteristics of SMEs in Malaysia, Based on Responses to the 1993 SME Census*

SME characteristic	Amount/Percentage[a]
Size	
Small scale[b]	88%
Average number of employees	19
Average annual sales revenue	$525,091[c]
Average book value of capital	$98,505[c]
Average factory built-up area	20,369 ft^2
Technology	
Completely manual production	10%
Main source of technology: Malaysia	41%
International connections	
Any exports	19%
Any foreign equity	6%
Formal status	
Registered business	94%
Located in industrial estate	9%
Interactions with government agencies	
Any dealings with technical advisory agencies in previous year	16%
Any dealings with management advisory agencies in previous year	10%
Any dealings with DOE in previous year	0.1%
Type of waste generated	
Solid	66%
Metallic	29%
Semi-toxic	15%
Liquid	12%
Toxic	2%
Waste disposal methods	
Trash cans	34%
Sold off	32%
Indiscriminate	11%
Special containers	11%
Recycled	7%
Normal drainage	6%
Gave away	3%

[a]Percentages are based on number of companies that provided full information (11,292).
[b]Definition: ≤ 50 employees, annual sales ≤ 10 million ringgit ($4 million at the 1993 exchange rate).
[c]Conversion based on the 1993 exchange rate (2.5 ringgit per dollar).
Source: PNB Corporate Development (1996), various tables.

Environmental Performance

Malaysian regulations related to water pollution and toxic and hazardous waste predate the SME census. The Sewage and Industrial Effluents Regulations, which went into effect in 1979, prescribe discharge standards for specific pollutants in wastewater. The Scheduled Wastes Regulations,[7] which went into effect in 1989, restrict the use and disposal of 107 types of toxic and hazardous substances. Both sets of regulations apply to SMEs as well as to larger companies, but a loophole that affects some SMEs exists in the Sewage and Industrial Effluents Regulations. Establishments that generate no more than 60 cubic meters of wastewater per day are exempt from these regulations, as long as the wastewater contains no toxic metals and no more than 6 kilograms of biochemical oxygen demand (BOD) or suspended solids. Most metal finishers and many dyeing and finishing houses do not qualify for this exemption because they use plating chemicals or dyes that contain heavy metals, but many other SMEs do.

The census data highlight the difficulties the Malaysian environmental authorities face in monitoring SMEs' compliance with these regulations. Despite the fact that the census respondents were overwhelmingly in the formal sector, fewer than 10% were located in industrial estates. Most SMEs in Malaysia are mixed into residential areas of cities and towns or dispersed across the countryside. Similarly small percentages had had "any dealings" with government agencies that provided assistance on technical or management issues. This suggests that the government had limited interaction with, and therefore limited direct knowledge about, the SME sector. The government tacitly acknowledged this in 1996, when it established the Small and Medium Industries Development Corporation (SMIDEC) as a specialized agency to serve SMEs. More to the point of this chapter, only 0.1% of respondents—just 14 out of 11,292—reported "any dealings" with DOE. As of 1993, even SMEs in the formal sector were evidently far beyond the reach of DOE's regulatory net.

The census contained only two questions specifically about SMEs' environmental performance:

"What type of waste material is produced by your operations?"

"How do you dispose of waste material?"

Each question included several potential responses, and respondents were allowed to check all that applied. Table 5-1 shows the percentage of respondents who checked each response. On the surface, the responses suggest that formal-sector SMEs were not significant pollution sources in the early 1990s. Only 2% of the respondents reported generating any toxic waste, and only 15% reported generating any semi-toxic waste. Just over a tenth reported disposing of their waste in an indiscriminate fashion, which was the most negligent option. Many more (over a third) reported using one or more of the three options related to recycling (sold off, recycled, or gave away).

There is a good reason to be skeptical about these responses, however: namely, the census was not anonymous. Respondents provided identifying information, including the name and address of the company and the name of the individual who completed the questionnaire, on their response sheets. It is reasonable to expect that they avoided giving responses that might have attracted greater scrutiny by government regulatory agencies, including DOE. It is also possible that the lack of definitions of *toxic* and *semi-toxic* in the questionnaire caused them to under-report wastes in those categories.

DOE monitoring and enforcement programs provide more objective data on a broader range of indicators of environmental performance by manufacturing industries, including noncompliance rates with pertinent regulations. DOE reports these data by industrial sector, and it includes metal finishing and textiles as distinct sectors. Unfortunately, it does not publish the data separately for SMEs and large companies, but as noted in the introduction, most companies in the Malaysian metal-finishing sector are SMEs. So are most dyeing and finishing houses, which no one disputes are the most polluting subsector of the textiles industry.

For these reasons, one might expect the DOE data to provide a reasonably accurate picture of the environmental performance of SMEs in the two sectors. In fact, the data likely *understate* the significance of SMEs as sources of water pollution and toxic and hazardous waste. This is because, as the census data suggest, DOE's monitoring and enforcement efforts have been directed more toward readily identifiable pollution sources: companies that are large and registered, not SMEs and especially not unregistered SMEs. DOE officers believe that larger companies generally perform better than SMEs and that registered SMEs perform better than ones that are unregistered. Moreover, with regard to compliance rates for the Sewage and Industrial Effluents Regulations, the data omit SMEs that qualify for the exemption noted earlier.

Table 5-2 presents a summary of the DOE data for 1997. Metal finishing and textiles were among the leading sectors—i.e., the worst sectors from an environ-

Table 5-2. *Environmental Performance of Textile and Metal Finishing Industries in 1997 (all establishments, not just SMEs)*

Criterion	Metal finishing	Textiles
"Significant water pollution sources," as defined by DOE		
Percent of total number	8%	7%
Rank[a]	4th out of 17	5th out of 17
Noncompliance with Sewage and Industrial Effluents Regulations		
Percent of establishments out of compliance	31%	17%
Rank	1st out of 19	6th out of 19
Industrial water pollution complaints		
Percent of total number	4%	12%
Rank[b]	5th	1st
Generation of toxic and hazardous waste		
Percent of total amount	11%	14%
Rank	4th out of 14	3rd out of 14

[a]Rank is from highest to lowest among the industrial sectors identified in the DOE data. A higher rank indicates worse environmental performance.

[b]The number of sectors was not given but is presumably comparable to those for other indicators of water pollution (i.e., 17–19).

Source: Department of Environment (1998), Figures 4.8, 4.11, 4.22, and 6.4.

mental standpoint—in terms of number of "significant water pollution sources"; noncompliance rates with the Sewage and Industrial Effluents Regulations; and generation of toxic and hazardous waste. In addition, the textile sector was the most common source of industrial water pollution complaints. In view of the probable downward bias in these statistics, there is little doubt that SMEs in the two sectors were important industrial sources of water pollution, including effluent contaminated by toxic and hazardous compounds, as of the late 1990s.

Net Costs of Pollution Prevention in Malaysia

As Figures 5-1 and 5-2 illustrate, the two Malaysian economic incentive programs that are the focus of this chapter—fiscal incentives and user fees—will be more effective if the net costs of pollution reduction are lower. As a prelude to the discussion of these two programs, this section presents evidence on the net costs of pollution prevention by Malaysian SMEs. The evidence comes from a technical assistance project that promoted pollution prevention by SMEs in the metal-finishing, textiles, and food processing sectors. This project, Promotion of Cleaner Technology in Malaysian Industry, was launched in 1996 by the Standards and Industrial Research Institute of Malaysia (SIRIM) with funding from the bilateral aid agency Danish Cooperation for Environment and Development (DANCED).

Advocates of pollution prevention often claim that the net costs of improved environmental management by manufacturing industries are negative: that manufacturing processes can be modified in ways that reduce the use of "dirty" inputs without sacrificing output, thus saving companies money on inputs while simultaneously generating less pollution. Referring to Figure 5-2, this would be the case if not only MC but also ATC were negative for some amount of pollution prevention. The prevalence of such "win–win" opportunities has been hotly debated,[8] but the controversy has not slowed the stream of technical assistance projects that promote pollution prevention. These projects often target small and medium enterprises,[9] and that was the case for the SIRIM/DANCED project.

Pollution-prevention projects typically target companies that have not upgraded their processing technology in many years. Win–win opportunities are believed to be most prevalent and most dramatic in these companies. The reasoning is that the companies are operating on old production frontiers that are no longer efficient: they are using unnecessarily large amounts of inputs to produce a given amount of output. According to this criterion, SMEs in the metal-finishing and textile sectors in Malaysia would appear to be good choices for the SIRIM/DANCED project. Industry experts interviewed during the ADB study commented that the fabricated metal sector, which includes metal finishing, is "behind the times," and they estimated that equipment used by dyeing and finishing houses is typically 10–15 years old. The *Second Industrial Master Plan* stated that "dyeing and printing facilities are out-dated" and have "not developed in line with the other sub-sectors" in the textile industry (Ministry of International Trade and Industry 1996, 95).

The SIRIM/DANCED project sponsored a variety of activities, including workshops for companies and industry associations, a newsletter and other information dissemination programs, and six demonstration projects. To identify candidates for the demonstration projects, SIRIM conducted environmental audits of 37 companies in the three sectors during late 1996 and early 1997. It used information from the audits to estimate the costs and benefits of hypothetical process modifications by the companies.

Table 5-3 presents information from the six audits in the metal-finishing and textiles sectors that contained the most detail on projected cost savings. According to SIRIM, the process modifications proposed in these audits are potentially applicable to many companies in each sector; they are not unusual cases. The estimated investment cost ranged from US$15,800 to $118,400. Total annual cost savings ranged from US$7,900 to $57,900, yielding simple payback periods (investment cost divided by annual cost savings) of less than half a year to a little more than two and a half years. Such short payback periods should make the process modifications extremely attractive to SMEs. Companies interviewed during the ADB study stated that payback periods must be shorter than 3–5 years to be financially viable.

Note, however, that the projected cost savings in all six cases included reduced use of wastewater treatment chemicals. This implies that the companies were operating wastewater-treatment equipment. According to officers at DOE, and consistent with the discussion about the downward bias in the noncompliance rates in Table 5-2, this is not the case for most SMEs in the two sectors. Electroplaters and dyeing and finishing houses commonly discharge untreated wastewater into nearby rivers or drains. To be more representative of conditions among SMEs in Malaysia, the estimated cost savings should exclude the reduced expenditures on treatment chemicals and should be based solely on savings related to production inputs: water, fuel oil, plating or fluxing chemicals, and pigments.

The information from SIRIM was sufficiently detailed to recalculate the cost savings in this manner for four of the six companies. The last two columns of Table 5-3 show the production-related savings and associated payback periods. Production-related savings accounted for far less than half of total savings in two cases and around half in a third case. The revised payback periods in these three cases were on the order of 5–15 years. Only in the fourth case did production-related savings dominate the total savings, and only in that case did the payback period (<0.5 years) remain well below SMEs' reported threshold.

The information in Table 5-3 pertains to just a handful of companies, and it refers to hypothetical process modifications instead of actual modifications. Yet according to SIRIM, the production technologies used by the six companies are common among SMEs in the two sectors in Malaysia. Moreover, SIRIM designed the modifications to be cost-effective as well as environmentally effective. On the basis of this evidence, it appears that many SMEs in the metal-finishing and textile sectors in Malaysia have a rational reason not to invest in pollution prevention: the investment cost exceeds the present value of savings on production inputs. Instead of being a "costless" first step toward pollution reduction, which companies should take before spending money on end-of-pipe pollution-control equipment, pollution prevention is financially attractive for SMEs in the two sectors only if the companies are already treating their wastewater. It then becomes financially attractive primarily because it reduces expenditure on expensive treatment chemicals.

Table 5-3. *Costs and Payback Periods for Pollution-Prevention Investments in Malaysia*

Industry	Product or Service	Process modification	Source of savings	Investment^a	Total savings		Production-related savings only^b	
					Annual amount^a	Payback period (yrs.)	Annual amount^a	Payback period (yrs.)
Metal finishing	Hot dip galvanizing	Countercurrent rinsing, Regenerate fluxing solution	Water, Treatment chemicals, Fluxing chemicals	$15,800	$7,900	2.0	NA	NA
Metal finishing	Zinc plating	Ion exchanger units	Water, Treatment chemicals, Plating chemicals	$44,700	$42,600	1.0	$3,200	14.2
Metal finishing	Aluminum anodizing	Countercurrent rinsing	Water, Treatment chemicals	$15,800	$27,400	0.6	$1,100	15.0
Textiles	Dyeing	Recycle rinsing and cooling water, Recover waste heat	Water, Treatment chemicals, Fuel oil	$105,300	$39,500	2.7	NA	NA
Textiles	Dyeing	Recycle rinsing and cooling water, Recover waste heat	Water, Treatment chemicals, Fuel oil	$118,400	$57,900	2.0	$26,300	4.5
Textiles	Screen printing	Recover and reuse pigments, Wash drums, screens, etc., immediately	Water, Treatment chemicals, Pigment	<$26,300	$57,900	<0.5	$52,600	<0.5

Note: NA = not available.

^a Conversions based on fixed exchange rate of 3.8 ringgit per dollar, in effect since late 1998.

^b Excludes savings related to wastewater treatment.

Source: Unpublished SIRIM estimates.

Under these circumstances, inducing SMEs to reduce pollution through pollution prevention requires the provision of additional incentives, to which we now turn.

Characteristics and Performance of Incentive-Based Programs in Malaysia

SIRIM did not include fiscal incentives or user fees in its cost–benefit analysis. For these reasons it might have understated the financial attractiveness of pollution prevention to SMEs. Fiscal incentives affect the cost side, by reducing the after-tax cost of materials and equipment used in process modifications (Figure 5-1). User fees increase the benefits of pollution prevention (Figure 5-2). If firms are paying user fees for centralized waste treatment, and if pollution prevention enables them to generate less waste, then it saves them money on waste treatment, just as it enables firms that are operating their own waste-treatment facilities to save money on treatment chemicals.

SIRIM left out user fees for centralized waste treatment because no operational examples of such fees existed in Malaysia when it conducted its environmental audits. Two examples now exist: user fees for the treatment and disposal of toxic and hazardous wastes at a centralized facility, the Bukit Nanas Waste Management Centre, which serves all of Peninsular Malaysia and is operated by a private company, Kualiti Alam; and, on a much smaller scale, user fees for common wastewater treatment at a specialized industrial park for electroplaters, Bukit Kemuning Electroplating Park, which is operated by a different private company, BI-PMB Waste Management. The reason SIRIM ignored fiscal incentives is unclear, as such incentives have existed since at least 1990. The Malaysian government offers companies fiscal incentives for modernization projects that improve environmental performance, and it offers even more incentives for end-of-pipe pollution control. Hence, it offers fiscal incentives that in principle should promote water pollution reduction through both pollution prevention and wastewater treatment.

This section describes the characteristics of the fiscal-incentive and user-fee programs and presents information on their effectiveness in reducing pollution by SMEs. As will be seen, only the user fees at Bukit Kemuning Electroplating Park appear to have had any incentive effect. The reasons for the variation in the programs' performance will be explored in a later section titled Factors Influencing the Performance of Incentive-Based Programs in Malaysia.

Fiscal Incentives

The Malaysian government introduced several fiscal incentives to promote improved environmental management by manufacturing industries during the 1990s. These incentives apply to all companies, not just SMEs. Table 5-4 classifies the incentives into two groups, direct and indirect. Direct tax incentives reduce corporate income taxes. They include accelerated depreciation allowances on pollution-control equipment and facilities for storing, treating, and disposing of toxic and hazardous waste. The initial and annual allowances are "accelerated," in that they are twice as large as the depreciation allowances for ordinary industrial invest-

Table 5-4. *Fiscal Incentives That Favor Environmental Management by SMEs in Malaysia*

Incentive	Comments	Legislative basis (effective date)
Direct tax incentives		
Accelerated Depreciation Allowance for Environmental Protection Equipment	Initial allowance of 40% and annual allowance of 20%, to enable the full amount to be written off within 3 years	Income Tax Act (tax year 1996)
Accelerated Depreciation Allowance for Facilities to Store, Treat, and Dispose Toxic and Hazardous Waste by Companies that Generate Waste	Initial allowance of 40% and annual allowance of 20%, to enable the full amount to be written off within 3 years	Income Tax Act (January 1, 1990)
Indirect tax incentives		
Import Duty and Sales Tax Exemptions for Machinery and Equipment Used for the Control of Environmental Pollution	Available to approved companies in the manufacturing and service sectors	Customs Act, Sales Tax Act (predates 1994 budget)
Import Duty and Sales Tax Exemptions for Machinery, Equipment, Raw Materials, and Components Used for the Storage, Treatment, and Disposal of Toxic and Hazardous Waste	Available to both waste-management companies and waste-generating companies	Customs Act, Sales Tax Act (January 1, 1990)
Import Duty Exemption for Spares and Consumables. Includes spares and consumables imported for expansion and modernization projects that result in improved compliance with legal requirements, such as environmental laws		Customs Act (date unknown)

Sources: Federation of Malaysian Manufacturers (1998), Ministry of Finance (1999).

ments. Hence, they allow firms to write off environmental management investments more quickly.

Indirect tax incentives pertain to goods as opposed to income. They include
import duty and sales tax exemptions on machinery and equipment used in controlling pollution, and similar exemptions on machinery, equipment, raw materials,
and components used in managing toxic and hazardous waste. These exemptions
are not automatic: A company must apply to the Malaysian Industrial Development Agency (MIDA), which grants the import duty exemption only if the equipment is not available locally. Companies can also apply for an import duty exemption on spares and consumables[10] used in expansion or modernization projects that
improve their compliance with environmental laws (e.g., adoption of pollution
prevention).

These various tax breaks should provide incentives for SMEs to reduce the
generation of water pollutants and to increase treatment of their wastewater, as
depicted in Figure 5-1. Yet, available evidence indicates that there has been little
demand by either large companies or SMEs for the tax breaks, despite the fact that
some of them have been available for a decade. Although the government does not
track the number of applications or the number of approvals (or, for that matter,
the number of approvals that are actually implemented), according to unofficial
estimates compiled by MIDA, only two companies were granted accelerated depreciation allowances for environmental investments during 1990–96. Representatives of the Inland Revenue Bureau agreed that applications for these incentives
are rare. MIDA officials and industry representatives report that companies do
not regularly apply for the environmental import duty and sales tax exemptions
either.

User Fees for Toxic and Hazardous Waste Management: Kualiti Alam

Kualiti Alam's user fees for the management of toxic and hazardous wastes are
linked to the Scheduled Wastes Regulations, which as noted earlier were introduced in 1989 and cover 107 types of toxic and hazardous wastes. In 1995, the
company signed a 15-year agreement with the government to build and operate a
national waste-management center designed to treat these wastes. The agreement
gave Kualiti Alam the exclusive right to transport, treat, and dispose of toxic and
hazardous wastes in Peninsular Malaysia. Kualiti Alam began construction of the
Bukit Nanas Centre in 1995 and completed it in 1998.[11]

Kualiti Alam has a schedule of user fees that are differentiated by type of service (transport, treatment, or disposal) and type of waste. Table 5-5 shows the
1999 schedule for waste treatment. According to Kualiti Alam, the variation in
fees across waste categories reflects differences in the unit costs of the treatment
technologies required (e.g., stabilization or solidification, physical or chemical
treatment, incineration). SMEs in the metal-finishing and textile sectors produce
waste in several of the categories shown in the table, in particular inorganic waste
requiring physical or chemical treatment. The user fees should in principle provide
an incentive for such SMEs to adopt pollution-prevention measures to reduce the
waste they generate, per Figure 5-2.

Table 5-5. *Kualiti Alam's Waste-Treatment Fees (rates are per metric ton and are valid through December 31, 1999)*

1. Organic and inorganic waste for incineration

Waste group	Packaged waste		Bulk waste	
	Pumpable liquid	Solid	Pumpable liquid	Solid
A	$210		$170	
B	$830	$950		
C	$360			
H/Z	$500	$734	$470	$710
T	$830	$950		

2. Inorganic waste for physical or chemical treatment

Waste group	800-liter pallet tank	200-liter drum
X: Acid waste without chromate	$380	$430
X: Alkaline waste without cyanide	$380	$430
X: Chromate waste	$470	$520
X: Cyanide waste	$470	$520
K: Mercury waste	$950	$1,000

3. Inorganic waste for solidification

Waste group	Packaged waste	Bulk waste
X/Z	$210	$200

4. Inorganic waste for direct landfill

Waste group	Packaged waste	Bulk waste
X/Z	$130	$120

Notes: A = mineral oil waste; B = organic chemical waste containing halogen or sulfur; C = waste solvents without halogens or sulfur (content <1%); H = organic chemical waste without halogens or sulfur; K = waste containing mercury; T = pesticide waste; X = inorganic waste; and Z = miscellaneous (including medical waste, lab packs, asbestos waste, mineral sludge, isocyanate, and batteries).

Source: Information provided by Kualiti Alam.

Early demand for Kualiti Alam's waste disposal services has been high, but this does not imply a high rate of compliance with the Scheduled Wastes Regulations by SMEs. The annual treatment capacity at the Bukit Nanas Centre is approximately 75,000 metric tons. In December 1998, Kualiti Alam estimated that its waste receipts would total 60,000 metric tons for 1998, and it projected receipts of 80,000 metric tons for 1999. These impressively large numbers are inflated, however, by a large backlog of waste that larger companies accumulated while waiting for the Bukit Nanas Centre to open. Some companies reportedly stored waste for up to 10 years, ever since the Scheduled Wastes Regulations were introduced in 1989. Only 900 of the approximately 3000 generators of toxic and hazardous wastes identified by DOE as operating in Peninsular Malaysia had registered with

Kualiti Alam as of late 1998, and only 300 had actually sent it any waste. Kualiti Alam believes that SMEs account for most of the 10-fold gap between its actual and potential customer base. Obviously, Kualiti Alam's user fees cannot create an incentive for SMEs to reduce pollution if SMEs opt out of using its services.

User Fees for Common Wastewater Treatment: Bukit Kemuning Electroplating Park

Bukit Kemuning Electroplating Park is off to a more promising start. Completed in 1998 and located in the state of Selangor, it is the first industrial park in Malaysia with a common wastewater treatment plant designed specifically for metal finishers.[12] It is a joint venture of a government-owned development bank, Bank Industri, and a private metal-finishing company, Press Metal Berhad. Each factory lot in the park contains tanks for collecting wastewater and underground pipes leading from the tanks to the treatment plant. The plant is owned and operated by a for-profit subsidiary of Bank Industri and Press Metal Berhad, BI-PMB Waste Management. It is designed to remove 98–99% of the four main pollutants in the wastewater: chromium, cadmium, acids, and alkali.

BI-PMB meters the amount of wastewater each factory generates and charges a monthly fee that depends on the amount of wastewater and the concentration of pollutants in it. Hence, companies that generate more wastewater, and wastewater that is more difficult to treat, pay a higher fee. BI-PMB bases the fees on its unit-treatment costs, which include capital and operating costs for the treatment plant, fees paid to Kualiti Alam for disposal of sludge from the treatment plant, and a 15% profit margin. It projects that the average monthly payment will be approximately US$530 per factory when the plant is operating at full capacity. As with Kualiti Alam's user fees, these payments should create an incentive for the factories to reduce the amount of pollution they generate.

All 32 lots in the park sold on the day they went on sale in 1998. As of late 1998, three companies had already moved in and begun operations. One electroplating company that was interviewed as it was preparing to relocate to Bukit Kemuning stated that the prospect of paying user fees for wastewater treatment had already prompted it to investigate recycling and other process changes as a way to reduce the amount of wastewater it generated and the amount of pollution in its wastewater. BI-PMB claims that its treatment plant has had a compliance rate with the Sewage and Industrial Effluents Regulations above 90% so far.[13] Encouraged by this experience, BI-PMB prepared plans for two more industrial parks with common treatment plants in Selangor: another one for metal finishers, and one for textiles and printing. The economic slump caused by the East Asian financial crisis forced it to put these plans on hold.

Factors Influencing the Performance of Incentive-Based Programs in Malaysia

The demand by electroplaters for factory lots at Bukit Kemuning stands in sharp contrast to the lack of demand by SMEs for the government's fiscal incentives and for Kualiti Alam's toxic and hazardous waste-management services. Although several factors have influenced the performance of the three programs, differences in the enforcement of environmental regulations provide a common explanation.

Fiscal Incentives

Industry and government representatives offer several explanations for the lack of demand for the available fiscal incentives. Some apply to both large companies and SMEs. One is that companies believe the government approves few applications for the incentives. Even in the seemingly straightforward case of the import duty exemption for pollution-control equipment, companies claim that the burden of proof is on companies to demonstrate that the equipment is *not* available locally, not on MIDA to demonstrate that it is. Another is that the financial benefits of the incentives are small. For example, most import duties are already so low (0–5%) that the environmental exemptions are superfluous. Moreover, much pollution-control equipment is made to order locally from general-purpose components, such as pumps, valves, meters, and filters, not imported as a complete unit. Most such components are already tariff-free, so the import duty exemption has no effect on their prices.

Several other explanations are specific to SMEs. One is a lack of information about either the fiscal incentives themselves or the pollution-control technology whose cost the incentives are intended to reduce. A survey conducted by the Malaysian central bank in the mid-1990s found that many SMEs were unaware even of fiscal incentives for productive (i.e., nonenvironmental) investments (Jabatan Ekonomi, Bank Negara Malaysia 1996). Similarly, Malaysian environmental engineers interviewed during the ADB project claimed that most SMEs are generally unaware of pollution-prevention and pollution-control technologies.

A second explanation specific to SMEs is that applying for the incentives can involve substantial nonpecuniary costs. Industry associations report that the paperwork required to apply for incentives is too time-consuming and too complex for SMEs. Some officers at MIDA are sympathetic to the view that the duty exemptions for environmental equipment involve excessive paperwork.

A third explanation is weak enforcement of environmental regulations. This appears to be the most fundamental explanation. If the risk of being caught out of compliance with environmental regulations is essentially zero, then even a fiscal incentive that reduces the after-tax cost of pollution-control equipment by nearly 100% would not prompt a company to buy the equipment. Nor would a company have a motive to search for information about incentives and environmental technologies or to seek help (e.g., from SMIDEC) in applying for the incentives. The vanishingly small number of respondents in the SME census who reported having had "any dealings" with DOE—just 0.1%—suggests that SMEs did indeed face a tiny risk of being caught out of compliance. And as noted earlier, the census included mainly SMEs in the formal sector. The risk of being caught out of compliance with environmental regulations was surely even lower for SMEs in the informal sector.

Certain statutory provisions reduce the pressure of environmental regulations on SMEs. The exemption for small volumes of wastewater in the Sewage and Industrial Effluents Regulations is one. Another pertains to the 1975 Industrial Co-ordination Act. This law requires all manufacturing companies with shareholders' funds above US$660,000[14] to obtain a manufacturing license to operate. In the mid-1990s, MIDA revised the license application to require detailed descriptions of the types and quantities of pollutants generated, pollution discharge points, and proposed pollution-control equipment. A DOE officer stationed full-time in MIDA reviews these parts of the license application. This revision has reportedly made an important contribution to improved awareness about and management of industrial pollution by licensed manufacturing companies. However, because SMEs typically have shareholders' funds below $660,000, it has had no impact on them. Indeed, until January 1998, the government defined SMEs as companies with shareholders' funds below US$660,000.

Problems with the enforcement of tax laws have also undermined SMEs' demand for fiscal incentives. Unregistered SMEs surely do not want to reveal themselves to the authorities by applying for fiscal incentives. By evading taxes, they are already receiving the maximum tax break. According to the Tax Analysis Division of the Ministry of Finance, even many registered SMEs do not file income tax returns, due to a lack of coordination between the Registrar of Companies and the Inland Revenue Bureau.[15]

User Fees

Unlike the Sewage and Industrial Effluents Regulations, the Scheduled Wastes Regulations contain no exemptions for establishments that generate small amounts of toxic and hazardous waste. All companies that generate such waste are obliged either to use Kualiti Alam's services or to treat the waste themselves in ways that comply with the regulations. Even in the latter case companies that generate wastewater would likely need to contract with Kualiti Alam to dispose of the sludge from their treatment plants.

Yet, as noted in the section titled User Fees for Toxic and Hazardous Waster Management: Kualiti Alam, a large number of SMEs are evidently flouting the Scheduled Wastes Regulations by not using Kualiti Alam's services. As in the case of fiscal incentives, the low risk of being caught out of compliance provides a straightforward explanation for this behavior. There is no loophole, but the regulations are not being effectively enforced against SMEs.

But then why did 32 electroplaters express such keen interest in relocating to Bukit Kemuning Electroplating Park? BI-PMB and SMEs give two reasons. One is the opportunity to operate in modern factory lots.[16] This enables SMEs to upgrade their technology and the quality of their plating operations. One SME that has purchased a factory lot at Bukit Kemuning stated that it will be able to reduce its work force by two-thirds and its use of plating solution by a significant amount. The same SME expects to be able to upgrade from double to triple plating, which will enable it to gain new customers (e.g., multinational companies) and fetch a higher price for its products.

The second explanation is regulatory pressure. Although DOE's monitoring of SMEs has been weak overall, it strengthened its enforcement effort against electroplaters in the late 1990s, especially in the capital city of Kuala Lumpur and the surrounding state of Selangor. One electroplating shop visited during the ADB project had been hit with two fines in quick succession; the second fine was four times the size of the first. Several industry representatives, including one with a company relocating to Bukit Kemuning, cited such sanctions as the overwhelming reason that electroplaters are considering relocating to industrial parks with common wastewater treatment plants.[17] This targeted enforcement effort is a key difference compared to the case of the low demand by SMEs for Kualiti Alam's services: SMEs in other industrial sectors have not been subject to as much scrutiny, and so Kualiti Alam is receiving little waste from SMEs in general.

Economies of scale in wastewater treatment make relocation to Bukit Kemuning a more attractive option for electroplaters than building and operating their own individual treatment plants. BI-PMB estimates that an individual electroplating shop that decided to build its own treatment facility would incur capital costs of about US$26,300. This estimate is comparable to ones cited by metal-finishing companies. The aggregate cost for 32 factories would thus be $840,000. This is about 60% more than the cost of the treatment equipment at Bukit Kemuning. Studies in other countries have also found that common treatment plants reduce the aggregate costs of wastewater treatment (Chiu and Tsang 1990).

Conclusions

The absence of a credible threat of punishment has undermined the impact of incentive-based programs for reducing water pollution from SMEs in Malaysia. Short payback periods for pollution prevention investments in the Malaysian metal-finishing and textiles sectors apparently depend on cost savings related to wastewater treatment chemicals, but the low risk of being caught out of compliance with the Sewage and Industrial Effluent Regulations and the Scheduled Wastes Regulations induces SMEs to save even more money by not installing treatment equipment at all. For the same reason, the user fees that Kualiti Alam charges for toxic and hazardous waste management are not providing much incentive for SMEs to invest in pollution prevention either. Instead, SMEs have avoided these fees by not registering with Kualiti Alam, despite their legal obligation to do so under the Scheduled Wastes Regulations.

The low risk of being hit by the enforcement stick has also led to low demand for the numerous fiscal-incentive "carrots" that the government offers related to virtually every tax that SMEs pay or, more to the point, are supposed to pay. Despite the evident lack of effectiveness of fiscal incentives for environmental management, the government continues to favor fiscal incentives as an instrument for addressing industrial pollution problems. For example, the government's *National Economic Recovery Plan*, which was prepared in response to the East Asian financial crisis, recommended that the "industrial sector should be given incentives for wastewater treatment and recycling to reduce pollution and water consumption" and that "financial [sic; fiscal] incentives should be provided to facilitate the transfer of 'clean' technology and the importation of pollution control equipment" (National Economic Action Council 1998, 141). Without stronger enforcement, it is hard to see how additional fiscal incentives will have any effect.

Bukit Kemuning Electroplating Park, to which nearly three dozen existing electroplaters were willing to relocate voluntarily despite needing to pay user fees for wastewater treatment, is the exception that proves the rule. Although DOE's monitoring and enforcement programs have fallen short of the mark for SMEs in general, they were recently boosted in the specific case of electroplating. Electroplaters' dash for the factory lots at Bukit Kemuning is a direct response to the teeth that DOE has included in this targeted pollution-control effort. This finding is in line with evidence from the brickmaking industry in Mexico, which indicates that managing pollution from small and medium enterprises by relocating the enterprises to industrial parks "is only feasible when regulatory authorities enjoy considerable bargaining power" (Blackman 2000, 18).

Other researchers have recently emphasized the importance of enforcement in incentive-based environmental policy programs (Blackman and Harrington 1999; Bell and Russell 2002). This lesson has a precedent in Malaysian environmental history. Malaysia was one of the first countries in the world to implement economic incentives for industrial pollution control when, in 1978, it introduced charges on effluent from palm oil and rubber mills (Vincent et al. 2000). This effluent charge system is still functioning today. The aggregate load of BOD pollution discharged by crude palm-oil mills declined dramatically within a few years after the charges were introduced. Some environmental economists have concluded from this coincidence that the charges were responsible for the decline. An analysis by Vincent et al. (2000, 188) suggests otherwise:

> The government's commitment [to solving the palm-oil effluent problem] was illustrated most strikingly by its well-publicized actions to suspend the operating licenses of mills that violated the regulations. Such actions, coupled with … the imposition of mandatory standards after the first year [of the Crude Palm Oil Regulations], strongly suggest that the risk to a mill of having its operating license suspended, not the financial incentive created by the effluent charges, was primarily responsible for the reduction in BOD discharge. This was probably true even in the first year, as the mandatory standards were pre-announced, and mills knew they had just a one-year grace period.

The enforcement challenge was much easier in this case than in the case of water pollution from SMEs, given that the number of crude palm-oil mills was smaller and the locations of all mills were known.

The Malaysian government recognizes the need to strengthen environmental enforcement. The *National Economic Recovery Plan* recommended that "enforcement sections and activities of environmental agencies should be given priority" and that "DOE [must be given] greater enforcement powers, and more control over the discharge of waste into water systems," and it included several specific measures to strengthen DOE (National Economic Action Council, 1998, 138–41). This was not cheap talk: the government included an additional $1.3 million in DOE's operating budget in 1998. DOE allocated nearly all this amount to its Control Division, which increased the division's budget by 28% between 1997 and 1998. The increase in DOE's operating budget contributed to the reversal of the longstanding erosion of DOE's budget relative to the size of the manufacturing sector. Figure 5-3 shows the ratio of DOE's operating expenditure (not just

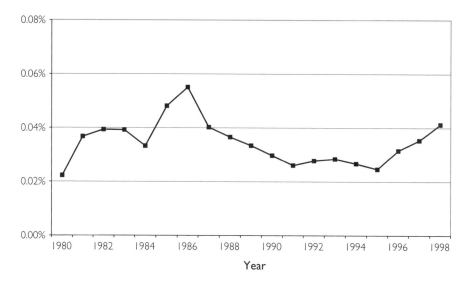

Figure 5-3. *DOE Operating Expenditure Relative to Manufacturing GDP*

the budget of the Control Division) to manufacturing GDP (all companies, not just SMEs) during 1980–98. The ratio rose until the mid-1980s and then declined until 1996. The increase in DOE's budget suggests an impressive commitment to environmental protection during a time of economic hardship—the Malaysian economy was battered during 1997–98—which stands in contrast to the budget cuts that environmental agencies suffered in other East Asian countries, in particular Indonesia (Vincent et al. 2002).

The message of this chapter is not that incentive-based approaches have no role to play in managing pollution from small and medium enterprises, but rather that the design of incentive systems must take into account the limitations of a country's regulatory system. As Panayotou (1998, 107) observes, "Large numbers of scattered, small-scale economic units imply high monitoring and enforcement costs. A country with limited monitoring and enforcement capability will opt for indirect instruments such as product taxes over effluent charges …." Eskeland and Devarajan (1996) have succinctly described this indirect approach as "taxing bads [pollutants] by taxing goods [e.g., production inputs]." The Malaysian government signaled support for this approach in the *Seventh Malaysia Plan 1996–2000* (Economic Planning Unit 1996) by stating that "This legal and regulatory framework [i.e., the Environmental Quality Act and associated regulations] will be complemented by the use of innovative economic and tax instruments such as presumptive charges which collect payment based on presumed annual total pollution discharge …." (Economic Planning Unit 1996, 606). Existing taxes can sometimes be recast as presumptive pollution charges simply by adjusting their rates. For example, the Malaysian government could in principle levy higher import and excise duties on dyestuffs containing greater amounts of toxic and hazardous substances, to encourage dyeing and finishing houses to use less damaging dyes.[18]

Presumptive charges might even provide the basis for a prepaid disposal fee system that would reduce the perceived cost of Kualiti Alam's waste-management services to SMEs. Continuing with the example of dyestuffs, the government could set the presumptive charge for a given dye equal to the cost of treating and disposing of the estimated residual portion of the dye that winds up in the sludge generated by dyeing and finishing operations. Kualiti Alam would not charge dyeing and finishing houses directly for collecting and treating the sludge; instead, it would invoice the government. Dyeing and finishing houses would already have paid for these services implicitly, when they purchased the dye, and these prepayments would generate the revenue needed by the government to pay the invoices from Kualiti Alam. The appearance of free waste-management services should make dyeing and finishing houses more willing to use Kualiti Alam's services.[19] A similar presumptive charge cum prepaid disposal system could be developed for plating chemicals used by SMEs in the metal-finishing sector.

Notes

1. Kneese and Bower (1968) provide perhaps the earliest discussion of fiscal incentives for pollution reduction. For a more recent textbook exposition, see Kolstad (2000, 124–28).

2. This formulation is similar to the "expected marginal penalty" function depicted in Figure 1 in Dasgupta et al. (2000), with a difference being that the horizontal axis in that figure is pollution, not pollution reduction as in Figure 5-1 in this chapter.

3. This result contradicts Blackman's (2000, 5) claim that "communal treatment creates no incentives for pollution prevention," although he may be referring to government-operated common treatment plants that do not charge user fees.

4. This is the approximate dollar-equivalent of the actual amount, 25 million Malaysian ringgit. Since late 1998, the ringgit has been fixed at RM3.8 per U.S. dollar. Unless otherwise noted, all monetary values cited in this chapter that were originally in ringgit have been converted to U.S. dollars using this exchange rate.

5. *Fiscal incentives* refer to tax breaks, whereas *financial incentives* refer to subsidized loan programs.

6. The actual amount stated in the definition is 10 million ringgit.

7. "Scheduled waste" is the Malaysian term for toxic and hazardous waste.

8. See Porter and van der Linde (1995), Palmer et al. (1995), and Reinhardt (2000, Chapter 4).

9. For example, Asia-Pacific Economic Cooperation (APEC) issued a series of eight industry-specific manuals in a 1998 series titled *Eco-Efficiency in Small and Medium Enterprises*. These reports are available online at www.apec.org/apec/publications/all_publications/small___medium_enterprises.html.

10. Consumables are materials used up during production, e.g., catalysts in the chemical industry.

11. And in 2002, Kualiti Alam became the first Malaysian company to receive ISO 9002 and ISO 14001 certifications simultaneously.

12. See O'Connor (1994, 168–71) for examples of industrial parks with common wastewater treatment plants in Indonesia and Thailand.

13. Of course, a high compliance rate for the treatment plant does not constitute evidence that none of the electroplaters are circumventing the plant and dumping their waste illegally, which is one way they might respond to high user fees (O'Connor 1994). BI-PMB is confident that it can detect such behavior, given the relatively small size of the park and the metering data

it regularly collects on individual electroplaters' wastewater generation. More important is the fact that it operates the treatment plant on a for-profit basis, which gives it a strong incentive to ensure that illegal dumping does not occur.

14. The actual amount given in the act is 2.5 million Malaysian ringgit.

15. This parallels a finding from Blackman's (2000, 17) study of brickmakers in Mexico, that "simply registering informal polluters is not sufficient to facilitate enforcement of command and control regulations".

16. The Malaysian government's Industrial Adjustment Fund offers SMEs in selected sectors, including machinery and engineering (which includes electroplating), soft loans that can be used to finance many of the costs of relocating to industrial estates. Some of the companies that have relocated to Bukit Kemuning have reportedly applied to this fund.

17. The owner of one electroplating shop also cited informal regulatory pressures: being shunned by neighbors who believed that her plant was creating health hazards for their families. The effect of informal regulatory pressures on polluting behavior has been studied in several developing countries but not, to our knowledge, in Malaysia. See World Bank (2000) for an overview of informal regulation of industrial pollution in developing countries.

18. The Tax Analysis Division of the Ministry of Finance pointed out that international trade laws might place limits on the level of import duties implemented for environmental reasons. Violations of international laws are less likely, however, if excise duties on the same goods manufactured locally are set at the same level.

19. On the other hand, the presumptive charge could make them more likely to use black market dyes (Biller and Quintero 1995), especially if the charge accounted for a large share of dye price. Data necessary to estimate the presumptive charge for dyes commonly used in Malaysia were unfortunately not available.

References

Bell, Ruth Greenspan, and Clifford Russell. 2002. Environmental Policy for Developing Countries. *Issues in Science and Technology* (Spring): 63–70.

Biller, Dan, and J.D. Quintero. 1995. Policy Options To Address Informal Sector Contamination in Latin America: The Case of Leather Tanneries in Bogota, Colombia. LATEN dissemination note 14. Washington, DC: World Bank.

Blackman, Allen. 2000. Informal Sector Pollution Control: What Policy Options Do We Have? Discussion Paper 00–02–REV. Washington, DC: Resources for the Future.

Blackman, Allen, and Winston Harrington. 1999. The Use of Economic Incentives in Developing Countries: Lessons from International Experience with Industrial Air Pollution. Discussion Paper 99–39. Washington, DC: Resources for the Future.

Chiu, H., and K. Tsang. 1990. Reduction of Treatment Costs by Using Communal Treatment Facilities. *Waste Management & Research* 8: 165–67.

Dasgupta, Susmita, Hemamala Hettige, and David Wheeler. 2000. What Improves Environmental Compliance? Evidence from Mexican Industry. *Journal of Environmental Economics and Management* 39(1): 39–66.

Department of Environment. 1998. *Malaysia Environmental Quality Report 1997*. Kuala Lumpur.

Economic Planning Unit. 1996. Seventh Malaysia Plan 1996–2000. Kuala Lumpur: Prime Minister's Department.

Eskeland, Gunnar, and Shanta Devarajan. 1996. *Taxing Bads by Taxing Goods: Pollution Control with Presumptive Charges*. Washington, DC: World Bank.

Federation of Malaysian Manufacturers. 1998. *FMM Business Guide. SMIs: Small and Medium-Size Industries,* 4th ed. Kuala Lumpur.

International Business & Technical Consultants, Inc. 1999. A Proposed Strategic Framework for Malaysian Small and Medium Scale Industrial Pollution Control Management. Report prepared for the Asian Development Bank, under ADB Technical Assistance Project No. 2856-MAL. Manila: Asian Development Bank.

Jabatan Ekonomi, Bank Negara Malaysia. 1996. Laporan Kaji Selidik Syarikat-Syarikat Perkilangan, 1995: Small and Medium-Scale Enterprises (SME). Typescript. Kuala Lumpur.

Kneese, Allen V., and Blair T. Bower. 1968. *Managing Water Quality: Economics, Technology, Institutions*. Baltimore: Johns Hopkins Press.

Kolstad, Charles. 2000. *Environmental Economics*. New York: Oxford University Press.

Ministry of Finance. 1999. *Economic Report 1998/99*. Kuala Lumpur.

Ministry of International Trade and Industry. 1996. *The Second Industrial Master Plan 1996–2005*. Kuala Lumpur.

National Economic Action Council. 1998. *National Economic Recovery Plan*. Kuala Lumpur.

O'Connor, David. 1994. *Managing the Environment with Rapid Industrialization: Lessons from the East Asian Experience*. Paris: Organisation for Economic Co-operation and Development.

Palmer, Karen, Wallace Oates, and Paul Portney. 1995. Tightening Environmental Standards: The Benefit–Cost or the No-Cost Paradigm? *Journal of Economic Perspectives* 9(4): 119–32.

Panayotou, Theodore. 1998. *Instruments of Change: Motivating and Financing Sustainable Development*. London: Earthscan Publications Ltd.

PNB Corporate Development. 1996. *Small and Medium-Scale Industries Study Final Report: Technical Report Volume II (Census Computer Tabulations)*. Kuala Lumpur.

Porter, Michael, and Claas van der Linde. 1995. Toward a New Conception of the Environment-Competitiveness Relationship. *Journal of Economic Perspectives* 9(4): 97–118.

Reinhardt, Forest. 2000. *Down to Earth*. Cambridge, MA: Harvard Business School Press.

Stavins, Robert N. 2003. Experience with Market-Based Environmental Policy Instruments. In *Handbook of Environmental Economics, Volume 1*, edited by Karl-Göran Mäler and Jeffrey R. Vincent. Amsterdam: North-Holland.

Sterner, Thomas. 2003. *Policy Instruments for Environmental and Natural Resource Management*. Washington, DC: Resources for the Future.

Vincent, Jeffrey R., and Rozali Mohamed Ali, with Khalid Abdul Rahim. 2000. Water Pollution Abatement in Malaysia. In *Asia's Clean Revolution: Industry, Growth and the Environment*, edited by David P. Angel and Michael T. Rock. Sheffield, U.K.: Greenleaf Publishing.

Vincent, Jeffrey R., Jean Aden, Giovanna Dore, Magda Adriani, Vivianti Rambe, and Thomas Walton. 2002. Public Environmental Expenditures in Indonesia. *Bulletin of Indonesian Economic Studies* 38(1): 61–74.

World Bank. 2000. *Greening Industry: New Roles for Communities, Markets, and Governments*. Oxford, U.K.: Oxford University Press.

CHAPTER 6

Improving Environmental Performance of Small Firms through Joint Action

Indian Tannery Clusters

Loraine Kennedy

*I*N THE MID-1990s, following a series of orders from the Supreme Court of India, hundreds of mainly small-scale tanneries in the Palar Valley of Tamil Nadu were threatened with closure if they failed to comply quickly with regulations requiring them to treat their effluents. In this crisis situation, the vast majority of tanneries cooperated with each other to build and operate common effluent treatment plants (CETPs), an option encouraged by government subsidies for these plants. The result has been a dramatic reduction in tannery water pollution. This experience offers valuable insights into the role that joint action—cooperation among industrial enterprises—can play in greening clusters of small-scale enterprises (SSEs). In particular, it holds lessons regarding the factors that facilitate and deter such cooperation. It also demonstrates how the threat of sanctions can be combined with inducements and subsidies to encourage improved environmental performance.

This case study of the Palar Valley experience is based largely on field work conducted in 1997–98, including more than 75 interviews with stakeholders at different levels. Subsequent field work in the region has allowed partial updating. The chapter is organized as follows. The next section offers a brief introduction to the literature that informs the analysis. The section titled Small-Scale Leather production in the Palar Valley provides background information about the organization and internal structure of the small-scale leather tanning industry in the Palar Valley. It pays special attention to the social organization of local actors involved in this activity. The section titled Cooperative Capital: Previous Experience with Joint Action briefly discusses an example of past joint action, which allowed the clusters to generate cooperative capital. The section titled The Pollution Crisis Sparked by Judicial Activism introduces the crisis sparked by the Supreme Court rulings and examines past efforts by state authorities to promote pollution control. The section titled The Response of the Palar Valley Clusters: Common Effluent Treatment Plants discusses the response of the Palar Valley leather producers and analyzes determinants of success and failure among and within the clusters. The section titled Problems with Collective Treatment outlines some of the main problems encountered in setting up CETPs and monitoring their performance. The paper concludes with a brief summary of the factors that facilitated the largely successful response, as well as some deterrents, which threaten sustainability.

The Industrial Cluster Framework

Recent literature on small-firm clusters provides a useful framework for this study (Schmitz 1995, 1997, 2000). This literature emphasizes the role that joint action plays in bolstering the competitiveness of small-scale enterprise (SSE) clusters. In the ideal, exemplified by Italian case studies, clusters of small enterprises are vertically integrated in the manner of one large firm.[1] Individual firms specialize in one or several stages of production to capture economies of scale. This type of industrial organization generates positive externalities through greater flexibility, lower fixed capital requirements, lower transaction costs, and heightened learning effects. Beyond specialization in production, firms may also act collectively through a consortium or a producers' association. The latter can provide "real services" by circulating trade-related information and by representing the interests of the local producers in their relations with labor unions and regulators. However, it should be remembered that cooperation among the enterprises of a given cluster coexists with competition, a factor that may in some cases inhibit joint action.

Studies of industrial clusters have shown that firms are more likely to cooperate with each other when economic agents are bound by social ties based on community, kinship, shared local identity, and ethnicity (Nadvi 1999). Such ties form the basis for trust, which reduces transaction costs by limiting business risks (Humphrey and Schmitz 1998). Indeed, the likelihood of fraud and breach of contract is much smaller when economic agents belong to the same locality, especially to the same community. Social control, with its implicit threats of exclusion and loss of reputation, operates to check opportunistic behavior.

Small-Scale Leather Production in the Palar Valley

The Palar Valley in the state of Tamil Nadu is a major leather-tanning center in India, contributing about half of the country's total output of finished leather.[2] Approximately 600 small, mainly family-owned enterprises make up this local industry, the roots of which go back more than a century. Most of the tanneries are clustered in and around five small towns. Basic information about the tannery clusters is presented in Table 6-1.

Small-scale firms dominate the Indian leather industry, constituting approximately 90% of the total number of tanneries (CLRI 1998). An important reason is that tanning and footwear production until recently were reserved by the Indian government for the small-scale sector.[3]

As indicated above, most tanneries in the Valley are located in a cluster. In some cases, they are situated literally side by side, with contiguous compound walls.

Table 6-1. *Population and Size of Firms in the Palar Valley Tannery Clusters*

Town	Population (2001)	Number of tanneries 1998	Percentage very small ≤1000 kg/day	Percentage small 1001–1500 kg/day	Percentage medium 1501–3000 kg/day	Percentage large >3000 kg/day
Ambur	99,855	67	43	16	27	13
Melvisharam	36,675	37	24	38	30	8
Pernambattu	41,323	18	33	28	39	0
Ranipet	47,236	202	80	9	7	3
Vaniyambadi	103,841	136	89	8	2	1

Source: Population data from Government of India (2001). Data on size and number of tanneries was collected by the author from common effluent treatment plant managers in 1998–99.

Note: The number of tanneries includes both existing and planned units. Approximately 50 tanneries situated outside the main clusters have not been included for lack of data. For Pernambattu, only the Bakkalapalli subcluster is included.

This spatial configuration is a defining feature of the local leather industry and has arguably played a major role in its development. Indeed, drawing on insights from the industrial cluster literature, there is ample evidence that these clusters have enjoyed gains from both agglomeration effects and joint action.

Industrial Organization of the Local Leather Industry

In the Palar Valley, the organization of the leather industry has undergone substantial changes in the past 25 years. Traditionally, the industry was made up of low-technology firms that specialized in semifinished, vegetable-tanned leather. Local firms began finishing leather in the early 1970s. Subsequently, a number of firms moved further up the value-added chain into the manufacture of leather products such as footwear, shoe uppers, and gloves. However, the tannery clusters have a pyramid structure with numerous small tanneries forming the base. As Table 6-1 indicates, more than 80% of the tanneries in the Valley fall in the small and very small categories. Many of these are so-called primary tanneries, processing raw hides and skins into semifinished leather, an intermediate good.[4] A step up from the small tanneries are a smaller number of larger firms, most of which are composite factories, that is, factories equipped to process leather from raw to finished stage. At the summit of the pyramid, there are a few large firms, many of which have integrated forward and manufacture leather goods, either locally or in nearby areas (Chennai and Bangalore). They produce primarily for export, frequently in partnership with foreign firms.

According to most accounts, interfirm cooperation, in the form of subcontracting and job work, has been on the rise. Medium and large tanneries increasingly subcontract the primary processing phase to smaller tanneries so that they can focus on finishing and manufacturing.[5] There are also numerous small firms, notably on the industrial estate in Ranipet, specializing in finishing leather, that is, they process semifinished leather into finished leather. They often produce on a contract basis for leather goods manufacturers, charging by the piece, but in some cases they sell their output on the open market or use it to feed their own garment or footwear factories. Finishing leather is more complex than primary tanning and usually requires an array of machines. Unlike primary tanning, it can be broken down into distinct processes, which need not be performed under one roof. This has allowed a certain degree of process specialization, and in recent years the large clusters especially have witnessed the creation of tiny units doing "machine job work." Even composite tanneries rent out their finishing machines when they are not in use, rather than leave them idle.

Whereas these practices point to a certain flexibility in production within the leather sector as a whole, interfirm production relations among primary tanneries do not appear to be particularly intense. The reason is that the production of semifinished leather cannot be easily broken into distinct processes, and almost all firms use the same technology. There is little product differentiation at this stage and therefore strong price competition.

Ethnic and Religious Factors Contributing to Social Cohesiveness

Tanning in the Palar Valley and elsewhere in India is largely associated with the Muslim community, a historical fact linked to Hindu religious beliefs and specifically to the caste system, which establishes a social hierarchy on the basis of ritual purity. Handling carcasses and making leather are occupations traditionally relegated to the lowest castes (former untouchables). This explains why Hindus were, and are still to a certain extent, reluctant to invest in the leather industry. Although the Muslim minority represents less than 6% of the total population of Tamil Nadu, Palar Valley's tannery towns have a sizable proportion of Muslims, a majority in several cases. They tend to form tight-knit communities infused by extensive kinship relations. Tannery owners identify strongly with Islamic religion and culture and often participate actively in community-based social organizations, such as charities and educational trusts. Secular associations, such as Lions and Rotary Clubs, are also prevalent. Through these organizations, local business people, whatever their religious affiliation, have frequent interaction. Moreover, tanners come together in professional bodies, such as tanners' associations, which have existed for decades in all the study towns. Their functions include circulating sector-specific information, providing diverse services, and representing tanners in regional bodies and government.

Another factor that contributes to social cohesion among tanners is a shared local identity. Generally speaking, tanners are attached to their towns and are quick to discourse on the differences that distinguish them from the inhabitants of neighboring towns. Many prefer, for example, to contract marriage alliances within their town whenever practical.

Interviews with local producers confirmed that these diverse social ties facilitate economic cooperation. Sociocultural and kinship ties and shared local identities clearly contribute to regulating individual behavior because belonging to a small and tight-knit community involves adhering to rules. Sanctions and the threat of ostracism dissuade transgression, although patterns of social control vary from one place to another. Traditional Muslim authority structures such as *jamaths*, whose function is to manage the mosques but also to dispense justice, remain prominent in all of these towns, again to varying degrees. One small town with a large Muslim population boasts of not having a police station and of solving all disputes internally, through the *jamath*. Although this is an exceptional case, it suggests the degree of social control that exists in these localities, at least within the Muslim community. This collective leverage extends to the economic sphere and is exercised, as we shall see, in the management of treatment plants, which requires compliance to difficult rules.

It is important to underscore that inasmuch as the local sociocultural milieu operates as a regulatory mechanism, ensuring compliance to rules and norms, it does so primarily within a given religious community. In the tanneries of the Palar Valley, the majority of tanner owners are Muslim, whereas the majority of workers are Hindu. Intrafirm relations are often antagonistic. This is often the case in India, where employers' attitudes and working conditions are largely unfavorable for labor and where unionism is limited to the formal sector of the economy (large firms, government service)[6], but labor–managment tensions are exacerbated here by that fact that some sections of the Hindu population resent the success of Muslims in the leather industry. It is significant that the local voluntary association that petitioned the Supreme Court about tannery pollution indulges in anti-Muslim rhetoric. So Muslims and Hindus live peacefully in the Valley, but they cannot be said to share a political subculture, an important element of local regulation in Italian cases that helped to establish a "social compromise" (Trigilia 1986).[7]

Cooperative Capital: Previous Experience with Joint Action

This section briefly examines an example of joint action on the part of tanners that preceded the pollution crisis. In the early 1970s, the Indian government decided to phase out the export of raw and semifinished hides and skins to enhance domestic capacity to produce finished leather and leather products and to thereby increase value added in the leather sector. This policy decision was extremely destabilizing for the local industry, which at the time specialized in semifinished leather. Finishing leather required tanners to acquire entirely new equipment and skills and to locate new markets.

Nevertheless, the government's policy of encouraging finished leather and leather products dramatically changed the industrial structure of Palar Valley clusters.[8] Several lead firms played a decisive role in opening the way for others, by moving first into finishing leather and then into manufacturing leather products (Ramasami 1982). Today a sizable number of firms in the Valley produce finished leather for both the domestic and international product markets, in the medium to high value-added range. In national contests, firms from the Palar Valley are generally among the winners in almost all categories (e.g., overall exports, finished leather, footwear, uppers, garments).[9]

The 1970s were a turning point for the industry in terms of joint action. As tanneries diversified their production and clusters became increasingly differentiated, there was a marked increase in interfirm transactions, within and among clusters alike. Also, the 1970s saw the creation of cooperative societies in several clusters to provide finishing services, mainly small tanners. Finally, local tanners' associations began to play a more significant role; their main functions were to network with other regional and national bodies and to relay information, for example, regarding government support measures.

The Pollution Crisis Sparked by Judicial Activism

In the mid-1990s, the Indian Supreme Court ordered the tanneries of the Palar Valley to comply with environmental regulations or face closure. Laws for regulating water pollution had existed since the mid-1970s, including standards governing the release of tannery effluents. The Environment [Protection] Act of 1986 was intended to enforce existing laws and coordinate various regulatory agencies. However, it is clear from this study case that state regulators did not effectively enforce environmental legislation, perhaps especially in the case of SSEs. In general, regulators had been more demanding with large firms, and consequently most of these were equipped with in-house effluent treatment plants (ETPs) before the crisis, even if their performance was below today's standard. This conforms to a general trend in India, whereby medium and large firms are more stringently regulated than small ones, most notably with respect to labor management. As mentioned above, small firms have received special treatment from the government on a number of fronts.

Officials at the Tamil Nadu Pollution Control Board (PCB), established in 1982, contend that before the Supreme Court rulings, high-level political commitment to pollution control was lacking, and therefore the PCB did not have the means to compel industry to comply.[10] In effect, successive deadlines for setting up effluent treatment plants had been allowed to expire.[11] Local testimonies corroborate the lack of political will in enforcement and underscore the collusive behavior between tannery owners and regulatory authorities, including local inspectors. Clearly, client–patron relationships between industry and politicians and widespread corruption, consistent with patterns found elsewhere, facilitated the circumvention of pollution-control regulations.

The 1996 Supreme Court ruling on tannery pollution was the outcome of a public interest petition, provided for in Article 32 of the Constitution of India, submitted in 1991 by a small civic association in Vellore.[12] The association contended that tannery pollution had caused considerable damage to the water resources of the Palar basin, depriving the population of an adequate supply of drinking water and affecting the fertility of agricultural land. Discussions with the plaintiffs suggest that there may have been ethnic motivations behind the petition.[13] Be that as it may, the problem of untreated tannery pollution was real and had been raised in a number of reports appearing over the years.[14]

Before its final ruling in 1996, the Supreme Court released a series of interim orders. These were based on information provided by the Tamil Nadu Pollution Control Board about the degree to which individual tanneries were complying with existing environmental regulations. These orders gave tanneries three months to complete construction of a treatment facility (individual or collective). Beyond that period, they would be liable to pollution fines on the basis of past production levels and also liable to closure. Under pressure, most clusters mobilized; meetings were called and collective decisions taken.

As successive grace periods reached their term, the Supreme Court started ordering the closure of tanneries that had failed to take any steps toward implementing pollution treatment, either individually or in association with other firms. By 1995, more than 200 tanneries in Vellore District, roughly one-third of the total, had been closed by order of the Supreme Court.

In its final ruling on August 28, 1996, the Supreme Court suspended its previous closure orders and granted the tanneries in the five affected districts a final grace period of three months to set up collective or individual treatment plants. If they failed to do so, they would be permanently closed or directed to relocate. In addition, the final judgment directed the central government to constitute a special authority to determine the "loss to ecology" and environmental degradation in the affected areas, identify the victims of pollution and assess the amount of compensation to be paid to them, and evaluate the amount to be collected from the polluters to cover the cost of reversing damage to the environment. It also imposed a pollution fine of 10,000 Indian rupees on all the tanneries in the districts of the state concerned by tannery pollution. This fine and the compensation amount were to be pooled to form an Environment Protection Fund, which would be used both to compensate the individuals and families identified by the special authority and to restore the environment.

The Supreme Court ruling essentially ordered the state government to enforce existing environmental legislation, mainly the Environment Act passed in 1986. This decision exemplifies the enhanced role that the Supreme Court has assumed over the past two decades. According to some analyses, growing judicial activism is a result of decisions made by the Supreme Court that have effectively enlarged its jurisdiction (Anant and Singh 2002). In particular, by expanding various fundamental rights and easing of procedural requirements, exemplified by the Public Interest Litigation, conditions were created for the courts to enter the policy sphere. On a broader societal level, other factors can also be cited, notably the decline of the Congress party, which previously dominated the political scene, and the advent of greater political pluralism. These developments have contributed in checking the disproportionate influence exercised by the ruling party over the country's institutions, including the judicial machinery, opening the way for increased judicial activism.

The Response of the Palar Valley Clusters: Common Effluent Treatment Plants

In the face of the new determination on the part of the state machinery to enforce compliance, the leather producers of the Valley, usually acting through their local tanners' association, overwhelmingly chose to build CETPs. Indeed, CETPs were often the only viable option for technical and financial reasons. Moreover, the spatial organization of the Palar Valley industry, i.e., small-firm clusters, lent itself quite naturally to CETPs.

Table 6-2 below gives an indicative picture of the response of the main clusters of the Palar Valley tanneries to regulations. It shows the number of tanneries in each cluster just before the Supreme Court rulings and the number of tanneries that were closed by court order in 1995–96. It provides an indication of the situation in 2003, including the number of tanneries linked to CETPs and those using an ETP for effluent treatment. These data are not readily available and were compiled on the basis of information collected from cluster associations.

Of the 200 tanneries closed by court order in Vellore District, including many tanneries outside the main clusters, most have never reopened because they have been unable to join a CETP. Those that have resumed operations have managed to do so by investing in individual treatment facilities. Significantly, of the eight CETPs that were planned or under construction in 1997, only one was actually completed by 2003. On a more positive note, the seven CETPs that were functioning in 1997 continued to function in 2003. This suggests that CETPs that gathered enough momentum to get off the ground in the immediate aftermath of the crisis have survived, whereas those that ran into problems early on did not manage to find sustainable solutions.

From the point of view of an individual tannery, CETPs have a number of advantages, which are magnified for the small firm. CETP membership is generally less costly than building an ETP, enables small tanneries to capture economies of

Table 6-2. *Tanneries and Treatment Status before and after the Supreme Court Rulings*

Tannery cluster	Tannery subcluster[a]	No. of tanneries before Supreme Court order	No. of tanneries closed following Supreme Court order 1996	No. of tanneries in operation 2003	Operational/connected to ETP 2003	Operational/connected to CETP 2003
Ambur	Maligaithope	17	17	18	11	7
	Thutipet	49	0	44	10	34
	Other	7	0	7	7	0
Melvisharam		25	25	26	4	22
Pernambattu[b]		38	28	18	8	10
Ranipet	SIDCO	86	0	87	1	86
	Ranitec	77	0	77	0	77
Vaniyambadi	Udayendram	10	0	10	0	10
	Vanitec	110	6	110	0	110
	Other	79	79	28	28	0
Total		498	155	425	69	356

Note: These figures are indicative, and some could not be reconfirmed in the field. They were compiled by J. Hannak.

[a]These figures do not include tanneries situated outside the main clusters, numbering approximately 50.

[b]These figures do not cover the entire V. Kota subcluster of Pernambattu, which had approximately 60 tanneries before the court ruling. The CETP planned for this sector has not been completed, and approximately 48 tanneries remain closed. The others have built ETPs.

scale in wastewater treatment, and does not require in-house technical expertise in waste treatment. Members of a CETP do not have the worry of maintaining an ETP and ensuring that regulatory parameters are respected. However, a CETP may not always be a possibility. Because it requires conveyance pipes for wastewater, it may not be practical in a situation where factories are separated from each other by distance or physical barriers, e.g., streams or roads. Despite its advantages, a CETP has a distinct disadvantage in that its sustainability depends on the cooperation of all who belong to it. A member of a CETP depends on the other members for its survival. If the CETP does not function adequately, all of the members face closure.

One important difference between this and the earlier crisis stemming from the ban on exports of semifinished leather was that all tanners were forced to act or perish. In the previous crisis, some entrepreneurs took the lead, some followed, and some did not. The tanners who did not follow could still pursue their livelihood, albeit in more restricting conditions. Now any tannery that did not take immediate steps was faced with indefinite closure.

Significantly, the PCB had floated the idea of CETPs for the tanning industry long before the judicial decision that sparked the crisis was announced. After the petition was filed with the Supreme Court, public officials came forward with a substantial financial assistance package for CETPs. Grants from the federal and state governments (in equal shares) were to cover half of the total cost, tanners were to contribute 10–20% of the cost in the form of share capital, and the remainder was to be borrowed by the CETP, often at subsidized rates of interest. The state's response was clearly targeted at assisting the industry through the crisis, but authorities were also driven by their concern about the social cost of closing factories. It is mainly socially disadvantaged groups who depend on tannery work for their livelihood, and their access to alternative employment opportunities is extremely limited because of the segmented labor market.

Characteristics of CETPs

Initially, it was assumed that each town would construct a single CETP for the tanneries located there. In reality, however, this was not feasible, either because some tanneries were too far from the planned facility or because they were separated from it by a highway, a river, or a railroad track, making the connection too complicated or costly. Consequently, the towns were divided into sectors of various sizes, ranging from 9 to 110 tanneries. In some cases, the various sectors in a given town have continued to belong to a single company and maintain a central management facility.

Most CETPs in the Valley adopted a similar institutional design: They are limited companies owned collectively by the shareholders. Before construction, to determine plant capacity, member tanners were required to declare their current and planned production levels. The tanners then contributed share capital accordingly. Once the CETP is in operation, members pay monthly operating charges that are usually based on production levels. They elect from among themselves a managing director and a board, on which also sits a government nominee. The managing director and the board members tend to be successful tanners and are often individuals who enjoy high social status.

Even though the day-to-day management is usually left to hired technical staff, the board is ultimately responsible for the proper functioning of the plant and answers to the regulatory authorities. Among its most difficult tasks is peer monitoring. In effect, there is high performance ambiguity because CETPs do not have reliable information about the actual quantity or quality of wastewater arriving from individual tanneries.[15] To prevent free riding, it is necessary to monitor member tanneries to ensure that they are producing effluents within their limits. In the seven CETPs that were surveyed for this study, each had a monitoring committee in charge of conducting periodic inspections. The choice of leadership is crucial: These individuals must possess both technical knowledge—to detect signs of overproduction, for instance—and moral authority. However, peer monitoring is an onerous task in small towns where tanners know each other personally, and managers expressed their desire to find technical solutions, such as individual flow meters, to preclude the need for peer monitoring. They corroborated the point made in the collective action literature, namely in small communities, punishment is costly to the punisher.

Most CETPs reported infractions among their members, including overproduction compared to declared capacity, late payment of maintenance fees, and improper disposal of waste. In some cases, CETP leaders have taken punitive action, ordering tanneries to cease production for a specified time period or imposing fines. However, it appears that verbal warnings usually suffice to rectify the situation. One managing director indicated that when he encounters noncooperative behavior, he starts by applying pressure on the individual through personal appeals. If that fails, he approaches the member's close relatives and requests them to intervene, which is usually effective. This underscores the importance of social control—the threat of losing one's reputation and being ostracized—as an efficient means of inciting cooperation in a close-knit community.

In this context, the manager of one large CETP spoke of the importance of maintaining a "family atmosphere" to ensure successful cooperation in the day-to-day running of the plant. Problems frequently arise, requiring funds for repairs and improvements, including compulsory modifications required by the regulatory agency. Frequent meetings are called to discuss these problems and convince the members of the necessity for action. Managers indicated that despite a certain degree of resistance, there was overall cooperation. Until now, the threat of disconnection or closure of the collective plant appears to have been a sufficient inducement to cooperate.

It is noteworthy that many larger units already equipped with ETPs at the time of the Supreme Court orders decided nonetheless to join a CETP. One reason was to avoid the risk involved with treating effluents. Not only is it difficult and expensive to monitor a treatment plant, but it is also perceived as risky in the event that parameters are not met.[16] A second reason is directly linked to the crisis context. Vellore District was declared a polluted area[17], and it was announced that authorizations for new tanneries or expansions to existing plants would not be granted. Hence, tanners faced the prospect of zero expansion, a serious constraint for any business and all the more disconcerting in the context of recent heavy investments in leather product manufacturing. However, in joining a CETP, tanners were given the opportunity to declare future production plans to ensure that the plant would have sufficient capacity to accommodate them. Thus, joining a CETP offered a way around the ban on new authorizations.[18] Finally, large firms had an incentive to join CETPs to ensure that smaller firms survived. Given that large firms often subcontract their orders to smaller firms, the disappearance of the latter would reduce the overall flexibility of production on which the cluster depends for its efficiency. The participation of large plants in CETPs has arguably played a decisive role: They can mobilize capital quickly when necessary, collecting later from less endowed members, and they have provided crucial leadership.[19]

Determinants of Success and Failure of Joint Action

Sociocultural factors clearly play an important role in initiating and sustaining co-operation, but given that all five of these clusters present similar sociological characteristics, they do not explain the failure of some clusters to form CETPs. What explains this variation? Geographic factors account for the poor performance of certain clusters—in some cases, there were physical obstacles preventing tanneries from connecting to a CETP. Also, peripheral subclusters often lacked critical mass, and many have had difficulty getting treatment operations off the ground. Absentee ownership of the tanneries, rivalry among firms, and an absence of leadership in some clusters hampered the formation of CETPs. Finally, some clusters lacked cooperative capital generated by previous experience with joint action. As noted above, the Palar Valley tanneries suffered an earlier exogenous crisis when the government banned the export of semifinished leather, their stock in trade. Most of the clusters adapted with government support and by following the example of lead firms.[20] Most—but not all—of the tannery clusters in the Valley met this first challenge and gained firsthand experience with joint action, experience that may have played a critical role in their capacity to meet the pollution crisis.

Pernambattu represents the most serious case of failure in meeting the challenge of pollution control. Two subclusters within the city were designated for CETPs. One of these CETPs (Bakkalapalli) has been built, but the other (V. Kota), designed to serve a group of 60 tanneries, was partially constructed and then abandoned due to financial and institutional problems. As a result, all the tanneries in this second sector were closed by order of the PCB. Today, approximately 50 of the original 60 tanneries in this sector remain closed, and the others have built ETPs. A combination of social and economic factors explains Pernambattu's overall poor performance.

Historically, Pernambattu was one of the major tanning centers in the region, renowned for its high-quality buffalo and cow leather. Today, however, it is the least dynamic tannery town in the Valley. It has not modernized its industry to the same extent as the other clusters, nor increased the value added of its production. The majority of tanners continue to produce a low-technology product used to make soles for sandals for the domestic market. One reason may be that Pernambattu is not situated on the main communication routes, a factor that may depress investment. A logical question is whether Pernambattu failed to respond effectively to the pollution crisis for the same reasons that it failed to modernize its industry.

A close look at socioeconomic conditions prevailing in Pernambattu reveals some unusual characteristics. The most remarkable is the large number of tanners in Pernambattu who do not own their factories but lease them, albeit often for periods spanning several generations. Evidently, many of the owners of Pernambattu's tanneries chose not to continue in the industry, moving to the cities to pursue education and other professions, while holding on to the tanneries for rental income. This ownership pattern has probably had a dampening effect on entrepreneurship and on the reinvestment of profits.

Absentee ownership has clearly had an effect on the ability of Pernambattu's tanners to raise their contribution for the treatment plant. They do not have collateral and are hence compelled to turn to the owners, who are often unable or unwilling to provide the funds. On a psychological level, more than elsewhere in the Valley, tanners expressed skepticism about the treatment plants and distrust about their necessity and their viability. There is an obvious lack of cooperation in the cluster, a situation that may be linked to the fact that it largely missed the modernization wave. Consequently, it also missed a firsthand experience with joint action, and this may help explain the leadership vacuum observed in this cluster. Although there are some relatively successful large tanneries, they have not taken the lead in meeting the pollution crisis collectively. A number of mainly large firms in the V. Kota subcluster, some of which were fed up with the delays, built their own ETPs and are no longer committed to realizing the CETP.

Local Changes as a Result of Joint Action

Joint action has changed the organizational environment of the local industry. The vast majority of local tanners now belong to a CETP, which they own collectively with other tanners. The CETPs created a forum for communication and exchange about problems and challenges facing the cluster or the industry at large. CETPs have supplanted the tanners' associations as the main professional organization at the local level. In fact, the legitimacy of a number of tanners' associations was diminished as a result of their failure to anticipate or attenuate the pollution crisis. Today, CETP directors have become the main interlocutors of decisionmakers in regional-level professional bodies and also in government and research institutions. Dynamic individuals, often at the head of prominent firms, characterize the new CETP leadership.

It seems likely that the new institutions and leaders will be more effective and proactive than their predecessors. In particular, the direct involvement of lead industrialists in the CETPs means that environmental issues are more likely to be integrated into line management in their respective firms, hence into the overall business strategy, a factor that could favor environment-friendly innovations.

Evidence gleaned from interviews, professional meetings, and trade magazines suggests that, aside from these concrete changes in organization and management, the pollution crisis has left the tanning community of the Palar Valley much more environmentally aware.[21] For example, trade magazines and association newsletters report that discussions are underway to develop an "eco-label" for leather produced in Tamil Nadu. This strategy, which aims to capitalize on the Valley's investments in treatment facilities, reflects awareness that such labeling could appeal to Western consumers and also a readiness to anticipate what may become an import requirement in certain countries or trading blocs. However, the local tanning community does not appear to be universally mobilized to pursue this strategy collectively.

Problems with Collective Treatment

The collective response that enabled the local industry to meet the pollution crisis has brought problems as well as benefits. Firms have become extremely interdependent, and there are new rigidities with respect to production levels. For instance, CETPs were designed to operate with a fixed capacity and cannot easily adjust to the changing circumstances of member firms. Whereas some tanneries are expanding their business and would like to acquire a larger effluent quota, others would like to reduce theirs. However, at present, the regulatory authorities do not allow adjustments of capacity within the CETP. Despite this, several plant managers admitted that they had allowed internal arrangements between members. All emphasized the need to find a way to institutionalize a practice whereby members can buy or sell back "effluent shares" to the company.

Another problem is linked to treatment technology. Because most tanneries pay for treatment on the basis of the quantity of leather that they process, and not on the quantity or quality of effluent they produce, there are no built-in incentives for firms to adopt cleaner technologies. As Dasgupta has noted, installing end-of-pipe abatement measures without ensuring a shift to less polluting production processes does not allow industry to make the connection between environmental benefits and economic gains (2000, 18).

Moreover, given the current design of CETPs, one key pollution parameter cannot be properly addressed, i.e., totally dissolved solids (TDSs). TDSs in tannery effluent consist mainly of common salt, used to preserve hides and skins during the period between flaying and tanning.[22] Different solutions are being studied. For instance, it was initially suggested that tanneries should be physically relocated to the coast because standards for the discharge of TDSs into the sea are less stringent than for surface water. This idea was firmly rejected by local producers, and policymakers recognized that it was not feasible on social or environmental grounds. Similarly the idea of a pipeline for conveying treated effluent to the sea was ruled out. Many CETPs have required their members to build shallow cement beds to collect the soaking liquid that contains high concentrations of TDSs. Even when there is space for these solar evaporation pans, as they are called, they represent additional costs and are beset with difficulties.[23] More promising is research on reverse osmosis technology for reducing TDS loads from wastewater so that it can be released into surface water bodies.[24] At the present time, cost is the major obstacle to this solution.[25]

Yet another problem is disposal of sludge generated in the CETPs, a solid waste classified as hazardous. The state government is in the process of selecting safe sites, but in the meantime CETPs are stocking it in the open, following guidelines from the PCB.

Many tanners are uncomfortable with the increased interdependence that CETPs have created. Indeed, each firm's survival depends on the behavior of its neighbors, on their willingness to comply with regulations and abide by internally devised rules. This is one of the major deterrents to collective treatment and explains why large tanners equipped with ETPs may be tempted to pull out of the CETP if they obtain permission to use their independent facilities.[26] If such defection takes place, it could have grave consequences for the remaining members.

Concluding Remarks

In a broad sense, this case study of the Palar Valley leather industry has demonstrated that joint action can improve the environmental performance of small firms. What more specific policy lessons can be distilled from this study?

A first remark is that without judicial coercion, tanneries in the Palar Valley would not have implemented pollution control measures in such a swift and forthright manner. Forced closure was an efficient method for stopping environmental pollution, but the greater challenge was to find a solution that is both economically and socially viable. In the case examined here, the state came to the assistance of the local industry, providing both technical guidance, with regard to the CETP model for instance, and substantial financial assistance. Hence, this example demonstrates that strict sanctions can be successfully combined with a cooperative approach to promote environmental protection.

The Palar Valley experience also sheds light on the factors that facilitate joint action. First, social ties between tanners facilitated cooperation; in these small towns, personal, religious, and kinship bonds overlap, as well as a shared place identity. Social control, the implicit threat of losing reputation and community, was an effective method for extracting cooperation from CETP members. Second, most tanneries in the Valley are small and did not possess the financial means to construct individual facilities. Third, tanneries are located close to each other, a necessary condition for centralized treatment. Finally, large tanneries had incentives to cooperate to ensure the survival of smaller firms, which represented a vital component of the supply chain.

Finally, this case study suggests that joint action aimed at pollution control can have a number of side benefits unrelated to the environment. In the Palar Valley, a collective response to pollution control has required new institutions, notably CETPs collectively owned and managed by the tanners themselves. The leadership, usually owners of large tanneries, is generally more dynamic and representative than that of the tanners' associations. They have become the main interlocutors of decisionmakers at the regional level, reflecting the current importance of pollution control for the industry.

Acknowledgments

This research was carried out in the framework of a joint project sponsored by the Social Sciences Department of the French Institute of Pondicherry (India) and

CNRS-REGARDS in Bordeaux, France. Many of the issues discussed here were developed in Kennedy (1999). I would like to thank Allen Blackman for his useful suggestions in editing this chapter and D. Chandramouli and Jurgen Hannak at the Central Leather Research Institute in Chennai for their precious help with the data. My sincere thanks go also to G. Venkatasubramanian for his competent and cheerful assistance throughout this study and to all the people in the Palar Valley and in Chennai who kindly took time to talk with me.

Notes

1. A useful introduction to this literature is Pyke et al. (1990). For the application of this framework to developing country clusters, see Nadvi and Schmitz (1994) and the special issue of World Development (1999) that they organized.

2. Precise statistics are not available. This estimate is based on diverse sources, such as exports from Chennai's port, and on projections from industry specialists.

3. The rationale for this policy, which is being progressively dismantled, was that compared to large industries, SSEs create more employment because they are labor-intensive, promote balanced regional development because they are relatively abundant in rural areas and small towns, and tend to provide inexpensive consumer goods. A less explicit motivation for this reservation policy was to limit investments for the consumer-goods sector to channel scarce capital to the capital-goods sector. Inspired largely by the Soviet model, Indian planners emphasized industrialization from the early 1950s as a motor for economic growth. One of the consequences for small-scale industries is low productivity and low efficiency levels, which have seriously limited their capacity to create gainful employment. For a critical review of these policies, see Bala Subrahmanya (1998) and Kennedy (2001).

4. There is not, however, a clear correlation between firm size and the processes carried out by the firm. For instance, according to a study by the Central Leather Research Institute (1990), although the vast majority of firms in Vaniyambadi are small or very small, only 28% are "primary" tanneries. Conversely, in Ambur, where tanneries tend to be larger, 38% are "primary".

5. Usually, they supply the raw material to the job-work units to ensure the quality of the end products.

6. The literature on labor and working conditions in India highlights the extreme tendency toward division of labor and hierarchy, a reflection of social organization in general. On the Agra footwear industry, see Knorringa (1996).

7. Moreover, local communal harmony has been adversely affected by increasing communal tensions at the national level, notably in the aftermath of the destruction of the Babri mosque in Ayodhya in 1992.

8. For a critical reading of the success of this policy at the national level, see Sinha and Sinha (1991).

9. The winners of these contests, organized annually by the Council for Leather Exports, are published in *Leder Informant,* a Chennai-based trade magazine.

10. Interview by author with the member secretary of the Tamil Nadu Pollution Control Board, Chennai, February 5, 1998.

11. See Subrahmanian (1989).

12. Vellore Citizens Welfare Forum vs. Union of India, Writ Petition 914 of 1991. Judgment issued on August 28, 1996.

13. Interview with the office bearers of the Vellore Citizens Welfare Forum, Vellore, June 24, 1997. This association made public complaints about a planned Muslim religious congregation that were aired by a leading daily, *The Hindu*, in its Madras edition dated May 13, 1997. The

association alleged that the congregation organizers planned to "slaughter 10,000 cows," a statement likely to offend Hindu sentiment. In my interview with them, the office bearers admitted that they had not verified the information but had acted on the basis of a letter they received from a private party.

14. The earliest report I located, marked "For Official Use Only," is from 1982 (Soil Survey and Land Use Organisation 1982). It indicated, inter alia, that almost 4000 hectares of land were severely affected by untreated tannery effluents and that farmers had been shifting over to crops more resistant to salinity.

15. There has been much discussion among CETP managers and state officials about the necessity for monitoring output of member tanneries.

16. In this context, it is noteworthy that authorities at the PCB in Chennai expressed an unambiguous preference for private individual treatment facilities, precisely because they facilitate the task of attributing individual responsibility in the event of noncompliance.

17. This is not due solely to the leather industry. A number of large chemical units located in Vellore District do not treat their effluents. See Krishnakumar (1997).

18. This explains why there are so many planned units in the CETP membership lists (as many as existing units in some cases). The opportunity to declare additional capacity carries a price: Declarations of intentions have to be backed by financial commitment, namely, share capital at the time of constructing the treatment facility and in some cases, full monthly maintenance charges.

19. In addition to social pressure to take up positions of leadership, large tanners admitted that they did so to look after their own business interests. Even though it makes demands on their time, the stakes are perceived to justify the demands.

20. See Ramasami (1982).

21. A contributing factor has been links to the global community. The local leather industry has not as yet been exposed to direct global pressures in areas such as environmental protection, but indirect pressures come from clients who translate new consumer demands, for instance, with respect to chemical inputs.

22. Usually, applying salt lasts not more than two or three months. Salt is reapplied to the flesh side every week or so to prevent putrefaction.

23. Tanners mentioned that evaporation is a long process and requires numerous beds. Also rain disrupts the evaporation process and causes the beds to overflow.

24. The Vanitec CETP in Vaniyambadi was planning to install a pilot plant in 2002. Interview with N. Abdur Rahman, plant manager, Vaniyambadi, March 13, 2002.

25. According to recent research, a less costly alternative for the TDS problem is the "high rate transpiration system," under experimentation at a CETP in Ranipet. However, uncertainties remain with regard to this method. See Sankar (2000, 11–12).

26. Such views were expressed by several large firms in interviews.

References

Anant, T.C.A., and J. Singh. 2002. An Economic Analysis of Judicial Activism. *Economic and Political Weekly Mumbai*, 37(43): October 26.

Bala Subrahmanya, M.H. 1998. Shifts in India's Small Industry Policy. *Small Enterprise Development* 9(1): 35–45.

Central Leather Research Institute (CLRI). 1990. *Report on Capacity Utilisation and Scope for Modernisation in Indian Tanning Industry.* Prepared for Industrial Bank of India and State Bank of India, Chennai, India.

———. 1998. *Directory of Tanneries in India.* Chennai, India.

Dasgupta, N. 2000. Policy Implications for Environmental Improvements in India's SSIs. *Small Enterprise Development* 11(2): 15–27.

Government of India. 2001. *Census of India.*

Humphrey, J., and H. Schmitz. 1998. Trust and Inter-Firm Relations in Developing and Transition Economies. *Journal of Development Studies* 34(4): 32–61.

Kennedy, L. 1999. Cooperating for Survival: Tannery Pollution and Joint Action in the Palar Valley (India). *World Development* 27(9): 1673–91.

———. 2001. Protégée ou Condamnée? Les Politiques Publiques à l'Egard de la Petite Industrie en Inde. *Revue Tiers Monde* 42(165): 105–28.

Knorringa, P. 1996. *Economics of Collaboration. Indian Shoemakers between Market and Hierarchy.* New Delhi: Sage Publications.

Krishnakumar, A. 1997. Pollution Unchecked. *Frontline* September 19: 97–99.

Nadvi, K. 1999. Shifting Ties: Social Networks in the Surgical Instrument Cluster of Sialkot, Pakistan. *Development and Change* 30(1): 143–77.

Nadvi, K., and H. Schmitz. 1994. Industrial Clusters in Less Developed Countries: Review of Experiences and Research Agenda. Discussion paper 360. Brighton, U.K.: Institute of Development Studies.

Pyke, F., G. Becattini, and W. Sengenberger (eds.). 1990. *Industrial Districts and Inter-Firm Cooperation in Italy.* International Institute for Labour Studies. Geneva: International Labour Organization.

Ramasami, K.S. 1982. Entrepreneurship and Modernization of Industry: A Study of the Tanners of North Arcot. Doctoral Thesis. University of Madras.

Sankar, U. 2000. Common Effluent Treatment Plants: An Institutional Arrangement for Pollution Control in Small Scale Tanneries in India. Second International Conference on Environment and Development. Stockholm: Royal Swedish Academy of Sciences, September 6–8.

Schmitz, H. 1995. Collective Efficiency: Growth Path for Small Scale Industry. *Journal of Development Studies* 31(4): 529–66.

———. 1997. Collective Efficiency and Increasing Returns. IDS working paper 50. Brighton, U.K.: Institute of Development Studies.

———. 2000. Does Local Co-operation Matter? Evidence from Industrial Clusters in South Asia and Latin America. *Oxford Development Studies* 28(3): 323–36.

Sinha, S., and S. Sinha. 1991. Leather Exports: An Illusory Boom? *Economic and Political Weekly* 26(35): 111–18.

Soil Survey and Land Use Organisation. 1982, A Study on the Influence of Tannery Effluents on Soils, Water and Crops in North Arcot District. Unpublished report, North Arcot District Collectorate, Vellore.

Subrahmanian, P.S. 1989. Relevance of Environmental Laws and Article 48-A of the Constitution of India on the Functioning of Tanneries in India. *The Madras Law Journal* July–December(II): 5–13.

Trigilia, C. 1986. Small-Firm Development and Political Subcultures in Italy. *European Sociological Review* 2(3): 161–75.

World Development. 1999. Special issue on Industrial Clusters in Developing Countries. 27(9).

Using Supply-Chain Networks to Help Small and Medium-Sized Enterprises Adopt Environmental Management Systems

The Guadalajara Environmental Management Pilot

Kulsum Ahmed[1]

I N DEVELOPING COUNTRIES, small and medium-sized enterprises (SMEs) typically receive little or no appropriate technical assistance aimed at improving their capacity for environmental management. There are a number of reasons. Given chronic scarcities of technical, administrative, and financial resources, policymakers typically target a few large companies for assistance rather than a multitude of SMEs. Even when technical assistance centers and funds for pollution control and prevention are made available to both small firms and large ones, they are usually accessed by larger, more sophisticated companies because these companies are aware of these resources, and because they have the time and know-how to negotiate application procedures. Moreover, technical assistance programs typically promote end-of-pipe treatments or pollution-prevention activities, a higher level of intervention than simple good housekeeping measures, which can reduce the use of raw materials and utilities at low cost and which are often particularly attractive to SMEs.

To maximize scarce enforcement resources, many developing countries' governments are increasingly using innovative approaches to promote compliance with environmental regulations. For example, Indonesian regulators have instituted a program to publicize the environmental performance ratings of large water polluters, a mechanism that appears to have significantly boosted public pressures to comply with environmental regulations (World Bank 2000). However, it is not clear that such programs, which exploit multifaceted relationships between the public and large firms, are an effective means of improving SMEs' environmental performance. SMEs' most important linkages are probably with downstream large company clients, not with the public. Indeed, large companies often offer financial and technical assistance to their smaller suppliers, typically in the form of free training in quality assurance. Such assistance not only enhances the quality of the

SME suppliers' products, but also the large companies' own products, as the former constitute the large companies' raw material.[2]

The Guadalajara Environmental Management Pilot (GEMP), carried out in Guadalajara, Mexico, between 1997 and 2000 was an innovative program that sought to reach out to the SME sector to improve environmental management and did so by relying on supply-chain networks and focusing mainly on good housekeeping measures. This chapter describes this pilot and discusses its implications for policymakers.

The rest of the chapter is organized as follows. The next section discusses the historical and institutional context of the GEMP, at both the national and local levels. The section titled The Guadalajara Environmental Management Pilot describes the GEMP, including its origins, participants, principal activities, and results. The section titled Outcomes and Lessons discusses the pilot project's outcomes in more detail and distills lessons. The last section discusses design recommendations for future programs.

The Context

National Environmental Regulatory Reform

In Mexico, at the national level, a number of regulatory reforms during the 1990s laid the institutional and intellectual groundwork for the GEMP. These included the separation of standard setting and enforcement within the national environmental ministry via the creation of the office of the Federal Attorney General for Environmental Protection (*Procuraduría Federal de Protección al Ambiente*, PRO-FEPA) and the National Institute of Ecology (*Instituto Nacional de Ecología*, INE) in 1992, followed by the regrouping of environmental responsibilities under a new Ministry of Environment, Natural Resources and Fisheries (*Secretaría de Medio Ambiente, Recursos Naturales y Pesca*, SEMARNAP) in 1994.[3] Associated with these institutional changes was a major reform of the framework environmental law in 1996. One of several objectives of this reform was to promote voluntary environmental programs and standards. These legal and institutional changes laid the groundwork for voluntary environmental management programs involving both public- and private-sector participants.

One outcome of the early 1990s national environmental reforms directly anticipated EMS standards. This was the creation of a program of voluntary environmental audits for firms in high-risk sectors. In effect, these audits promoted adoption of environmental management systems or EMSs (see Box 7-1 for a definition). The program was administered by the office of the Deputy Attorney General for Environmental Audits, created as part of PROFEPA in 1992.[4]

Shortly after the start of GEMP, in 1997, two other interrelated programs were also launched that aimed to improve the management of industry's impact on the environment. The first was the award of Clean Industry (*Industria Limpia*) certificates to the first 115 companies to complete the action plans developed as a result of the PROFEPA audits program.[5] The second was a regulatory reform initiative that, among other things, established a program to promote voluntary EMSs. The goal of the latter was to encourage continuous improvement in environmental performance based on pollution prevention and the sustainable use of natural resources throughout the production chain.[6]

Guadalajara

Guadalajara, in the state of Jalisco, is Mexico's third largest city, with a population of almost 3 million. It is also one of Mexico's major industrial centers and is rapidly acquiring a reputation as Mexico's "Silicon Valley" due to the large influx of multinational electronic companies. Its pleasant weather and relatively smaller size make it one of Mexico's more popular locations for multinational industry siting. As a result, the city has grown rapidly in recent years.

Guadalajara's leading industrial sectors are electronics, food processing, shoes, oil, metalworking, textiles, leather, plastics, chemicals, and cement. Jalisco's *State Development Plan 1995–2000* noted that 7,300 potentially contaminating firms were located within the metropolitan area of Guadalajara. Industrial pollution has been compounded by a lack of infrastructure for handling and disposing of solid wastes and a lack of municipal water treatment plants in the metropolitan area.

The need for environmental management in Guadalajara became eminently clear in April 1992 after five miles of sewer lines exploded, resulting in an official death toll of 200, permanent injuries to an additional 53 people, and severe damage to more than 500 houses. The cause was determined to be the dumping of several thousand gallons of gasoline into the sewer system by the local state-owned petrochemical facility. In 1995, dumping of hazardous materials into the sewage system by a local SME resulted in more than 12,000 people being evacuated from their homes. These two incidents sharply altered the Guadalajaran public's perception of environmental risks.

SMEs and Environmental Management in Mexico

In many countries, SMEs make up a significant portion of the industrial sector. In Mexico, 89% of manufacturing establishments are so-called "micro" facilities, with fewer than 15 employees, and an additional 10% are SMEs, with fewer than 250 employees. Together, micro and SME facilities account for about 50% of employment in the manufacturing sector (AMBIO 1995).

In Mexico, as in many developing countries, there is an enormous disparity between the environmental management capabilities of large and small companies. This disparity was documented by a 1995 INE- and World Bank-sponsored survey of the status of environmental management in Mexican industry, based on in-person interviews with representatives of 236 industrial facilities chosen to represent a variety of potentially polluting sectors, geographic locations, and plant sizes. Econometric analysis of the survey data indicated that the factor that most strongly differentiated companies with positive environmental performance was the existence of EMS elements (see Box 7-1 for a definition of EMS elements) (Lexington Group 1997). Fewer than 20% of small firms surveyed had EMSs, compared to 70–80% of large Mexican and multinational companies (see Figure

Box 7-1. Environmental Management Systems

An environmental management system (EMS) is a systematic approach to controlling a facility's environmental impacts. An EMS standard does not set specific pollution targets but establishes the required elements of an effective pollution control system. It provides the tools for a holistic approach to environmental management. In doing so, it prevents technological predeterminism, in that clean technologies, nor end-of-pipe treatment, nor good housekeeping are encouraged per se. It also places the responsibilities for operating the system squarely in the hands of the organization itself, its management, and its employees. Promoting EMSs does not obviate the need for strong environmental regulation, nor does the adoption of an EMS substitute for compliance with such regulation. Rather, an EMS should be viewed as a tool to help ensure cost-effective compliance and to encourage the continuous improvement of environmental performance.

The ISO Standard for Environmental Management Systems

In recent years, a number of voluntary EMS standards have been developed, including the British Standard Institute's BS7750, published in 1992, and the European Union's Eco-Management and Audit Scheme, published two years later. In 1992, the International Standard Organization (ISO), an international nongovernmental organization, made a commitment to identify ways it might help promote "sustainable business development" in support of the U.N. Conference on Environment and Development, held in Brazil in June of that year, and to prevent trade barriers from being raised by competing environmental standards. Toward these ends, ISO formed the Strategic Advisory Group on the Environment (SAGE), which recommended the formation of a technical committee to develop voluntary international standards for environmental management systems and tools. Through an iterative process of consultation, building partnerships between governmental and private-sector representatives from its 112 member countries, ISO published the ISO 14001 standard on Environmental Management Systems in 1996. Whereas each EMS model presents its own strengths and weaknesses, the ISO standard has attracted particular attention, largely because of its importance in the global marketplace.

The ISO 14001 standard identifies a series of elements as requirements of an effective EMS, including:

- an environmental policy, defined by top management and communicated throughout the organization, specifying commitment to compliance with environmental legislation, pollution prevention, and continual improvement in environmental performance;
- planning, starting with the identification of environmental aspects and legal requirements, from which objectives and targets are set and incorporated into an environmental management program that defines responsibilities, means, and time frame;
- mechanisms for implementation and operation of the environmental program, covering the structure of responsibilities, training, communication, documentation, and emergency preparedness;
- procedures for checking and corrective action, especially for monitoring and measurement, correcting nonconformance, maintaining records, and conducting periodic audits; and
- management review of the EMS to ensure its continuing effectiveness.

This model was developed through a protracted process of international negotiation and as a result reflects a number of compromises for which it has subsequently been criticized. Among these, two weaknesses have attracted particular attention. First, the ISO 14001 standard does not require that a certified organization be in compliance with environmental legislation, only that the environmental policy include a commitment to compliance, and that the EMS include a mechanism for identifying regulatory requirements and establish a plan for achieving them. Second, an ISO 14001 certified organization is only required to publicly communicate its environmental policy, not its environmental aspects and program.

7-1). Moreover, many of the small companies that did have EMSs belonged to larger corporate entities.[7]

The World Bank survey also helped determine the factors that increase the likelihood of an SME implementing an EMS (Lexington Group 1997). It suggested that companies concerned about regulatory requirements were more likely to adopt elements of an EMS. In this regard, SMEs posed a particular challenge because two-thirds of those surveyed reported that they had little knowledge of environmental regulatory requirements, and one-third claimed they had no sources of environmental information. Partly because of this, only one-third of the SMEs surveyed claimed to have met or exceeded regulatory requirements, compared to two-thirds of the large companies. Independent of concern about regulatory requirements, firm size was also found to be a strong determinant of the extent to which an industrial facility had implemented an EMS, with SMEs less than half as likely as large companies to have EMS elements in place (Lexington Group 1997). These results clearly demonstrated a need to enhance the environmental awareness of Mexican SMEs and to boost their use of EMSs.

The Guadalajara Environmental Management Pilot[8]

Origins

On November 19, 1996, 11 large companies in Guadalajara, Mexico, signed a voluntary agreement with SEMARNAP to mentor small suppliers in implement-

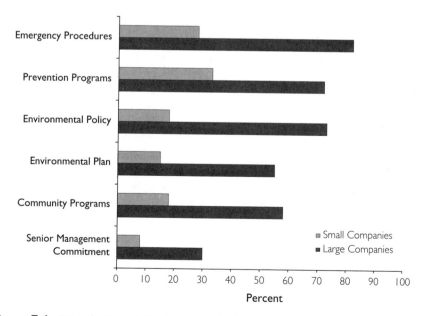

Figure 7-1. *Distribution of Environmental Management Capabilities in Mexican Industry (Lexington Group 1997)*

ing EMSs. This voluntary agreement was one of several pilots encouraged by INE, in line with the changes to the Ecology Law, under SEMARNAP's *Programa de Competitividad Industrial y Protección Ambiental.*

Just as the groundwork for the pilot was laid by a number of intersecting national and local trends in environmental public policy, the more immediate motivations for the GEMP were the product of several interactions, associations, and interests, and they evolved over time. The first seeds for the project were planted in a presentation on environmental management made by the Lexington Group, which administered the 1995 World Bank survey of the status of environmental management, to several industry leaders in Guadalajara. Discussions among these stakeholders led to a plan for the Lexington Group to provide the Guadalajara companies with EMS training as a group to cut costs. Given the government's emphasis on voluntary programs, the companies decided to share the plan with SEMARNAP—more specifically INE within SEMARNAP—to demonstrate their environmentally responsible behavior. Simultaneously, the companies, together with the Lexington Group, asked the World Bank to finance the training. Given the results of the 1995 industry survey, the World Bank suggested shifting to promoting EMSs in SMEs. SEMARNAP, for its part, was supportive. The pilot initiative was seen to complement the agency's emphasis on voluntary regulation.

Participants

The pilot, as it was finally implemented, used networks among SMEs, large companies, universities, and government agencies to promote implementation of EMSs by SMEs. The participants in GEMP included

- Eleven large companies, each of which invited one to three of their small suppliers to participate. The 11 companies committed to providing the SMEs with mentoring assistance and to providing partial financing for the pilot. By attending the EMS training sessions, the large companies also hoped to benefit from the training;
- SMEs, which committed to implementing EMSs;
- The Lexington Group, which committed to providing EMS training and guidance to project participants;
- The *Instituto Tecnológico de Estudios Superiores de Monterrey* (ITESM) and the *Universidad de Guadalajara* (UdG), two local universities that provided 17 staff members to assist the SMEs;[9]
- The *Centro de Investigaciones y Estudios Superiores en Antropología Social* (CIESAS), one of Mexico's most prestigious anthropological research institutes, committed to conducting a separate study, financed by the World Bank, on the role that culture change plays in the introduction of EMSs;
- Mexican federal, state, and local government officials, who participated as observers in the pilot. INE and PROFEPA committed to participate as observers in periodic evaluations and to use these review sessions for discussion of pertinent aspects of national environmental policy. PROFEPA also committed to avoid any duplication of effort with its environmental audit program; and

- The World Bank, which provided partial financing and agreed to participate as observers in planning, training, and review sessions.

Recruited by a Guadalajara industry leader involved in the original meetings with the Lexington Group, the 11 companies that signed the November 1996 voluntary agreement were *Acietera la Junta*, Aralmex, *Casa Cuervo, Celulosa y Derivados, Cementos Guadalajara, Compañia Siderúrgica de Guadalajara, Honda de Mexico, IBM de México,* Lucent Technologies, Quimikao, and SCI Systems. These companies each contributed US$5,000 to share part of the consultant costs with the World Bank.

A total of 22 SMEs participated in this pilot at one stage or another. Each of these firms was invited by a large company and was required to meet two criteria: Each had to be an independent Mexican company, not a subsidiary of a larger company; and each could not have more than 250 employees, the upper limit of the official Mexican definition of a medium-sized business. The participating SMEs ranged in size from 3 to 230 employees and represented a variety of industries, including construction, metalworking, chemical manufacturing, automobile parts, environmental services, and printing.

The pilot started in February 1997 and officially came to a close in November 2000. It consisted of two distinct phases, which are described below. The rationale was to set up the pilot's framework and provide consultant support in the first phase, with active supervision by the World Bank and its consultants. The second phase was a period to monitor sustainability of GEMP with only minimal involvement of the World Bank and its consultants. It was therefore an opportunity to see whether a pilot of this type was sustainable without external support.

Phase One[10]

From February to May 1997, the participants in the GEMP held several joint sessions to lay the groundwork for the project. The Lexington Group presented a three-day training course that described the ISO 14001 model in general terms so that large companies could compare their environmental management systems to this model and so that all participants could decide whether the model was suitable for SMEs. Ultimately, the parties decided to use the ISO 14001 EMS as a model without simplification (see Box 7-1 for a description of ISO 14001). This was an important decision because, at the time, formal EMSs were generally considered to be too complex and expensive for use by SMEs in developing countries. In addition, SMEs were thought to have limited incentives to adopt ISO 14001 because they predominantly sell to domestic markets that are less concerned about environmental issues than the international markets targeted by large companies. Despite these constraints, the industry participants in the planning sessions decided to use ISO 14001, mainly because the aim of GEMP was to implement EMSs in SMEs, not to certify the companies in ISO 14001. The stakeholders in GEMP viewed certification as a decision that each company should make based on its own circumstances.

For the most part, however, this decision was based on the fact that most ISO 14001 requirements flow from the significant environmental aspects (SEAs) identified by the organization itself. These SEAs vary based on the size and type of organization. Generally the SMEs participating in the project identified fewer than 10 SEAs, and often fewer than 5, a tiny number compared to a large, complex chemical or refining operation, which may identify several hundred SEAs. It was therefore felt that the ISO 14001 application could serve as a feasible EMS model.

During the spring of 1997, the participants in GEMP also decided that convincing SME senior management of the importance of developing an EMS should be an explicit phase of the project. Finally, reporting formats were developed by the companies for recording significant environmental aspects of the project, as well as for objectives and targets.

Aside from the preliminary planning process in the spring of 1997, the core of GEMP during Phase One was a series of plenary training and smaller review sessions that lasted from May 1997 to February 1998. During this 10-month period, training and progress review sessions were held every 3 months. At the suggestion of the companies themselves, the first training was preceded by a senior management briefing to build awareness of GEMP. In each training session, participants received training in a subset of EMS elements that they were thought to be able to implement (with the assistance of their mentors and university consultants) in an 8–10-week period. At the end of each implementation period, the group reconvened, first in small work groups (with companies chosen at random) to review progress with implementation, and then as one large group to receive training on additional EMS elements.

The GEMP used several tools to monitor the progress of implementation by SMEs. These included progress review sessions, which provided the SMEs with an opportunity to learn from each other and network during EMS implementation; a self-assessment survey carried out on a periodic basis to monitor the status of implementation, as well as environmental performance data (including efficiency of use of raw materials, water, and energy); a self-assessment compliance checklist developed by the participating large companies to facilitate review with environmental regulations; visits to the SMEs' facilities by the university consultants, in some cases, together with the large company mentors; and finally, the culture change study conducted by CIESAS, the anthropological research institute.

The CIESAS team used a variety of sociological methods to study the environmental awareness and culture of the participating firms. These methods included formal questionnaires administered to a sample of firms before and after the training course; focus group discussions of environmental problems, policies, and procedures; observation of production processes and administrative systems; and case studies of selected firms. This study provides an indication of the sustainability of environmental performance improvements that took place during the GEMP (CIESAS 1998).

Phase Two

A number of important institutional developments took place during Phase Two of the GEMP, which lasted from March 1998 to November 2000. The most important was the creation of the Project Guadalajara Association under the leadership of the original industry champion of GEMP. The association's purposes were to support the participating companies in implementing their EMSs and also to meet formal requirements of the two-year agreement with the Mexican government.[11] Each participating company, large and small, was required to send a formal letter from its legal representative confirming its continued participation in GEMP. Whereas 10 large companies and 16 SMEs confirmed their participation, 1 large company and 5 SMEs left the project. Both ITESM and UdG were invited to continue their participation by the association. ITESM accepted formally and UdG accepted informally, although its participation in Phase Two turned out to be minimal. The Project Guadalajara Association nominated a coordinating committee composed of representatives of three large companies, two SMEs, ITESM, and UdG.

A number of other institutional changes occurred during Phase Two. ITESM formally took on the roles of information clearinghouse and provider of technical assistance on environmental management. The World Bank and its consultants were more distant observers, monitoring progress during three site visits to Guadalajara. Also, four new SME subgroups were established based on the level of EMS implementation they had achieved and their desired level of further support. One group worked directly with its mentor, two groups with university consultants, and the third without consultants. In August 1998, the association set up a peer-review system for its members, whereby association members with experience of EMS verification audited and verified the EMSs established by other GEMP companies. Teams of ITESM consultants and mentor company representatives performed audits on a few of the SMEs.

After September 1998, there was a gradual reduction in the activity of the coordinating committee because participants reduced the time they put into the GEMP. The committee held its last meeting in March 1999. During the same period, participation of some SMEs also tailed off. Six SMEs suspended EMS development, and three SMEs dropped out of the project. Of the seven SMEs that continued EMS development, only two did so with the help of their mentors, whereas five opted for individual consultancies with ITESM. In general, during this period, the SMEs moved toward consulting help from individual consultants on the ITESM team. Some SMEs paid for this assistance. In March 1999, six SMEs successfully passed a preaudit carried out by the Mexican Institute for Standards and Normalization.

On November 21, 2000, the participants of the pilot held a final meeting to formally close the pilot and to discuss lessons learned. Certificates of appreciation from SEMARNAP, signed by INE's president, were also handed out to all pilot participants.

Results

GEMP's success in encouraging SMEs to improve their environmental management practices were mixed. On the positive side, GEMP clearly generated a number of important outcomes. At the final meeting of the pilot in November 2000, GEMP's key achievements, as defined by the participants, included the following:

• ISO 14001 certification (completed or in process) for six large companies;

- successful formal preaudits in six SMEs[12] in 1999 and a planned preaudit in one SME in March 2001;
- wide acknowledgment by the SME participants that the pilot taught them to understand the environmental effects of their organizations and the concept of sustainability;
- the continuation of good environmental practices established during the pilot by many of the SMEs, even if they did not continue to formally implement an EMS, thus implying a culture change on the part of the participants; and
- creation of a network of like-minded people to share ideas and move the environmental agenda forward.

On the negative side, though, participation in GEMP clearly diminished over time. Also, some of the participating SMEs did not experience particularly dramatic improvements in environmental management. The participation of these companies in GEMP, as well as those that were later inactive, were also useful, as they provided a better understanding of SMEs and their approach to environmental matters.

In conclusion, GEMP was an important learning experience, providing a number of policy lessons about the effectiveness of this type of approach. The specific outcomes that GEMP generated and the lessons that can be learned from the program are discussed below.

Outcomes and Lessons

Environmental Performance

Based on self-reported data, GEMP demonstrated that EMSs can improve the environmental performance of SMEs. Every SME that attended the review visit in August 1998 reported at least one significant improvement in its environmental performance. In some cases, these improvements, which included "good housekeeping" measures as well as process changes, brought substantial reductions in materials and energy use and in environmental impact, achieved at low cost and yielding a net monetary savings. The actual environmental improvements self-reported by the SMEs as of August 1998 are identified in Box 7-2 and categorized in Figure 7-2. More than three-quarters of the facilities reduced releases to the environment, 70% had improved the work place environment, and about two-thirds had reduced energy and/or materials use, improved waste handling, and improved regulatory compliance. In some cases, this self-reported data was verified by site visits or by the university consultants supporting the SMEs. However, detailed measurements of emissions or wastewater quality were not undertaken.

It is also interesting to note that many of the SMEs that pulled out of the GEMP still continued with the process changes that were implemented as a result of their EMSs.[13] This suggests that GEMP had some impact on the environmental management capabilities of these SMEs, despite the short period of their involvement, and that these process changes were sustainable. Also noteworthy is that the SMEs most successful at realizing environmental and economic performance improvements generally had a high level of worker participation in their EMSs.

Box 7-2. SME Environmental Performance Improvements

Custom manufacturer of machine parts (20 employees)

- Oil use halved through better machine maintenance (replacement of old seals)
- Reclassified as nonhazardous waste generator
- Work area cleaner and safer
- Small garden built within facility

Environmental services group specializing in effluent analysis and manufacture of water-treatment products (12 employees)

- Improved work environment
- Extraction hood reduced waste of raw material and dust
- Water-treatment system improved quality of effluent

Plastic manufacturer (100 employees)

- Reduced energy consumption
- Reduced number of health and safety incidents

Manufacturer of packaging materials (100 employees)

- Reduced VOC emissions by gradual shift from polyurethane using volatile adhesive to molded polyethylene
- Reduced scrap from 1% to 0.5%

Print shop (210 employees)

- Paper waste cut 30% by buying paper in custom sizes
- Greater use of recycled paper
- Designed waste collection system into new layout
- Contaminated effluent reduced by 90% (from 700 to 60 liters/month) by separation of aqueous hazardous wastes

Construction company specializing in construction of gas stations (45 employees)

- Increased tarpaulin use and sprinkler application (now required of subcontractors) reduced dust emissions
- Modified construction plan saved several native trees
- Cut wood consumption by 30%

Manufacturer of hot sauce and sangrita (30 employees)

- Vehicles better maintained to reduce emissions
- Change in cleaning process reduced use of iodine-based stainless steel sanitizer by 11,000 liters per year (overall effluent discharge also reduced)
- Requiring suppliers to use stronger containers reduced raw material waste
- 3,000 lb of orange juice concentrate (6% of annual use) recovered annually by spraying scooped-out containers with water and using resulting juice

Print shop (21 employees)

- Four 55-gallon containers of paper recycled each week
- Reduced paper consumption by reducing trial runs and using both sides of test paper

Company that shapes, cuts, and prints customer logos on PVC to make safety seals (70 employees)

- Changed the incentive structure in the printing area (to reflect quality as well as quantity) to reduce waste
- Reduced hazardous rag waste (from 5.5 to 1.7 kilograms of rags per ton of product)
- Significantly reduced machine noise
- Reduced electricity consumption
- Offer used-battery collection program to employees

Environmental services company, including wastewater analysis and production of chemical products for water treatment (10 employees)

- Separation and proper disposal of hazardous waste
- Reduced evaporation and additional waste of hexane and reduced generation of other gases through changed analytical procedures
- Cut water consumption by 50%

Environmental services company offering laboratory analysis and chemical products for water treatment (20 employees)

- Less effluent generated
- Separation and appropriate disposal of hazardous effluent and waste, including chloroform and hexane
- Precipitation and/or neutralization of heavy metals

Company performing analysis of hazardous industrial waste (8 employees)

- Changed location to improve ability to separate and treat effluent
- Installed carbon filter to improve quality of air discharge

Manufacturer of seat belts and air bags (120 employees)

- All used maintenance oil now treated as hazardous waste
- Reduced consumption of maintenance oil

Mixer and distributor of chemical products such as chlorine (3 employees)

- Use of personal protective equipment
- Reduced transportation risk by purchasing new truck (to take place of family car) to separate chemical drums from each other and from driver
- Reduced number of chemical spills by labeling storage drums and using alternative drums that make it easier to transfer product

Mixer and distributor of concrete (45 employees)

- Cut water consumption 1,800,000 liters/month (40%) by recycling water used to wash out mixers
- Reduced dust emissions

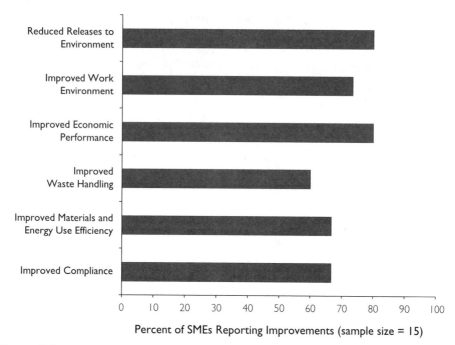

Figure 7-2. *Environmental and Economic Improvements by Category (based on Data from the 15 SMEs That Attended the August 1998 Review Sessions)*

Changes in Environmental Attitudes

EMS implementation brought about important changes in environmental attitudes of employees at all levels (Figure 7-3). Unlike traditional environmental improvement techniques, such as pollution prevention or clean technologies, EMSs do not target the environmental impacts of the organization. Rather, they target its procedures and attitudes, which collectively constitute its organizational culture, in the hope that these changes will result in consistent environmental improvements. An EMS might first affect the attitudes of senior management, middle management, and workers, then the organization's overall commitment to environmental improvement, and finally its environmental performance. The data presented in Figure 7-3 are consistent with the hypothesis that this progression occurred in many of the SMEs participating in GEMP. Because the project initially targeted senior managers, changes in their attitudes were most evident: two-thirds of the SMEs reflected important or very important changes at this level. SMEs embraced formal commitments to environmental improvement by adopting environmental policies (signed by the companies' CEOs) and environmental objectives and targets. By August 1998, all but one SME had taken both of these steps.

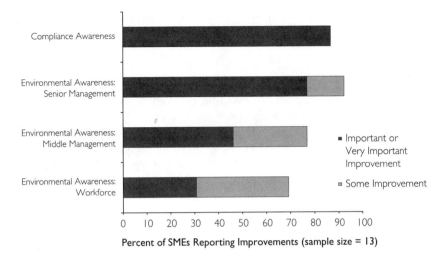

Figure 7-3. *Improvements in Environmental and Compliance Awareness (based on Data from the 15 SMEs That Attended the August 1998 Review Sessions)*

Economic Performance

The environmental performance improvements in SMEs led to improvements in economic performance at 80% of the SMEs. Many of these improvements were simple, low-cost housekeeping measures that resulted in reduced use of raw materials, energy, or water. Unfortunately, it proved difficult to quantify economic performance improvements.[14]

Compliance Awareness

EMS implementation and compliance fulfillment are complements, not substitutes. For this reason, GEMP never presented EMSs as an alternative to regulation, nor was there a thorough study of the effect of EMS implementation on compliance. However, the ISO 14001 model, as taught to the SMEs, requires companies to include a commitment to full compliance in their environmental policies and to develop compliance management systems. The participating SMEs did in fact make commitments to full compliance and also chose to use a "compliance checklist" developed by the large companies to monitor their progress toward this goal. At the start of GEMP, many SME representatives were not aware of all relevant regulatory requirements. The process of implementing an EMS heightened this awareness. In fact, as this awareness increased, the number of items not checked on the compliance checklists of several SMEs initially increased. Furthermore, many SME representatives commented in the February 1998 review session that the process of implementing an EMS significantly improved their capability to comply with the law because it helped to set up a framework within which they could identify and tackle noncompliant areas. However, as mentioned above, GEMP did not focus on verifying whether compliance with regulations actually improved.

Use of ISO 14001 by SMEs

The GEMP experience suggests that ISO 14001 is an appropriate EMS for all sizes of SMEs, as long as technical assistance is provided. In June 1999, six SMEs participated successfully in an ISO 14001 preaudit, a group that included the smallest participating SME (3 employees) as well as the largest (230 employees). It is important to note, however, that the SMEs in GEMP were provided with significant implementation support, including simplified formats, discrete milestones, and staff assistance.

Effective and Sustainable EMSs for SMEs

GEMP holds a number of lessons regarding the implementation of EMSs by SMEs. First, to be effective, EMSs needed to be incorporated into the overall business strategies of the SMEs. At the end of the pilot, participating SMEs indicated that their reasons for continuing to implement their EMSs included a desire to increase the value of the company, to expand market opportunities with multinational and local clients, and to improve business systems (this applied especially to the laboratories, which have to comply with a systems-oriented laboratory analysis standard).

Second, successful EMS implementation did not depend on the size of the SME. This was the major finding of the CIESAS culture change study (CIESAS 1998). Third, senior management support was a critically important determinant of whether an SME dropped out of the pilot. Evidently, the economic and environmental benefits achieved through EMS were not sufficient to ensure long-lived management interest in implementing EMSs. Two of the SMEs that dropped out were among the most advanced SMEs in terms of EMS development and had realized impressive environmental and economic performance improvements. In each case, the firms dropped out after a change in senior management. The reduced activity of the committee during Phase Two of GEMP—which made it difficult for the new management of these SMEs to learn about GEMP and its purposes—was probably also a factor.

Fourth, supply-chain networks are an important mechanism to ensure SME participation in programs promoting environmental management systems. The invitation from the large mentor companies was critical in getting the SMEs to participate in GEMP. This point was underscored in Phase Two, as several SMEs quit active participation in the pilot after their mentor companies' level of commitment flagged. The large companies that had supplier development programs and EMSs were the most successful SME mentors.

Fifth, peer-review arrangements for SMEs—whereby EMSs are audited by large company mentors, university consultants, or a peer group of SME staff—have a great deal of merit because they can be a means of providing third-party verification of EMSs at a much lower cost than formal certification. This verification could help to open up domestic markets for the firm, in addition to acknowledging the quality of a firm's EMS without an expensive certification procedure.

Sixth, the experience of GEMP suggests that active participation in and promotion of such schemes by the government is important. The government's contribution to GEMP could have been enhanced through a clearer initial agreement on the exposure of the participating companies to regulatory sanctions. Appropriate official recognition of the participating companies was only made at the end of the pilot. Earlier recognition could have served as an incentive for continual involvement by the large companies.

Replicating the Pilot: Project Design Recommendations

Based on the lessons learned from GEMP, this section presents a number of recommendations for governments interested in designing similar environmental initiatives that reach out to SMEs or development agencies supporting governments to implement such schemes.

Large Company Mentors

The link between the large company mentor and the SME needs to be maintained over time by creating incentives for the large company to remain involved. These incentives could be generated by an industry association with particular interest in the environment or by the government, for example, through official recognition of companies participating in such programs. Future initiatives should also require large companies to develop their own EMSs alongside their SME protégés and provide them with the necessary support, so that they can function more effectively as mentors.

SMEs

How can SMEs' incentives to participate be strengthened? Clearly there are economic gains from adopting an EMS, for example, from reduced raw material and utility use. Although GEMP makes a start, such gains need to be better documented through case studies. But even documentation by itself may not be enough to keep SMEs interested. Here the role of the large company mentor, as well as the close linkage with the business strategy of the firm, is crucial.

Two factors can help enhance an SME's performance during the course of a GEMP-like project. First, SMEs should be provided greater practical legal expertise on the national environmental regulatory framework. Also, EMS documentation should be stressed throughout the course.

Consultants

GEMP's university consultants turned out to be more important than originally envisaged, particularly in providing the SMEs with continuous access to assistance, most importantly in management system design and legal analysis, and less so in the technical aspects of their processes. In future pilots, a number of improvements could be made to enhance consultant participation. First, local university consultants should meet predetermined qualifications, should be organized under a single management structure, and should have defined responsibilities. Second, local consultants should be trained as a group in EMSs and in general consulting techniques before training industry participants, so that they are more effective at supporting their clients regardless of their specialization. Third, the program designer should establish a formal structure to manage and support the university consultants. For example, a local EMS center could be set up in future projects and could be in charge of selecting the consultants based on established qualifications, making sure that they fulfilled their responsibilities and providing administrative (and possibly financial) support for their work. Such a center could also serve as the local administrative home for the project as a whole. Furthermore, if the center were based at a learning institution, such as a university, then in the course of providing extension-type services to SMEs, it would also enhance the training of its students and faculty, thereby improving the environmental management capabilities in the country over the long term. For these reasons, such a center may merit government support until it is firmly established.

Linkage with Regulatory Framework

For all companies, large and small, involved in an effort to promote EMSs, it is important to define in advance the relationship between regulatory programs and the participating companies. GEMP demonstrated that EMSs are potentially a powerful tool for reaching the SME sector when used in combination with other tools in the government's compliance and enforcement system. However, governments should not mandate the implementation of EMSs. A government mandate would be hard to enforce. Also, close linkage between a firm's EMS and its business strategy is essential for success. A government mandate might inhibit such close linkage, resulting in an ineffectual EMS.

Leadership

Setting up a coordinating committee (similar to that established in GEMP's Phase Two) at project initiation should help to better establish a clear structure for project leadership and a channel for open communication among all parties.

Ensuring Continuity in Such Programs

Finally, could a program or activity similar to GEMP be replicated by local stakeholders without external funding? In the case of GEMP, the World Bank partially financed the international consultant providing the EMS training. But this funding was less than the total financing contributed by the large companies, so World Bank funding was probably not necessary. The more important roles of the World Bank were to ensure continuity and progress over time and to resolve conflicts between different parties. The pilot involved more than 70 participants at any one time, each with their own interests. The fact that reduced participation of the Bank in Phase Two corresponded with reduced participation by the companies indicates the importance of putting a mechanism in place to ensure continuity. The government could play such a role by creating incentives for companies to participate and by creating a national EMS center. In this way, responsibility for promoting better environmental management could be shared across the public, private, and nongovernmental sectors.

Acknowledgments

The author wishes to thank Francisco Giner de los Rios, the Mexican government official who was the counterpart for GEMP, for his valuable comments on this chapter. She also wishes to thank the many GEMP participants, without whom this pilot and all the learning associated with it, could not have taken place.

Notes

1. The views represented in this chapter are entirely those of the author and should not be attributed in any way to the World Bank, to its affiliated organizations, or to members of its Board of Executive Directors or the countries they represent.

2. This statement is based on the author's personal experience as an environmental and quality control manager in a multinational firm in a developing country.

3. SEMARNAP was restructured during the Fox administration in 2000–2001. In this restructuring, INE was changed from a regulatory and licensing agency to a think tank. Regulatory and licensing functions were transferred to two separate under-secretariats in the Ministry. SEMARNAP also became SEMARNAT as Fisheries (*Pesca*) was transferred to the Ministry of Agriculture.

4. In many respects, Mexico's environmental audits program anticipated the environmental management system (EMS) standards subsequently published by the British Standards Institute, the European Union, and the International Standards Organizations. The environmental audits covered the identification of potential environmental risks, the definition of systems to minimize such risks, the design of emergency response plans, and a review of compliance with regulations governing industrial safety, occupational health, and environmental protection. Once an audit was completed, an action plan was formulated, providing the basis for a voluntary agreement between PROFEPA and the audited facility. Under this agreement, the facility assumed the obligation to resolve any irregularities encountered through the audit. By 1997, when the Guadalajara pilot began, PROFEPA had undertaken environmental audits at more than 900 facilities, focusing on the highest risk sectors of production. In 1997, PROFEPA augmented the audits program by awarding Clean Industry (*Industria Limpia*) certificates to the first 115 companies to complete the action plans developed as a result of the initial audits. Such public recognition underscored SEMARNAP's support for EMSs as a valuable tool for improving industrial environmental performance.

5. PROFEPA's Clean Industry Program continues under the Fox administration.

6. This was never fully implemented and did not progress further under the new priorities of the Fox administration.

7. This report used the official Mexican definition of a large company (i.e., more than 250 employees).

8. The preliminary findings of the pilot from February 1997 to February 1998 are described in World Bank (1998).

9. ITESM's initial involvement was through a contract with the Lexington Group, and UdG joined the project subsequent to its start-up at the request of some of the large companies. The participation of UdG staff was underwritten by the university.

10. A detailed description of the chronological events of Phase One can be found in World Bank (1998).

11. The association did not have a legal basis. It was an informal entity.

12. This sample included the largest (with 230 employees) and the smallest SME (with 3 employees).

13. This information is based on interviews with personnel from these companies in April 1999.

14. This weakness is discussed in greater detail in World Bank (1998).

References

AMBIO. 1995. Ciudades y Giros Prioritarios en Relacion con la Contaminación Industrial en México. Report for the World Bank, September.

CIESAS. 1998. Cultura Ambiental y la Industria en Guadalajara. Report for the World Bank.

Lexington Group. 1997. Industrial Environmental Management in Mexico: Results of a Survey. Report to the World Bank on a survey funded by a grant from the Japanese government administered by the World Bank.

World Bank. 1998. *Mexico: The Guadalajara Environmental Management Pilot*. Report 18071–ME. September 8.

World Bank. 2000. *Greening Industry. A World Bank Policy Research Report*. Oxford: Oxford University Press, 64–75.

CHAPTER 8

Clean and Competitive?

Small-Scale Bleachers and Dyers in Tirupur, India

Michael Crow and Michael B. Batz

ESPITE PRESSING POLLUTION PROBLEMS, policymakers in developing countries are often reluctant to enforce environmental regulations because they fear that doing so will have adverse economic impacts. This is particularly true when the polluters in question are small and medium enterprises (SMEs). According to conventional wisdom, such firms may face difficulty complying with environmental regulations due to a number of factors that are commonly understood to handicap small firms. The literature indicates that small firms typically lack access to credit (Bianchi and Noci 1998); are vulnerable to exogenous cost pressures due to thin profit margins (Berry 1997; Mead and Liedholm 1998); face difficulties learning and acquiring new technologies due to limited informational and human resources (Levy 1993; Bianchi and Noci 1998); often lack physical space needed to install new technologies (NEERI 1992; McCormick et al. 1997); and are disadvantaged compared to larger firms due to a lack of economies of scale (Schmitz 1982; U.S. EPA 1995).[1]

For these reasons and others, governments worldwide protect SMEs from environmental regulations. In the United States, for example, small firms enjoy regulatory exemptions and special considerations in regulatory standard setting and enforcement (Brown et al. 1990; Dole 2001). Although appealing in light of the aforementioned arguments, such exemptions are not based on strong empirical evidence that environmental regulations have had a disproportionate effect on small firms (Brock and Evans 1986).

To shed light on the question of whether forcing small firms in developing countries to comply with environmental regulations necessarily has adverse economic impacts, this chapter examines a recent natural experiment in Tirupur, India. The city is dominated by a cluster of approximately 8,000 small and medium-sized firms producing low-cost cotton knitwear. Approximately 800 of these firms bleach and dye cloth, a process that has been responsible for extensive pollution of local surface and groundwater. In 1996, the Madras High Court ordered Tirupur's bleachers and dyers to install pollution-control devices or be shut down. Soon thereafter, approximately one-fifth of the bleachers and dyers closed down voluntarily or were closed by the government for failure to install pollution-control devices. Ultimately, however, the vast majority of bleachers and dyers installed effluent treatment plants. This transformation undoubtedly imposed significant costs on the bleachers and dyers. Yet, there are few visible signs of serious economic distress. As of 2002, the number of bleachers and dyers has returned to approximately 800 firms (Prithiviraj 2002). Also, the knitwear cluster to which the firms belong has remained competitive, exhibiting growth in absolute exports as well as in share of overall Indian knitwear exports. Thus, although considerable uncertainty remains as to the effects of the court order mandating water pollution control, it appears *not* to have had serious economic impacts.

Our analysis is based on primary and secondary sources, including 80 on-site interviews with various stakeholders, and a firm-level, nonrandom survey of 18 bleaching and dyeing firms. Firms were interviewed and surveyed in strict confidence, so references to interviews and survey data are only noted specifically when the subject granted permission. Surveyed firms were targeted according to production capacity to ensure an informative cross-sampling, as shown in the section called The Bleaching and Dyeing Subcluster. Because they were not selected randomly, however, data culled from the surveys cannot be statistically extrapolated to the larger population of firms. Whenever possible, survey data have been supplemented by other sources. More detailed information about the survey, interviews, and secondary research can be found in Crow (1999).

Our analysis is organized as follows. The section titled Background describes the Tirupur knitwear cluster, the bleaching and dyeing subcluster within it, and the pollution problems that the subcluster creates. The section titled Environmental Regulation discusses recent efforts to compel bleachers and dyers to comply with environmental regulations. The section titled Economic Impacts of Pollution Control discusses the private costs of this regulation and its economic impacts. The section titled Mitigating the Economic Impact of Regulation describes two factors that have enabled bleachers and dyers to avoid significant economic impacts from this regulation: their ability to finance effluent treatment and collective action. The last section summarizes lessons for policymakers.

Background

The Tirupur Knitwear Cluster

Tirupur, a city of 500,000 located in the southernmost Indian state of Tamil Nadu, is renowned for its thriving knitwear industry. In 1989, the city was home to 8000 registered firms—and countless unregistered firms—90% of which were directly engaged in garment production, and almost all of which were on a small or medium scale (MIDS 1997). The Indian government explicitly reserves knitwear production for small-scale industries (SSIs), which are defined by a ceiling on investment.[2]

Tirupur's knitwear cluster is well-known for its flexibility and low production costs, which enable it to efficiently fill small orders and meet short deadlines (Cawthorne 1995; MIDS 1997). These characteristics are partly attributable to the preponderance of small firms in the cluster and to its reliance on subcontracting (field interview with a Canadian buyer 1998), which is consistent with the literature on small firms (Piore and Sabel 1984; Schmitz 1995). Approximately 80% of the firms employ "job-working" in contracts, in which subcontracted firms perform a specified stage in the production process using raw materials supplied by the contractor (Gulati 1997).

Tirupur is India's dominant producer of cotton knitwear for both domestic consumption and export. It produces about 80% of the cloth sold in domestic markets (field interview with United Nations Industrial Development Organization [UNIDO] cluster experts 1998), 80% of the country's exports of cotton knitwear, and 50% of its knitwear exports of all types (*Business Line* 2000).

The volume of the cluster's direct exports increased more than six fold in only eight years between 1987 and 1995, with 1995 direct exports exceeding $440 million in 1998 inflation-adjusted U.S. dollars (Table 8-1). Note, however, that export growth plateaued in 1994–95 and value per piece began to decline around the same time. The corresponding exports for the period during and following the principal changes to environmental regulation, from 1996 through 2001, are described in the section titled Economic Impact of Regulatory Enforcement.

Table 8-1. *Growth in Tirupur Knitwear Direct Export Volume and Value, 1987–1995*

	Volume		Value		Value per piece	
Year	Number of pieces (millions)	Growth over previous year (%)	1998 US dollars (millions)	Growth over previous year (%)	1998 US dollars (millions)	Growth over previous year (%)
1987	33.36		48.2		1.45	
1988	45.91	38	60.5	25	1.32	−9
1989	61.40	34	87.7	45	1.43	8
1990	88.87	45	136.4	56	1.54	7
1991	90.51	2	186.5	37	2.06	34
1992	139.90	55	311.0	67	2.22	8
1993	189.30	35	435.2	40	2.30	3
1994	196.40	4	425.2	−2	2.16	−6
1995	217.10	11	440.3	4	2.03	−6

Sources: Apparel Export Promotion Council (1998, 2005).

Note: Converted to constant 1998 U.S. dollars using Indian Ministry of Commerce and Industry (2004) and Tata Services (1998).

The Bleaching and Dyeing Subcluster

Because it is responsible for a vital stage of garment production, the bleaching and dyeing subcluster's growth has paralleled that of the knitwear cluster as a whole. The subcluster grew from fewer than 100 firms in the early 1980s to 866 firms in early 1998.[3] Of the 866 firms in operation in 1998, approximately 180–250 were bleachers, engaged only in bleaching of cloth, while the remaining firms were dyers, engaged in both the bleaching and dyeing of cloth (field interviews with Tirupur Bleachers and Dyers Associations 1998; Cawthorne 1995). Some 78% of bleachers and dyers are job-working subcontractors. The remaining 22% are generally larger firms that tend to be vertically integrated in supply chains (Madras School of Economics 1998; field observations 1998).

The subcluster has two major trade associations, the Tirupur Dyers Association (TDA) and the Tirupur Bleachers Association (TBA), which in 1998 had membership rates of 96% and 72%, respectively, and which provide the subcluster with assistance in such areas as legal and political representation, labor, taxes, equipment, and pollution control.[4]

Table 8-2 shows the size distribution of the subcluster in terms of processing capacity, employment, and capital investment and indicates that most subcluster firms appear to satisfy the definition for SMEs, especially in terms of employment. Furthermore, most SSIs, as all firms surveyed other than the largest dyers, reported capital investment (exclusive of effluent treatment) less than Rs 6 million ($150,000), far less than the Rs 50 million ($1.25 million) SSI designation.[5]

Bleaching and Dyeing Pollution

Bleaching and dyeing require copious amounts of water—between 80 and 250 liters of water per kilogram of cloth—and generate considerable water pollution. By 1996, Tirupur firms were discharging more than 13 million liters of effluents per day, up from one million liters per day in 1986 (field interviews and survey data 1998; Krishnakumar 1998). Left untreated, these effluents contain hazardous chemicals and exceed Indian emissions standards (Blomqvist 1996; Madras School of Economics 1998).[6] Effluents have contaminated local rivers and groundwater, as well as the Orathu Palayam reservoir downstream, a primary source of irrigation water for local farmers (Blomqvist 1996; field interview with K. Sivasubramaniyan of MIDS 1998).

Anecdotal evidence of the impact of this pollution is plentiful. Farmers around Tirupur have reported significantly reduced soil fertility due largely to high salinity and have also noted increased health problems in cattle (Blomqvist 1996; Ragunathan 1997; Krishnakumar 1998; Madras School of Economics 1998). Water in the Orathu Palayam Reservoir has become so polluted that, since 1993, local farmers have lobbied against using it for irrigation and fishermen using the reservoir complain of degraded fish stocks (field interview with Nelliyat and Menon of MIDS 1998). Local hospitals report increased incidence of skin disease (Krishnakumar 1998). In reaction to decreasing water quality, Tirupur's population has essentially stopped using local ground and surface water for drinking, relying instead on semiweekly delivery of potable water (Madras School of Economics 1998; field interview with N.P. Paul 1998).

Table 8-2. *Size Distribution of Tirupur Bleaching and Dyeing Firms*

Madras School of Economics data			Corresponding field research data		
Processing capacity (kg cloth or yarn/ day)	Type of firm	% of firms	Number of firms contacted	Labor employed (high season)	Capital investment of surveyed firms (US$ 1998)
0–1000	Dyers	47.2	11	3–25	$500–150,000
	Bleachers	24.8	3	10–12	$6,250–10,000
1001–2000	Dyers	17.9	3	25–100	$62,500–125,000
	Bleachers	3.1	2	12	$12,500–15,000
>2000	Dyers	6.8	6	70–220	$37,500–2,300,000
	Bleachers	0.1	1	24	$12,500
Total		100	26	3–220 range	$500–2,300,000 range

Note: US$ 1998, current value of capital.

Sources: Madras School of Economics (1998) statistical data; field interviews; survey data.

Environmental Regulation

Early Pollution-Control Efforts

Efforts to regulate bleachers and dyers in Tirupur are relatively recent and correspond to the explosive growth of the subsector in the past two decades. As late as 1982, there were only about 70 bleachers and dyers in Tirupur, so the Tamil Nadu Pollution Control Board (TNPCB—a new state agency created to enforce environmental regulations) focused its resources on larger enterprises (Blomqvist 1996; field interview with TNPCB officer 1998; Madras School of Economics 1998). The TNPCB did not post an officer in Tirupur until 1989, by which point the number of bleachers and dyers had climbed to 300 (Blomqvist 1996).

By 1989, promoting and subsidizing common effluent treatment plants (CETPs) was a key element of the Indian national government's environmental policy toward small firms. The members of a CETP typically form a corporation to build and operate an effluent treatment plant that receives discharges via pipes and/or trucks. Compared to individual effluent treatment plants (IETPs), CETPs offer a number of perceived advantages, including economies of scale, reduced demand for technical expertise, and more efficient use of scarce land. They are also expected to significantly reduce the monitoring burden placed on the enforcement agency (Prasad No date; NEERI 1992; Prabhu 1998). Hence, investments in CETPs were subsidized. In 1989, Indian CETPs could receive a 50% subsidy on capital costs—25% each from the central and state governments—as well as loans at subsidized interest rates from the Small Industries Development Bank of India (SIDBI) and the Industrial Development Bank of India (IDBI) (Blomqvist 1996).[7]

In 1989, the TNPCB began to promote CETPs in Tirupur. The recently established TDA tentatively cooperated in this effort to forestall more drastic regulatory action and began collecting small equity share contributions from member firms

(Blomqvist 1996; field interview with a TDA representative 1998). However, most firms remained opposed to further action because the PCB was unwilling to use its closure power. Politics undoubtedly motivated this hands-off regulatory policy (field interviews with dyers and a TNPCB official 1998). PCB leaders are politically appointed and often represent vested interests (Sapru 1998). The TNPCB does not shut down firms unless it has political support to do so.

The political landscape began to shift in the mid-1990s, when the TNPCB was pressured to step up enforcement of water pollution regulations. A number of newspaper and magazine articles highlighted the pollution problems in Tirupur (field interview with a TDA representative 1998). These articles were spurred by protests of environmental groups and occasional calls from the national government to enforce environmental legislation (Blomqvist 1996).

The TNPCB increased pressure on the TDA to begin construction of CETPs. In response, the TDA organized firms into 12 CETPs and selected firm owners to lead them. In 1995, the TNPCB again demanded that firms make contributions to CETP equity share accounts and issued closure notices to firms that did not. Few closure notices were issued, however, and even those firms that received these notices often continued to operate illicitly and openly. This half-hearted enforcement reinforced the perception that the TNPCB was a "lackadaisical paper tiger" (Blomqvist 1996; field interviews 1998), and by early 1996, construction on CETPs had yet to begin (field interview with a larger dyer 1998).

Judicial Action

In February 1996, a farmer downstream from Tirupur filed a lawsuit against all bleaching and dyeing firms in both Tirupur and nearby Karur, charging them with operating in violation of state pollution laws and severely damaging the environment. The Madras High Court quickly ruled in the petitioner's favor and ordered the PCB to force firms to comply with regulations (field interview with V. Prakash 1998).

Bleachers and dyers took the court ruling seriously. The same court had ordered tanneries near Madras shut down the year before. Also, dyestuff manufacturers in another jurisdiction had recently been shut down for noncompliance (causing a short-term shortage of dyes to the Tirupur dyers). Therefore, firms believed that the TNPCB would be under pressure to show results or face the wrath of the court (field interviews with two TDA members and representatives 1998).

Of the 12 CETPs that the TNPCB worked to set up, 8 CETPs made up of 299 individual firms began construction within the year of the court action (Blomqvist 1996; field interviews 1998). The remaining four CETPs disbanded before construction began. In addition, 567 firms decided to install IETPs instead of joining CETPs. Some of these firms were located in areas where CETPs were being built (*Business Line* 1998a; Gulati 1998). In the section titled Mitigating the Economic Impact of Regulation, we discuss the reasons that firms chose CETPs or IETPs.

By early 1998—two years after the court ruling—a majority of CETPs and IETPs had significant construction under way. However, none were completed. Because three court deadlines for completion had passed since the original judicial action, reflecting a compromise between the TDA and the TNPCB, the Madras

High Court ordered 103 firms with incompleted IETPs to be shut down.[8] In November 1998, the Madras High Court ordered another 40 firms that had opted for IETPs shut down for lack of progress. Although the TDA claimed that all such firms remained closed, field research suggests that as many as 50% of them continued to operate illicitly.

In early 1999, 8 CETPs connected to 278 firms commenced operations, and all 424 remaining IETPs had completed construction and began treating effluent. Thus, there were 702 firms still operating, meaning that 164 firms (19% of the original 866) had either been shut down by the Madras High Court or shut down on their own accord (Peace Trust 2001).[9]

Compliance?

Although the widespread installation of ETPs in Tirupur was a significant achievement, it does not follow that the environmental problems were entirely resolved, or even that bleachers and dyers were fully complying with regulatory mandates. Although the CETPs and IETPs used primary treatment facilities designed to remove organic wastes (BOD and COD), few have used secondary treatment facilities to remove inorganic wastes, such as chloride, used in dye fixation.

Moreover, it is not clear that CETPs or IETPs have been continuously or all properly operated since they were installed. We found no evidence to the contrary from either the TNPCB or from media reports. Still, follow-up research is needed to make a reliable determination.

Unfortunately, little data are available to address the question of whether the operation of the new ETPs in Tirupur has improved water quality. The only known study is an analysis performed in 2001 on samples from eight separate locations in the area, including wells, the Noyyal River, the Orathu Palayam Reservoir, and two CETPs (Prithiviraj 2002). This study found that TDS, chloride, and other measures of water quality were far above World Health Organization standards and TNPCB effluent standards. Although limited and preliminary, this analysis suggests that substantial enforcement may still be needed to ensure that CETPs and IETPs have sufficient treatment capabilities and are operating continuously and properly.

The impression of partial compliance is reinforced by continued public- and private-sector concern about water pollution in Tirupur. In the early spring of 2002, downstream farmers complained to their district of groundwater contamination, due largely to high levels of TDS and salinity (*Business Line* 2002a). As a result, the TNPCB issued notices to members of seven Tirupur CETPs, threatening them with closure for not installing secondary treatment facilities (*Chemical Weekly* 2002). The deadline passed without event at the end of May, however. The TNPCB did not want to pursue the matter out of concern for the industry (*Business Line* 2002b). However, in early 2003, the TNPCB took serious action against larger firms for apparently the first time, temporarily cutting off the power supply to 2 larger firms until they promised to install secondary treatment within four months (Gurumurthy 2003).

Economic Impacts of Pollution Control

Private Costs of ETPs

Researchers at the Madras School of Economics (1998) predicted ex ante that combined capital and operating costs for ETPs would increase bleachers' and dyers' production costs by 5–25%. As discussed in depth in Crow (1999), field data suggest that for many of Tirupur's bleachers and dyers, installing IETPs or participating in CETPs was indeed costly. People at 20 firms were questioned, either through the survey instrument or through field interviews, about capital investment in productive equipment, IETPs, and CETPs. ETP capital costs ranged from a low of Rs 150,000 ($3,750), for a bleacher sharing an IETP, to Rs 10 million ($250,000) for the largest firm contacted, which had invested in both an IETP and a CETP.[10] ETP investments averaged approximately Rs 1.3 million ($33,000), with a median of approximately Rs 900,000 ($23,000).

The magnitude of these figures becomes clear when expressed as percentages of existing capital outlays and of annual profits. For all but the largest and smallest of the 20 sample firms, investment in ETPs increased capital expenditures by anywhere from 20% to more than 100%, with an average of 66% and a median of 60%. Not surprisingly, ETP capital expenditures appear to tend to be a higher percentage of total investment—that is, a greater relative burden—among the smaller firms. ETP investment is also significant when compared to annual profits, as investment represented between 82% and 500% of annual profits among surveyed firms, with an average of 192% and a median of 150%.[11]

Economic Impact of Regulatory Enforcement

Did the court order requiring bleachers and dyers to install ETPs generate significant adverse economic impacts? If so, evidence might include the exit of firms from the industry, interruptions in supply of bleaching and dyeing services, and reductions in export competitiveness. We found no such evidence, however. With regard to exits, as noted in the opening text of the chapter, by 2001 the number of bleachers and dyers in Tirupur had risen back to 800, the number of firms in the city at the time of the court order (Prithiviraj 2002).

With regard to shortages, officers of the Tirupur Export Association (TEA) asserted in May and June of 1998 that there had been none (field interview 1998; *Business Line* 1998a). A number of factors likely minimized the effects of firm closures on the supply of bleaching services. First, only approximately 20% of the bleachers and dyers were closed, and as many as half of them may have initially continued to operate illicitly. Also, there are indications that the industry was operating below full capacity at the time of the court order. Finally, the flexibility inherent in the job-working system allowed production to be reallocated from closed firms to open ones.

With regard to export competitiveness, according to a major firm owner,

> The court case hasn't yet caused any difficulties to the industry … Our export turnover has not gone down. It's still increasing, although our rate

of growth has decreased since the early 1990s. For example, [our company] increased exports from 1.5 million pieces [in 1995] to 2.07 million pieces [in 1998] (field interview 1998).

This firm's experience parallels that of the knitwear cluster as a whole, although data suggest this growth had leveled off after 1999. As Table 8-3 shows, exports continued to increase following the court case, from 218 million pieces in 1995 to 370 million pieces in 2003. In value terms, the cluster exported more than $800 million in 2003, up from around $444 million in 1996 (in 1998 dollars). Furthermore, Tirupur's knitwear producers continued to outpace other knitwear producers in India. Even in years with decreases in exports, the cluster's share of Indian garment exports increased steadily, rising from 48% in 1996 to 55% in 2003 (AEPC 2005). The cluster performed especially well in the low-cost market of undergarments, in which costs may be particularly difficult to pass forward (*Business Line* 1998b).[12]

A number of factors may explain why the court-ordered enforcement of regulations appears not to have had significant adverse economic impacts on Tirupur's bleachers and dyers. One is that during the period in question, exogenous market conditions made the industry more profitable. However, available evidence contradicts this explanation. Labor costs in Tirupur have been rising since the late 1980s, cotton and dye prices increased substantially in the 1990s, and groundwater has become ever scarcer and more expensive during this period (field interview with a large dyer and with Padmini Swaminathan 1998). In addition, real value per exported piece of knitwear began to decline in 1993, and export growth slowed significantly starting in 1994 (AEPC 1998).[13] Furthermore, because of intense competition within the cluster, bleachers and dyers are typically price-takers, just as the garment manufacturers hiring them are price-takers in the export market

Table 8-3. *Growth in Tirupur Knitwear Export Volume and Value*

| Year | Volume | | Value | | Value per piece | |
	Number of pieces (millions)	Growth over previous year (%)	1998 U.S. dollars (millions)	Growth over previous year (%)	1998 U.S. dollars	Growth over previous year (%)
1996	257.4	19	443.9	1	1.72	−15
1997	294.3	14	548.2	23	1.86	8
1998	338.5	15	635.0	16	1.88	1
1999	368.0	9	742.6	17	2.02	8
2000	410.4	12	824.8	11	2.01	0
2001	372.4	−9	805.1	−2	2.16	8
2002	344.80	−7	772.6	−4	2.24	4
2003	370.40	7	825.5	7	2.23	−1

Source: Apparel Export Promotion Council (2005).

Note: Converted to 1993–94 Indian rupees using Indian Ministry of Commerce and Industry (2004) and Tata Services.

because of competition from other low-cost competitors in Bangladesh, Egypt, Turkey, and elsewhere (Cawthorne 1995; field interview with a larger dyer 1998). Thus, bleachers and dyers appear to have weathered the court order despite prevailing market conditions—not because of them.

A second possible explanation for the court order's lack of obvious economic impact is that bleachers and dyers participating in CETPs received significant government subsidies for pollution-control investments. However, subsidies only marginally improved CETPs' capital cost advantage relative to IETPs, and only 35–40% of bleachers and dyers participated in CETPs. In addition, as discussed below, CETPs faced substantial delays in receiving subsidies and, in the short run, have had to rely principally on firms' equity share payments, unsubsidized commercial loans, and high-rate informal loans.

An additional explanation for the seeming lack of adverse economic consequences from the court order is that the full impacts have yet to be felt. ETPs have only recently become routinely operational on a widespread basis, and many entrepreneurs may not yet be operating their ETPs to reduce costs. Furthermore, in the coming years, firms may have to install and operate costly secondary treatment facilities, and loans will have to be paid back. Nonetheless, the cluster's apparent continuing competitiveness is surprising, given the arguably significant initial challenges (cost and otherwise) that ETP installation has imposed to date. Only time and more research will demonstrate whether the cluster can continue to thrive in the face of new challenges.

The data presented in this section only suggest, but do not make a definitive case, that environmental regulations had no serious economic impacts on bleachers and dyers. Nevertheless, considering that complying with environmental regulations is thought to be particularly burdensome for SMEs, even this evidence is somewhat unexpected and begs explanation.

Mitigating the Economic Impact of Regulation

The economic resiliency of the bleachers and dyers in the face of sudden enforcement of environmental regulation is partly explained by the manner in which these firms financed investments in pollution control and also by their willingness and ability to engage in collective action.

Financing Effluent Treatment

Whether installing IETPs or participating in CETPs, all bleachers and dyers needed to raise significant investment capital to comply with the court order. Our field research suggests that for the most part, bleachers and dyers relied on owner assets or retained earnings for these investments. Of 18 firms surveyed, almost half financed their investments in ETPs using only their own funds, and almost 90% financed at least half of these investments exclusively with their own funds. This investment pattern is consistent with the literature, which indicates that small firms rarely borrow funds from banks, relying instead on personal or family savings (Berry 1990; Hansohm 1992).

However, the literature also suggests that SMEs generally lack sufficient savings for large capital investments because of working capital deficits, a lack of savings, and thin profit margins. Tirupur bleachers and dyers, on the other hand, were largely able to overcome these constraints and remain in business. Three factors contributed to this success: the job-working system, CETP equity share installment payments, and the modernization of equipment and reorganization of operations.

The Job-Working System. The job-working system in Tirupur eases working capital difficulties for many bleachers and dyers because they do not have to purchase cloth, an input that would otherwise account for more than 70% of production costs (Madras School of Economics 1998). Also, job-working enables firms to avoid trade credit imbalances, whereas small firms typically grant much more trade credit than they receive, inhibiting their ability to make capital investment (Harper 1979; field interviews and surveys 1998).

CETP Equity Share Installments. In Tirupur, CETP equity share installments served as a vehicle for saving. The TDA collected funds from firms throughout the 1990s to be used later for capital investment. The Rs 60,000 ($1,500) contributed by many dyers in 1994 typically represents at least 20% of the estimated minimum outlay for either a CETP or IETP (Blomqvist 1996). Because the TDA returned contributions to participants who declined to participate in CETPs, such firms were able to reinvest those funds in IETPs. Furthermore, financially weaker firms were permitted to delay their equity share payments (field interviews 1998), a provision that enabled them to divide their investment into what Schmitz (1997) calls "small riskable steps."

Modernization and Vertical Integration. Bleachers and dyers were also able to generate investment capital by maintaining healthy profits. Despite the increasing financial pressures discussed above—rising input prices, decreasing export prices per piece, and slowing export growth—profit margins in the subcluster (which typically average approximately 20%) remained steady and may even have increased in the 1990s (Blomqvist 1996; Madras School of Economics 1998). This phenomenon can be explained by investments in improved productivity and product quality and by a nascent trend toward vertical integration.

During the rapid growth of the 1980s and early 1990s, firms in the subcluster funneled profits into efforts to improve productivity, product quality, and capacity (Swaminathan and Jeyaranjan 1994). The TDA, TBA, and SIDBI all reported that firms in the subcluster had been investing in more modern equipment and using quality control procedures to fight falling output prices by capturing greater value added per piece. To learn such approaches, larger firms often sent their managers—usually family members—to foreign graduate programs in textile production. Smaller firms appear to have relied overwhelmingly on vendors and industry associations for information on industrial improvements (field interviews and survey data 1998).

A growing trend toward vertical integration (i.e., acquisition of firms engaged in other stages of production) also allowed some bleachers and dyers to cope with cost pressures (field interviews 1998). The persistence of the job-working system in Tirupur is partly rooted in the reluctance of owners to manage large work forces because of concerns about labor unrest (Cawthorne 1995; field interview with the owner of a vertically integrated firm 1998). Firms in the cluster have begun to overcome this reservation, however, to save on margins, transport, and packing; to improve quality control; and to eliminate profit margins at multiple stages. Although the job-working system is still dominant, the number of vertically integrated firms in Tirupur increased from less than 1% to as much as 20% in the early and mid-1990s (Gulati 1997; field interview with an owner of a vertically integrated firm 1998).[14]

Collective Action

Job-working, CETP equity share payments, modernization, and vertical integration all helped bleachers and dyers finance effluent treatment. However, collective action, in the form of industry associations and effluent treatment collectives, may have been the most important factor that allowed bleachers and dyers to overcome economic barriers to compliance. Through collective action, Tirupur's bleachers and dyers were able to obtain political and legal representation, acquire the knowledge and skills needed to operate ETPs, ensure widespread enforcement through peer monitoring, deal with land scarcity, acquire government subsidies, and use economies of scale. These experiences mirror the recent literature suggesting that collective action can enable clusters of small firms to weather economic and competitive crises (Nadvi 1997; Schmitz 1997).

Industry Associations. As discussed in the section titled The Bleaching and Dyeing Subcluster, Tirupur bleachers and dyers have been largely represented by the Tirupur Dyers Association (TDA) and, to a lesser extent, by the Tirupur Bleachers Association (TBA), which acceded to the TDA's leadership.

Unified Political and Legal Representation. The TDA provided political and legal representation for the entire subcluster, including bleachers and nonmember firms, and therefore gave the subcluster bargaining power in its dealings with the government and courts. Unity is a key factor because other authors have observed that elsewhere in the world, such as the Sinos Valley in Brazil, competing interests among specialist groups have diluted the unified voice of industry associations (Tewari 1990; Schmitz 1995). This benefit is illustrated by the contrasting outcomes of two 1996 court cases brought against bleachers and dyers—one in Tirupur and a second in Karur, a nearby city whose bleachers and dyers were far less effectively organized. The Pollution Control Board ultimately shut down far more firms in Karur. Also, bleachers and dyers in that city were granted fewer deadline extensions (field interviews 1998).

Technical Assistance. The TDA and TBA also provided information and technical assistance to their members. Acquiring technical information and learning new technologies are difficult for small firms, who are commonly ignorant of environmental management issues (Allybokus et al. 1997; Bianchi and Noci 1998) and who can ill afford human resources for investments that do not boost profits (Levy 1993; Grosh and Somolekae 1996). Also, industry organizations often have had difficulty providing technical assistance to large numbers of small-scale members (Semlinger 1993; Humphrey and Schmitz 1995). In Tirupur, many business owners are poorly educated and have a background in traditional farming rather than industry. However, the TDA and TBA had sufficient membership and dues to run full-time offices and reached out to small firms by holding meetings, seminars, and workshops to disseminate information about ETPs. The TDA and TBA also helped to connect bleachers and dyers with ETP consultants and state-run agencies for technical and financial assistance, and they provided assistance to multiple research efforts, including that of the authors (field interviews with TDA and TBA staff 1998). A majority of surveyed firms in Tirupur cited either the TDA or TBA as one of their two most important sources of information about ETPs (field survey data 1998).

Enforcement. The TDA also worked closely with the TNPCB to facilitate widespread enforcement. It did so by collecting and sharing data about firm locations and water usage, as well as hosting a TNPCB officer in its offices. Led by larger firms, the TDA cooperated for several reasons: fear that shut-down would be more likely if it was uncooperative; a desire to level the playing field by helping regulators find small firms as well as large ones, and hopefully drive many small competing firms out of business; and a concern that Western markets might soon demand better environmental performance from Tirupur suppliers (Blomqvist 1996; field interviews with large dyers 1998).[15] This cooperation significantly enhanced TNPCB enforcement efforts and bolstered TDA's reputation in the cluster as an important intermediary. This status boosted the TDA's status, political clout, and even its membership, enabling it to better protect its members. The TNPCB benefited as well—working through the TDA, it was able to deal with the hundreds of firms in the subcluster (Blomqvist 1996; field interviews 1998). By all accounts, the TDA and the TNPCB both grew stronger through their relationship.

CETPS: New Collectives. As discussed earlier, in addition to acting jointly through the TDA and TBA, the bleachers and dyers formed CETP corporations to cope with environmental regulations. In 2000, the CETPs represented approximately 35–40% of the subcluster's firms (see the section titled Judicial Action). The CETP corporations have provided services to their members similar to those provided by the TDA, including legal representation and technical assistance. In addition, they have helped address land scarcity issues, have served as savings vehicles, and have enabled member firms to access subsidies from the government not available to firms building IETPs.

Political and Legal Representation. The CETPs conferred a number of political advantages. First, because of CETPs' importance to the government and the leadership role in CETPs played by large firms, CETPs further enhanced the political influence of the largest firms. In fact, the leaders of CETPs formed a special trade association to represent solely CETPs. Second, they prevented firm closures. CETP member firms are rarely shut down, because poor performance cannot easily be attributed to a single firm. Therefore, the TNPCB would be forced to shut down the entire CETP when infractions occur, an unlikely result because it would be a public failure for a government so supportive of the CETP approach (field interviews with V. Prakash and U. Sankar 1998).[16] Third, the CETPs secured subsidies. These subsidies were increased by 73% in late 1998, after significant lobbying (*The Hindu* 1998; Madras School of Economics 1998; SIDBI 1998). This windfall reduced total capital costs actually borne by CETP members to approximately 22%.

Information Needs. CETPs also served an informational function. They virtually eliminated the need for smaller firms to acquire knowledge about ETPs. The CETPs hired technical staff to operate the pollution-control equipment so that the participation of small member firms mainly consisted of their providing CETP equity share payments (field interview with a CETP board member 1998). Despite these advantages, CETPs may not always treat effluent properly, either because the mix of effluent being treated is unknown, or because individual firms concentrate their effluent before transport to reduce operating costs (NEERI 1992; U.S. EPA 1995).

Land Scarcity. Many bleachers and dyers in Tirupur are located in high-density urban areas and therefore faced a scarcity of land on which to build IETPs (NEERI 1992; McCormick et al. 1997). To address this issue, approximately 50 firms relocated, and other firms joined CETPs. Had CETPs not been available, it is likely that many more firms would have had to relocate or close. CETPs faced their own land scarcity problems, however. Finding and procuring large centrally located tracts of land was a major problem for CETP planning and reportedly played a significant role in the failure of the four CETPs that disbanded (field interviews with a large dyer and a TDA representative 1998). Of 10 CETP members contacted, 3 cited land scarcity as a prime reason for joining. Also, a CETP board member cited land scarcity as a reason that most firms had joined his CETP (field interviews and survey 1998).

Financing Arrangements. In addition to serving as savings vehicles as discussed above, CETPs helped in financing pollution-control investments because they were eligible for government subsidies and also had access to low-rate subsidized loans. CETP corporations were eligible for subsidies from state and national governments, originally capped at Rs 10 million each, but eventually equal to fully half of capital costs. CETPs have also had access to loans from government and state banks, often at subsidized rates lower than those available from commercial banks or informal moneylenders (field interviews and surveys 1998). CETPs, however, faced substantial delays in receiving subsidies and low-interest loans from government and quasi-government agencies (Crow 1999). As a consequence, CETPs have had to rely more extensively in the short run on firms' equity share payments, unsubsidized commercial loans, and high-rate informal loans, thus diminishing some of their financing advantages. Even commercial banks were also initially reluctant to lend to CETPs, out of fears that effluent treatment would reduce profitability of firms and that CETPs would not be able to recoup operating costs from their members (Gurumurthy 1997; *Business Line* 1998a; field interview with a larger dyer 1998).

Economies of Scale. According to their promoters, lower capital and operating costs were to be principal benefits of CETPs. However, thus far, available evidence does not support this argument. With respect to capital costs, when subsidies are not considered, Tirupur's CETPs appear to have been more costly on average per unit capacity than IETPs. The average total unsubsidized capital cost per kiloliters per day (kld) of capacity among CETPs is Rs 6,468 ($162), whereas the average among IETPs is Rs 4,554 ($114), a difference of 42% (Crow 1999). This analysis is based on cost data for 6 CETPs and 11 IETPs presented by Madras School of Economics (1998). Cost data for the other 2 CETPs was received from the Small Industries Development Bank of India, Tirupur Branch. The Madras School of Economics' (MSE's) IETP data does not fully reflect random sampling. MSE randomly sampled IETPs but presented data only from the 11 that had completed installation of IETPs. The data are strongly supported by assertions of several firm owners, who cited high costs of CETPs as a reason for investment in IETPs (field interviews and survey data 1998). In addition, a CETP board member verified that CETP unit capital costs had not been cheaper than those for IETPs (field interview 1998). Under the original subsidy arrangement—on which firms' decision-making was based—CETPs and IETPs had similar capital costs per unit of treatment capacity, perhaps explaining why both CETP and IETP participants cited lower cost as the reason for their choice (field interviews and surveys 1998). Only under the new subsidy arrangement granted in late 1998, which provided an additional Rs 60 million ($1.5 million) windfall to Tirupur CETPs, does the average cost per kld among CETPs drop below that of the IETP sample (Crow 1999).

Capital costs for CETPs have not been as low as expected, partly because CETPs invested in better and more expensive technology than IETPs. This in turn stems from the fact that, as recipients of wastewater from multiple sources, they are subjected to a much more rigorous design review process than IETPs (U.S. EPA 1995; field interviews 1998). Also, some observers suspect that CETP designers and leaders may have artificially inflated costs to extract greater subsidies from the government, but this could not be independently confirmed (field interviews 1998).

As for operating costs, potential economies of scale at CETPs largely have been offset by the significant costs of transporting effluent via trucks or pipes from individual firms to a central location. It is possible that CETPs might have long-term economies of scale over IETPs, however. Due to better equipment and maintenance, they may have lower costs of repair and replacement.

Fairness Within the Subcluster: Small Firms and CETPs

Although the Indian government promotes CETPs in part because of the expectation that they will help small firms, these benefits may be overstated. In fact, most of the smallest firms in Tirupur opted to install IETPs instead of joining CETPs, and those that chose CETPs found financial arrangements of these institutions biased in favor of large firms. Although CETP members pay for capital and operating costs according to volume of effluents, they are also required to invest a minimum financial equity share, often exceeding their percentage share. Thus, the smallest firms typically pay a higher cost per unit of effluent than larger firms (field interviews with a TDA representative and a small dyer 1998).

The CETP leaders justify this apparent inequity on three grounds. First, the largest firms essentially perform all of the management activities of the CETP, from administering the organization and supervising construction to providing political representation and acquiring the subsidies. Second, CETP leaders argue that financial equity share should not be based solely on effluent levels because not all capital costs are directly proportional to effluent volume; specifically, the installation costs of effluent transport pipes are much more a function of distance than they are volume; therefore, smaller firms should not necessarily pay less than large firms. Third, CETP leaders argued that large firms would have had scale and knowledge advantages over smaller firms if all firms had built IETPs and that those larger firms, therefore, have the right to retain a competitive advantage. Some large dyers privately hoped that the high costs of effluent treatment might force smaller firms to fail, minimizing competition in the subcluster (Blomqvist 1996; field interviews with a TDA representative and a CETP board member 1998).

Conclusion

We have argued that the case of Tirupur's bleachers and dyers suggests that forcing small firms in developing countries to comply with environmental regulations will not necessarily have significant adverse economic impacts. This case study offers a number of lessons for policymakers.

Judicial Action

Environmental regulations would likely never have been enforced in Tirupur were it not for the Madras High Court, which was independent of both the TNPCB and the industry. Although the TNPCB officially had the power to close firms, it did not possess the political will to do so. Only when the court threatened widespread closures did firms begin to install ETPs. In the United States, the courts have long played a similar role in responding to citizen suits against industry and implementing agencies, and courts in India have increasingly done likewise in the past several years (Sathe 2002). In situations like Tirupur's, a similarly powerful and independent third party may prove necessary to force compliance.

Focusing Enforcement on Clusters

Tirupur's case suggests that focusing enforcement on small-firm clusters may be sensible for three reasons: they generate significant environmental damage; working with clusters may confer enforcement economies to regulators; and the collective efficiencies of firms may lead to more successful adaptation to compliance costs. On this last point, the firms' geographic proximity facilitated information sharing and may have helped the TDA to grow rapidly. Furthermore, strong local ties to other firms in the knitwear cluster supply chain, along with a job-working network, may have made the subcluster more stable and better able to bear increased costs without losing business partners. Finally, the proximity of firms within the cluster made CETPs feasible for those who chose that path.

Collective Action

Collective action was critical to the success of Tirupur bleachers and dyers. The TDA provided a number of benefits, including political and legal protection, technical and regulatory information, and access to effluent treatment contractors. The TDA also intermediated between bleachers and dyers and the TNPCB. The firms of Tirupur were suspicious of the Pollution Control Board and wary of corruption, and they sought the protection and representation of the TDA.

Likewise, the TNPCB used the TDA to efficiently interact with the hundreds of firms in the cluster. The TNPCB worked with the TDA to disperse technical and regulatory information, to identify firms, and to monitor progress. In general, regulators may be able to extend their enforcement resources by working with trade associations in such a manner, although they must be wary of either being unduly influenced by the trade association or of bolstering an ineffective organization (Layzer 1998; Rosenbaum 1998).

The TDA helped ensure widespread compliance through peer monitoring. The TDA shared details about firms with the TNPCB, in part to placate the enforcement agency, but also to ensure that no firms had an unfair competitive advantage because they had not installed or operated costly pollution-control equipment. In situations like Tirupur, where there are too many firms for the regulatory agency to assess individually, peer monitoring may be essential both for widespread compliance and for ensuring a level playing field.

CETPs: Limited Dividends

CETPs did not live up to promoters' advertisements on a number of counts. They failed to provide advertised economic benefits to most firms because of higher than anticipated capital and operating costs. (CETPs may yet offer economies of scale in operating costs, although no data are available to confirm this.) Large firms led Tirupur CETPs, even though smaller firms paid higher costs per unit of effluent than larger firms. Whether this is equitable, considering the larger firms' more prominent contribution to leadership, is an open question, but it is also important to recognize that more than a third of Tirupur's firms chose to join CETPs.

The extent to which CETPs benefited regulators is also not clear. CETPs appeal to regulators because they promise to reduce the costs of monitoring hundreds of small enterprises and because professional management at CETPs is expected to lead to better treatment. In fact, subsidizing CETPs relative to IETPs is only justified if it reduces governmental monitoring costs and/or improves environmental performance. However, as discussed in the section titled Compliance?, preliminary evidence suggests that these assumptions do not necessarily hold.

To ease the regulatory monitoring burden, CETPs must be effective peer monitors by ensuring that member firms are actively participating in effluent treatment. Although some Tirupur CETPs reported to the TNPCB when equity share payments by members were substantially delayed, it is unclear that this peer monitoring was widespread or is continuing in the operational phase. CETPs elsewhere in Tamil Nadu and other Indian states have failed to demonstrate that they can and will force the overwhelming majority of their members to participate (Sarangi and Cohen 1995; Mehta et al. 1997), and the TNPCB has shown a reluctance to threaten CETPs or members with serious action for slow compliance of member firms.

In fact, in Tirupur's CETPs, the TNPCB has created a tiger difficult to tame—both because of CETPs' collective power and because of pressure to avoid criticizing a strategy it has long promoted. In fact, whereas the TNPCB arguably avoided "regulatory capture" when working with the TDA, it may have ensnared itself by creating CETPs. If the subsidization of CETPs is to be justified from a regulatory point of view, the TNPCB must demonstrate that CETPs effectively collect and treat the overwhelming majority of members' effluent. The PCB may accomplish this via CETP effluent monitoring and perhaps through random sampling of CETP members. If such monitoring fails to show progress, the TNPCB must take action.

The experience in Tirupur suggests the need for a comprehensive evaluation of the efficacy of India's CETP policy, focusing on two questions. First, are CETPs the answer for firms, given that the majority of Tirupur's firms chose to install IETPs and that CETP benefits have been uneven and unreliable, particularly to the smallest firms? Second, is CETP promotion the best approach for regulators to improve small-firm environmental performance, especially given the questionable environmental performance of CETPs and the political difficulties of regulating them? If CETPs were deemed desirable from a public policy point of view, it would further be important to examine how best to promote them. The current subsidy strategy has obviously been problematic (Mehta et al. 1997; Crow 1999). The next two sections suggest additional approaches that policymakers might consider, in either case.

Overcoming Financial Hurdles

We have argued that three factors contributed to the success of Tirupur's bleachers and dyers in financing ETPs: CETPs served as savings vehicles; job-working limited capital requirements; and investments in improved efficiency and quality kept profit margins stable. Thus, the Tirupur case suggests that policymakers in similar situations may wish to encourage early savings and provide vehicles and incentives for doing so. They may also wish to provide general business technical assistance to small firms to help them minimize working capital difficulties and to encourage a dynamic and creative drive toward improved efficiency.

Flexibility

Tirupur's firms had considerable flexibility in choosing how to comply with regulations requiring ETPs. They could join a CETP or build an IETP. This decision was made by each firm based on their own perceptions of the costs and risks involved, as well its constraints on land availability, financial capital, and human capital. Such flexibility may have allowed a greater number of firms to stay in business. Policymakers may wish to follow Tirupur's example in allowing technological flexibility and encouraging private-sector innovation.

Cleaner Production

A promising regulatory strategy is notably absent from the PCB's approach: cleaner production—also known as pollution prevention, waste minimization, and eco-efficiency. Cleaner production is a business-oriented problem-solving approach focused on improving production efficiency. More efficient use of input materials and energy also reduces waste, conserves resources, and cuts pollution.

From a regulatory point of view, cleaner production should be the compliance strategy of first resort. In Tirupur's case, cleaner production promotion would have offered several advantages. First, it would have offered firms the opportunity to make environmental improvements cost-effectively. As shown by DESIRE, a UNIDO-sponsored waste-minimization project in India involving 12 demonstration companies drawn from small-scale industries, opportunities for cleaner production are often commonplace and can result in significant cost savings over alternatives (Van Berkel 2004). Second, because cleaner production integrates into the production process itself, such improvements do not typically require regulatory monitoring. Third, such cost-cutting improvement efforts would have dovetailed with the industry's other efforts in process improvement. Fourth, cleaner production would have offered an opportunity for immediate improvements in areas that to date have not been dealt with effectively: TDS pollution, water conservation, and ETP waste disposal.

In light of these opportunities, and in light of the cluster's evident success at adopting other types of new technologies, the TNPCB's omission of cleaner production is glaring. Unfortunately, this failing is common among PCBs in India (Dasgupta 1997, 2000).[17] In the future, the authors recommend that Indian PCBs work with traditional business service providers—including government and international agencies, trade associations, and other private-sector actors—to identify and promote cleaner production opportunities for fundamentally addressing environmental problems. Businesses are often more likely to trust such traditional service providers, who are also able to more effectively communicate the business advantages of cleaner production.

Dynamic Analyses

Finally, Tirupur's story indicates that ex ante analyses of the economic impacts of environmental regulation should take into account the frequently demonstrated capacity of small firms to adapt in the face of regulatory and cost pressures. Basing analyses solely on current estimated compliance costs, capital investment and profits will invariably overestimate impacts. The dynamic adjustments observed in Tirupur defy conventional wisdom, as do similar studies of sawmills in the U.S. Pacific Northwest (Layzer 1998) and of wood product firms in Brazil (Bianchi 1997). Studies of the dynamics of cluster responses to exogenous pressures suggest a need for such analyses to also consider the history of cooperation and adaptation, markets served, and the growth trend (e.g., Nadvi 1997; Schmitz 1997).

In closing, although this case presents uncertainties about the Tirupur cluster's continued ability to thrive and questions about its ultimate ability to reverse long-term natural resource degradation, it challenges the long-held notion that environmental progress necessarily comes at the expense of small enterprises, and it presents lessons for citizens and governments seeking to effectively manage sustainable economic growth among SMEs.

Notes

1. References in this chapter have been limited to two per parenthetical citation; further references can be found in the original study on which this chapter is based (Crow 1999). Unless otherwise noted, all currency figures are in constant 1998 Indian rupees, converted using the Indian Wholesale Price Index (WPI) for Textiles (Indian Ministry of Commerce and Industry 2004), or U.S. dollars, converted using international exchange rates (Tata Services 1998).

2. This ceiling was Rs 7.5 million ($187,500) in 1997 and was raised to Rs 50 million ($1.2 million) in 1999 (SIDBI 1999). It is higher than the range generally used to define SMEs. The literature classifies SMEs as having investment levels from $850–$8,500 (1989 US$) (Anderson 1982) to $5,500–$140,000 (Berry 1990); the literature also classifies SMEs as having fewer than 100 employees. The original Indian SSI designation was 10–49 employees (Cawthorne 1990). Some Tirupur firms employ up to 200 people during the high season.

3. Counts do not include cottage-sized firms that operate out of households and dye little cloth or yarn. The best estimate is that there are anywhere from 50 to 200 such firms (field interview, TDA representative 1998). As a consequence of their hidden nature and low effluent volume, they have not been a focus of the efforts of the Tamil Nadu Pollution Control Board and will not be discussed in this chapter.

4. See the section titled Collective Action for more information on the role of trade associations.

5. These investment numbers are significantly higher than reported by Blomqvist (1996), who estimates that firms processing less than 2,000 kg per day have investment limits closer to Rs 400,000 ($10,000) and that 90% of firms are SSIs.

6. Chemicals include sodium hydroxide, sodium hypochloride, sodium sulfide, hydrochloric acid, reactive dyes, and peroxide. Regulatory limits exceeded include those for pH, color, chemical oxygen demand (COD), biological oxygen demand (BOD), total suspended solids (TSS), total dissolved solids (TDS), and chlorides. BOD and COD are measures used to estimate biological matter present in effluent, which effectively reduces the oxygen available to organisms naturally occurring in the receiving body of water, reducing their viability. Because dyers use substantial amounts of salt to improve fixation of dyes, violation of TDS standards is a particular concern.

7. This subsidy has changed over time and will be discussed in greater detail in the section titled Collective Action.

8. Under the compromise, only those firms that had completed less than 50% of IETP installation were shut down. Of the 103 firms shut down, 69 were bleachers and 34 were dyers.

According to representatives of the TDA and TBA, these firms were representative of the entire population of firms (i.e., not overwhelmingly the smallest firms), although bleachers typically have less capital investment than dyers.

9. There is no explicit record that traces individual firms. Rather, we rely on aggregate counts of firms from multiple data sources, some of which are inconsistent. To the best of our knowledge, 164 firms shut down between 1998 and 1999, of which the Madras High Court explicitly ordered the closure of 143.

10. This firm was not alone among larger firms in choosing to invest in both an IETP and a CETP. Such firms typically cited at least one of three reasons for doing so: a responsibility to the subcluster to lead the CETP; a desire to have a back-up effluent treatment system in the event that the IETP stopped working; and a desire to have extra treatment capacity to handle growth in the volume of production (and, therefore, effluent).

11. A CETP manager reported that direct investment in effluent treatment plants now accounts for 40–50% of total capital investment at most firms (field interview 1998). For comparison, field survey data (1998) show investment in ETPs representing anywhere from 17% to 55% of total capital investment, with a median of 38%. Furthermore, these percentages are likely to be understated because CETP amounts reflect only equity share contributions, not loan repayments.

12. The average cost per piece of directly exported undergarments was approximately 25% of the average cost per piece of all directly exported garments from Tirupur. Continued strong export performance is particularly remarkable when one considers that the Indian government in winter 1997–98 reduced the export rebate (i.e., the "drawback") available to firms from 21% to 13% (field interview with a TEA officer 1998).

13. Field research seconds this finding. One large dyer reported that exporters were having trouble getting good orders, and the value added per piece had dropped 30% in recent years (field interview with a larger dyer 1998).

14. Cawthorne also suggests that the advantages of being an SSI also encouraged firms to maintain the job-work system. This argument is probably valid for horizontal job-working (i.e., within the same subsector, such as knitting, which Cawthorne directly researched). However, it does not appear to be an explanation for vertical job-working: according to the owner of an integrated unit, firms within different subsectors have separate capital ceilings for SSI purposes, even if they are integrated under the same owner. Thus, a large vertically integrated operation can still maintain SSI status for each individual operation.

15. Such market demands had not materialized on any noticeable scale by the time of field research in 1998. Only one firm contacted in 1998 had a foreign buyer who was actively concerned about the environmental performance of its supplier (See Crow 1999, Appendix E). However, the subcluster's concerns may be better understood by considering that, in 1994–95, the Tirupur knitwear cluster was receiving negative press in Europe after a researcher exposed its child labor practices on a BBC special. At least one large department store stated that it would not buy from suppliers that used child labor. Firms in Tirupur largely reacted by placing local Lion's Club signs on their gates, certifying "No Child Labor Employed Here," and continuing to employ children (London Mail on Sunday 1995; Blomqvist 1996; field interviews with multiple subcluster sources and Padmini Swaminathan 1998).

16. The TNPCB reportedly even told firms that those belonging to CETPs would receive more sympathy than those opting for IETPs (field interview 1998). As noted in the section titled Compliance?, there are some suggestions that this political protection may be weakening, however. In 2002, the TNPCB threatened to shut down the firms at seven Tirupur CETPs for failing to install the secondary treatment required to meet TDS standards in effluents (Chemical Weekly 2002). Though they did not shut down firms at that time, they did temporarily shut off electricity to two large firms the next year (Gurumurthy 2003).

17. Only in 2004 is cleaner production becoming a highlighted environmental problem-solving approach in the sector, under a new World Bank project (*New Indian Express* 2004).

References

Apparel Export Promotion Council (AEPC). 1998. Quantity and Value of Garment Exports from Tirupur, 1987–1997. Chart. New Delhi, India: AEPC.

———. 2005. Tirupur Knitwear Exports as a Percentage of All India Knitwear Exports. Chart. http://www.aepcindia.com/portal/tirupur.asp (accessed November 14, 2005).

Allybokus, M., et al. 1997. Environmental Auditing of a Mauritian Textile Dyeing Factory. *Industry and Environment* 201–02.

Anderson, D. 1982. Small Industry in Developing Countries: A Discussion of Issues. *World Development* 10(11): 913–48.

Berry, A. 1990. On the Dynamism of Small and Medium Industry in Colombia: Some Possible Lessons. In *The Other Policy*, edited by Frances Stewart, et al. London: Intermediate Technology Publications.

Berry, A. 1997. Small-Scale Non-Agricultural Exports as a Route to Employment Creation and Poverty Alleviation. *Konjunkturpolitik* 43(2).

Bianchi, R., and G. Noci. 1998. "Greening" SME's Competitiveness. *Small Business Economics* 11: 269–81.

Bianchi, T. 1997. Supply-Led Technology Adoption in Maranhao, Brazil: A Case of Developmental Trade in the Small-Scale Furniture Sector. Master's Thesis. Department of Urban Studies and Planning, Massachusetts Institute of Technology. Cambridge, MA.

Blomqvist, A. 1996. *Food and Fashion: Water Management and Collective Action among Irrigation Farmers and Textile Industrialists in South India.* Linkopeng, Sweden: Linkopeng University.

Brock, W., and D. Evans. 1986. *The Economics of Small Business: Their Role and Regulation in the U.S. Economy.* A CERA Research Study. New York: Holmes & Meier.

Brown, C., et al. 1990. *Employers Large and Small.* Cambridge, MA: Harvard University Press.

Business Line. 1998a. India Delay in Setting Up ETPs Costs Tirupur Dyeing Units Dear. May 19.

———. 1998b. Cotton Undergarment Exports from Tirupur Double. November 2.

———. 2000. India: Tamil Nadu: Tirupur Units Seek SEZ Status. April 6.

———. 2002a. Effluent Discharge into Noyal River—Erode Farmers Complain Against Tirupur Units. March 23.

———. 2002b. TNPCB Deadline Lapses; No Relief in Sight for Tirupur Dyeing Units. June 2.

Cawthorne, P.M. 1990. *Amoebic Capitalism as a Form of Accumulation: The Case of the Cotton Knitwear Industry in a South Indian Town.* Ph.D. Thesis, Open University. Milton Keynes, United Kingdom.

———. 1995. Of Networks and Markets: The Rise and Rise of a South Indian Town, the Example of Tirupur's Cotton Knitwear Industry. *World Development* 23(1): 43-56.

Chemical Weekly. 2002. TNPCB Issues Notices to Tirupur Dyeing Units. 4736: 96. April 30.

Crow, M. 1999. Successfully Adjusting to Environmental Regulation: The Small-Firm Cluster of Tirupur, India. Master's Thesis. Department of Urban Studies and Planning, Massachusetts Institute of Technology, Cambridge, MA.

Dasgupta, N. 1997. Greening Small Recycling Firms: The Case of Lead Smelting Units in Calcutta. *Environment and Urbanization* 92: 289–305.

———. 2000. Environmental Enforcement and Small Industries in India: Reworking the Problem in the Poverty Context. *World Development* 285: 945–67.

Dole, D. 2001. Measuring the Impact of Regulation on Small Firms. U.S. EPA, National Center for Environmental Economics. Working paper 01–03. November.

Grosh, B., and G. Somolekae. 1996. Mighty Oaks from Little Acorns: Can Micro-Enterprise Serve as the Seedbed of Industrialization? Draft paper.

Gulati, M. 1997. *Restructuring and Modernisation of Small Medium [sic] Enterprise Clusters in India.* Vienna, Austria: United Nations Industrial Development Organization.

———. 1998. Personal communication: UNIDO field notes supplied by author.

Gurumurthy, G. 1997. India: Tirupur Effluent Treatment Plant Promoters Float Forum. *Business Line.* November 8.

———. 2003. PCB Restores Power to Two Tirupur Units. *Business Line.* January 10.

Hansohm, D. 1992. *Small Industry Development in Africa—Lessons from Sudan.* Hamburg: Lit Verlag.

Harper, M. 1979. The Employment of Finance in Small Business. *Journal of Development Studies* 11(4): 366–75.

The Hindu. 1998. India—Tirupur CETPs All Set To Start Operation. November 25.

Humphrey, J., and H. Schmitz. 1995. Principles for Promoting Clusters and Networks of SMEs. Paper commissioned by Small and Medium Enterprise Branch of UNIDO. Sussex, U.K.: Institute of Development Studies, University of Sussex.

Indian Ministry of Commerce and Industry. 2004. *Handbook of Industrial Policy and Statistics.* New Delhi, India: Office of the Economic Advisor, Ministry of Commerce and Industry.

Krishnakumar, A. 1998. A Pollution Challenge. *Frontline* (July) 66–73.

Layzer, J. 1998. *Case Studies in Environmental Politics.* MIT Project on Environmental Politics and Policy.

Levy, B. 1993. Obstacles to Developing Indigenous Small and Medium Enterprises: An Empirical Assessment. *The World Bank Economic Review* 71: 65–83.

London Mail on Sunday. 1995. We Want No Part in Child Labour. January 8.

Madras Institute of Development Studies (MIDS). 1997. *Tamil Nadu's Urban Environmental Challenge: A Study of Eight Secondary Cities/Towns,* edited by Ajit Menon et al. Draft report. November. Chennai, India: MIDS.

Madras School of Economics. 1998. *Economic Analysis of Environmental Problems in Bleaching and Dyeing Units and Suggestions for Policy Action.* Supported by UNDP Project LARGE. Chennai, India.

McCormick, D., et al. 1997. Growth and Barriers to Growth Among Nairobi's Small and Medium-Sized Garment Producers. *World Development* 25(7): 1095–110.

Mead, D.C., and C. Liedholm. 1998. The Dynamics of Micro and Small Enterprises in Developing Countries. *World Development* 26(1): 61.

Mehta, S., et al. 1997. *Controlling Pollution: Incentives and Regulations.* New Delhi: Sage Publications.

Nadvi, K. 1997. The Cutting Edge: Collective Efficiency and International Competitiveness in Pakistan. IDS discussion paper 360. Sussex, U.K.: Institute of Development Studies.

National Environmental Engineering Research Institute (NEERI). 1992. Common Effluent Treatment Plant: State of the Art. Report sponsored by the Indian Ministry of Environment and Forests. Nagpur, India: NEERI.

New Indian Express. 2004. Dyeing Units Put Heads Together To Clean Noyyal. February 12.

Peace Trust. 2001. The Ruined River Basin Ecosystem in Tamil Nadu, India. Press Release for International Conference on Freshwater 2001. December 3–7.

Piore, M., and C. Sabel. 1984. *The Second Industrial Divide: Possibilities of Prosperity.* New York: Basic Books.

Prabhu, S. Indian Minister of Environment and Forests 1998. Speech at Harvard University, Cambridge, MA.

Prasad, B.M. No date. An Overview of Common Effluent Treatment Plants (CETPs) in India. Delhi: Indian Central Pollution Control Board.

Prithiviraj, S.M. 2002. Dirty Shirts: A Study of Health, Safety, and Environmental Concerns in the Context of the Garment Industry in Tirupur Region, India. Netherlands: Consumers' Association Goede Waar & Co. September.

Ragunathan, A.V. 1997. ETPs—Textile Units Face Hobson's Choice. *The Hindu.* April 28.

Rosenbaum, W. 1998. *Environmental Politics and Policy.* Washington, DC: Congressional Quarterly Press.

Sapru, R.K. 1998. Environmental Politics and Policy in India. In *Ecological Policy and Politics in Developing Countries: Economic Growth and Environment,* edited by Uday Desai. Albany, NY: SUNY Press. 153–82.

Sarangi, S., and G. Cohen. 1995. A Tale of Two Industrial Estates. *Economic and Political Weekly* June 17.

Sathe, S.P. 2002. *Judicial Activism in India: Transgressing Borders and Enforcing Limits,* 2nd ed. Oxford, U.K.: Oxford University Press.

Schmitz, H. 1982. Growth Constraints on Small-Scale Manufacturing in Developing Countries: A Critical Review. *World Development* 10(6): 429–50.

———. 1995. Small Shoemakers and Fordist Giants: Tale of a Supercluster. *World Development* 231: 9–28.

———. 1997. Collective Efficiency and Increasing Returns. Brighton, United Kingdom: Institute of Development Studies, University of Sussex. Working paper 50.

Semlinger, K. 1993. Public Support for Small Firm Networking in Baden-Wurttemberg. In *The Embedded Firm,* edited by G. Grabher. London: Routledge. 161–78.

Small Industries Development Bank of India (SIDBI). 1998. Annexure III: Comparative Statement for CETPs. Lucknow, India: SIDBI.

———. 1999. http://www.sidbi.com/english/corporate/corpprofile/profile/profile.asp (accessed April 1, 1999).

Swaminathan, P., and J. Jeyaranjan. 1994. The Knitwear Cluster in Tirupur: An Indian Industrial District in the Making. Working paper 126. Chennai, India: Madras Institute of Development Studies.

Tata Services, Ltd. 1998. *The Statistical Outline of India: 1997–98.* December. Tables 186 and 187.

Tewari, M. 1990. Understanding the Organization of Work: The State, Intersectoral Linkages, and the Historical Conditions of Accumulation in Ludhiana's Industrial Regime. Mimeo. Cambridge, MA: Department of Urban Studies and Planning, Massachusetts Institute of Technology.

———. 1995. *Centralized Treatment Facilities for Hazardous and Nonhazardous Waste Generated by Small- and Medium-Scale Industries in Newly Industrialized Countries.* Cincinnati: U.S. EPA.

Van Berkel, R. 2004. Assessment of the Impact of the DESIRE Project on the Uptake of Waste Minimization in Small Scale Industries in India 1993–1997. *Journal of Cleaner Production* 123: 269–81.

CHAPTER 9

Small Firms and Clean Technologies

Part I: Informal Brickmaking in Ciudad Juárez, Mexico

Allen Blackman and Geoffrey J. Bannister

As DISCUSSED IN CHAPTER 1, weak institutions, limited political support, and a host of other constraints hamper environmental management in developing countries, and these limitations are magnified when polluters are small-scale and informal. Recently, clean technologies—new technologies that mitigate environmental impacts without significantly raising production costs—have received considerable attention as a means of surmounting such problems. The hope is that firms will adopt such technologies voluntarily, or at least with minimal prodding, easing the burden on regulatory authorities. General endorsements of clean technologies are contained in both the seminal Brundtland Commission Report to the U.N. (World Commission on Environment and Development 1987) and the equally influential 1992 World Bank Development Report: Development and the Environment (World Bank 1992), and a number of anecdotal studies have emerged in the past several years (e.g., Maltzou 1992; Almeida 1993). Yet, to our knowledge, there has been no rigorous research on why informal firms (or even small-scale firms) do and do not adopt clean technologies. The well-developed empirical and theoretical literature on the diffusion of small-scale cost-saving innovations in developing countries is certainly broadly relevant, but it does not have much to say about the regulation, externalities, and peculiar political and economic considerations that undoubtedly have a significant impact on the diffusion of clean technologies.

As a first step toward filling this gap, we present the results of an econometric analysis of the diffusion of propane among informal "traditional" brickmakers in

Parts of this chapter were published as "Community Pressure and Clean Technology in the Informal Sector: An Econometric Analysis of the Adoption of Propane by Traditional Mexican Brickmakers" *Journal of Environmental Economics and Management* 35(1): 1–21, 1998.

Ciudad Juárez, Mexico. Our overall aim is to identify the principal determinants of the adoption of propane in Ciudad Juárez and to explore the implications for environmental management in developing countries.

The two key policy implications of our analysis are that it is possible to successfully promote the adoption of a clean technology by intensely competitive informal firms even when the new technology significantly raises variable costs, and community pressure applied by competing firms and private-sector local organizations can generate incentives for adoption, presumably even in the absence of formal regulatory pressure.

This chapter is organized as follows. The next section provides some background on traditional brickmaking in Ciudad Juárez. The section titled The Literature reviews the literature on the adoption of clean technologies and small-scale productivity-enhancing technologies. The section titled Model describes analytical and econometric models. The section titled Data and Variables discusses data. The section titled Results discusses our results. And the last section summarizes and concludes.

Background: Traditional Brickmaking in Ciudad Juárez

Chapters 2 and 4 provide detailed background on traditional brickmaking in Ciudad Juárez and on the early 1990s effort to introduce propane into the city's brickyards. We briefly summarize this material here, adding some new information that will prove relevant to the econometric analysis that is the focus of this chapter.

Principally fired with refuse such as used tires and scrap wood, which is often impregnated with toxic varnishes, Ciudad Juárez's approximately 330 traditional brickkilns are a leading contributor to air pollution in both Ciudad Juárez and its sister city, El Paso, Texas (See Chapter 2). Kiln emissions contribute to an urgent environmental problem as air quality in Ciudad Juárez and El Paso is the worst on the U.S.–Mexican border and among the worst in North America (Nuñez et al. 1994).[1] In addition, traditional kilns are a serious local health hazard to those living in and near Ciudad Juárez's eight brickmaking *colonias*.[2]

Traditional brickmaking in Ciudad Juárez is an extremely labor-intensive, low-technology activity. The four main tasks—mixing earth and clay, molding the mixture into bricks, drying the bricks in the sun, and firing them in a primitive adobe kiln—are all performed by hand. It is also small-scale and low-paying. On average, each kiln has a capacity of approximately 10,000 bricks, employs six workers, and generates profits on the order of $100 per month.[3] Socioeconomic conditions are poor. The majority of brickmakers live next to their kilns in primitive houses with no sewers or running water. On average, kiln owners have three years of schooling, and approximately a quarter are illiterate (FEMAP 1991).

Most of Ciudad Juárez's brickmakers are associated with one of two rival political factions. The first is made up of organizations affiliated with the historically dominant Institutional Revolutionary Party (PRI).[4] The second faction is dominated by the Committee for Popular Defense (CDP), which is linked to the national Worker's Party. The CDP has traditionally been opposed to the political establishment and has resisted all attempts to regulate brickmaking. In a July 1995 survey of 76 owners and managers of brickkilns in Ciudad Juárez (described below), 44% belonged to a PRI affiliate, 18% to the CDP, and the remaining 38% were independent.

As described in Chapter 4, in the early 1990s, a binational multisector coalition, led by a Ciudad Juárez-based nonprofit, the *Federación Mexicana de Asociaciones Privadas de Salud y Desarrolo Comunitario* (FEMAP), began an effort to introduce clean-burning propane into the brickmaking *colonias* of Ciudad Juárez. Faced with a daunting array of obstacles, including brickmakers' financing constraints; their seeming indifference to the adverse health impacts of burning debris; strong competitive pressures to use cheap, dirty fuels; and a virtual absence of regulatory pressure, the coalition put in place a number of inducements and sanctions aimed at encouraging adoption. Local propane companies provided free access to the equipment needed to burn propane.[5] Universities developed technical extension and health education courses. To improve enforcement of a widely ignored ban on the burning of debris, the municipal government of Ciudad Juárez set up a peer monitoring mechanism, wherein police were dispatched in response to citizen complaints about specific kilns burning toxic materials. Violators were fined and sometimes jailed. Finally, project organizers worked with leaders of local trade and community organizations to pressure brickmakers to adopt propane. In March 1993, the leaders of key brickmaker organizations were brought together to hammer out an agreement on clean fuels and to set a deadline for the adoption of propane. The PRI affiliates were in general quite cooperative, enforcing strict rules on permissible fuels in some brickyards. One important impetus for adoption developed autonomously as adoption proceeded—in an effort to avoid being undercut by competitors using cheap dirty fuels, those brickmakers who adopted pressured their competitors to switch as well.

Although adoption was frustratingly slow at first, by October 1993, an estimated 40–70% of brickmakers in Ciudad Juárez were using propane, a significant achievement given the obstacles involved. Unfortunately, almost all of this progress has been reversed since 1994 because of the nationwide reductions of longstanding Mexican subsidies on propane and a consequent dramatic increase in the price of propane relative to debris. Though relatively short-lived, this episode of adoption offers a rare opportunity to study clean technological change in the informal sector.

Note that the adoption of propane is best viewed as technological change rather than simple fuel switching because most brickmakers who adopted (hereafter "adopters") incurred substantial fixed costs in doing so and also made significant adjustments to the production process. Fixed costs consisted of transactions costs, learning costs, the costs of procuring a burner (the one piece of equipment that propane companies did not supply), and for most adopters, the costs of modifying the kiln to enable it to withstand the intense heat generated by propane.[6] A common change in the production process was a reduction in the number of laborers hired to help fire the kiln because propane eliminates the need to continuously shovel fuel into the firebox.

The Literature

This section briefly reviews relevant findings from the thin academic literature on the adoption of clean technologies in developing countries, as well as related literatures on the adoption of clean technologies in industrialized countries and on the adoption of small-scale productivity-enhancing technologies in developing countries.

The literature identifies two determinants of technological change that are unique to clean technologies: regulatory pressure and awareness of the private health benefits of adoption. The link between formal regulatory pressure and clean technological change is well-established in the theoretical literature (for a review, see Ecchia and Mariotti 1994) and recently, a number of researchers have found some empirical evidence for it (e.g., Jaffe and Stavins 1995). Even though financial and institutional constraints often preclude effective formal environmental regulation in developing countries (World Bank 1992), a growing body of recent research shows that community pressure—also known as "informal regulation"—applied by private-sector groups such as neighborhood organizations, nongovernmental organizations, and trade unions can substitute for formal regulatory pressure. For example, Pargal and Wheeler (1996) analyze data on releases of water pollution by Indonesian factories during a period when there was no effective national regulation for water pollution and find that lower releases were correlated with a set of proxies for community pressure, including per capita income, education, and population density in the vicinity of the plant (See also Hartman et al. 1997).

A second potential determinant of clean technological change is awareness of the private health benefits associated with adoption. For example, in a review of studies on the determinants of the adoption of improved cooking stoves in developing countries, Barnes et al. (1993) found that adopters often perceived reduced exposure to smoke to be the principal advantage of new stoves. Similarly, research on the diffusion of low-chemical pest control technologies shows that farmers often view reduced exposure to chemicals as an important benefit of adoption. (e.g., Antle and Pingali 1994)

The well-developed empirical and theoretical literature on the adoption of small-scale productivity-enhancing innovations in developing countries (for reviews, see Fransman and King 1984 and Feder et al. 1985) identifies a number of determinants of adoption that are potentially relevant, including input prices, firm size, credit availability, and human capital. Obviously, firms that face different input prices will have different technological preferences. For example, firms with access to cheap labor may prefer relatively labor-intensive technologies (e.g., Hill 1983).

The majority of the evidence indicates that large firms adopt many new technologies faster than small ones (e.g., Hayami 1984). The most obvious explanation is that adoption involves fixed costs that imply economies of scale. Fixed costs may arise from a capital indivisibility or from more subtle informational and transactions costs (Feder et al. 1985).

Considerable evidence suggests that lack of access to credit is a binding constraint on technological change for small firms (e.g., Levy 1993), even when fixed pecuniary costs of adoption are not large (e.g., Bhalla 1979).

Finally, there is a good deal of empirical evidence to support a positive correlation between adoption of new technologies and human capital as proxied by education, experience, or exposure to extension services (e.g., Lin 1991). The key idea is that to adopt new technologies, firms must first acquire the requisite technical and economic information—a costly enterprise. Information acquisition may be passive, with firms absorbing information via day-to-day contact with business associates, or it may be active, with firms engaging in training and technical extension programs. The oldest and best-known models of technology diffusion focus on the dissemination of information about new technologies via day-to-day contact among firms, likening this process to the spread of a disease (Mansfield 1961).

Model

This section develops analytical and econometric models of a brickmaker's choice between a clean firing technology and a dirty firing technology, models that formalize the discussion of the determinants of clean technological change in the section titled The Literature. We assume that each brickmaker chooses a firing technology and a vector of input quantities to minimize the discounted present value of the total cost of firing a kiln load of premolded bricks subject to a production function. Brickmakers choose between a clean technology and a dirty one indexed by $i \in (c,d)$. Time is indexed by $t = (0,1 \ldots \tau)$. Total costs are made up of variable costs and fixed costs. Variable costs, paid by both adopters and nonadopters, are equal to the dot product of a vector of input quantities, $\mathbf{X}_{it}$, and a vector of input prices, $\mathbf{V}_{it}$. In addition, adopters must pay a one-time fixed cost of adoption, which is broken down into two components: nonpecuniary fixed transactions and learning costs, $T_{c0}(\bullet)$, and pecuniary fixed costs, $F_{c0}(\bullet)$. Nonadopters obviously do not pay fixed adoption costs but must pay fixed perceived health costs, H_{dt}, and fixed regulatory costs, $R_{dt}(\bullet)$, in each period. All recurrent costs—H_{dt}, $R_{dt}(\bullet)$, and $\mathbf{X}_{it}\mathbf{V}_{it}$—are discounted using a subjective discount rate, θ.

Some of the fixed costs are functions of underlying brickmaker characteristics. Pecuniary fixed costs are assumed to be decreasing in wealth, w_t, because poor brickmakers lack collateral that would enable them to finance investment at prime interest rates. In addition, pecuniary fixed costs are assumed to be increasing in output, y_t, because larger kilns require more modification. Nonpecuniary fixed costs are assumed to be decreasing in human capital, u_t, because more educated and experienced brickmakers learn the new technology more quickly. Finally, regulatory costs are assumed to be an increasing function of formal government regulatory pressure, g_t, and community pressure, o_t.

The restricted production function, $y_{it}(\mathbf{X}_{it}; u_t, k_t)$ is a twice differentiable, increasing concave function of input quantities holding constant levels of human capital and physical capital, k_t.

Thus the brickmaker's optimization problem may be written

$$\min_{(\mathbf{X}_{it},i)} \int_0^\tau [\mathbf{X}_{it}\mathbf{V}_{it} + H_{it} + R_{it}(g_t,o_t)]e^{-\theta t}dt + F_{i0}(y_0,w_0) + T_{i0}(u_0) \quad (9\text{-}1)$$

subject to

$$y_{it} = y_i(\mathbf{X}_{it}; u,k) \quad t = (0, 1, \dots \tau)$$

where for nonadopters,

$$F_{d0}(w_0,y_0) = T_{d0}(u_0) = 0$$

and for adopters,

$$H_{ct} = R_{ct}(g_t,o_t) = 0 \qquad t = (0, 1, \dots \tau)$$

The brickmaker will choose vectors of cost-minimizing input quantities for each period, that, in turn, imply restricted (variable) cost functions of the form

$$C_{it}(k_t,u_t,\mathbf{V}_{it},y_t) \quad i = (c,d) \; t = (0, 1, \dots \tau) \tag{9-2}$$

Thus, the present discounted value of minimized total costs for each technology may be written

$$D_i(g_t,k_t,o_t,u_t,\mathbf{V}_{it},w_0,y_t) =$$

$$\int_0^\tau [C_{it}(k_t,u_t,\mathbf{V}_{it},y_t) + H_{it} + R_{it}(g_t,o_t)]e^{-\theta t}dt + F_{i0}(y_0,w_0) + T_{i0}(u_0) \quad i = (c,d)$$

$$\tag{9-3}$$

To be able to write D_i as a function of period 0 costs, we assume that brickmakers know the intertemporal paths of the costs H_{ct}, R_{ct}, and C_{it}.[7] More specifically, we assume that the time path of each of these costs may be described by an equation of the form

$$R_{ct} = R_{c0}f_R(t)$$

where $f_R(t)$ is a bounded, nonnegative function of time. Then total minimized costs may be written

$$D_i(g_0,k_0,o_0,u_0,\mathbf{V}_{i0},w_0,y_0) =$$

$$S_{iC}C_{i0}(k_0,u_0,\mathbf{V}_{i0},y_0) + S_R R_{i0}(g_0,o_0) + S_H H_{i0} + F_{i0}(w_0,y_0) + T_{i0}(u_0) \quad i = (c,d) \tag{9-4}$$

where

$$S_{iC} = \int_0^\tau f_{Ci}(t)e^{-\theta t}dt \qquad i = (c,d)$$

$$S_H = \int_0^\tau f_H(t)e^{-\theta t}dt$$

$$S_R = \int_0^\tau f_R(t)e^{-\theta t}dt$$

The brickmaker chooses between the two technologies by calculating the difference between the present discounted value of the minimized total costs associated with each, a quantity we shall call I^*, that is,

$$I^* = D_d(g_0, k_0, o_0, u_0, \mathbf{V}_{d0}, y_0) - D_c(k_0, u_0, \mathbf{V}_{c0}, w_0, y_0) \tag{9-5}$$

The brickmaker will adopt as long as $I^* > 0$. Using equation 9-4, I^* may be written as

$$I^* = S_{dC}C_{d0}(k_0, u_0, \mathbf{V}_{d0}, y_0) - S_{cC}C_{c0}(k_0, u_0, \mathbf{V}_{d0}, y_0) + \{S_H H_{i0} + S_R R_{i0}(g_0, o_0) - F_{i0}(w_0, y_0) - T_{i0}(u_0)\} \tag{9-6}$$

Our econometric model is a reduced form of equation 9-6.[8] We estimate

$$I^*_j = \beta_d C^*_{dj} - \beta_c C^*_{cj} + \mathbf{Z}_j \gamma + e_j \tag{9-7}$$

where

j = an index for individual brickmaking firms;

I^*_j = an unobserved latent variable;

C^*_{dj} = firm j's true variable cost of using the dirty technology;

C^*_{cj} = firm j's true variable cost of using the clean technology;

$\mathbf{Z}_j$ = a vector of firm-specific variables that influence fixed costs;

β_i = a parameter;

γ = a vector of parameters; and

e_j = an error term.[9]

Though I^*_j is latent and unobserved, we do observe an indicator variable, I_j, which takes the value of 1 if the clean technology is adopted and 0 otherwise, that is, we observe

$I_j = 1$ if $I^*_j > 0$

$I_j = 0$ if $I^*_j \leq 0$

Note that the observed variable cost depends on whether the brickmaker has adopted, that is, we observe

C^*_{cj} if $I^*_j > 0$

C^*_{dj} if $I^*_j \leq 0$

but we never observe both C^*_{cj} and C^*_{dj}. Therefore, to generate the variable-cost terms in equation 7 for the entire sample, we estimate variable-cost functions for adopters and nonadopters. We use a simple restricted Cobb–Douglas functional form:

$$C^*_{cj} = \alpha_c + \mathbf{P}_{cj}\partial_c + \mathbf{K}_j\psi_c + \phi_c Y_j + \eta_{cj} \tag{9-8}$$

$$C^*_{dj} = \alpha_d + \mathbf{P}_{dj}\partial_d + \mathbf{K}_j\psi_d + \phi_d Y_j + \eta_{dj} \tag{9-9}$$

where

$\mathbf{P}_{ij}$ is a row vector of logarithms of variable input prices for each firm, some of which depend on i, the index of c, d;

$\mathbf{K}_j$ is a row vector of measures of fixed factors;

Y_j is the logarithm output;

α_i is a parameter;

ϕ_i is a parameter;

∂_i is a vector of parameters;

ψ_i is a vector of parameters; and

η_{ij} is an error term.

   Equations 9-7, 9-8, and 9-9 constitute a simultaneous equation model. A simple recursive approach—estimating equations 9-8 and 9-9 using ordinary least squares, using the parameters to generate the relative cost terms on the right-hand side of the adoption equation, and finally estimating the adoption equation as a probit— will *not*, in general, yield consistent parameter estimates because of sample selection bias. Technically, selection bias exists if the expected values of the error terms in the cost regressions conditional on the choice of technology are not zero, that is, if $E(\eta_{ij} \mid I^*_j = 1) \neq 0$. Intuitively, selection bias may arise because we do not observe both C^*_{gj} and C^*_{dj} for each brickmaker in the sample; we observe C^*_{gj} only for one subset of the sample (adopters) and C^*_{dj} only for a second subset (nonadopters). These subsets are not likely to be randomly constituted. Rather, the group of adopters may well posses certain *unobserved* characteristics, such as managerial skills and political ties that predispose them to have relatively low costs no matter which technology they use. Therefore, in a simple recursive model, selection bias could generate a spurious correlation between variable cost and adoption.

   To correct for possible selection bias, we use the two-stage estimation procedure proposed by Lee (1981). The object is to adjust the error terms of the cost functions so that they have zero means. In the first stage, we substitute equation 9-8 and equation 9-9 into equation 9-7 to obtain a reduced-form adoption equation:

$$I^*_j = \mathbf{P}j\lambda_1 + \mathbf{K}_j\lambda_2 + \lambda_3 Y_j + \mathbf{Z}_j\lambda_4 + \upsilon_j \tag{9-10}$$

where the λs are parameters or vectors of parameters and υ_j is an error term. In the second stage, we use ordinary least squares (OLS) to estimate

$$C_{gj} = \alpha_c + \mathbf{P}_{gj}\partial_c + \mathbf{K}_j\psi_c + \phi_c Y_j + \delta_c\{-n(p_j)/N(p_j)\} + \mu_{gj} \tag{9-11}$$

$$C_{dj} = \alpha_d + \mathbf{P}_{dj}\partial_d + \mathbf{K}_j\psi_d + \phi_d Y_j + \delta_d\{n(p_j)/[1-N(p_j)]\} + \mu_{dj} \tag{9-12}$$

where $N(\bullet)$ is the cumulative distribution function of the standard normal, $n(\bullet)$ is its density function, p_j is the predicted value of the indicator variable in equation 10, and δ_i is a parameter. As long as the joint density of η_{gj}, η_{ij}, and υ_j is multivariate normal, these modified cost functions will have the property that $E(\eta_{ij} \mid I^*_j = 1) = E(\eta_{ij} \mid I^*_j = 0) = 0$ and will yield consistent parameter estimates. We use equations 9-11 and 9-12 to generate the predicted cost terms. Finally, we estimate equation 9-7 as a simple probit.

Data and Variables

We use data from an original July 1995 survey of the owners or managers of 95 traditional brickkilns in Ciudad Juárez.[10] Of these, 19 records were later dropped because of missing information, leaving 76 complete records. Table 9-1 presents summary statistics for the complete sample, as well as for subsamples of adopters (n = 47) and nonadopters (n = 29). Because by July 1995, virtually every brickmaker in Ciudad Juárez who had been using propane had already reverted to debris (again, due to the elimination of subsidies on propane), the survey solicited recall data for a uniform base month—October 1993—judged to be the month during which most brickmakers in Ciudad Juárez were using propane.

To estimate cost functions we use data on six variables: output (CAPKLN); two variable inputs, labor (L) and fuel (F); a measure of physical capital, truck ownership (TRK); and two measures of human capital, years making bricks (BKYRS) and years of formal education (EDYRS). Output is measured as the average number of standard-size bricks produced per firing less breakage (output is equal to

Table 9-1. *Variables in the Econometric Model*

		Adopters (n=47)		Nonadopters (n=29)		All (n=76)	
		Mean	S.D.	Mean	S.D.	Mean	S.D.
Endogenous							
LPG	Adopt (1/0)	1	0	0	0	0.62	0.49
VC	Variable cost ($N)	927.05	297.64	380.65	174.84	718.55	370.16
Exogenous							
BKYRS	Experience (years)	18.04	10.98	12.33	8.91	15.86	10.56
EDYRS	Education (years)	3.54	2.87	2.69	2.75	3.22	2.84
GREG	Awareness of government regulations (1/0)	0.74	0.44	0.79	0.41	0.76	0.43
HEALTH	Propane "healthier" (1/0)	0.17	0.38	0.03	0.19	0.12	0.33
HOUSE	Owns house (1/0)	0.87	0.34	0.83	0.38	0.86	0.35
CAPKLN	Capacity of kiln (1000 bricks)	10.62	3.10	8.38	2.44	9.76	3.05
LORGPRI	Member of a PRI affiliate (1/0)	0.60	0.50	0.21	0.41	0.44	0.50
LD-SAT	*Colonia* Satelite (1/0)	0.32	0.47	0.03	0.19	0.21	0.41
LD-M68	*Colonia* México 68 (1/0)	0.28	0.45	0.52	0.51	0.37	0.49
LD-K20	*Colonia* Kilómetro 20 (1/0)	0.17	0.38	0.41	0.50	0.26	0.44
LD-FV/DN	*Colonia* Francisco Villa/División del Norte (1/0)	0.23	0.43	0.03	0.19	0.15	0.37
PL	Price labor ($N/firing)	104.06	34.45	97.14	53.21	101.42	42.39
PFP	Price LPG ($N/1000 liters)	414.77	117.22	n/a	n/a	414.77	117.22
PFD	Price debris ($N/truckload)	n/a	n/a	147.37	70.17	147.37	70.17
TRK	Owns truck (1/0)	0.85	0.36	0.66	0.48	0.78	0.42

kiln capacity because the kiln is only fired when full). Therefore, inputs are measured in units per firing. Quantity of labor is measured as the total number of workers used to fire the kiln adjusted for the contribution of the owner. If the kiln is fired with family or unpaid labor, wages are those that the owner reported he would have paid for hired labor. Wages are in pesos (N) per laborer per firing.[11] For propane, quantity is measured in thousands of liters per firing. Prices are in pesos per thousand liters. For debris, quantity data was poor because the common metric was a truckload of variable size. We used survey data on total cost of debris per firing and price per truckload to derive quantity measured in an arbitrary unit we call truckloads. Prices are in pesos per truckload.

To estimate the probit adoption function, we use data on 13 variables that are associated with fixed health, regulatory, and transactions costs in the manner hypothesized in the analytical model presented in the section titled The Literature. Fixed regulatory costs for the dirty technology are hypothesized to depend on both formal regulatory pressure and community pressure and, as discussed in the section titled Background: Traditional Brickmaking in Ciudad Juárez, both types of pressure seem to have had some real impact. Unfortunately, finding a good exogenous firm-specific measure of formal regulatory pressure proved difficult. The most easily observed measure, instances of enforcement, is obviously correlated with adoption because nonadopters are more likely to have experienced such instances. We use a dichotomous variable that indicates simple knowledge of the existence of laws banning certain types of fuel (GREG).

Our proxy for community pressure, a dichotomous variable indicating membership in a PRI-affiliated local organization (LORGPRI), purports to capture the pressure that PRI affiliates applied on their members to adopt propane. Recall that 44% of the brickmakers in our sample belonged to PRI-affiliated neighborhood and trade organizations, which actively cooperated with efforts to promote the adoption of propane, in some cases enforcing strict rules on permissible fuels.

To proxy for perceived fixed health costs associated with burning debris, we use a dichotomous variable (HEALTH), indicating an affirmative response to the question, "Is burning propane healthier than burning debris?"

In the analytical model, fixed pecuniary transactions costs associated with adoption of the clean technology are a function of firm size and wealth, whereas nonpecuniary fixed transaction costs are a function of human capital. We use kiln capacity (CAPKLN) to proxy for firm size. To measure wealth, we use a dummy variable for home ownership (HOUSE). We use the same measures of human capital in the adoption regression as in the cost functions: years making bricks (BKYRS) and years of formal education (EDYRS).

Finally, we control for fixed location effects in a separate model using location dummies for *colonia* Satelite (LD-SAT), *colonia* México 68 (LD-M68), *colonia* Kilómetro 20 (LD-K20), and an amalgamation of two small neighboring *colonias*, Francisco Villa and División del Norte (LD-FV/DN).

Results

Table 9-2 presents the OLS selectivity-corrected estimates of the parameters of the cost functions. The selectivity term is constructed from the residuals of a reduced form probit (equation 9-10) and as a result depends on the specification of the adoption equation. Therefore, we report cost function parameter estimates for each of our two adoption models.

For adopters, regression results are consistent across both models. Estimated coefficients for both input prices are significantly different from 0 at the 1% level and have the expected sign. None of the coefficients on either the output or the capital measures are significantly different from zero. The selectivity variable is significant in Model 2.

For nonadopters, the estimated coefficient for labor prices is significantly different from 0 at the 1% level and has the expected sign in both models. However, the coefficient for fuel prices is not significantly different from 0 in either model. The most likely explanation is that, having been imputed from total costs, debris prices were measured with error.[12] None of the coefficients on the output or capital

Table 9-2. *Cost Function Estimates Corrected for Selection Bias*

Variable		Adopter		Nonadopter	
		Model 1	Model 2	Model 1	Model 2
	Intercept	-0.463	-0.015	2.445	2.722
		(1.135)	(1.108)	(2.023)	(2.210)
PL	Ln price labor	0.357**	0.385**	0.871**	0.821**
		(0.097)	(0.093)	(0.108)	(0.116)
PF	Ln price fuel	0.643**	0.615**	0.129	0.179
		(0.097)	(0.093)	(0.108)	(0.116)
CAPKLN	Ln output	0.177	0.137	-0.153	-0.188
		(0.122)	(0.118)	(0.222)	(0.243)
EDYRS	Education	0.014	0.014	0.009	0.005
		(0.015)	(0.014)	(0.023)	(0.025)
BKYRS	Experience	0.002	-0.001	0.008	0.008
		(0.004)	(0.004)	(0.007)	(0.008)
TRK	Owns truck	0.058	0.075	0.007	0.003
		(0.097)	(0.093)	(0.136)	(0.149)
$-n(p_i)/N(p_i)$ or $n(p_i)/[1-N(p_i)]$	Selectivity term	0.00005	0.02560†	0.035†	0.006
		(0.00182)	(0.01313)	(0.018)	(0.013)
	Sample size	47	47	29	29
	F value	5.667	6.839	4.060	3.003
	Adjusted R^2	0.378	0.432	0.396	0.300

**Significant at 1% level two tailed test.

†Significant at 10% level two tailed test.

measures are significantly different from 0. The coefficient for selectivity variable is significantly different from 0 in Model 1.

The cost functions confirm evidence indicating that propane was considerably more costly to use than debris. For the two models, the average ratio of the mean predicted variable cost of firing with propane to the mean predicted variable cost of firing with debris is 2.13 (see Table 9-3). Evidently, any savings in labor costs that accrued to propane users were swamped by the higher energy costs.

Table 9-4 reports the results of the two probit adoption models. Of our proxies for nonpecuniary transaction costs associated with adoption—years of experience (BKYRS) and years of education (EDYRS)—the coefficient on the former has the expected sign and is significantly different from 0 at the 1% level in both models, and the coefficient on the latter has the expected sign and is significantly different from 0 at the 5% level in the second model.[13] Thus, more experienced brickmakers and more highly educated ones were more likely to adopt.

The coefficients on our proxies for pecuniary transaction costs associated with adoption—house ownership (HOUSE) and kiln size (CAPKLN)—are insignificant in both models. This result is not surprising. Other studies have found that wealth and firm size are correlated with adoption when adoption entails substantial fixed pecuniary costs that large, wealthy firms can pay more easily than small, poor firms. However, in the present case, local community groups heavily subsidized the fixed pecuniary costs of adoption by providing free propane equipment, greatly reducing the advantages conferred by size and wealth.[14]

The coefficient on our proxy for the perceived fixed health costs associated with burning debris, HEALTH, has the expected sign and is significantly different from 0 at the 10% level in both models. Though suggestive, this result should be interpreted cautiously for two reasons. First, only 8 of the 47 adopters in our sample believed that firing with propane was healthier than firing with debris, so that this belief cannot have played a role in the adoption decisions of most brickmakers. Second, this result does not necessarily imply that brickmakers who believed that burning propane was relatively healthy adopted propane as a result. The causation may have run in the opposite direction—adopters may have concluded that propane was healthier than debris after they adopted.

The coefficients on our predicted variable cost terms are not significantly different from 0 in either model. We strongly suspect that at bottom this result stems from the fact that, although our price and quantity data are undoubtedly noisy, *true* cross-sectional variation in factor prices and factor productivities was limited

Table 9-3. *Average Predicted Variable Costs of Using Propane and Debris per 1000 Bricks ($N) (average for Models 1 and 2)*

	October 1993	July 1995 (imputed)
Propane	98.56	147.59
Debris	46.32	51.97
Ratio	2.13	2.84

Note: $n=76$.

Table 9-4. *Probit Adoption Function Estimates*

	Variable	Model 1	Model 2
	Intercept	−2.476*	−0.698
		(1.121)	(1.459)
BKYRS	Experience	0.052**	0.056**
		(0.020)	(0.022)
EDYRS	Education	0.090	0.197*
		(0.070)	(0.093)
HEALTH	LPG "healthier"	1.293†	1.302†
		(0.766)	(0.812)
HOUSE	Owns house	0.375	0.066
		(0.540)	(0.668)
GREG	Aware of city regulations	−0.655	−0.433
		(0.454)	(0.536)
CAPKLN	Capacity of kiln	0.095	0.095
		(0.082)	(0.099)
PVCLP	Predicted cost of LPG	0.026	0.028
	($N 100)	(0.138)	(0.170)
PVCD	Predicted cost debris	0.076	−0.091
	($N 100)	(0.175)	(0.233)
LORGPRI	Member of a PRI affiliate	0.908*	0.481
		(0.414)	0.502
LD-SAT	*Colonia* Satelite		0.033
			(1.045)
LD-M68	*Colonia* México 68		−1.916*
			(0.817)
LD-K20	*Colonia* Kilómetro 20		−1.383*
			(0.796)
	Sample size	76	76
	Log likelihood	−35.421	−29.267

*Significant at 5% level two tailed test.

**Significant at 1% level two tailed test.

†Significant at 10% level two tailed test.

because factor markets within Ciudad Juárez were competitive and simple firing technologies were more or less uniform across brickmakers. As a result, the ratio of the per-brick variable costs associated with the two technologies was approximately 2 to 1 for all brickmakers. Hence, cross-sectional differences in variable costs did not drive the pattern of adoption observed in October 1993. Rather, this pattern was shaped by cross-sectional differences in fixed costs, namely, regulatory costs, perceived health costs, learning costs, and transaction costs.[15]

Given the evident lack of true cross-sectional variation in variable costs, our cross-sectional analysis cannot tell us much about the sensitivity of adoption to changes in variable costs. However, we can get a rough idea of this sensitivity by noting that in July 1995, by which time propane had disappeared from the brick-yards of Ciudad Juárez, the ratio of the per-brick variable costs of using propane vs. debris was 25% higher than it had been in late 1993, when the majority of brickmakers were using propane (see Table 9-3).[16] Thus, the 2-to-1 ratio of per-brick variable costs that existed in October 1993 was probably approximately the maximum that was politically sustainable.

The coefficient on our proxy for the formal regulatory costs associated with burning debris, GREG, is not significantly different from 0 in either model. We suspect that the data for GREG was corrupted by measurement error. Although almost one-quarter of our survey respondents claimed to have been ignorant of any formal regulation regarding permissible fuels, leading us to believe that GREG would be a good proxy for formal regulatory pressure, there are indications that a number of these respondents were feigning ignorance, perhaps because they were hesitant to admit awareness of rules that had been violated. If this is in fact what happened (i.e., if virtually the entire sample was aware of government regulation), then GREG, even if accurately measured, would not be a particularly good proxy for formal regulation.

Finally, in Model 1, our proxy for the informal regulatory costs associated with burning debris, LORGPRI, is significantly different from 0 at the 5% level. This suggests that community pressure brought to bear by PRI-affiliated local organizations played an important role in brickmakers' adoption decisions.

However, alternative explanations are possible. Because membership in PRI-affiliated local organizations is correlated with location (see Table 9-5), LORG-PRI may proxy for location-specific effects that promote adoption. To test this hypothesis, we introduce location dummies in Model 2. In this new model, the coefficient on LORGPRI is not significantly different from 0, but the coefficients on two of the three location dummies are. This suggests that location-specific effects were in fact important.

What exactly were these location-specific effects? One candidate is localized information dissemination, long a principal focus of technology diffusion research

Table 9-5. *Survey Respondents, Percent Adopters, and Percent PRI Affiliate Members by Colonia*

Colonia	Survey respondents	% Adopters	% PRI affiliate members
México 68	28	46†	36
Kilometro 20	20	40*	20*
Satelite	16	58	58†
Francisco Villa/ División del Norte	12	92*	42
Total	76	62	43

Note: n=76.

*Significantly different from sample mean at 5% level.

†Significantly different from sample mean at 10% level.

(e.g., Mansfield 1961). Put more concretely, the spatial concentration of adoption may have stemmed from the fact that brickmakers in *colonias* where a select few adopted early on were able to acquire information about the new technology from their neighbors at relatively low cost and were therefore apt to adopt themselves.

A second possibility is that the spatial concentration of adoption arose from a type of community pressure that is not captured by LORGPRI: the pressure to switch to propane that adopters placed on all nonadopters—regardless of their political affiliation—to avoid being undercut by brickmakers using cheap, dirty fuels. The intensity of this pressure would have been location-specific because the proportion of adopters differed markedly across *colonias* (see Table 9-5).

A third possibility is that community pressure applied by local organizations did actually drive the spatial pattern of adoption, but that location dummies capture this effect better than LORGPRI does. This could happen if, in *colonias* like Fransisco Villa that were dominated by PRI affiliates, PRI leaders were able to induce brickmakers of all political persuasions to adopt.[17]

Ultimately, our data do not allow us to disentangle the effects of localized information dissemination and community pressure in the econometric analysis. However, additional survey data support the hypothesis that community pressure was in fact an important, if not a critical, determinant of adoption. Some 25% of the adopters we surveyed identified "outside pressure" as the most important factor affecting their decision to adopt, as high a percentage as chose any other factor, whereas only 9% picked "information provided by various parties" (see Table 9-6). In addition, 64% of the 48 local organization members we surveyed said that a local organization (not necessarily their own) had an influence on their current (July 1995) choice of fuels, and a third of these respondents volunteered the information that the local organization prohibited the use of dirty fuels, such as tires and plastics. We would expect that, in October 1993 at the height of the propane initiative, pressures applied by local organizations to burn clean fuels would have been stronger and more pervasive.

Table 9-6. *Seven Factors Affecting Adoption: Percent of Adopters Identifying Each as "Most Important"*

Factor	Percent
Outside pressure	25
Good for environment	25
Access to free LPG equipment	21
Information provided by city et al.	9
LPG is more convenient	8
LPG suppliers extended credit	6
Other	7
Total	100

Note: n = 44.

Conclusion

To sum up briefly, our econometric results indicate that, first, on average, the variable cost of burning propane was more than two times greater than the variable cost of burning debris in October 1993. Second, the adoption of propane was correlated with the brickmakers': human capital, awareness of the health costs of burning debris, location, and (most likely) exposure to community pressure. And finally, for reasons discussed above, we observed no significant correlation between adoption and our measures of the brickmakers': wealth, firm size, exposure to government regulation, and variable costs. What are the policy implications of these findings?

One important implication is that it is possible to successfully promote the adoption of a clean technology by intensely competitive informal firms even when the new technology significantly increases variable costs and imposes considerable one-time fixed costs. In Ciudad Juárez, this success was the result of an organized effort to simultaneously lower the fixed costs of adoption and raise the costs of nonadoption by supplying equipment, training, and education free of charge and by ratcheting up both formal and informal penalties for continuing to burn debris.

Our finding that the adoption of propane is likely to have been correlated with the intensity of community pressure extends a growing body of recent research that shows that even in countries where financial and institutional constraints preclude effective public-sector monitoring and enforcement, community pressure can take up at least some of the slack. Most of the existing research concerns large-scale polluters, and some authors (e.g., Almeida 1993) have suggested that because small-scale firms have a relatively low profile and are generally viewed more sympathetically than large firms, they are not likely to be susceptible to community pressure. Our findings suggest otherwise.

Ironically, one reason that community pressure may work in the informal sector has to do with the intense competition among small-scale firms. In Ciudad Juárez, adopters were at a competitive disadvantage compared to nonadopters. Therefore, they had an incentive to ensure that at least neighbors and fellow union members switched to propane as well. This suggests that, in general, if enough informal firms can be convinced by hook or crook to adopt a clean technology, eventually competition will ensure that diffusion becomes self-perpetuating, even if the clean technology increases costs.

Several qualifications regarding community pressure in the informal sector are in order. First, as discussed above, because we cannot disentangle the impacts of location-specific information effects from community pressure, our results must be interpreted cautiously. Second, our results should not be interpreted as evidence that community pressure can be effective without public-sector support because in Ciudad Juárez the municipal government was instrumental in providing both carrots and sticks, which led PRI-affiliated organizations to cooperate with the propane effort. Third, in our case study, effective community pressure depended largely on the fact that neighbors could easily observe violations because they could see or smell emissions from burning debris. Other types of informal-sector pollution, such as the dumping of waste oil into sewers by mechanics, is not as easy to detect.

Finally, our finding that the adoption of propane was correlated with human capital and was weakly correlated with the perception that burning debris is relatively unhealthy echoes the conclusions of other studies of technological change in developing countries and suggests that training and education, in particular the dissemination of information about the health risks associated with dirty technologies, can be an effective means of promoting adoption.

Acknowledgments

We are grateful to Billy Pizer, Anna Alberini, Ray Kopp, two anonymous referees, our excellent research assistants, Brian Kropp and Maria Elena Meléndez, and our student enumerators in Ciudad Juárez, Magda Alarcon, Pablo Reyes, and Simon Vega. Special thanks to FEMAP, Octavio Chavez, Nancy Lowery, Carlos Rincon, and the brickmakers of Ciudad Juárez. Finally, we gratefully acknowledge the financial support of the Tinker Foundation.

Notes

1. In 1995, the city of El Paso was classified by the U.S. Environmental Protection Agency as a "moderate" nonattainment area for both carbon monoxide and particulate matter, and El Paso County was classified as a "serious" nonattainment area for ozone.

2. These *colonias* are Anapra, División del Norte, Francisco Villa, Fronteriza Baja, Kilómetro 20, México 68, Satelite, and Senecu 2.

3. This compares to the March 1996 monthly minimum wage in the north of Mexico of about $64 (Banco de Mexico 1996).

4. The three principal PRI affiliates are the Federation of Mexican Workers (CTM), the National Federation of Citizens' Organizations (FNOC), and the PRI-affiliated Brickmakers' Union.

5. In most cases, the equipment was attached to a trailer that was moved from kiln to kiln as needed. Although enforcement during this period was relatively vigorous, it was never universally effective; at least 30% of brickmakers continued to burn debris throughout.

6. Modifications generally consisted of reinforcing kiln walls, rebuilding the firebox with high-quality bricks, or changing the height of the firebox. Some 54% of the adopters in our sample made such modifications.

7. We require a model in which D_i is a function of period 0 costs because we do not have a panel of data that would enable us to estimate a true intertemporal model. The assumption that brickmakers know the intertemporal path of costs is less restrictive than the alternative assumptions, which yield the same result: agents choose a technology by simply comparing the costs and benefits that accrue in period 0 (e.g., Lin 1991; Shrestha and Gopalakrishnan 1993); or costs are stationary, in which case agents' input demands are identical in each period and the intertemporal model collapses to a static one. We are grateful to Billy Pizer for discussions on this point.

8. Our model is similar to those used by Pitt and Sumodiningrat (1991) and Shrestha and Gopalakrishnan (1993).

9. To be able to estimate the model with our data, we are forced to make a number of assumptions and abstractions. First, we implicitly assume that the discount factors, S_{iCj}, S_{Hj}, and S_{Rj}, and therefore discount rates, θ_j, are constant across brickmakers. We note, however, that the

literature suggests that discount rates may vary considerably across producers (Pender 1996). Second, we abstract entirely from uncertainty, which is often a significant influence on investment decisions (Pindyck 1991) and may have been a factor here, given movements in propane prices. If uncertainty about propane prices did discourage adoption, then our model is misspecified because our measure of the stream of variable costs associated with the clean technology, C^*_g, does not include the monetized utility costs of this uncertainty. As a result, β_c may be biased away from zero. Finally, we abstract from variations in producers' risk attitudes, which may also have been significant (Antle 1987).

10. The survey was administered by personal interview. The interviews were conducted by the two coauthors and four paid assistants. Some 89% of the respondents in our sample were kiln owners and the remainder were managers. We interviewed managers only when kilns had absentee owners and declined to interview hired workers when managers were absent. Because they were relatively inaccessible, we did not sample in three brickmaking *colonias* in Ciudad Juárez—Anapra, Fronteriza Baja, and Senecu 2. According to the Municipal Environmental Authority, only 9% of the kilns in Ciudad Juárez are located in these *colonias* (Dirección Municipal de Ecología de Ciudad Juárez 1995).

11. Most of the tasks involved in brickmaking other than firing—molding bricks, loading and unloading the kiln, and transporting bricks—are performed by hired laborers who are paid standard piece rates. As a result, there is little variation in the per-brick costs of these tasks across firms. Moreover, these tasks are functionally independent from firing. For these reasons, we assume that the cost function is separable between firing and the piece rate tasks and disregard the latter. Thus, the cost function gives the variable costs of firing, holding all other costs constant.

12. Measurement error would also explain why estimated cost shares for fuel seem to be biased downward: The estimates are 13% and 18%, although the actual average cost share is 57%.

13. The insignificance of years of education in Model 1, which does not control for location effects, suggests that this variable is a good predictor of adoption within *colonias* but not across them.

14. Our finding that wealth is not a significant predictor of adoption is robust to our choice of a wealth proxy. Our data set includes dummy variables indicating whether each brickmaker owns a television, a fan, a car, and a truck, and whether each has an alternative source of income. When substituted for HOUSE in the adoption regressions, none of these dummy variables was significantly correlated with adoption.

15. This finding does not imply that *intertemporal* changes in variable costs had no effect on brickmakers' adoption decisions—they obviously did—only that *cross-sectional* variation in variable costs does not explain which brickmakers had adopted in October 1993 and which had not.

16. For 1995 factor quantities, we used 1993 values. For 1995 debris and labor prices, we used actual survey data on 1995 prices. For 1995 propane prices, we used 1993 values adjusted by a growth factor based on a propane price series that FEMAP has provided. Finally, we assumed that kiln capacity, years of education, years of brickmaking experience, and number of trucks are at the 1993 levels.

17. Access to propane equipment did not differ significantly across *colonias* and is therefore not likely to have driven the spatial concentration of adoption. Our survey data suggest that access to equipment was universal; every adopter in our sample acknowledged using free equipment, and no nonadopters cited lack of access to equipment as having played a role in their decision not to adopt.

References

Almeida, C. 1993. Development and Transfer of Environmentally Sound Technologies in Manufacturing: A Survey. United Nations Conference on Trade and Development (UNCTAD) discussion paper 58. Geneva: UNCTAD.

Antle, J. 1987. Econometric Estimation of Producers' Risk Attitudes. *American Journal of Agricultural Economics* 69: 509–22.

Antle, J., and P. Pingali. 1994. Pesticides, Productivity, and Farmer Health: A Philippine Case Study. *American Journal of Agricultural Economics* 73: 418–30.

Banco de Mexico. 1996. *The Mexican Economy 1995*. Mexico City: Banco de Mexico.

Barnes, D., et al. 1993. What Makes People Cook with Improved Biomass Stoves: A Comparative International Review of Stove Programs. World Bank technical paper 242, Energy Series. Washington, DC: World Bank.

Bhalla, S. 1979. Farm and Technological Change in Indian Agriculture. In *Agrarian Structure and Productivity in Developing Countries,* edited by R. Berry and W. Cline. Baltimore: Johns Hopkins University Press.

Dirección Municipal de Ecología de Ciudad Juárez. 1995. "Complaints According to Their Origin" and "Juárez Kiln Distribution." Ciudad Juárez: Dirección Municipal de Ecología de Ciudad Juárez.

Ecchia, G., and M. Mariotti. 1994. A Survey on Environmental Policy: Technological Innovation and Strategic Issues. Nota di lavoro 44.94. Milan: Fondazione Eni Enrico Mattei.

Feder, G., R. Just, and D. Zilberman. 1985. Adoption of Agricultural Innovations in Developing Countries: A Survey. *Economic Development and Cultural Change* 33: 255–98.

Federacion Mexicana de Asociaciones Privadas de Salud y Desarrolo Comunitario (FEMAP). 1991. *Summary of Brick Kilns Census*. Ciudad Juárez: Federacion Mexicana de Asociaciones Privadas de Salud y Desarrolo Comunitario.

Fransman, M., and K. King (eds.). 1984. *Technological Capability in the Third World*. London: Macmillan.

Hartman, R., M. Huq, and D. Wheeler. 1997. Why Paper Mills Clean Up: Determinants of Pollution Abatement in Four Asian Countries. Policy Research Department (PRD) working paper 1710. Washington, DC: World Bank.

Hayami, Y. 1984. Assessment of the Green Revolution. In *Agricultural Development in the Third World*, edited by C. Eicher and J. Staatz. Baltimore: Johns Hopkins University Press.

Hill, H. 1983. Choice of Technique in the Indonesian Weaving Industry. *Economic Development and Cultural Change* 31: 337–53.

Jaffe, A., and R. Stavins. 1995. Dynamic Incentives of Environmental Regulations: The Effects of Alternative Policy Instruments on Technology Diffusion. *Journal of Environmental Economics and Management* 29: S43–S63.

Lee, L.-F. 1981. Simultaneous Equations Models with Discrete and Censored Dependent Variables. In *Structural Analysis of Discrete Data with Econometric Applications,* edited by C. Manski and D. McFadden. Cambridge, MA: MIT Press.

Levy, B. 1993. Obstacles to Developing Indigenous Small and Medium Enterprises: An Empirical Assessment. *World Bank Economic Review* 7: 65–83.

Lin, J. 1991. Education and Innovation Adoption in Agriculture: Evidence from Hybrid Rice in China. *American Journal of Agricultural Economics* 73: 714–23.

Maltzou, S. 1992. Constraints to Clean Technology Transfer to Developing Countries. In *Environmentally Sound Technology for Sustainable Development*. New York: United Nations.

Mansfield, E. 1961. Technical Change and the Rate of Imitation. *Econometrica* 29: 741–65.

Nuñez, F., D. Vickers, and P. Emerson. 1994. Solving Air Pollution Problems in Paso del Norte, El Paso. Presented at the Conference on Border Environment, El Paso, TX, October 3 and 4.

Pargal, S., and D. Wheeler. 1996. Informal Regulation of Industrial Pollution in Developing Countries: Evidence from Indonesia. *Journal of Political Economy* 104: 1314–27.

Pender, J. 1996. Discount Rates and Credit Markets: Theory and Evidence from Rural India. *Journal of Developmental Economics* 50(2): 257–296.

Pindyck, R. 1991. Irreversibility, Uncertainty, and Investment. *Journal of Economic Literature* 29: 1110–52.

Pitt, M., and G. Sumodiningrat. 1991. Risk, Schooling and the Choice of Seed Technology in Developing Countries: A Meta-Profit Function Approach. *International Economic Review* 32: 457–73.

Shrestha, R., and C. Gopalakrishnan. 1993. Adoption and Diffusion of Drip Irrigation Technology: An Econometric Analysis. *Economic Development and Cultural Change* 41: 407–18.

World Bank. 1992. *World Development Report: Development and the Environment.* Washington, DC: Oxford University Press.

World Commission on Environment and Development. 1987. *Our Common Future.* New York: Oxford University Press.

CHAPTER 10

Small Firms and Clean Technologies
Part II: Leather Tanning in León, Mexico

Allen Blackman

*A*S DISCUSSED IN CHAPTER 1, given that in many developing countries, a host of financial, institutional, and political factors hamstring conventional environmental regulation, a promising strategy for controlling pollution from small firms (SFs) is to promote the voluntary adoption of clean technologies. Although this strategy has received considerable attention in policy circles, empirical research on the adoption of clean technologies by SFs in developing countries is limited.

This chapter presents historical background and original survey data on the adoption of five clean tanning technologies by a sample of 137 small- and medium-scale leather tanneries in León, Guanajuato, Mexico. León is an archetype of a city where clean technological change represents the best hope for fighting pollution control. The city's leather tanneries have caused severe environmental harm, and attempts to mitigate the problem using conventional regulation have repeatedly failed. Recently, however, a significant percentage of León's tanneries have voluntarily adopted clean technologies. The present study is the first to examine this phenomenon.

The remainder of the chapter is organized as follows. The next section provides background on leather tanning in León. The section titled Clean Tanning Technologies describes the five clean technologies. The section titled Survey discusses our survey methods. The section titled Survey Results presents the survey results, and the last section offers conclusions. (Readers interested in the literature on the drivers of clean technology adoption are referred to the review in Chapter 9).

Efforts To Regulate Leather Tanning in León

The city of León in north central Mexico produces about two-thirds of the country's tanned leather. Almost all of it is used in shoemaking, León's other hallmark industry. Although exact numbers are not known, local regulators estimate that León is home to approximately 1200 tanneries. At least three-quarters of these tanneries are small-scale, employing fewer than 20 workers, and about a quarter are unregistered and informal (Villalobos 1999).

Historically, León's tanneries have dumped untreated effluents directly into municipal sewers, which then deposit them into the Gómez River, a tributary of the Turbio. The main pollutants from tanneries are salt (used to preserve rawhides), various chemical compounds of sulfur (used to dehair hides), chromium III—commonly known as chrome—(used to render hides biologically inert), dissolved and suspended solids, and solid wastes impregnated with tanning chemicals. Tannery pollution has contaminated surface and groundwater and has damaged irrigated agricultural land. A 1987 study found chromium VI—a highly toxic by-product of chromium III—in three-quarters of the city's drinking water wells (Hernández 1987). León's water pollution problems attracted international attention in 1994 after a die-off of tens of thousands of migratory aquatic birds wintering in a local reservoir contaminated by the city's wastewater (Commission for Environmental Cooperation 1995).

Regulations governing tannery pollution have been on the books for decades. Among other things, they require tanneries to register with environmental authorities, install sedimentation tanks and water gauges, handle most solid wastes as hazardous materials, and—most important—pretreat wastewater so that daily concentrations of various pollutants do not exceed set standards. For the most part, however, these regulations are simply not enforced. By all accounts, the main reason is that leather tanneries are a mainstay of the local economy and therefore enjoy considerable political power.

Concerted efforts to control tannery pollution in León began in July 1987 when tannery representatives signed a voluntary agreement to comply with written regulations within four years. But when it became apparent in 1991 that the tanners had not taken any action aside from installing crude sedimentation tanks urgently needed to prevent sewers from clogging, the agreement was renegotiated.[1] In October 1991, a new voluntary agreement essentially granted tanners a second three-year grace period. It also committed the city of León to build both a common effluent treatment plant for biological (but not chemical) wastes and a facility for handling solid and hazardous wastes. By the end of this second grace period, these facilities had not been built, and tanneries had made no progress in reducing discharges. A third voluntary agreement was negotiated in June 1995, and a fourth in March 1997. None of these efforts produced any concrete progress in treating tannery industrial wastes.

For the most part, public-sector ineffectiveness in using top-down pressure to force compliance with environmental regulations has been matched by private-sector disinterest in and resistance to such strategies. Interviews and focus groups with a wide variety of stakeholders in León—including environmental advocates, tanners, politicians, and regulators—indicated that environmental advocacy groups and neighborhood organizations have not placed significant pressure on tanners to improve their environmental performance. The following anecdote illustrates the complacency of León's citizens with respect to tanneries. In 2002, the municipality received a complaint about odors from 22 tanneries operating in a working-class neighborhood, a rare event. In response, the municipality organized a neighborhood referendum on a proposal to relocate these tanneries. 188 resident families voted against the referendum and only 8 voted in favor of it (*Correo de Hoy* 2002).

Surprisingly, the one exception in this regard has been the *Cámara de la Industria de Curtiduria del Estado de Guanajuato* (CICUR), the principal trade organization representing León's tanners. Notwithstanding its general opposition to promulgating and enforcing pollution-control regulations, CICUR has encouraged—and on occasion even pressured—its members to cut pollution. In addition, it has promoted clean technological change in meetings and trade publications (*Dinámica de la Curtiduría* Various years).

Given that León's tanneries have yet to install end-of-pipe treatment facilities needed to comply with emissions standards, to date the most significant progress in controlling tannery emissions has resulted from the voluntary adoption of clean tanning technologies. The next section provides background on these technologies, as well as a brief overview of the process of leather tanning.

Clean Tanning Technologies

Leather tanning consists of two meta-processes: wet blue production and finishing. The former involves removing unwanted substances (salt, flesh, hair, and grease) from a rawhide, trimming it, treating it to impart the desired grain and stretch, and finally soaking it in a chrome bath to prevent decomposition.[2] Finishing involves splitting, shaving, retanning, and dyeing the wet blue. The wet blue process and finishing process are technologically and economically separable, and many tanneries in León specialize in one or the other. The wet blue process is far more polluting than finishing, generating 90% of the water pollution associated with leather tanning. Two substages of this process are particularly dirty: dehairing, in which rawhides are soaked in a bath of lime and sodium sulfide to dissolve hair and flesh, and tanning, in which hides are soaked in a chrome bath.[3]

Of the five clean technologies we consider here, two are associated with dehairing and two with chrome tanning (for technical details, see UNEP 1991). The technologies are the following:

1. High exhaustion. Using special inputs and procedures to ensure that more of the chrome in the tanning bath actually affixes to the hide, and less ends up in waste streams. Although this technique requires a more expensive type of chrome ("self-basifying") and a longer soaking period, it offers significant cost savings because of reduced overall chrome use (UNEP 1991).
2. Enzymes in the dehairing bath. Substituting biodegradable enzymes for lime and sodium sulfide.
3. Precipitation of chrome. Using alkalis to precipitate out the chrome in the tanning bath, collecting the resultant sludge, and processing it with sulfuric acid to recover the chrome.
4. Recycling the dehairing bath. Saving and reusing the contents of the dehairing bath instead of discharging them into the sewer after a single use. This simple

technology only requires fixed investments in a holding tank, a pump, and a filtering system to remove suspended solids—usually a simple wire mesh screen. Because the chemical inputs into the dehairing bath are relatively inexpensive, only minor cost savings accompany the environmental benefits. According to UNEP (1991), a tannery that produces 1000 wet blues per day could expect to save only US$8,000 per year.

5. Recycling the chrome tanning bath. Reusing contents of the tanning bath instead of discharging them into the sewer after a single use. Like recycling the dehairing bath, this simple technology only requires fixed investments in a holding tank, a pump, and a simple filter. It can reduce chrome use by up to 20% (UNEP 1991).

Survey

In January 2000, a team of enumerators administered a (face-to-face) question-naire to the owners or managers of 164 tanneries in León. Respondents were asked to provide information on whether or not they had adopted each of the five clean technologies described above, whether they had received technical training in the use of the technologies, and their views on costs and benefits of adopting each. Twenty-seven records were ultimately eliminated because of missing or in-consistent responses, leaving a total of 137 records.

Unfortunately, the conventional approach for randomizing survey samples—randomly selecting firms from a complete list—proved impractical because so many of León's tanneries are informal and are not included on any public or private registries. Just as important, in preliminary surveys, randomly selected tan-neries often declined to participate. As a result, we relied on so-called convenience sampling, a technique commonly used in industrial sectors with large numbers of informal firms. We identified participants by setting up interviews with firms on a list of 766 formal tanneries maintained by Centro de Investigación y Asesoría Tecnológica en Curteo y Calzado (CIATEC), the local leather tanning and shoe-making research institute, and by going door to door in neighborhoods in León where tanneries are plentiful. Given our reliance on these second-best methods, there is no guarantee that our survey sample is representative of the population of tanneries in León.

Survey Results

This section presents summary statistics from our survey data. Most of our respon-dent firms were small-scale, reflecting the population of tanneries in León. The average tannery in our sample had 16 employees and produced 499 wet blues per week.

Familiarity with Clean Technologies

More than 70% of our respondents had heard of each of the five clean tanning technologies (Table 10-1). They were least familiar with the enzymes and the precipitation of chrome and were most familiar with recycling of the chrome bath and high exhaustion. Those respondents who had heard of the five technologies claimed a relatively high level of familiarity with technical details. In each case, the average respondent rated his or her familiarity higher than 3 on a scale of 1 to 5 (where 1 = no familiarity and 5 = very familiar). Although most tanners were familiar with the five technologies, this knowledge appears to have been relatively new. In each case, fewer than half the respondents had known about the technology for more than five years. With the exception of enzymes, the plurality of respondents first learned about each technology from CICUR, the tannery trade association. In the case of enzymes, the key source of initial information was input suppliers. Input suppliers were also an important source of information in the case of high exhaustion.

Table 10-1. *Familiarity with Clean Technologies (n)*

	High exhaustion	Enzymes	Precip. Chrome	Recycle dehairing	Recycle Chrome	Average
Heard of technology? (% yes)	95	72	77	81	91	83
	(137)	(137)	(137)	(137)	(137)	
Familiar with technical details?	3.73	3.54	3.32	3.43	3.37	3.48
[scale 1 = none to 5 = very]	(128)	(98)	(104)	(111)	(125)	
Years since first heard of technology (% each category)						
This year/never	5	28	23	19	9	17
Less than five years	47	46	45	51	56	49
5–9 years	29	20	16	20	21	21
10–14 years	14	3	9	8	12	9
15–20 years	4	2	4	1	1	2
More than 20 years	1	0	1	1	1	1
	(137)	(137)	(137)	(137)	(137)	
Source of initial info. about (% each category)						
Tanner	15	9	16	19	23	16
Input supplier	21	46	14	8	9	20
CICUR	30	19	27	32	35	29
CIATEC	9	12	16	13	12	12
Other	23	13	24	27	22	22
Do not recall	2	0	2	2	0	1
	(130)	(98)	(104)	(111)	(124)	

Adoption of Clean Technologies: Rates, Timing, and Reasons

Table 10-2 presents survey data on rate and timing of adoption for the five clean technologies and the reasons the respondents gave for either adopting or not adopting. With regard to rates of adoption, the two technologies that have diffused most widely are high exhaustion and enzymes: 59% of the respondents have adopted the former and 35% have adopted the latter. About one-fifth of the respondents adopted the remaining three clean technologies.

These technologies are fairly new to the adopters in our sample, a finding that is not surprising, considering that, as discussed above, most adopters only recently learned about them. Most adopters acquired the technologies in the mid-1990s. Recycling the dehairing bath was adopted earliest (on average 1994), and enzymes were adopted most recently (on average 1997). Figure 10-1 shows precisely when our survey participants adopted.

What reasons did the adopters in our sample give for their choice? The reasons were similar for the three technologies that do not involve recycling—high exhaustion, enzymes, and precipitation of chrome—and for the two that do—recycling of the chrome bath and recycling of the dehairing bath.[4] For the three

Table 10-2. *Adoption of Clean Technologies* (n)

	High exhaustion	Enzymes	Precip. chrome	Recycle dehairing	Recycle chrome	Average
Adopted? (% yes)	59	35	20	18	20	30
	(137)	(137)	(137)	(137)	(137)	
Year adopted (average)	1995	1997	1995	1994	1995	1995
	(81)	(48)	(28)	(24)	(27)	
Reason adopted? (adopters only; % each category)						
Reduces variable costs	20	6	25	32	41	25
Improves product quality	31	71	36	4	7	30
Law requires it now	11	4	4	8	7	7
Law will require	0	2	0	0	7	2
Reduces pollution	36	15	32	44	37	33
Other	2	2	4	12	0	4
	(81)	(48)	(28)	(25)	(27)	
Reason have NOT adopted? (nonadopters only; % each category)						
Lack of technical info	49	44	46	41	37	43
Uncertainty	6	14	5	12	10	9
Fixed costs too high	23	12	21	25	24	21
Variable costs too high	4	2	5	1	4	3
Ruins quality	0	4	8	2	9	5
Other	17	24	14	19	15	18
	(47)	(50)	(76)	(85)	(97)	

Figure 10-1. *Timing of Adoption of Clean Technologies by 137 Survey Respondents*

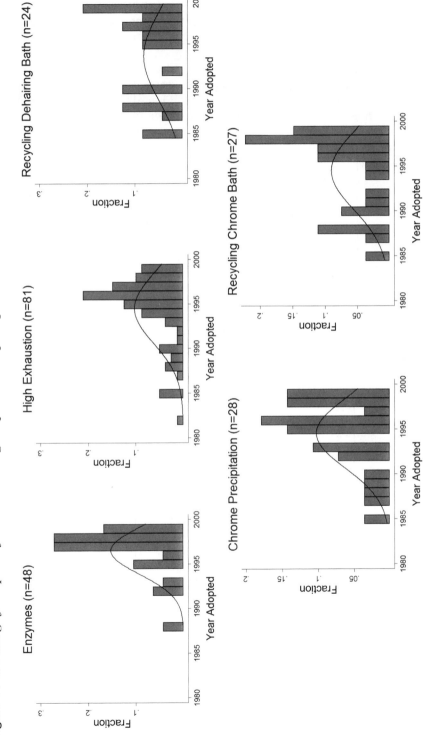

nonrecycling technologies, the majority of adopters cited private nonenvironmental benefits—improving product quality and reducing variable costs—as the most important reason for adopting (Table 10-2). Improving product quality was clearly viewed as the most important reason in the cases of enzymes—more than two-thirds of adopters cited it as most important. This factor also appears to have played a key role in the adoption of precipitation of chrome and high exhaustion—more than one-third of respondents in each case said that it was the most important reason for adopting. Although environmental benefits of adopting the nonrecycling technologies were cited as most important by a significant percentage of respondents, few cited current or expected future regulatory pressure as a factor. As for the two recycling technologies, the plurality of respondents who adopted recycling the dehairing bath—and a near plurality of those who adopted recycling the chrome bath—cited environmental benefits as the most important reason for adopting. Even so, few of these adopters cited current or expected future regulatory pressure as a factor.

What reasons did nonadopters give for their choices? Here there was a striking degree of consistency across the five technologies. The plurality of respondents in every case cited a lack of technical information as the most important reason for not adopting. Fixed costs were also often cited as a barrier to adoption.

Technical Assistance in the Use of Clean Technologies

The majority of tanners in our sample received some instruction in the use of each of the five clean technologies (Table 10-3). Almost three-quarters of the tanners received instruction in the use of high exhaustion and enzymes. More than half received instruction in the remaining technologies. In each case, more than 60% of the respondents received some type of formal instruction. We do not have information on whether the instruction coincided with adoption or preceded it. Clearly, however, more tanners received instruction than actually adopted. Presumably, then, for many respondents, instruction preceded adoption.

Surprisingly, the most important sources of instruction were not public regulatory agencies but private-sector entities, namely, input providers, CICUR, and CIATEC. Input providers were the most important sources of instruction in the use of high exhaustion and enzymes, whereas CICUR was the most important source in the case of the remaining technologies: the precipitation of chrome, recycling the dehairing bath, and recycling the chrome bath.

Conclusion

Although a rigorous statistical analysis of the determinants of the adoption of clean technologies by León's tanneries is beyond the scope of this study, the summary statistics and historical information presented in the sections titled Efforts to Regulate Leather Tanning in León and Survey Results paint a fairly compelling and coherent picture of the important factors at play. Clearly, formal and informal regulatory pressure have not been key factors. As the historical overview makes clear, notwithstanding continuing official hullabaloo, formal regulatory pressure has been quite weak if not completely superficial. The survey results support this hypothesis. Few of the respondents in our sample cited such pressure—either current or expected—as the most important reason for adopting.

Informal regulatory pressure to adopt clean technologies also has been limited. Anecdotal evidence indicates that pressure from neighborhood associations, environmental NGOs, and the media has been quite weak. None of the adopters in our sample cited pressure from such organizations as a motivating factor. Although two private-sector organizations—CICUR, the tannery trade association; and CI-ATEC, the tannery research organization—have been instrumental in disseminating technical information about the clean technologies, apparently they have stopped short of applying significant social, political, or economic pressure.

The data presented here suggest that, rather than top-down regulatory pressure, the key factor driving the adoption of clean tanning technologies in León has been the somewhat haphazard, bottom-up dissemination of information about the cost and quality benefits of the technologies. For three of the five technologies—including the two technologies with the highest adoption rates—the majority of adopters cited quality and cost advantages as the most important reason for their decision, whereas for all five technologies, the plurality of nonadopters cited lack of technical information as the most important reason for their decision. Furthermore, our survey results suggest that the technologies have only recently

Table 10-3. *Technical Assistance in the Use of Clean Technologies (n)*

	High exhaustion	Enzymes	Precip. chrome	Recycle dehairing	Recycle chrome	Average
Received instruction? (% yes)	72	74	59	54	56	63
	(130)	(98)	(105)	(111)	(125)	
Received instruction from:						
another tanner? (% yes)	5	6	6	3	6	5
	(93)	(72)	(62)	(59)	(70)	
an input provider? (% yes)	30	51	18	17	13	26
	(93)	(72)	(62)	(59)	(70)	
SAPAL? (% yes)	3	0	2	3	1	2
	(93)	(72)	(62)	(59)	(70)	
Ecologia Municipal? (% yes)	2	0	0	0	0	0
	(93)	(72)	(62)	(59)	(70)	
CICUR? (% yes)	27	19	32	37	39	31
	(93)	(72)	(62)	(59)	(70)	
CIATEC? (% yes)	17	13	24	22	27	21
	(93)	(72)	(62)	(59)	(70)	
Other? (% yes)	24	18	24	31	23	24
	(93)	(72)	(62)	(59)	(70)	
Formal instruction? (% yes)	65	60	66	73	71	67
	(93)	(72)	(62)	(60)	(70)	

been introduced in León and have yet to be discovered by many tanners. Finally, the survey results clearly demonstrate that trade associations, input suppliers, and tanners—not public-sector institutions—have been primarily responsible for disseminating information about the technologies.

What are the policy implications of these findings? We begin with our negative results. Our finding that top-down regulatory pressure was unimportant runs counter to the literature's emphasis on such pressure as a driver of clean technological change. That formal regulatory pressure was not important in León is not all that surprising given that such regulation is typically weak in developing countries. That informal regulatory pressure is not important is somewhat more surprising. Two factors may explain this result. One has to do with the nature of the pollution in question. Although emissions from industrial sources of air pollution are relatively easy to detect and also affect some neighborhoods disproportionately, damages from individual tanneries (odors aside) are not easy to detect and are not concentrated around the source. Tannery effluents are discharged into common sewers, where they are mixed with effluents from other sources before being deposited in a river miles away. Thus, it is difficult for private-sector organizations, such as neighborhood organizations, to identify particularly dirty tanneries, and moreover, they have little incentive to do so. A second explanation for the lack of top-down informal regulatory pressure has to do with the political economy of León. As discussed above, tanneries are a leading employer and a powerful political force in the city, and they are able to derail efforts to enforce environmental regulations. Unfortunately, neither one of these two factors is likely to be unique to our case study: one would expect them to be present in most large clusters of water polluters.

Our key positive result is that factors related to information acquisition drove the adoption of clean tanning technologies in León. In many respects, clean technological change in León resembles productivity-enhancing technological change worldwide—many firms adopt to improve quality or cut costs, and they do so after having been exposed to requisite technical and economic information by various private-sector contacts. From a policy perspective, this is welcome news. It implies that clean technological change can occur absent strong regulatory pressure or even significant public-sector assistance. As a result, it may be—as proponents argue—an effective means of ratcheting up environmental performance in developing countries with weak environmental regulatory institutions. Furthermore, our findings imply that an effective means of promoting clean technologies in developing countries is to disseminate technical information through the trade associations, input suppliers, and other private-sector institutions that are already helping to perform this function.

Finally, we briefly recast this discussion to emphasize its relevance to the debate about whether and how private-sector institutions can help to "green" industry in countries where public-sector regulatory institutions are weak. On one hand, our results suggest that the ability of private-sector institutions, such as neighborhood associations, to use sanctions or threats of sanctions—i.e., "sticks"—to accomplish this goal is limited. Such approaches are only likely to be feasible in specific political and geophysical settings. However, on the other hand, our findings suggest that the private-sector institutions can play a key role in facilitating improved environmental performance through less coercive means, namely by providing "carrots" such as technical assistance.

Acknowledgments

Thanks to the Tinker Foundation for financial support; Arne Kildegaard, Edgar Isusquiza, Nicolas Sisto, CICUR, PPAEG, and CIATEC for assistance with field research; and our enumerators at the University of Guanajuato—Federico Arturo, Jorge Barrio, Federico Cantero, Juan Días, Julio Gasca, Claudia Gomez, Erika del Carmen Gonzalez, Jeremy Heald, Edgar Isusquiza, Cid Rodríguez, Arcelia Rodríguez, Fabiola Romero, and Eduardo Vargas—for their assistance in administering the survey.

Notes

1. Sedimentation tanks are the only end-of-pipe abatement devices commonly used in León. These inexpensive, low-technology concrete barriers enable suspended solids to settle out of waste streams. To prevent the city's sewers from clogging, the municipal water authority has strictly enforced regulations requiring sedimentation tanks since the late 1980s.

2. The resulting semifinished hide is called a wet blue because the chrome bath imparts a bluish tint.

3. A small percentage of tanneries in León use an alternative to chrome tanning called vegetable tanning, which involves soaking hides in tree bark extracts. This process produces low-grade leather used primarily as shoe soles. Our survey sample does not include any tanneries that use this process.

4. Adopters in our sample were asked to choose the one most important reason from a list of reasons, one of which was a catchall "other." Like all of the multiple-choice questions in our survey, this one was constructed from feedback tanners provided in focus groups and open-ended preliminary surveys.

References

Commission for Environmental Cooperation. 1995. The Death of Migratory Birds at the Silva Reservoir (1994–95). CEC Secretariat: Montreal, Quebec. www.cec.org (accessed March 5, 2005).

Correo de Hoy. 2002. Permite Cabildo Uso de Suelo a Tenerías Instaladas en Colonia La Piscina, Guanajuato. December 5: 19.

Dinámica de la Curtiduría. Various years. León, Guanajuato: Cámara de la Industria de Curtiduria del Estado de Guanajuato.

Hernández, J. 1987. Situacion Actual del Problema de Contaminación en la Región Calzatecnia 9. León, Guanajuato: Centro de Investigación y Asesoría Tecnológica en Curteo y Calzado. Jaffe, A., R. Newell, and R. Stavins. 2003. Technological Change and the Environment. In Handbook of Environmental Economics, edited by K.-G. Mäler and J. Vincent. Amsterdam: North-Holland/Elsevier Science.

United Nations Environmental Programme (UNEP). 1991. Tanneries and the Environment: A Technical Guide. Paris: UNEP.

Villalobos, J.L. (Subprocurador de Verification Normativa, PROFEPA, Guanajuato.). 1999. Personal communication with Allen Blackman, January 27.

CHAPTER 11

Small-Scale Agroindustry, Trade, and the Environment

Coffee Processing in Honduras

Robert R. Hearne,[1] José Manuel Gonzalez, and Bruno Barbier

*A*LTHOUGH TRADITIONAL AGRICULTURAL SYSTEMS are rarely pollution-intensive, Honduran coffee is an exception. The country's small-scale coffee growers, who are mostly located in mountainous areas, use upland rivers both as a source of water for processing raw coffee and as a repository for wastewater and organic by-products. During coffee harvest, mountain waterways are inundated with untreated wastes. This pollution has severe impacts on water supplies and riverine ecology in both upstream and downstream areas.

Clean coffee-processing technology—consisting of simple effluent treatment ponds, water recycling, and composting of organic wastes—is available to mitigate this problem. Unfortunately, however, for a variety of economic and institutional reasons, it is only cost-effective in medium- and large-scale centralized processing plants, not in the small-scale farm-level plants that predominate in Honduras. Honduran stakeholders have identified the development of centralized, environmentally friendly coffee processing as a priority. Yet efforts to establish these plants have largely failed.

Other Central American countries have had more success with centralized processing. One reason is that such processing has improved quality control, which in turn, has enabled exporters to obtain higher prices on the international market. This experience begs the question of whether centralizing coffee processing in Honduras could boost coffee profits enough to make it attractive to the key stakeholders in the coffee market.

This chapter presents a minimum-cost processing and transportation model to demonstrate that an environmentally friendly system of centralized coffee processing in Honduras does in fact have this property. We show that if such a system leads to the elimination of the export price "penalty" currently imposed on Honduras' coffee because of poor quality, then it will be Pareto superior to the current system, that is, it will make all the principal participants in the coffee market—growers, middlemen, and processors—better off. This chapter also discusses the challenges involved with converting a decentralized system of small-scale processors into a centralized system of medium- and large-scale processors.

The remainder of the chapter is organized as follows. The section titled Background provides additional detail about coffee processing in Honduras. The section titled Pollution Control Policy Options reviews pertinent policy options. The section titled Feasibility of Centralized Processing presents a minimum-cost plan to implement centralized environmentally friendly coffee processing in the Rio Frío Basin in west-central Honduras. The section entitled Implementation Issues covers many issues in Honduras and in neighboring countries. The chapter concludes with a discussion of the challenges of implementing such a system.

Background

Coffee's share of Honduran export earnings has declined in recent years because of damage from Hurricane Mitch in 1998, steep declines in the international price of coffee in the 1990s, and rapid growth in the manufacturing sector. Nevertheless, it remains Honduras' most important export crop. It contributed 24% of the country's export earnings in 2000 (CEPAL 2002).

In Honduras, approximately 250,000 hectares of coffee are cultivated on 85,000 separate plots on hillside terrain between 700 and 1500 meters above sea level. The vast majority of coffee farms are small-scale—more than 92% of growers plant less than 7 hectares and produce less than 100 quintals (1 quintal = 45.36 kg, see Table 11-1). Because much of Honduras' coffee is grown on the hillsides in the upland watersheds, it uses land that would be economically and environmentally unsuitable for the production of other crops. Coffee cultivation has been a key factor in reducing poverty and maintaining rural social stability in Honduras.

Slightly more than half of Honduras' 85,000 coffee growers process coffee themselves, mostly using inefficient traditional technology. Only a few dozen large producers have constructed modern processing plants. A number of factors constrain small farmers' ability to adopt environmentally friendly technologies. Such farmers generally have limited savings and lack access to formal bank credit. Also,

Table 11-1. *Distribution of Coffee Producers in Honduras by Annual Production*

Annual coffee production (46.36 kg quintals)	Producers (%)
<10	30
10–25	50
25–100	13
100–500	6
>500	1

Source: IHCafe 1999a.

cooperatives made up of small farmers often suffer from poor management and lack of financial resources (Pineda et al. 1998; Peyser 1999).

Coffee is generally processed by farmers and then sold to intermediaries in nearby market towns. The intermediaries contract with truck owners to transport the coffee to the exporters who, in turn, prepare lots of 500 60-kg bags. These lots are purchased by international coffee brokers.

Previous government efforts to improve coffee processing have largely failed. In the 1970s, the Honduran Coffee Institute (IHCafe), a parastatal marketing agency, wholly owned by the Honduran government, constructed 13 large processing plants located in 8 of the 15 coffee-producing departments in Honduras. Unfortunately, the choice of the location was motivated more by politics than by efficiency. Some plants were situated more than 40 km from coffee plantations, which greatly increased the costs of transporting the relatively heavy unprocessed coffee. Processing cooperatives were established, but cooperative leaders often did not have the managerial or financial capacity to administer them effectively. Producers were often not consulted in these decisions, and the initiative was perceived to be an institutional mandate. Systematic disinformation, mistrust, and bad management resulted. As a result, only 3 of the original 13 centralized processing plants are still operating. The failure of this initiative has led to a persistent aversion to centralized processing and cooperatives (Palma et al. 1997; Pineda et al. 1998).

Coffee Processing and Coffee Quality

Coffee processing can be dry or wet. In wet processing, water is used to depulp and wash beans. This technique is used in Colombia, Central America, and the Caribbean—all countries producing *arabica* coffee, which has a softer taste and fetches a higher price than the *robusta* coffee produced in Brazil and Africa. Wet processing is reputed to conserve *arabica*'s quality by reducing bitterness and increasing acidity (Jaquet 1993; IHCafe 1995).[2] That said, quality control during processing depends critically on the effort, skills, and equipment of individual processors. During washing, beans must be floated in tanks of water, and the low-quality beans must be removed. A number of problems can alter quality during wet processing. Immature beans produce a bad taste and are difficult to depulp. Also, water used by small-scale processors is usually contaminated by upstream plants (Bailly et al. 1992).

The average quality of Honduran coffee is relatively low because of inadequate processing and quality control. The typical small farmer has no more than a manual depulping machine and a barrel for fermenting and washing. The problem of poor quality control by small-scale processors is exacerbated by the fact that small farmers generally sell to multiple middlemen, who mix coffee from different sources. Therefore, it is difficult for individual farmers to obtain higher prices by improving quality control.

Honduran farmers have had strong financial incentives to process coffee themselves rather than relying on centralized processing, which could improve quality control. In 1995, unprocessed beans sold at 54–56% of international market prices, whereas processed beans (called *pergamino seco*) sold at 70% of international prices. In addition, small farmers are often not treated fairly when they sell unprocessed beans to processing plants. They generally need to deliver 286 kg of unprocessed beans to be paid for 245 kg (IHCafe 1995).

Because of poor quality control, Honduran coffee exporters do not receive full international prices for their product. They pay a "penalty" ranging from 9% to 16% of the international price. This penalty was initiated in the late 1990s after a U.S. broker received unsatisfactory coffee. The resulting bad publicity has affected all of Honduras' coffee exports (except for a cooperative in Marcala that uses centralized processing and maintains high standards). Despite efforts to ameliorate this problem, quality control remains inadequate, and Honduran coffee is widely considered "filler" (Peyser 1999; Gonzalez 2000; Luxner 2000, 2001).

Environmental Impacts of Coffee Production and Processing

Coffee production in Honduras has both positive and negative environmental impacts. More than 85% of the coffee produced in the country is traditional shade-grown coffee, that is, it is cultivated in the shade of the existing forest canopy. Shade-grown coffee is considered to be environmentally friendly because trees maintain soil quality, prevent erosion on the steep slopes where coffee is typically cultivated, provide habitat for birds and thus support biodiversity conservation, and provide valuable inputs into the household economy, such as fruits, firewood, and lumber, which reduce the stress on forested area. Also, shade-grown coffee requires fewer chemical inputs than more modern intensive monoculture systems.

However, coffee cultivation in Honduras also comes at an environmental cost, given that processing is done at the farm level using water-intensive technology and no environmental controls. One kg of dried coffee produces 2.5 kg of wet pulp and 12.4 kg of effluent (Echeverría and Cleves 1995). In Honduras, more than 272,000 metric tons of pulp and 136,000 metric tons of mucilage are produced as waste in postharvest processing. Currently, this waste is dumped into nearby streams and rivers without control or treatment. Coffee waste discharges contain high concentrations of all manner of water pollutants, and are also acidic (Table 11-2). The organic matter in these waste streams is sufficient to cause eutrophication of upland rivers, with the subsequent loss of plant and fish life, strong odors, and increased population of mosquitoes and other harmful insects (González Besteiro and Obando 1994; Osorio 1997). The level of pollution in

Table 11-2. Water Quality in Honduras

	Potable water	Untreated wastewater	Coffee processing effluents
pH	7.0	6.5	3.7
COD (mg/L)	2	500	15,000
BOD (mg/L)	2	250	9,000
Soluble solids (mg/L)	0	500	3,600
Total solids (mg/L)	500	800	12,000

Source: SERNA 1995.

Honduras' rivers and streams is directly related to the quantity of coffee processed and the processing technology (Jacquet 1993).

Other environmental and natural resource problems can be attributed to traditional coffee processing. Water, and therefore soils, are acidified, leading to reduced agricultural productivity in irrigated areas (Salas et al., 1983; Blanco and Perera 1999). Acidity and organic sediments also damage hydraulic equipment (Alfaro and Cárdenas 1988). Pollution of mountain streams and strong odors from coffee processing diminish the ability of the coffee-processing areas to attract tourists. Consumption of fuelwood for drying coffee promotes deforestation (Blanco and Perera 1999).

Finally, coffee production exacerbates water scarcity. Wet processing requires 40 liters of water for each kg of processed coffee (Bailly et al. 1992). Approximately 40% of the water used during the process is wasted. This extraction of river water occurs from February through April—the dry season in Honduras—when rivers have their minimal flow. Human consumption of water reaches its peak during these months because of the immigration of migrant labor for the coffee harvest (Bailly et al. 1992; González 1996).

Pollution Control Policy Options

Current Regulatory Environment for Coffee Processing in Honduras

Honduras' water pollution policy is codified in the 1993 General Law of the Environment and subsequent administrative decrees. This law declares that the state will protect the environment and that any individual can denounce an activity that they consider harmful to the environment to the Department of Denouncements of the Secretariat of Natural Resources and the Environment (SERNA).

All new coffee-processing plants are required to apply for a license from SERNA. Coffee processors producing more than 800 quintals per week are required to submit a full environmental impact statement as part of the application procedure. Smaller traditional processors and large "ecological" processors are allowed to submit a less formal statement of environmental impact with their license application. These applications are reviewed by municipal authorities and SERNA. SERNA can require mitigation before a license is granted. Fees are collected from the applicants to cover the costs of this licensing process. Generally, these regulations do not apply to established processing plants.

The decentralized structure of the coffee-processing sector makes it difficult to enforce these regulations, however. Although the country's approximately 44,000 farm-level processors are technically point sources, from the standpoint of environmental regulators, they resemble nonpoint pollution sources. Identifying small-scale processing plants and monitoring them is costly, and it is quite difficult to attribute ambient pollution levels to any specific plant. Also, regulating thousands of individual processors entails considerable transaction costs.

Not surprisingly, enforcement of environmental regulations governing coffee processing is inconsistent. In recent years, the Honduran government has made an effort to place environmental officers in more municipalities, and some municipalities have attempted to enforce environmental restrictions on coffee processing. In some cases, established processing plants have been relocated to protect municipal water intakes. However, small municipalities are often unable to enforce environmental controls, whereas larger downstream municipalities have little control over pollution that occurs in upstream coffee-growing regions.

It is also important to note that, in general, Honduras does not have a strong tradition of environmental regulation. Corruption and poor governance limit the feasibility of many pollution-regulation strategies, especially those that involve fees and payments. Fee collection can invite corruption, robbery, and mistrust. For all these reasons, using conventional regulatory instruments, such as technology standards, emissions fees, and tradable permits would be problematic.

Low-Emissions Coffee-Processing Technology

Honduran coffee processors use five different types of coffee-processing technologies. These differ by their capacities (from 25 to 5000 quintals per year) and their water requirements (Pineda 1997a). Each of these five technologies can be modified to conserve water and reduce water pollution. Thus, IHCafe has proposed five types of environmentally friendly plants, which feature water recycling, effluent treatment, reduced use of water in the transport of by-products, composting of organic by-products, rapid fermentation, improved de-pulping, and low energy use. In Honduras, these types of processing plants are called "ecological" processors. Figure 11-1 presents the pertinent steps in coffee processing, including the important pollution-mitigation features. Table 11-3 presents the features of these IHCafe-approved plants, including output, costs, water use, effluent and environmental controls.

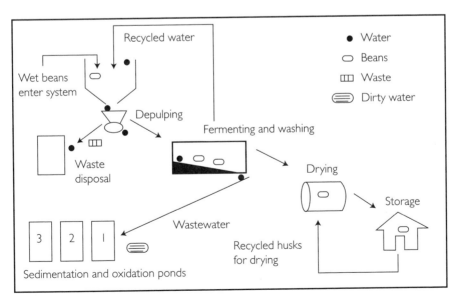

Figure 11-1. *Ecological Coffee Processing*

Table 11-3. Attributes of Five Proposed Coffee-Processing Plants

Plant model	Annual capacity (quintals)	Water use (L/quintal)	Effluents (kg/quintal/year)	Fixed cost[a] ($/quintal)	Variable cost ($/quintal)	Technical characteristics
1	25	507	171	21.88	1.89	• Manual de-pulping • Wooden fermentation sinks • Manual waste pulp transport
2	100	501	171	12.31	1.84	• Manual de-pulping • Cement fermentation sinks • Manual waste pulp transport
3	500	300	171	10.94	1.75	• Mechanized de-pulping • Cement fermentation sinks • Hydraulic waste pulp transport • Water recycling • Oxidation ponds
4	1000	300	151	12.31	0.98	• Mechanized de-pulping • Cement fermentation sinks • Hydraulic waste pulp transport • Siphon receptor • Water recycling • Hydraulic coffee transport • Classification canal • Water recycling • Oxidation ponds
5	5000	300	151	14.23	0.61	• Mechanized de-pulping • Cement fermentation sinks • Archimedes' screw transport • 1 or 2 chute receptor • Water recycling • Water storage dam • Drying patio • Cylindrical dryer • Oxidation ponds

Source: Pineda 1997a, 1997b.

[a]10-year loan at 28% interest.

As Table 11-3 illustrates, type 1 plants have the smallest capacity and type 5 plants the largest. Depulping is manual in type 1 and type 2 plants and is mechanized in all other plants. A key pollution-reduction feature of type 1 and 2 plants is "vertical" transport of raw materials, wastes, and coffee, using manual labor. By contrast, most small processing plants use large quantities of water for transport. In addition, type 1 and type 2 plants compost waste, again using manual labor.

Type 3 and type 4 plants rely on hydraulic transport, whereas type 5 plants use an Archimedes' screw for this purpose. However, three plants (types 3, 4, and 5) also recycle water. Types 3, 4, and 5 plants use oxidation ponds to treat their wastewater. Also, these plants collect organic matter produced in the depulping, fermentation, and washing stages. After treatment and composting, most of these by-products can be recycled as fertilizer (Jaquet 1993; Barrios 1995; Urive et al. 1997).

As seen in Table 11-3, the larger ecological processing plants are associated with significant economies of scale. These processors have lower per-unit costs, use less water, and produce fewer effluents per unit of output. Of course, the necessity of transporting unprocessed beans to a centralized processing plant implies greater transportation costs and more transport-related air pollution.

Feasibility of Centralized Processing

IHCafe has had a goal of introducing a network of centralized, environmentally controlled processing plants to reduce water pollution and water consumption, improve product quality, and raise export prices.[3] Because it would not be practical for the Honduran government to mandate centralized processing, a necessary condition for successful implementation of a centralized system is that all participants in the market, including growers, processors, and middlemen either have positive financial incentives to switch to the new system or at least remain financially neutral. Although centralized processing will entail increases in some types of costs—most notably transportation costs—these cost increases might be offset if improved quality control associated with centralized processing led to higher coffee prices.

To provide a rough assessment of the financial feasibility of centralized ecological processing, we first use a mathematical programming model to characterize a minimum cost centralized processing system. Then we analyze whether market participants have appropriate financial incentives to support such a system. This research does not address how the network of processing plants should be initiated nor who should own and operate these plants. Rather the focus is on determining the optimal location and type of plants.

The Model

The problem is to simultaneously determine the cost-minimizing size and location of the processing plants in a watershed, given the need to process all existing coffee production, meet environmental standards, and observe limits on water supplies. This problem is solved by mathematical programming. We define the following:

i = index of plant types (1 to 5);

f = index of farms;

p = index of processing plant locations (1 to 7 per river segment);

r = index of river segments (1 to 7);

$X_{i,p,r}$ = number of plants of type i in location p on river segment r;

F_i = fixed cost for each processing plant type i (US$);

T^γ = transport cost per km per quintal of unprocessed beans (US$);

T^ϕ = transport cost per quintal per km per quintal of processed beans (US$);

V^c_i = variable cost per quintal for centralized processing plant type i (US$);

$D_{f,p}$ = distance from the farm f in river segment r to plant location p in river segment r (km);

$D_{p,e}$ = distance from plant location p in river segment r to buyer e (km);

Q^ϕ_f = processed coffee produced by farm f;

$Q^{\phi*}_f$ = processed coffee produced by farm f during 30-day peak period;

R_i = processing capacity of plant type i during 30-day peak period;

W_i = water used by plant type i (liters of water per second at peak capacity); and

S_r = water available (liters per second).

The social planner's problem is to select $X_{i,p,r}$ to minimize total costs, thus:

$$\sum_{r,p,i} \left(F_i + V^c_i \sum_f Q^\phi_f + \sum_f T^\gamma D_{f,p} + \sum_p T^\phi D_{p,e} \right) X_{i,p,r} \tag{11-1}$$

subject to the following restrictions. First, in each river segment r, the total processing capacity of the proposed plants is sufficient to handle all the coffee produced in the relevant river segment during the peak period.

$$\sum_{p,i} R_i X_{i,p,r} \geq \sum_f Q^{\phi*}_f \quad \forall r \tag{11-2}$$

Second, the distance between each coffee field and its corresponding plant is less than 25 km.

$$D_{f,p} \leq 25 \quad \forall f,p,r \tag{11-3}$$

Third, peak water consumption by coffee-processing plants does not exceed the water available in the river during low-flow periods.

$$S_r \geq \sum_{p,i} W_i X_{i,p,r} \quad \forall r \tag{11-4}$$

Finally, X must be an integer:

INTEGER $(X_{i,p,r})$ \hfill (11-5)

With regard to the first constraint, note that capacity needs to be sufficient to handle all the coffee harvested during any given day. Thus, demand during the peak harvest period determines plant capacity and therefore affects plant type and water demand. The distance constraint is needed to ensure that processing begins within five hours of harvest. Raw coffee cherries need to be processed shortly after harvest to preserve taste.

This is a partial equilibrium model. That is, it assumes all parameters—including farm-level outputs, transportation costs, production costs, and farm-level coffee prices (used in the feasibility analysis below)—are exogenous, that is, they will not change under a centralized-processing regime, even though they are based on data from a decentralized regime. Furthermore, this analysis relies on average costs as opposed to marginal costs. These are admittedly strong assumptions, but they are consistent with our aim to provide a rough analysis of the economic feasibility of a centralized ecological processing system. However, it is fair to note that a switch to centralized processing would significantly increase the transportation needs in the upper watershed, and this might lead to increasing marginal transportation costs. Also, the human capital required to manage centralized processing may lead to increased costs.

Study Area

The cost-minimization model was constructed for the Rio Frío watershed in the department of Santa Barbara, within the boundaries of the municipality of San Nicolas in western Honduras. The watershed covers an area of 86 square km between 550 and 1600 meters above sea level. Overall, the area boasts good conditions for coffee.[4]

Coffee plantations are located in the upper part of the watershed and make up its main economic activity. Farmers also produce livestock, sugar cane, vegetables, maize, and beans. About 1137 families produce coffee in the watershed, but only 569 families reside there for the entire year. Approximately 40,000 quintals of *pergamino seco* coffee is grown on 2527 hectares, an average of 16 quintals per hectare.

Data

Our data come from a variety of sources. IHCafe has collected an impressive amount of data related to coffee production in the Rio Frío watershed, including information on prices, production costs, processing, transaction costs, water use, and water quality (IHCafe 1995, 1999a, 1999b). Data on transportation costs come from the authors' interviews with local growers, middlemen, and extension agents. Finally, local banks provided data on conditions and costs of credit from local banks. (The investment for new plants requires a loan for 7–10 years at 28%, with 2 years of grace and 5–8 years of capital reimbursement).

A digitized map and a geographic information system from the International Tropical Agriculture Center (CIAT 1999) were used to identify roads and rivers and to estimate distances among farms, possible plant sites, and the export depot. These distances were validated during a tour of the watershed. Also, the final selection of potential locations for processing plants was done in consultation with local growers and extension agents to ensure access to roads and water.

The Rio Frío watershed can be divided into seven river segments. Data on water availability in each segment is based on measurement of the stream flows by Pineda et al. (1998). Because the stream flows are measured at the outlet of each river segment, the measured stream flow is net of all water consumed in the river section. Water is withdrawn from the river segments to be used in coffee processing and human consumption. For purposes of establishing a water consumption constraint, human consumption is assumed to be constant.

Table 11-4 presents some of the key cost data used in the model. Harvest cost per quintal is US$11.49, independent of the size of the farm. The cost of transporting beans within the farm was estimated at US$0.62 per km per quintal. And the cost of transporting beans on secondary roads was estimated at US$0.05 per km per quintal. This cost reduces to $0.04 per km on improved roads. It takes 5 quintals of unprocessed beans to make a quintal of processed beans. Processing costs differ across plant types because of economies of scale and differences in technology. For example, water is not recycled in plant models 1 and 2, which implies no recycling costs but a greater use of water.

Harvested unprocessed coffee cannot be stored for long periods. The initial stages of processing should begin within five hours of the harvest. This implies that processing plants need to be relatively close to the plantations. Also, the processing capacity needs to be sufficient to receive all the coffee harvested during any day. In the watershed, 70% of the production is harvested in 30 days. During this 30-day peak period, all fixed inputs and variable inputs are used fully in harvesting and processing. This implies that processing capacity much be sufficient to receive 1381 quintals per day.

Table 11-4. *Harvest, Transportation, and Processing Costs by Plant Type (US$/quintal)*

Activity	Type 1	Type 2	Type 3	Type 4	Type 5
Harvest	11.49	11.49	11.49	11.49	11.49
Transportation (per km)					
Unprocessed beans	0.62	0.62	0.62	0.62	0.62
Processed beans	0.05	0.05	0.05	0.05	0.05
Plant to exporter	0.04	0.04	0.04	0.04	0.04
Processing					
De-pulping	0.20	0.23	0.13	0.23	0.15
Washing	0.79	0.79	0.58	0	0
Washing and recycling	0	0	0.84	0.17	0.03
Wrying	0.90	0.82	0.78	0.58	0.43
Subtotal for processing	1.89	1.84	2.25	0.98	0.61

Source: Pineda 1997a, 1997b.

Simulation Results

Given seven river segments and seven locations within each segment, there are 49 possible plant locations. Given five different types of processing plants, this implies 245 possible combinations of processing plants and locations. The General Algebraic Modeling System (GAMS) optimization software was used to determine the cost-minimizing combinations. The results are shown in Figure 11-2. The cost-minimizing solution is to build eight large type 5 plants and seven small type 2 plants. These plants have a peak period capacity of 40,700 quintals. Most of the plants are located in the upstream portions of the watershed because of the favorable conditions for coffee production and proximity to farms. A total fixed investment of US$667,000 is required to construct these 15 plants.

Financial Incentives

A necessary condition for the feasibility of a centralized system of processing is that all participants in the coffee market have positive financial incentives to support it, or at least do not have disincentives. In other words, farmers, processors, and intermediaries need to be at least financially neutral between the current system and the proposed changes. Farmers need to receive a price from new centralized plants for unprocessed beans that compensates them for the loss of the value added that they traditionally receive from their own processing enterprises. The new processing plants need to receive a price for processed beans that covers all of their costs, including the cost of transporting beans to exporters now provided by middlemen. Intermediaries, who currently advance the cash needed to purchase the coffee at the farm and manage the transaction with the exporters, need to receive a return for bringing coffee to the export market comparable to that in

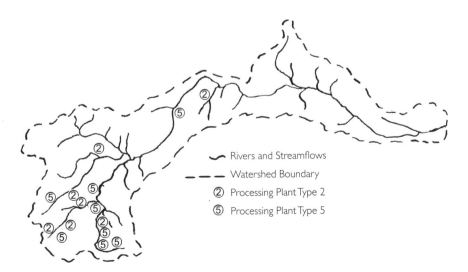

Figure 11-2. *Plant Locations as Determined by Cost-Minimization Model*

the current system. We find that these feasibility constraints can be met if the new centralized processing system allows for a reduction in the price penalty paid by Honduran exporters.

The following notation is needed for this analysis:

V^d_f = variable cost per quintal for decentralized (on-farm) processing plant (US$);

Q^γ_f = farm output of processed coffee beans (quintals);

Q^ϕ_p = plant output of processed coffee beans (quintals);

P^ϕ_f = price paid to farm for processed coffee beans (US$ per quintal);

P^γ_f = price paid to farm for unprocessed coffee beans (US$ per quintal);

P^ϕ_p = price paid to centralized processing plant for processed coffee beans (US$ per quintal); and

I = intermediaries' per-quintal return in decentralized system (US$).

To ensure that growers participate, the farm price they receive for selling unprocessed coffee should be greater than the farm price they would receive for selling processed beans, net of the average variable costs of decentralized (on-farm) processing. Fixed investments in decentralized processing are, for this analysis, considered to be sunk costs, which are not recoverable. This implies that farmers must receive a price for unprocessed coffee such that

$$P^\gamma_f \geq \frac{\left(P^\phi_f - V^d_f\right)Q^\phi_p}{Q^\gamma_f} \quad \forall f \tag{11-6}$$

Intermediaries must receive a per-quintal profit comparable to the one they get in the current decentralized processing system, I. These per-unit returns are estimated to be the price of processed coffee paid by exporters, less the farm-gate price and the transportation costs.

$$I = P^\phi_e - T^\phi \sum_f D_{f,e} - P^\phi_f \quad \forall r, \forall e \tag{11-7}$$

To ensure that new processing plants participate, each plant will need to pay for unprocessed beans, the fixed and variable costs of processing, and the transportation costs from the farm to the plant and from the plant to the export depot, including payments to intermediaries (who actually provide the transportation services) sufficient to enable them to match their profit margins under the current system. This implies that the processor must receive a per-quintal price from the exporter, P^ϕ_p, such that

$$P^\phi_p \geq \frac{P^\gamma_f \sum_f Q^\gamma_f + V^c_i Q^\phi_p + F_i + T^\gamma \sum_f D_{f,p} + T^\phi \sum_p D_{p,e} + IQ^\phi_f}{Q^\phi_f} \quad \forall p, \forall i \tag{11-8}$$

A centralized processing regime will be feasible if the international price for Honduran coffee is sufficient to pay prices that growers, the new processing plants, and intermediaries need to receive to participate in the new system, i.e., sufficient to enable equations 11-6 and 11-8 to be satisfied.

Rather than testing these constraints for every farmer and every processing plant in our study area, we only test them for those farmers and those centralized processing plants for which equations 11-6 and 11-8 are least likely to be satisfied. If the feasibility constraints are met for these agents, then we can be certain that they will be met for all other remaining agents. Thus, to determine whether equation 11-6 is met, we use data for a farm-level decentralized processing plant with the lowest variable costs, since such a plant has the least to gain from a system of centralized processing. Such low-cost decentralized processors are best represented by plant type 3 but without water recycling (see Table 11-3). To test equation 11-8, we use data for plant type 5, which has the highest fixed and variable cost, since such a plant would have the most difficulty satisfying this constraint (see Table 11-4). Furthermore, in all of our calculations, we use the greatest allowable distances between plants and farms (25 km). And to ensure that intermediary returns are as high as possible, we use the greatest distance between farms and export depots (95 km).

Table 11-5 shows the results of this financial analysis. The data come from both published sources and the local interviews conducted during 2000. As noted above, this analysis assumes that all parameters are exogenous, except for the export price. As shown in Table 11-5, a farmer with low-cost on-farm processing technology would need a farm-level price of US$48.79 per quintal of unprocessed beans to forgo his or her current processing operation and remain financially indifferent to the new centralized processing system. Intermediaries would need to maintain their returns of US$2.28 per quintal to be financially indifferent. And a processor using the most costly, centralized, ecological processing plant would need to receive US$74.96 per quintal of processed coffee at the export depot to be able to cover payments to farmers for unprocessed beans, fixed and variable processing costs, transportation costs, and payments to intermediaries.

This US$74.96 per quintal depot price is not sufficient to make centralized processing financially feasible for all current participants. As long as the US$12.00 per quintal quality penalty imposed on Honduran coffee exports persists, a subsidy of US$11.96 per quintal would be required to provide all market participants with the incentives needed to maintain 2000 production levels. However, centralized processing is feasible if the US$12.00 penalty is eliminated. If centralized processing plants improved coffee quality and eliminated this penalty, the international price of coffee (US$75.00) would exceed the price required to make centralized processing feasible for every participant. It is worth pointing out that the US$0.04 per quintal figure in Table 11-5—the amount by which the international price exceeds the total feasible return—is not an average for all coffee produced in the Rio Frío watershed. Rather, it is the difference for farmers and plants that require the highest feasible returns. Thus, this analysis demonstrates that with the elimination of the US$12.00 price penalty, a system of centralized processing would be Pareto superior to the old system, and no growers or intermediaries would suffer financial losses.

Table 11-5. *Financial Analysis of Centralized Coffee-Processing System in 2000*

Label	Parameter	Source	Cost (US$ per quintal)
	Relevant price and cost data		
a	Farm price for processed beans	Local interviews	56.67
b	Farm-level processing costs (without project, includes in-farm transport costs)	Pineda 1997a	7.88
c	International price of processed coffee	IHCafe data	75.00
d	Price penalty applied to Honduran exports	IHCafe data	12.00
e	Transport cost for unprocessed beans (25 km)	Local interviews	6.25
f	Transport cost for processed beans from plant to depot (70 km)	Local interviews	2.80
g	Transport cost for processed beans from farm to depot (95 km)	Local interviews	4.05
h	Fixed cost of processing plant type 5	Pineda 1997a	14.23
i	Variable cost of processing plant type 5	Pineda 1997a	0.61
	Necessary returns		
A	Necessary price to small farmers for sale of unprocessed beans (right-hand side of eq. 11-6)	a − b	48.79
B	2000 return to intermediaries (right-hand side of eq. 11-7)	c − d − a − g	2.28
C	Centralized processing and transport costs	e + f + h + i + B	26.17
D	Necessary export price for processed coffee (right-hand side of eq. 11-8)	A + C	74.96
	International price versus total feasible return		
E	Current international price of Honduran coffee (with penalty) minus necessary export price	(c − d) − D	−11.96
F	International price coffee (with no penalty) minus necessary export price	c − D	0.04

Implementation Issues

Domestic Issues

Although centralized processing may be financially feasible if Honduras' export penalty is removed, implementing such a system presents a number of challenges. One has to do with continued softness in international coffee prices, which begs the question of the survivability of the Honduran coffee sector. But to the extent that coffee prices are cyclical, this may be a transitory problem. In any case, Honduras' small-scale coffee growers have continued to produce despite reports that Central American growers cannot afford to harvest their beans (Brosnan 2002). Coffee cultivation remains an important activity in rural Honduras that many groups would want to continue to support to maintain rural livelihoods.

A related set of issues concerns attracting new investors and managers into centralized coffee processing. Private-sector investors, working with the limited number of licensed coffee exporters might be able to establish competitive processing plants. Because of the environmental and financial benefits of centralized processing, as well as the economic and social importance of the Honduran coffee sector, development banks, such as the Central American Development Bank or the Inter-American Development Bank, may be interested in helping to finance such investment. As for management, existing coffee cooperatives may be able to operate the processing plants. Although coffee cooperatives in Honduras have historically been characterized by poor management, with the expansion in higher education in Honduras in the past 20 years, this problem may be waning.

A third problem concerns the social transformation involved in a switch from decentralized to centralized processing. Once plants are built, it would be necessary to encourage farmers to abandon farm-level processing. More research is needed to understand the household implications of this type of transformation.

A fourth issue has to do with environmental controls. Additional measures are needed to ensure that centralized processing plants control pollution. A variety of strategies can be employed to achieve this aim, including watershed management projects, certification, and export controls. Currently, watershed management programs in Honduras provide farmers with incentives to maintain vegetation and practice erosion control. These programs stress land management as opposed to water management and often neglect coffee processing, even though it is a chief determinant of water quality and stream flows. International aid agencies, development banks, and national institutions have become heavily involved in these projects. These agencies could expand their interest in watershed management to include mitigating coffee-processing effluents.[5]

Certification is another possible means of enhancing incentives for clean coffee processing. There is some evidence that coffee certified as "shade-grown," "organic," and "fair trade" sells for a premium on the international market. Therefore, certification could theoretically create economic incentives for environmentally friendly processing (Kotchen et al. 2000; Peyser 2001; Economist 2002). Indeed, one Honduran coffee certification program affiliated with the Rain Forest Alliance requires water conservation and treatment of wastewater (Sustainable Agriculture Network 2002). However, other certification programs ignore environmental issues related to coffee processing. This allows coffee processed with high-organic-effluent, low-conservation technology to be certified as a "green" product. For example, the International Federation of Organic Agriculture Movements' standards for organic production and processing do not mention wastewater treatment for food processing (IFOAM 2002). It may be possible to promote clean coffee processing by making certification agencies more aware of the water pollution issue.

Although enforcing effluent standards and quality control at numerous point sources can be difficult, the Honduran government and IHCafe might be able to use economic incentives to give coffee exporters—of which there are only 40 in the country—incentives to ensure that their suppliers use clean methods (Luxner 2000). One alternative is to make export licenses contingent on a record of compliance with an environmental standard. Such a policy would shift enforcement costs onto the coffee sector. Exporters would have an incentive to enter into coffee processing—or at least to facilitate the strengthening of coffee-processing cooperatives—to ensure compliance. They would have incentives to promote and maintain the identity of coffee processed with clean technology. Small producers who continue to use dirty farm-level processing would be able to sell to the lower-priced domestic markets.

A fifth problem associated with implementation concerns a "chicken-and-egg" problem: centralized processing is needed to improve export prices, and improved export prices are needed to make centralized processing feasible and to finance new capital investment. Thus, sequencing is a significant concern. The initial stages of any large-scale national program to centralize coffee processing will require significant financial capital, as well as the will to enforce pollution-abatement requirements. Thus, once ecological plants are constructed, environmental regulations need to be enforced, either at the point of export, or in the coffee producing highlands. This step would ensure that farmers sell their unprocessed beans to the centralized processing plants.

Tax relief for coffee processed with pollution-abatement technology could also provide some of the needed financial capital. A U.S.$6.00 tax per quintal has been placed on Honduran coffee exports. It is used to support IHCafe and the National Coffee Fund, as well as to repay a loan that the government gave to producers as part of a post-Hurricane Mitch relief effort. Governments are of course reluctant to reduce tax revenue. But a temporary reduction in export taxes could be considered a mechanism to support the initial fixed costs of the ecological processing plants.

An alternative strategy would phase in the adoption of centralized ecological processing over time using pilot projects. Pilot projects will have a greater potential for success in areas where farmers, community watershed management projects, certification agencies, and exporters can present an integrated effort. Pilot projects in the upper watersheds have two advantages. High-altitude coffee is most likely to command a higher price for better quality (Brosnan 2002). Also, water quality improvements in upper watersheds have greater environmental benefits than those in lower areas. With the support of certification agencies, these pilot projects might be able to successfully differentiate themselves from low-quality producers and to gain an improved price. Indeed, this is the strategy adopted by the Marcala cooperative, which has managed to avoided the U.S.$12.00 price penalty.

Coffee Processing Pollution in Neighboring Countries

How have other Central American countries dealt with environmental issues in coffee processing? Most neighboring countries have both centralized and decentralized processing (Table 11-6). Costa Rica employs only centralized processing and has maintained a pollution-control system since 1990. Most of El Salvador's production is processed in centralized plants.

Table 11-7 presents information about pollution-control programs in the coffee sector in Central America. Standards have been established by the countries' respective private sector or parastatal coffee institutes. Honduras and Nicaragua have relatively strict standards, although neither country has an enforcement pro-

Table 11-6. *Number of Large and Small Coffee-Processing Plants in Central America*

Type of plant	Guatemala	El Salvador	Honduras	Nicaragua	Costa Rica
Centralized (>500 quintals./year)	20	93	20	95	95
Small (≤500 quintals./year)	16,125	ND	44,000	27,900	0
Total	16,145	ND	44,020	27,995	95

Source. Ibarra et al. 1999.

Note: ND = not determined.

Table 11-7. *Coffee Processing Pollution-Control Programs in Central America*

	Guatemala	El Salvador	Honduras	Nicaragua	Costa Rica
Pollution-control program	Yes	Yes	No	No	Yes
Standards	Proposed by ANACAFE	Proposed by PROCAFE	Proposed by IHCafe	Proposed by UNICAFE	Proposed by ICAFE
COD (mg/L)	1500	400-800	200	300	1500
BOD (mg/L)	500	ND	50	150	1000
pH	6.5–8.5	ND	6.9	8.8	5.9

Source: Ibarra et al. 1998.

Note: ND = not determined.

gram. Guatemala, El Salvador, and Costa Rica have established pollution-control programs with varying degrees of monitoring and enforcement.

These pollution-control programs can be effective. Costa Rica provides an instructive example. Before controls were established in 1990, the equivalent of 226 tons of biochemical oxygen demand (BOD) per day from coffee waste was dumped into the Virilla–Tarcoles watershed in Costa Rica. After controls were established, total emissions from coffee processing was reduced to 23 tons of BOD per day (Ramirez Corrales 2000).

The costs of Costa Rica's pollution control were not trivial. In 1996, a total of 95 processing plants processed 154,131 metric tons of processed coffee. The total cost of pollution control, including annualized payments for fixed costs and variable costs of water treatment and recycling, was estimated to be over US$3 million. This amounts to 1% of the value of the exported coffee. The 11 large plants with a capacity greater than 50,000 quintals had an average pollution mitigation cost of US$0.13 per cubic meter of water used. The 85 smaller plants had an average pollution-control cost of US$0.16 per cubic meter of water (Salguero 1996).

Notwithstanding these investments, Costa Rica initiated an ambitious voluntary program to reduce pollution and water use through an agreement between producers and governmental agencies. This agreement includes water recycling, reductions in suspended solids, and anaerobic treatment of wastewater (Vasquez 1997).

Conclusion

A first step in reducing water use and effluents from coffee processing in Honduras is to support the establishment of larger centralized processing plants with water recycling and wastewater treatment. The current system of farm-level plants is highly polluting, difficult to regulate, and leads to poor quality control and, as a result, low prices. A necessary condition for the successful implementation of a centralized system is that all participants in the coffee market must have financial incentive to support it. A mathematical programming analysis in a typical coffee-producing watershed suggests that this constraint can in fact be met if the price penalty imposed on Honduran exports can be removed by improving quality. The cost-minimizing solution requires an initial investment of U.S.$667,000 to construct the centralized processing plants, not a trivial sum for a relatively small watershed.

This research has focused on a cost-minimization problem and a feasibility analysis and has, therefore only addressed one of a larger set of economic, political, and institutional challenges related to implementing a centralized processing system. For example, although the coffee growers in the Rio Frío watershed and throughout Honduras have expressed their recent support for a centralized processing system, and although such a system has been identified by IHCafe as a priority, it is not clear how it would affect household production systems. Further research on this issue is needed.

Certification agencies and development projects can help to establish ecological processing plants, but a comprehensive solution would likely only come through the application of some governmental control and through financial incentives. The possibility of eliminating a price penalty on the international market could provide the financial incentive needed to facilitate a change to larger processing plants. With a relatively small number of processing plants, it would be feasible to enforce technology standards for wastewater treatment and recycling.

Acknowledgments

Field research was conducted while Hearne and Gonzalez were assistant professor and M.S. student, respectively, at the Tropical Agricultural Center for Research and Higher Education (CATIE), in Turrialba, Costa Rica. Barbier was a research fellow for The International Center for Tropical Agriculture (CIAT), in Tegucigalpa, Honduras. Research was supported by IHCafe and a scholarship provided by the German Academic Exchange Service (DAAD).

Notes

1. Corresponding author: Department of Agribusiness and Applied Economics, North Dakota State University, P.O. Box 5636, Fargo, ND 58105; phone: 701-231-6494; fax: 701-231-7400; email: robert.hearne@ndsu.edu.

2. In dry processing, which is generally used for *robusta* coffee, the fruit is dried initially and later the pulp is separated with a special machine.

3. With the sharp decline in international coffee prices after 2000, IHCafe has modified its strategy for pollution abatement and has recently promoted water recycling within traditional farm-level processing plants.

4. Temperatures vary between 18°C and 26°C. Annual rainfall is between 2300 and 2700 mm, and rainfall averages 120 to 160 days per year. The topography is mountainous, with slopes averaging 40–50%. Soil texture is clayish with good organic matter content.

5. For example, the watershed management programs sponsored by the Banhcafe Foundation establish and support community or cooperative managed ecological processing plants.

References

Alfaro, J., and A. Cárdenas. 1988. *Manejo de Cuencas.* Lima: Fundación Friederich Ebert.
Bailly, H., B. Salleé, and S. Garcia. 1992. Proyecto de Tratamiento de Aguas Residuales de Beneficios, Diagnostico de la Contaminación. Café Cacao. *Revista Trimestral, del Institut de Recherches du Café, du Cacao et Autres Plantes Stimulantes* (IRCC). 36: 2, April–June, 129–41.
Barrios, A. 1995. Ventajas Económicas del Beneficiado Ecológico. *Boletín IICA-PROMECAFE* 66–67: January–June, 19.
Blanco, J., and H. Perera. 1999. *Dilemas de la Reconversión del Beneficiado de Café en Centroamérica.* San José, Costa Rica: Biomas Users Network.
Brosnan, G. 2002. Hunger Stalks Guatemalan Coffee Farms. *The Washington Post.* December 9.
CEPAL (Comisión Económico Para Latín América y el Caribe). 2002. Anuario Estadístico de América Latina y el Caribe, 2001. Santiago: CEPAL.
CIAT (Centro Internacional de Agricultura Tropical). 1999. *Atlas de Honduras.* Tegucigalpa, Honduras: CIAT.
Echeverría, O., and R. Cleves. 1995. Beneficiado Ecológico del Café. *Revista Bimensual Agroindustria* 167: May–June, 32.
Economist. 2002. Berkeley's Coffee Wars. *The Economist.* August 24.
González, J. 1996. Determinación del Grado Optimo de Descomposición de Seis Substratos para Iniciar un Proceso de Lombricultura con *Eisenia foetida*. Undergraduate thesis. Catacamas, Honduras: Escuela Nacional de Agricultura.
———. 2000. Influencia de los Incentivos Economicos en la Reduccion de Contaminates de los Beneficios de Café en la Cuenca del Rio Frío, Honduras. M.S. thesis. Turrialba, Costa Rica: Centro Agronómico Tropical de Investigación y Enseñaza.
González Besteiro, A., and S. Obando. 1994. El Beneficiado Húmedo del Café, sus Residuos y la Contaminación Ambiental. *El Café de El Salvador* April–June: 20–34.
Ibarra, E., A. Barrios, G. Lardé, C. Pineda, P. Alcides, and W. Timon. 1999. Situación del Beneficiado del Café: Revisión y Avances Tecnológicos del Proceso Memoria. Seminario Regional de Consulta. February. Heredia, Costa Rica: PROMECAFE, IICA. Instituto Interamericano de Cooperación para la Agricultura
IFOAM (International Federation of Organic Agriculture Movements). 2002. Basic Standards for Organic Production and Processing. Final draft, September. http://www.ifoam.org/standard/index.html (accessed January 2003).
IHCafe (Instituto Hondureño del Café). 1995. *Beneficiado Húmedo del Café.* Manual para el Beneficiado del Café. Tegucigalpa, Honduras: Instituto Hondureño del Café.
———. 1999a. *Censo Nacional de Productores de Café.* Tegucigalpa, Honduras: Instituto Hondureño del Café.
———. 1999b. *Informe de Cierre de Precios del Café.* Unidad de Comercialización. Tegucigalpa, Honduras: Instituto Hondureño del Café.
Jaquet, M. 1993. Alternativas Tecnológicas del Beneficiado Húmedo en Relación con la Conservación del Medio Ambiente. In *Seminario Regional sobre Mejoramiento de la Calidad del Café.* San Pedro Sula, Honduras: IHCafe/PROMECAFE, September. *Boletín IICA-PROMECAFE* 61: October–December, 5–10.

Kotchen, M., M. Moore, and K. Messner. 2000. Green Products as Impure Public Goods: Shade Grown Coffee and Tropical Forest Deforestation. Selected paper presented at the American Agricultural Economics Association Annual Meetings, Tampa FL, August.

Luxner, L. 2000. Honduran Coffee Industry Finally Recovering from Mitch. *Tea & Coffee Trade Journal* 172: 61.

———. 2001. Coffee Smuggling in Honduras: Damage Worse than a Hurricane? *Tea & Coffee Trade Journal* 173: 27.

Osorio, F. 1997. Criterios para la Producción Sostenible de Café. In *Sexto Seminario Nacional de Investigación y Transferencia en Caficultura.* July. Tegucigalpa, Honduras: Instituto Hondureño del Café.

Palma, M., F. Oseguera, H. Rodríguez, and J. Chinchilla. 1997. Diagnostico Técnico del Beneficiado Húmedo y Sistemas de Comercialización en Honduras. In *Sexto Seminario Nacional de Investigación y Transferencia en Caficultura.* July. Tegucigalpa, Honduras: Instituto Hondureño del Café.

Peyser, R. 1999. The Honduras Journal. www.greenmountaincoffee.com/social_environmental/scripts/honduras.asp (accessed January 2003).

———. 2001. Coffee Project: Farmer-to-Farmer Volunteer Trip Report. January–February 2002. http://crs.uvm.edu/partners/coffee/coffee.html (accessed January 2003).

Pineda, C. 1997a. Determinación del Consumo de Agua en el Proceso de Beneficiado Húmedo del Café en Honduras. In *Sexto Seminario Nacional de Investigación y Transferencia en Caficultura.* July. Tegucigalpa, Honduras: Instituto Hondureño del Café.

———. 1997b. Evaluación del Sedimento de las Lagunas de Tratamiento de Aguas Mieles del Beneficiado en la Producción de Viveros de Café. In *Sexto Seminario Nacional de Investigación y Transferencia en Caficultura.* July. Tegucigalpa, Honduras: Instituto Hondureño del Café.

Pineda, W., C. Pineda, and M. Ordoñes. 1998. *Caracterización de Contaminantes en la Cuenca del Río Frí.* Tegucigalpa, Honduras: Instituto Hondureño del Café.

Ramirez Corrales, J. 2000. Cuantificacion de la Contaminacion de los Rios en la Cuenca 24: Virilla-Tarcoles. In *Proceedings of the XIX-Simposio-Latinoamericano-de-Caficultura.* October 2–6. San Jose, Costa Rica: Instituto del Cafe de Costa Rica (ICAFE), 483–91.

Salguero, E. 1996. Valoración Económica de la Contaminación de Fuentes de Agua por los Desechos del Beneficiado Húmedo de Café en Costa Rica. M.S. thesis. Turrialba, Costa Rica: CATIE.

Salas, W., F. Hernández, B. Chacon, and A. Rodriguez. 1983. Efectos de las Aguas Contaminadas en la Producción de Hortalizas. *Agronomía y Ciencias.* 1:13-21.

SERNA (Secretaría de Recursos Naturales y Ambiente) 1995. *Informe de Calidad de Aguas Residuales.* Tegucigalpa, Honduras: Secretaria de Recursos Naturales y Ambiente.

Sustainable Agriculture Network. 2002. Generic Standards for Coffee Farm Evaluation. http://www.rainforest-alliance.org/programs/cap/socios/coffee (accessed January 2003).

Urive, H., E. Echeverri, and H. Galindo. 1997. El Beneficio Ecológico del Café. *Revista Cafetera de Colombia* 46: January–June.

Vasquez, R. 1997. El Manejo de Efluentes en el Beneficiado del Café en Costa Rica. *Agronomía Costarricense* 21: 69–76.

CHAPTER 12

The Ancillary Carbon Benefits of SO_2 Reductions

A Small-Boiler Policy in Taiyuan, People's Republic of China

Richard D. Morgenstern, Alan J. Krupnick, and Xuehua Zhang

*I*T IS WELL UNDERSTOOD that greenhouse gas (GHG) reduction policies, which create incentives to alter the use of fossil fuels, can yield near-term environmental gains quite distinct from the long-term benefits directly associated with climate change. Significant ancillary reductions in local air pollution are predicted in studies of the U.S. economy, and even larger reductions are estimated for developing countries experiencing high pollution levels (Cifuentes et al. 2001; IPCC 2001). Despite the findings of net benefits when the ancillary gains are included, proposals for GHG reductions have been met with widespread skepticism in the developing world (Jin et al. 2000).[1]

A promising approach, particularly relevant for developing countries, is to reverse the policy logic and consider the ancillary carbon benefits of local air pollution control policies. A compelling case can be made for focusing on local pollution first: large health benefits can often be obtained at relatively modest cost, particularly in areas where air pollution levels grossly exceed international standards. The key questions are whether there are any carbon benefits associated with the local air pollution policies and, if such benefits do exist, are they large enough to justify a closer look at policies that take air pollution policies as their starting point?

Conventional wisdom holds that pollution abatement, e.g., the control of SO_2 emissions, requires additional energy to operate scrubbers or other equipment, thereby leading to an increase in carbon emissions. This concern, however, ignores the possibility of reducing SO_2 emissions without energy-using end-of-pipe controls, e.g., by fuel substitution or greater combustion efficiency. Skepticism about the size of the tangible, near-term benefits available to the local citizenry is understandable. Sources of significant carbon emissions in developing countries are often small, inefficient, and highly polluting, and they are found in the "informal" service and manufacturing sectors. Such sources are typically a challenge to regulate (Blackman 2000). According to a World Bank (1996) report, for example, as of 1990, 35% of China's coal use was in small- and medium-sized boilers with an average size of 2.3 tons per hour.

This chapter examines the case of Taiyuan, an industrial northern Chinese city heavily dependent on coal as a source of primary energy, which recently banned uncontrolled coal combustion in certain small boilers in the downtown area as part of its overall SO_2 control strategy. Because the implementation of the policy has been under way for two years (2000–2001), it is possible to go beyond the typical ex ante calculations and examine the actual ex post operation of the policy. SO_2 and carbon reductions are estimated via analysis of a recent survey of individual boilers designed and conducted by Resources for the Future and the Taiyuan Environmental Protection Bureau (EPB).

Overall, large reductions of both SO_2 and carbon occurred as a result of the decision to ban uncontrolled coal combustion in small boilers in certain classes of establishments in the central city of Taiyuan. The size of the estimated reductions depends on assumptions made about the future operation of recently shut down facilities and about the incremental emissions from large, centralized facilities used as replacement sources of energy. Not surprisingly, the marginal abatement costs per ton of SO_2 for banning uncontrolled coal combustion in small boilers are relatively high. Yet these costs are calculated to be less than the value of the marginal health benefits based on standard exposure, dose–response, and valuation assumptions. Adjustment for the indoor exposures associated with the use of small boilers in commercial establishments, or attributing any positive value to the carbon reductions, would clearly increase net benefits.

The next section of the chapter, titled Reversing the Policy Logic, reviews the literature on ancillary benefits and examines the rationale for reversing the policy logic by considering the ancillary carbon benefits of local air pollution control. The section titled The Policy To Shut Down Small Boilers in Taiyuan City introduces the specific policy adopted in Taiyuan in 1999 to close small boilers in certain classes of establishments and describes the conduct of the boiler survey, including the survey instrument used. The section titled The Survey Results presents estimates of the SO_2 and carbon emissions, both before and after implementation of the small-boiler policy, along with estimates of the marginal abatement costs for the SO_2 reductions. The section titled SO_2 Marginal Abatement Costs integrates the survey results with other information on damage costs associated with uncontrolled coal combustion, both indoor and outdoor. The section titled Implications explores the potential gains from expanding this policy to other classes of establishments and other locales in Taiyuan, as well as to other geographic areas. Given the evolving interest in using the Clean Development Mechanism[2] to obtain carbon reductions from small-scale projects, this broader assessment may have particular salience.

Reversing the Policy Logic

An extensive literature has developed on the ancillary benefits of GHG reduction policies.[3] The predominant finding from this work is that those benefits, which primarily consist of improved health from reduction in conventional air pollutants, can offset a significant fraction of carbon mitigation costs. Indeed, in some cases, carbon reduction can be justified on the basis of the ancillary air pollution improvements alone. This optimistic finding is generally more applicable to developing nations than to developed nations because of the lower (relative) costs of reducing carbon and the higher baseline pollution levels in developing versus developed countries.

Although these findings hold for China, in particular, they have yet to prove compelling in the policy arena. Although China was among the first nations to ratify the United Nations Framework Convention on Climate Change (in 1993), its official position in the international climate negotiations has been characterized as "conservative" (Buen 2000; United Nations Framework Convention on Climate Change 2002). In the Kyoto negotiations, China has emphasized "common, but differentiated responsibilities" for developing nations and has strongly argued that it should not be expected to limit its GHG emissions until its economy has reached the level of a developed country.

Notwithstanding its firm stand in the Kyoto negotiations, China's Agenda 21, adopted in 1994, established climate policy objectives, such as formulating a national program for controlling GHG emissions by afforestation and energy development.[4] Since 1995, China has adopted measures to reduce its carbon emissions, including participation in cooperative projects with Norway, Japan, the Netherlands, and the United States. For a variety of reasons, China's carbon emissions fell by almost 4% from 1995 to 1998 at a time when its GDP increased by 36%.

Despite the reluctance to embrace the ancillary benefits logic, there is, nonetheless, great concern about local air pollution levels in many urban areas. China has some of the highest pollution readings in the world for particulates and SO$_2$ (which converts to fine particulates in the air)—pollutants that are most significantly implicated in premature death and serious morbidity. The World Bank (1997) listed Taiyuan among the most polluted cities in the world in terms of ambient concentration of total suspended particulates and SO$_2$, based on 1995 data. Beginning in 1996, the Chinese government initiated a national policy of "One Control and Two Compliances," which set emissions standards in mass rather than concentration terms and required cities to implement so-called total emissions control. In principle, each province and city was required to bring its total emissions of particulates, SO$_2$, and other pollutants within the levels designated by the national government. The policy also required some key Chinese cities to meet the national ambient air quality standards by 2000, although the date was later extended.

Given the clear interest in reducing local air pollution and the clear reluctance to directly address carbon emissions, it seems reasonable to reverse the policy logic implicit in the ancillary benefits literature. That is, we consider whether the local air pollution policies that the Chinese government is already undertaking also may generate (ancillary) carbon benefits. If they do, how large, how cost-effective, and how cost-beneficial are these policies? What is the potential for expanding such efforts?

The Policy To Shut Down Small Boilers in Taiyuan City

The Policy

In June 1999, the Taiyuan City government issued the *Bulletin Controlling Air Pollution,* which covered a wide range of air pollution sources in the area, including both stationary and mobile sources. Among the issues covered in the *Bulletin* was a decision, supported by further administrative guidance, to shut down existing small coal-fired boilers operated by certain classes of establishments in a central zone established by the Taiyuan City government; "small boilers" were defined as those with a rated capacity of 2 tons or less of steam per hour.

All the heating boilers operating in areas served by central heating were required to connect to the district heating system. In addition, all the restaurants, entertainment centers, and public bathhouses located in the designated central zone were required to switch to less polluting fuels, such as coal gas, diesel oil, electricity, and liquid petroleum gas (LPG). The central zone was made up of high population density areas in each of the six districts in Taiyuan City. The policy was administered by the Taiyuan Environmental Protection Bureau.

The Survey

In cooperation with the Taiyuan EPB, we developed a survey instrument to assess the impact of the small boiler policy in the designated control zone. Specifically, we collected information on the boiler equipment in place before implementation of the new policy; the types, quantities, and costs of fuels used and hours of operation (before and after implementation of the new policy); and new investments undertaken to upgrade or replace the boilers in 2000–2001. The survey format is displayed in Appendix 12-1.

The survey was administered in November and December 2001 in the six districts supervised by the Taiyuan EPB.[5] In an initial meeting, the Taiyuan EPB reviewed the survey forms with the staff of the district EPBs. Each district EPB, in turn, designated "street" environmental personnel, who were individually in charge of administering environmental regulations on specific streets and visiting all the establishments with small boilers covered by the 1999 *Bulletin* in both 2000 and 2001. Each district EPB completed a survey form for these years.

In total, data were collected for 308 boilers that operated in the designated control zone at the end of 1999. It is our understanding that this number represents all the small boilers in the restaurants, entertainment centers, and public bathhouses in the designated zone, as well as those boilers used for (winter) heating located in the subzone where district heating became available in 2000–2001. As a form of quality control, a number of internal consistency checks were carried out.[6] Forty boilers were removed from the data set for a variety of technical reasons, leaving a total of 268 boilers for further analysis.[7]

The Survey Results

SO_2 and Carbon Emissions

Estimates of SO_2 and carbon emissions from the 268 boilers before and after implementation of the small-boiler shutdown policy are displayed in Table 12-1. According to the table, 99 of the enterprises reconfigured their boilers to burn other fuels, 98 reportedly stopped operation completely, and 71 switched to central heating. Among the 99 boilers that switched fuel, the fuels of choice were oil (69%), coal gas (21%), electricity (5%), and liquid petroleum gas (4%). For all boilers in the sample, SO_2 emissions were about 1,900 metric tons at the end of 1999. By way of comparison, the Taiyuan EPB estimates total SO_2 point-source emissions for the whole city, not just the zone designated for shutting down small boilers, at 258,000 tons in 1999 (Morgenstern et al. 2001). Thus, the emissions affected by the small-boiler shutdown policy implemented in 2000–2001 represent less than 1% of total point-source SO_2 emissions in the entire city.

When estimating emission reductions associated with the new policy, it is particularly important to account for those boilers reported as "shut down" and those switching to central heating. If one assumes that shutdown boilers are not subsequently reopened after the administration of the survey and that the services they perform are not taken up (with corresponding emission increases) in the remaining facilities, then a 100% emission reduction is implied.

We examined this issue by including in the survey a question on the motive for the shutdown. According to the answers, 3 of the 98 shutdown boilers were reported as going bankrupt, 8 of them were reported as combining with others, and 5 were reported as being removed from the premises. The large majority of the boilers (82) were reported as simply "shut down." With the possible exception of the 8 boilers in the survey reported as "combining with others," there is no

Table 12-1. *SO_2 and Carbon Emissions before and after Policy Implementation, Small Boilers in Taiyuan (2000–2001)*

| | Number of boilers | Emissions before policy response (tons) | | Emissions after policy response (tons) | | | |
| | | SO_2 | Carbon | Case A | | Case B | |
				SO_2	Carbon	SO_2	Carbon
Boilers continuing to operate	99	532.2	21,434.7	25.7	5,197.7	25.7	5,197.7
Boilers that stopped operation	98	515.4	20,636.8				
Centralized heating boilers	71	869.3	70,264.8	625.35	50,568.8		
All boilers	268	1,916.8	112,336.3	651.1	55,766.4	25.8	5,197.7

Notes: Case A counts SO_2 and carbon emissions of centralized heating as 72% of emissions before shutdown. Case B counts SO_2 and carbon emissions of centralized heating as zero.

credible basis to assume anything other than a complete cessation of operations, i.e., zero emissions.[8] If the 8 boilers reported as combining with others were in establishments covered by the *Bulletin*, their emissions would already be accounted for. If the boilers reported as combining with others were not in establishments covered by the *Bulletin* we would be overcounting the emission reductions. We acknowledge some uncertainty on this point, but we report the results separately, according to the reason for the boiler shutdown.

The situation involving centralized heating is somewhat more complicated. Based on a feasibility study developed for a district heating project in a nearby city (Datong), plus a site visit to Power Plant Number 1 in Taiyuan, Millison (2002) has estimated that central heating facilities generate 72% of both the SO_2 and carbon emissions of the typical small boiler per unit of output.[9] Using the Millison emissions estimate for central heating, along with fuel-specific emission estimates developed by the Taiyuan EPB, we calculate that as a result of the small boiler shutdown policy, SO_2 emissions were reduced by two-thirds, to about 650 tons per year (when calculated across all 268 small boilers in the survey).[10,11] These results are shown in Table 12-1 as Case A. Based on comparable assumptions, carbon emissions were reduced by 50% as a result of the small-boiler shutdown policy. For those boilers that switched fuels, higher reductions were obtained: 95% for SO_2 and 76% for carbon.

Interestingly, Taiyuan City officials reported that the energy replacing the 71 boilers converted to centralized heating was derived from waste heat, not from additional coal combustion, as assumed in Case A. Accordingly, we developed another case to reflect the assumption of zero emissions from the replacement district heating. Based on this assumption, we calculate that total SO_2 emissions were reduced by more than 98% as a result of the small-boiler shutdown policy. Based on comparable assumptions, carbon emissions were reduced by 95% as a result of the small-boiler shutdown policy. (These results are shown in Table 12-1 as Case B.)

SO_2 Marginal Abatement Costs

Marginal abatement costs represent the incremental costs per ton of emission reductions. Unfortunately, we only have complete cost information on a subset of 44 boilers that switched fuels in response to the policy to shut down uncontrolled combustion of raw coal.[12] Table 12-2 shows the distribution of fuels chosen by this subset of 44 boilers. More than 60% switched to oil; 30% switched to coal gas; and 10% switched to LPG. This distribution of (cleaner) fuels is similar but not identical to that of the full group of 99 boilers that switched fuel.[13] For this subset of 44 boilers, we summed the annualized investment costs for the new equipment and the *incremental* fuel costs.[14] This sum, divided by the reported emission reductions represents the average SO_2 marginal abatement costs of the 44 boilers for which we have complete data. As shown in Table 12-2, total investment in the 44 boilers amounted to about US$600,000 in 2000–2001. Annual fuel costs increased by more than a factor of five, from US$150,000 to more than US$800,000. Note that the SO_2 marginal abatement costs vary quite dramatically from the lowest (coal gas) to the highest (diesel oil) fuel type. LPG is considerably more expensive than

Table 12-2. Marginal Abatement Cost of SO₂ Reduction by Fuels

| | Number of boilers | Emissions before fuel switch | | Emissions after fuel switch | | % SO₂ reduction | Investment after (US$) | Energy Cost (US$) | | Average Marginal Abatement Cost (US$/ton) |
		Total SO₂ (tons)	Total carbon (tons)	Total SO₂ (tons)	Total carbon (tons)			Before	After	
Coal gas	13	1,115.49	4,287.36	44.18	709.95	96.38	212,875	60,963	265,500	2,029
(Diesel) oil	27	1,138.45	6,036.10	77.35	1,412.31	94.69	336,250	83,388	515,300	3,551
LPG	4	115.32	736.00	0.69	178.37	95.50	53,250	5,813	41,625	2,812
Total	44	2,369.26	11,059.46	122.22	2,300.63	95.52	602,375	150,163	822,425	2,797

coal gas per ton of SO_2 abated. Across the full group of 44 boilers, the average marginal abatement cost is US\$2,850 per ton of SO_2. [15,16] Of course, this policy also resulted in the incidental reduction of more than 8700 tons of carbon for these 44 boilers.

Implications

The findings reported in the previous section are striking: emissions of carbon fell by 50% to 95% from a baseline of 112,000 tons as a result of a policy to shut down small boilers in a single city center in only limited categories of establishments. The availability of waste heat to support district heating determines whether the percentage reductions are on the upper or lower end of this range. If reproducible in other parts of Taiyuan or in other Chinese cities, these results could have profound implications for carbon reduction throughout the country.

Of course, a policy that requires boilers to shut down is, on its face, likely to be inefficient. The cost for boilers that switched fuel was almost US\$2,900 per ton of SO_2.[17] This cost can be compared to other approaches for reducing SO_2 in Taiyuan, which we have estimated to be in the range of US\$60 (Taiyuan district heating) to US\$1,160 (coal washing) (Morgenstern et al. 2001). Estimated abatement costs for other areas of China developed by Liang et al. (1998) range from US\$75 to US\$250 per ton. Of course, actual marginal (as opposed to average) abatement costs for shutting down boilers were not estimated; neither was the cost of linking to a district heating system. A better designed, more flexible policy could doubtless lower average (and marginal) costs but, perhaps, would be harder to enforce.

At the same time, these per-ton costs may represent overestimates when considered in terms of "effective tons" reduced. When a boiler in a restaurant is replaced with district heating, for example, emissions from a short stack venting on the side or roof of a building, or perhaps even leaking into inhabited rooms, are eliminated. In its place are emissions from a tall stack of an electric power plant or another large facility. Recent air-quality modeling for point and surface nitrogen oxide (NO_x) emissions and their effects on particulate matter concentrations with diameter of 2.5 micrometers or less ($PM_{2.5}$) (Russell et al. 2002) shows that $PM_{2.5}$ concentrations in the local area are 60% higher than baseline per ton of emissions from the surface sources. If SO_2 has similar properties, then 1 ton of SO_2 eliminated from a small boiler is likely "worth" considerably more than a ton eliminated from a tall stack.

Another measure of whether this policy makes economic sense—again, even before accounting for the "free" carbon reductions—is to compare the costs of SO_2 reductions to the benefits. We performed a simple comparison using the results for the 44 boilers for which we had complete data. Total costs for reducing SO_2 by 257 tons per year are US\$732,500. Benefits are calculated based on a well-accepted practice termed the damage function approach (Krupnick and Morgenstern 2002), which links emissions changes to air-quality change, air-quality change to health effects, and health effects to monetary benefits, using estimates of individual preferences to reduce health risks. These steps were performed by HIID (2000) for another Chinese city and transferred to Taiyuan using simple assumptions. This analysis yielded an estimate of the total benefit per ton of SO_2 emissions reduced (Morgenstern et al. 2001). Estimated benefits ranged from US$4,677 to US$21,740 per ton of SO_2 reduction, depending on which of two daily time-series epidemiological studies of the effects of SO_2 on health are used (Xu et al. 1994, 2000 [cited in HIID (2000)]). Multiplying this figure by the 257 tons of SO_2 emission reduction, yields a total benefit of US$1.2 to 5.59 million. Thus, net benefits are positive for Taiyuan's small-boiler control policy, based on the 44 boilers for which data are available.

Another way of considering Taiyuan's small-boiler policy is to calculate the break-even value of carbon reductions that would offset the SO_2 abatement costs, even without counting any health benefits. This calculation involves dividing SO_2 abatement costs (US$732,500 per year) by the ancillary carbon reduction of 8,759 tons per year, for a break-even carbon-reduction value of about US$84 per ton. These figures are in the range of the values for marginal damages found in the literature. For example, the Union of the Electricity Industry (2001) lists damage values per ton of carbon ranging from 74 to 170 Euros per ton (1 Euro = about US$1.10). Note, however, that SO_2-related health benefits more than offset the full cost of the SO_2 emission reductions without counting carbon-reduction benefits.

Conclusion

Ancillary carbon benefits from local air pollution control—particularly by the "informal sector"—have not been widely explored in the literature. Given the reluctance of developing (and some developed) countries to adopt strong carbon abatement policies for their own sake, however, it is not unreasonable to consider other potential policy drivers. This ex post analysis of an actual policy to shut down certain classes of small boilers in the central area of a highly polluted Chinese city indicates significant carbon benefits in percentage terms—on the order of 50–95% reduction—associated with an SO_2 control policy.

We estimate that extending the small-boiler control policy adopted in downtown Taiyuan beyond restaurants, entertainment centers, and public bathhouses, as well as to other areas and to slightly larger boilers, could eliminate as much as 15% of total carbon emissions in the larger Taiyuan area.[18] If the estimates of 1990 coal use in small- and medium-sized boilers developed by the World Bank (1996) were representative of today's patterns, the potential savings could be considerably higher. Thus, although this small-boiler policy does not involve innovative technologies or major sources, the carbon reductions potentially achievable by such policies are not trivial. Given the demonstrated action of the city government to reduce SO_2 emissions from small boilers, these ancillary carbon reductions are truly free, from a social cost perspective. Of interest to policymakers is the shape of the supply curve of this untapped reservoir of potential carbon reductions—not just in Taiyuan, but in all of China. We have demonstrated that substantial emission reductions are available without cost, but how large a pool of reductions would be available if there was a market for the carbon?[19]

Of particular interest is the status of ongoing efforts to control small sources of SO_2 in other cities in Shanxi Province, as well as in areas in China. Conventional wisdom is that uncontrolled coal combustion from small sources is being phased out all over the country. Our survey in one city challenges this view. Only a small fraction of the eligible boilers in Taiyuan have been subject to regulation. Informal discussions with Taiyuan officials indicate that it may be many years before they are able to control all such sources. As noted, the economics of the small-boiler control policy are complex. Our estimates indicate that it is clearly not the most cost-effective way to achieve ambient SO_2 reductions in Taiyuan. However, when one considers the possible reductions in indoor exposures, or even the (conservatively) estimated benefits of ambient SO_2 reductions, the policy looks more attractive.

Whether the reduction of carbon emissions from small boilers could become eligible for CDM credits is an open issue. There are at least some policies in place to shut down these boilers. Thus, arguably, the baseline for any CDM calculations would be the non-coal boilers or the central heating facilities. Replacing or improving these installations would not likely yield cost-effective CDM credits. On the other hand, CDM baselines are generally defined as actual, on-the-ground practices.[20] The fact that only a small portion of the small boilers have been shut down in Taiyuan—and likely in other Chinese cities as well—means that tens or potentially hundreds of thousands of such boilers are still in operation. A good case could be made that significant financial barriers are impeding the transition away from these boilers. Thus, the CDM base case could well include a high proportion of old, inefficient coal boilers over the 10-year period typically used for CDM calculations. Although not offering as dramatic carbon reductions as certain other technologies, e.g., renewables, simple fuel switching for small coal boilers may represent relatively low-hanging fruit, particularly as the Clean Development Mechanism Board has recently issued guidelines favoring small sources (UNFCCC 2002).

Overall, we believe that further investigation is warranted of the potential for small-boiler control policies to improve local air quality and reduce carbon emissions. Incremental changes to ongoing policies with demonstrated local benefits may be an extremely effective way of starting down the long road of carbon mitigation, particularly in developing countries like China.

Acknowledgments

The authors would like to acknowledge the U.S. Environmental Protection Agency's Office of Air and Radiation and our project officer, Krishna Chivukula, for their support of this project. The survey would not have been possible without the dedication and hard work of Yuqi Xie of the Taiyuan Environmental Protection Bureau, who led the survey team. We would also like to thank Dan Millison for his work on estimating coal consumption at district heating plants, and Dong Cao of the Chinese Research Academy of Environmental Sciences for his help in various phases of the project.

Appendix 12-1. *Survey Form*

The boilers shut down

Name	Type	Size (tons)	Efficiency	District located	Operation time	Yearly coal consumption (tons)	SO$_2$ emission (tons)	Notes

Alternative boilers

Type	Size (tons)	Efficiency	Sources of energy use and consumption (tons)	SO$_2$ emission (tons)	Notes	Cost comparison (10,000 RMB)		
						Investment	Energy consumption	Operation cost

Note: RMB is renminbi (Chinese currency).

Notes

1. A key concern is that credits associated with inexpensive options for carbon reductions would benefit developed countries today, whereas developing countries would be left with more expensive options in the future.

2. The Clean Development Mechanism was established under Article 12 of the Kyoto Protocol for project-level activities to be carried out in developing (non–Annex I) countries.

3. See Davis et al. (2001) for a collection of papers and IPCC (2001) for a section on this topic in the Working Group III report.

4. As noted in China's Agenda 21, China "will actively seek investment from the international community for projects which assist in the slowing of climate change. These include projects for coal-fired power plants, hydroelectric power stations, coal gas projects, coal methane utilization and tree planting" (European Parliament 1996).

5. The six districts are Jiancaoping, Jinyuan, Wanbolin, Xiaodian, Xinghualing, and Yingze.

6. For example, we regressed the reported investment costs on a series of variables representing size, fuel type, and location (the subdistrict). Overall, the signs of the variables were as expected. The R_2 for the regression was 0.65.

7. Twenty-two boilers were replaced by larger units as part of a voluntary conversion for technological improvement and were thereby exempt from the 1999 *Bulletin*. Key information on energy use by the replacement units was missing for 18 of the boilers (primarily for electric-powered replacement boilers).

8. It is also true, as noted by one of the referees, that ample anecdotal evidence suggests that forbidden operations often resume once authorities stop looking. We cannot exclude this possibility in the case of small boilers reported shut down, but the interviewers were explicitly briefed on this issue in advance. Informal postsurvey discussions with the interviewers indicated that in most cases the old boilers had been physically removed from the premises.

9. The Millison memorandum is available from the authors of this chapter.

10. Assumptions used to calculate SO_2 emissions for replacement fuels: In oil-burning boilers, Taiyuan City usually uses light diesel oil. The polluting coefficient is 20 S/m^3 SO_2 emissions = fuel consumption × 20, where S is for sulfur. The sulfur content of light diesel oil is 0.2 lb per million Btu. The polluting coefficient of oil-burning boilers is 20 × 0.2/0.8 = 5kg/ton. For gas-burning boilers, the polluting coefficient is 630 kg/10^6 m^3. SO_2 emissions = fuel consumption × 630 kg/10^6 m^3. (Source: Taiyuan EPB.)

11. Assumptions used to calculate estimated carbon content for replacement fuels: For coal, ton × 0.8; for oil (diesel oil), m^3 × 0.94 × 0.85; for gas (coal gas), m^3 × 0.1125 × 0.75/1000; for electricity, kWh × 375 × 0.8/1000000; for LPG, m^3 × 0.542 × 0.807; and for centralized heating, kWh × 375 × 0.8 ×0.9/1000000 (same as for electricity, but heat transmission efficiency of 90% is assumed) (Millison 2002).

12. We also have (nominally) complete data for 8 additional boilers. However, because of internal inconsistencies in the responses, we eliminated them from the data set.

13. The full group had more oil and less coal gas and LPG. In addition, 5% of the full group switched to electricity, whereas none in this subsample did so.

14. Annual investment costs are taken to be 0.1% of total investment costs.

15. Weighting the average based on the distribution in the full sample of 99 boilers versus the 44 in this subsample raises the marginal abatement cost by 2.9% to about 30,000 RMB (renminbi is Chinese currency) per ton.

16. The US$2,850 figure is derived from the aggregate information in Table 12-2. Because the smaller boilers tend to have higher marginal abatement costs, the average of the marginal abatement costs of the individual boilers is somewhat higher (US$3,648). When the individual boilers are weighted by ex ante SO_2 emissions, the average marginal abatement cost falls to US$2,879, roughly the same as the average marginal abatement costs derived from the aggregate

information presented in Table 12-2. Although different calculations have relevance for different purposes, we believe that the marginal abatement costs derived from the aggregate data are most useful because they reflect social costs.

17. In all likelihood, the costs were lower for sources that were able to hook up to centralized heating.

18. Yuqi Xie of the Taiyuan EPB estimated that, in 1995, the total boiler population in the six EPB districts was about 4000. From the 4000 figure, one must subtract the 1000 boilers already shut down and boilers exceeding 10 tons, leaving about 2800 boilers that potentially could fall under an expanded shutdown policy. This does not count so-called tea stoves, which may number 700 in Taiyuan.

19. For example, if carbon credits could be sold for about US$7 per ton, the revenue from the sale of the reductions associated with the 44 boilers shown in Table 12-2 would cover the *annualized* costs of the fixed investments (excluding fuel costs). Presumably, offsetting the annual investment costs would make it more attractive to undertake such activities.

20. See UNFCCC (2002), Annexes A and B of the Simplified Modalities and Procedures for Small-Scale CDM Project Activities.

References

Blackman, Allen. 2000. Informal Sector Pollution Control: What Policy Options Do We Have? *World Development* 28(12): 2067–82.

Buen, Joerund. 2000. Can the Clean Development Mechanism Stimulate Green Innovation in Developing Countries? The Case of China. Conference paper presented at the second meeting of Sustainability, Technological Innovation and the Competitiveness of the Firm. France, May 27–28.

Cifuentes, L., V.L. Borja, N. Gouveia, G. Thurston, and D.L. Davis. 2001. Hidden Health Benefits of Greenhouse Gas Mitigation. *Science* 293: 1257–59.

Davis, D., A. Krupnick, and G. McGlynn (eds.). 2001. Ancillary Benefits and Costs of Greenhouse Gas Mitigation. Proceedings of an IPCC Co-Sponsored Workshop, March 27–29, 2000, in Washington, DC. Paris: Organization for Economic Co-Operation and Development.

European Parliament. 1996. *European Union—China Energy Cooperation*. Energy and Research Series W-24. Brussels, Luxembourg: Directorate General for Research, European Parliament.

Harvard Institute for International Development (HIID). 2000. Market-Based Instruments for Environmental Management. Report to the Asian Development Bank. TA 2951—PRC, April.

Intergovernmental Panel on Climate Change (IPCC). 2001. Climate Change 2001: Mitigation—Contribution of Working Group III to the Third Assessment Report of the Intergovernmental Panel on Climate Change. New York: United Nations.

Jin, Yunhui, Xue Liu, and Wanhua Yang. 2000. Prospects of CDM for Promoting Sustainable Development in China—Accelerating Foreign Investment and Technology Transfer. China Council for International Cooperation on Environment and Development Trade and Environment Working Group Reports and Papers. August. http://www.iisd.org/trade/cciced/cciced_rep.htm (accessed 2000).

Krupnick, Alan, and Richard Morgenstern. 2002. The Future of Cost–Benefit Analysis at EPA. *The Annual Review of Public Health* 23: 427–48.

Liang, Nian, Zhihong Liu, and Xiulan Gao. 1998. A Projection on Industrial Pollution Discharge and Abatement Cost in China. Presented at the Seminar on the Economics of Industrial Pollution Control in China. Beijing: World Bank, September 8.

Millison, Daniel. 2002. Taiyuan District Heating Network Coal Consumption (#2). Personal correspondence, April 3.

Morgenstern, Richard, Ruth Greenspan Bell, Alan Krupnick, Bob Anderson, Xuehua Zhang, Dan Millison, Steinar Larssen, Jinnan Wang, Jintian Yang, and Dong Cao. 2001. Inception

Report of Shanxi Air Quality Improvement Project to the Asian Development Bank (ADB). June. Washington, DC: Resources for the Future.

Russell, Armistead G., Michelle Bergin, Jhih-Shyang Shih, and Alan Kurpnick. 2002. *Source–Receptor Relationships for NO$_x$ and SO$_2$ Emissions to Fine Particulates and Ozone in the Eastern U.S.*, unpublished manuscript.

Union of the Electricity Industry. 2001. Pricing the Environment? An Update on ExternE. Proceedings of the EURELECTRIC Environmental Management and Economics Working Group. January 26. La Defense, Paris: Union of the Electricity Industry.

United Nations Framework Convention on Climate Change (UNFCCC). 2002. Principles, Nature and Scope of the Mechanisms Pursuant to Articles 6, 12, 17 of the Kyoto Protocol. Document FCCC/CP/2001/13/Add.2, Addendum, Report of decision 17/CP.7. January 21, agreed on from Conference of the Parties 7 in Marrakesh, Morocco.

World Bank. 1996. China: Efficient Industrial Boilers. Global Environment Facility, Project Document (mimeo), November.

———. 1997. *Clear Water, Blue Skies: China's Environment in the New Century.* Washington, DC: World Bank.

Xu, X., J. Gao, D. Dockery, and Y. Chen. 1994. Air Pollution and Daily Mortality in Residential Areas of Beijing, China. *Archives of Environmental Health* 49(4): 216–22.

Xu, Z. Y., X. Xu, B. Chen, and T. Kellstrome. 2000. Air Pollution and Daily Mortality in Shenyang, China. *Archives of Environmental Health.* 55(2): 115–120 (March–April).

CHAPTER 13

Conclusion

Allen Blackman

THE CHAPTERS IN THIS VOLUME address the three focus questions discussed in the introduction. What answers do they provide?

How Important Is Small-Firm Pollution?

The research presented in this book provides convincing evidence that from a
policy perspective, small-firm (SF) pollution is well worth worrying about—collectively, SFs can generate significant environmental damages that rival those
of large firms and that affect particularly vulnerable populations. Chapter 2, by
Blackman et al., demonstrates that in Ciudad Juárez, Mexico, particulate emissions
from small-scale brickkilns are responsible for significantly more human morbidity
and mortality than are two of the city's leading large-scale sources of this pollutant.
Several other chapters (6, 8, 10, and 11) present less rigorous, but still compelling,
evidence that clusters of SFs are leading sources of pollutants at the municipal or
regional level. Perhaps more surprising, in Chapter 3, Lanjouw finds that SFs can
also be leading source of pollution at the national level. Using data from Ecuador,
he shows that in a number of important economic sectors, including textiles and
iron manufacturing, SFs—not large firms—are responsible for the lion's share of
total pollution loads.

Two chapters in this volume also support the hypothesis that SF pollution
affects the poor disproportionately. In Chapter 2, Blackman et al. show that in
Ciudad Juárez, brickkiln air pollution principally affects the inhabitants of the
poor residential neighborhoods surrounding the city's brickyards. In Chapter 3,
Lanjouw demonstrates that in Ecuador, SFs create serious occupational hazards for
their employees who, by and large, are poor.

Will Forcing Small Firms To Comply with Environmental Regulations Exacerbate Unemployment and Poverty?

The economic consequences of SF pollution-control policies clearly depend on the design of the policies and the socioeconomic context—some policies in some contexts will undoubtedly adversely affect the poor. That said, the case studies presented here suggest that this certainly need not be the outcome, and in fact, may not be the most common outcome. In Chapter 8, which addresses this issue head on, Crow and Batz find that a regulatory crackdown in India targeting a cluster of small-scale bleachers and dyers had no discernable long-term impacts on the cluster's economic performance or presumably on employment. Successful efforts to control emissions from brickkilns in Ciudad Juárez, Mexico (Chapter 4) and from leather tanneries in Palar Valley (Chapter 6) also appear to have had no serious long-term employment consequences. Finally, in Chapter 3, Lanjouw finds that even if strictly regulating SFs in Ecuador were to result in significant unemployment, these job losses would only exacerbate poverty to a "very modest degree," in part because SF employees would be likely to find other work.

What Policy Options Are Available To Control Small-Firm Pollution?

Five of the chapters in this volume describe successful efforts to control severe SF pollution problems: Chapter 4 on Mexican brickkilns, Chapter 5 on Malaysian electroplaters, Chapter 6 on Indian leather tanners, Chapter 8 on Indian bleachers and dyers, and Chapter 12 on Chinese industrial boilers. Thus, these case studies clearly demonstrate that SF pollution-control policies can be successful. What specific lessons about policy design do the case studies hold?

The efforts to control SF pollution described in the case studies relied on a wide array of policies, including technology standards, relocation, communal treatment, economic incentives, informal regulation, and clean technologies. Rather than recapitulating the implications of the case studies for each of these options, this section describes three overarching lessons.

Collective Action

Although the studies of actual SF pollution-control initiatives presented in this book are quite diverse, one common element stands out clearly—in each case, conglomerations of SFs either opposed or cooperated with the initiative, and this negative or positive collective action drove the initiative's ultimate failure or success. In the two chapters detailing unsuccessful SF pollution-control initiatives—Chapter 4 on Mexican brickkilns in the cities of Saltillo and Torreón and Chapter 10 on Mexican leather tanneries in León—negative collective action took the same form: a powerful preexisting SF trade association torpedoed the effort. The positive collective action that was responsible for the success of pollution-control initiatives described in other chapters—Chapter 5 on Malaysian electroplaters,

Chapter 6 on Indian leather tanners, Chapter 8 on Indian bleachers and dyers, and Chapter 9 on Mexican brickkilns—was just as important, but far more heterogeneous. Both the purpose and form of the collective action varied. In some cases, the purpose was to ratchet up informal regulatory pressure to improve environmental performance, whereas in others it was to facilitate cost-effective communal pollution control. Furthermore, in some cases, collective action operated through preexisting associations whereas in others it was manifested in newly formed institutions or in less permanent mechanisms that enabled individual SFs to pressure each other to cut pollution. For example, in the Ciudad Juárez brickmakers project, described in Chapters 4 and 9, preexisting brickmaker trade unions pressured their members to adopt a clean technology. While in the cases of Indian leather tanners and bleachers and dyers (Chapters 6 and 8), small firms formed new associations to set up common effluent treatment plants.

Thus, the case studies suggest that harnessing positive collective action and deterring negative collective action are critically important in controlling SF pollution. Upon reflection, this is not at all surprising. SFs only create severe pollution problems when they are numerous, and when they are numerous, it is simply not practical for environmental management authorities to deal with them on an individual basis. The only workable approach is to deal with collections of SFs or to rely on SFs to place pressure on each other to cut pollution. Beyond this general point, the case studies shed light on how collective action can be promoted. For example, in Chapter 6, Kennedy argues that social cohesion among SFs greatly facilitates collective action; in Chapter 11, Hearne et al. focus on creating financial incentives for collective action; and in Chapter 7, Ahmed discusses the role that supply chains can play.

Alternative Environmental Management Strategies

The fact that conventional environmental regulatory instruments may not be a practical means of controlling SF pollution does not imply that the problem is intractable. Several of the case studies highlight the effectiveness of alternative environmental management policies. Specifically, Chapters 4 and 9 on Mexican brickmaking and Chapter 7 on supply chains demonstrate that informal regulatory pressure applied by private-sector and nongovernmental organizations can be quite effective—a point that is related to the above discussion of collective action. Chapters 9 and 10 on Mexican brickmaking and leather tanning demonstrate that clean technologies can also generate significant improvements in SF environmental performance.

Flexibility

Finally, the case studies collected in this volume clearly demonstrate that the political, socioeconomic, technological, and geophysical context in which pollution-control policies are implemented matters tremendously. As a result, no one approach or set of approaches to SF pollution control is likely to be universally effective. For example, the command-and-control technology standards that succeeded in dramatically reducing water pollution from leather tanneries in Palar

Valley, India (Chapter 6), were completely ineffective for controlling water pollution in León, Mexico (Chapter 10). Clean technological change initiatives that cut brickkiln emissions in Ciudad Juárez and Zacatecas fell flat in Saltillo and Torreón (Chapter 4). User fees for wastewater that were successful in promoting pollution prevention in an industrial park in Malaysia had no such effect when levied on hazardous waste in the same country (Chapter 5). Finally, common effluent treatment plants proved to be a viable approach to controlling water pollution for leather tanneries in some towns of the Palar Valley in India, but not in others (Chapter 6). Hence, policymakers need to be flexible and creative in designing pollution-control initiatives for SFs. They need to tailor their programs to the specific circumstances—and perhaps most importantly, the political realities—at hand.

Index